THE CHILDREN
OF COLUMBUS

THE CHILDREN
OF COLUMBUS

An Informal History
of the Italians in the New World

by Erik Amfitheatrof

Little, Brown and Company — Boston — Toronto

FIRST EDITION

The author is grateful for permission to quote the following works: The poems of Arturo Giovanitti are reprinted from *The Collected Poems of Arturo Giovanitti* by courtesy of E. Clemente and Sons, Publishers.

The anonymous poem on page 245 is translated by the author. The Italian version is quoted in Carlo Sforza's book, *The Real Italians* (New York: Columbia University Press, 1942), page 121, and is translated with the permission of the publishers.

Library of Congress Cataloging in Publication Data

Amfitheatrof, Erik.
   The children of Columbus.

   Bibliography: p.
   1. Italians in the United States--History.
I. Title.
E184.I8A527   917.3'06'51   72-12684
ISBN 0-316-03659-5

Published simultaneously in Canada
by Little, Brown & Company (Canada) Limited
PRINTED IN THE UNITED STATES OF AMERICA

21479

for Elvira

Contents

THE CHILDREN
OF COLUMBUS

Introduction

ON A FALL DAY in 1957, three men at the Yale library in New Haven sat examining a map drawn in brownish ink on a piece of ancient vellum. It was part of a volume that one of them, Laurence Witten, a New Haven antiquarian specializing in books and manuscripts, had recently purchased from a private collection in Europe. He had dropped by that day to show his acquisition to the library's curator of medieval and Renaissance literature, Thomas E. Marston, and its map curator, Alexander O. Vietor. The volume contained only twenty-one pages of Latin text, describing one of the earliest European journeys through Central Asia, made in 1245–1247 by the Italian friar Giovanni de Piano Carpini.[1] But it was a detail on the upper left-hand corner of the map that fascinated the Yale scholars.

It showed a tall, solitary island whose only distinguishing features were two slanting, saw-toothed bays. Above the island was a caption in script reporting that "Eric, legate of the Apostolic See and the Bishop of Greenland . . . arrived in this truly vast and very rich land . . . in the last year of our most blessed Father Pascal . . ." (Pope Pascal II died in January 1118).[2]

The import of the map was clear. If genuine, it meant that the Vikings had landed somewhere on the North American coast early in the twelfth century, nearly four hundred years before Columbus. Tales had long circulated that Leif Ericson's men had discovered the American continent and here, apparently, on this worm-eaten piece of vellum only eleven by sixteen inches, was the proof. After the coincidental discovery of a missing portion of the manuscript, Yale bought the precious map for a sum reportedly in the area of a million dollars.[3] On the eleventh of October, 1965, eight years after Witten had brought his little volume into the library, the university announced the existence of the Vinland Map, which its scholars were calling "the most exciting cartographic discovery of the century."[4]

To most people, hearing about it on their car radios or on the six o'clock telecast, the Vinland Map story was an unusually interesting news item, evoking visions of lean, rakish Viking ships tossing on the Atlantic swell, of Norse crews, bearded and horn-helmeted, going ashore to confront natives whom they called Skraelings rather than Indians. But to leaders of Italian-American communities across the nation, preparing to celebrate Columbus Day the very next morning, the news came as a stunning blow. The timing of Yale's announcement seemed a deliberate insult. Italian-language newspapers reacted with emotional denunciations, treating the news from New Haven as a vendetta against Columbus as if he were still in mid-Atlantic. Italian-American congressmen, under strong pressure from their irate constituents, sharply questioned the map's authenticity and Yale's motives in publishing it. The program chairman of one Columbus Day parade even suggested that the map might be a "Communist plot."[5] The reaction among Italian-Americans was in fact much more vehement than among Italians in Italy. Mayor Augusto Pedulla of Genoa, the city generally regarded as Columbus's birthplace, shrugged off the Yale map by noting that "every so often somebody turns up with that old rumor about the Vikings' trip to the New World. It represents nothing for human history."[6]

The fact is that Italian-Americans have always been notoriously defensive about their ethnic heritage. A proud people, they have had to struggle — like other minorities — against a debilitating sense of always having to measure themselves by Anglo-Saxon values and standards. Often, this process has meant rejecting one's own Italian past, or one's parents. The over fourteen hundred mutual aid societies that flourished among Italian-Americans in the early years of the century served in part as gathering places where successful Italian immigrants could meet and remind one another that they came from *Italia!* the heartland of art, beauty, knowledge. At innumerable smoke-wreathed dinners, speakers rose to proclaim the glorious achievements of Italian civilization and to sound the names of Dante, Leonardo, Michelangelo, Raphael, Galileo,

Manzoni, Marconi — names that fused into a drum roll of reassurance against the scorn of haughty Anglo-Saxons and, all too often, alas, of the immigrants' own American-born, American-educated children.

The initial popularity of fascism among Italian-Americans was due almost entirely to the feeling that Mussolini was remaking the image of the Italian race. Said a youthful member of an Italian-American street gang, "Whatever you fellows may think of Mussolini, you've got to admit one thing. He has done more to get respect for the Italian people than anybody else." [7]

The suspicion that they are being looked down on still embitters many Italian-Americans. As late as June 29, 1970, to the shock of responsible Italian politicians in New York, a crowd estimated at fifty thousand people thronged into Columbus Circle carrying signs belligerently proclaiming "I'm Proud to Be an Italian," and "25 percent of World War II Veterans were Italian-Americans." As an eight-piece orchestra serenaded the noisy, festive audience with the *Neapolitan Tarantella, Volare,* and *You've Got to Change Your Evil Ways,* Joseph Colombo, Sr., and other speakers accused the Justice Department, the press, and the advertising agencies of constantly depicting Italians either as criminal or comical, and called on all Italian-Americans to oppose this discrimination. The rally had nothing to do with the Mafia, Colombo affirmed, but with the self-respect of Italian-Americans. And as Colombo shouted, "This day belongs to you — to you the people!" the crowd's roar of approval melted into the surging chant of "one . . . one . . . one . . . ," denoting that henceforth there would be unity of purpose among Italian-Americans, that they would seek to develop an ethnic consciousness. New York *Times* correspondent Richard Severo wrote of the Italian-Americans at Columbus Circle that day, "After melting in the melting pot for all these years, they looked like they wanted to climb out." [8]

In truth, Italian-Americans have a right to feel misunderstood. Except for the Indians, they are actually the oldest of all Americans. Yet, ironically, the Italians were the last people to emigrate to America in great numbers, and they have yet to make those numbers count in the running of America. Their record in this New World discovered by their navigators remains opaque, confusing. In the days of the Sacco-Vanzetti trial, Italian workmen were regarded as subversives. Now, to suspicious liberals, they are angry flag-waving hard-hats. As Professor Richard Gambino pointed out recently in the New York *Times Magazine,* not even the Chinese are more mysterious to Main Street than are the Italian-Americans.[9]

They are a people composed of puzzling contradictions. On the one hand, they appear to be warm, emotional, exemplary in their attachment to family and to friends; and yet capable of being cold-bloodedly violent. Some are highly cultured, in the best European tradition; others seem almost willfully ignorant. While Italians are frequently physically gifted and beautiful, the Italian-Americans, Pietro Di Donato complained, often seem to be "a vociferous rotund breed; endomorphs in the anarchy of freedom over freedom."[10]

All of these contradictions, the real and the apparent, have roots deep in Italian history, and particularly in the intricate political history of southern Italy. Most of the peasants fleeing the age-old injustices and poverty of the Italian South from the 1870s onward were illiterate. As they shuffled in long, patient lines into cramped steerage compartments of ocean liners, they were literally entering a new world. Even the names of Leonardo and Michelangelo were unknown to most of these immigrants (they would learn those names in America); they thought in terms of flying saints, of all-powerful dukes, of angels and demons, of magic amulets and of goblins standing guard over caches of buried treasure at midnight. Yet the land that these peasants were fleeing was not some obscure, backward equatorial state. It was the pearl of Europe, the center of Western civilization, in whose lovely villas with their iridescent, fragrant gardens lived thousands of cultured foreigners — the Byrons, Shelleys, Keats, Brownings, Berensons. Anyone with an education, and at least a small private income, could discover that life in Italy was gayer, more fascinating, more beautiful and comfortable than anywhere else in the world.

As a group, then, the Italian-Americans reflect the tremendous social, economic, and regional contrasts of their backgrounds. "There is no one life-style you can point to as being theirs," said Professor John A. B. Faggi of Columbia. "They are not a closely knit group in any sense." [11] Bearing this out is the fact that most Italian-Americans approached Mario Puzo's *The Godfather* with as much avid curiosity and wonder as any other Americans; for them, too, a curtain had been lifted on an ethnic subculture more exotic than any hippie commune or Black Panther cell in the heart of Harlem. The Mafia of course involves only an infinitesimal fraction of the Italian-Americans; yet because of the Valachi hearings, the phenomenal success of *The Godfather,* the shooting of

Joseph Colombo, Sr., and of Joey Gallo, it sometimes appears that the Mafia has become the definitive mark of the Italians on American society.

This is a crippling distortion, one that robs many Italian-Americans of a sense of pride and security they might otherwise have.

It is also simply untrue. In the spring of 1970, for example, while Joseph Colombo, Sr., was making headlines each day picketing FBI headquarters in New York, some one hundred blocks farther downtown, in the financial district, another Italian-American, Ralph D. DeNunzio, thirty-eight-year-old executive vice president in the investment firm of Kidder, Peabody & Co., and vice chairman of the New York Stock Exchange, was meeting with a group of Wall Street's younger leaders to analyze the market slump that by midsummer would cut almost $200 billion from the value of shares listed on the exchange. Already, many brokerage firms had been wiped out or forced into shotgun mergers. Several major houses were on the point of collapse. For nearly half a century, a full-scale financial panic like that of 1929 had seemed unthinkable, but the speculative spree of the mid-1960s had uncovered Wall Street's endemic weaknesses. Many firms were poorly managed, and had so overinvested in glamour stocks and "go-go" securities for their own accounts that the sudden market drop, though mild in comparison with 1929, had been enough to bankrupt them. Clearly, Wall Street was ready for a major overhaul, and the structure of the Board itself needed changing. With that mandate, DeNunzio was appointed chairman of the New York Stock Exchange in May 1971, at thirty-nine the youngest man to have held that position in its 179-year history.*

The commander of Air Force One, who became the first American pilot to land in China in twenty years when he flew Henry Kissinger to Shanghai in October 1971, and who took President Nixon to Peking and Moscow for the 1972 summit meetings, is an Italian-American, Colonel Albert G. Albertazzie. When Alabama Governor George Wallace was shot on May 16, 1972, the cardiologist on the team of seven doctors who saved his life in a critical five-hour operation at the Holy Cross Hospital

---

* The New York Stock Exchange was reorganized in July 1972. Its Board of Directors was expanded to twenty, ten of whom are individuals selected from outside the securities business and who are charged with protecting the public's interest. In August 1972, James J. Needham became the first salaried chairman of the Board of Directors, replacing DeNunzio. In October 1972, the American Stock Exchange reorganized the structure of its Board of Directors along similar lines.

in Silver Spring, Maryland, was Dr. Herman C. Maganzini, an Italian-American.

It has become an outworn cliché that Italian-Americans are all blue-collar workers, gardeners, fish peddlers — and *Mafiosi*. They are a remarkably diverse people, with a dramatic, rich, and complicated history.

But the only way to truly make the point is to tell their story.

ONE

THE CRUCIBLE

1

The Navigators

HE CAME OUT of the Atlantic surf, wounded, falling exhausted on the darkened beach after having swum five miles. All that day, the thirteenth of August, 1476, a sea battle had raged off the Portuguese coast at Cape St. Vincent until seven vessels, blazing as they sank, had matched the sunset with their violence. At twilight a twenty-four-year-old common seaman from one of these ships, Christopher Columbus, had jumped into the ocean he would one day cross.

Two months earlier he had signed aboard a Genoese merchantman, part of a five-vessel convoy bound for Holland and the British Isles. After passing safely through the Strait of Gibraltar, the convoy was attacked by a dozen French and Portuguese warships, and by evening three of the five Genoese vessels and four of their attackers had been sunk. The townspeople of Lagos, on the Portuguese coast, spent the night on the beach looking for survivors, and towards morning the tall, strongly built seaman, his fiery red hair matted by the sea, was lifted and carried into a church where some of his shipmates were already being treated. The Franco-Portuguese attack had been more an act of piracy than of war. Columbus was given a meal, put to bed. He was not a prisoner. He had been cast ashore by destiny on a Portuguese beach, and now his great adventure would begin.

This was his first meeting with the Atlantic, although he had been at sea for several years, probably since his teens, starting out as a crewman aboard a small coastal packet making short trips from Genoa to Rapallo,

La Spezia, Leghorn; then aboard a bigger ship, sailing to Marseilles once, and once or twice to Greece.[1] He had never commanded anything. He was still a nobody, a plain sailor, ambitious, anxious to learn, but unschooled, having left his working-class parents' household in Genoa barely able to read and write. The battle off Cape St. Vincent, though he could not have known it at the time, would change all that. He was history's most fortunate castaway.

From Lagos, once his wounds had healed, Columbus went up the coast to Lisbon, where several hundred Genoese were living. Genoa was then one of the leading mercantile centers in the world, and its agents and bankers manned well-staffed offices throughout Europe. No post at the time was more important than Lisbon. The Portuguese king, known in English as Prince Henry the Navigator, had led all other Europeans in trying to open up new, faster-sailing routes for trade. Hoping to find a way to reach Europe's traditional markets in the Indian Ocean without an overland leg through Arabia, Prince Henry had sent expeditions down the West African coast to discover if the African continent extended south of the equator, and if its farthest extremity could be rounded. To aid his explorers the Portuguese king had established a complete maritime laboratory on the Sagres Peninsula, near Cape St. Vincent. There scholars prepared charts, discussed navigational aids, and debriefed returning captains.

Columbus had been washed ashore at that same Sagres Peninsula. In Lisbon, he found a job as a chartmaker, working with Portuguese navigators and the men who financed their voyages. "He was among people who could teach him everything he was eager to learn: Portuguese and Castilian, the languages of far-ranging seamen; Latin to read the geographical works of the past; mathematics and astronomy for celestial navigation; shipbuilding and rigging; and above all, discovery." [2] When his Genoese friends took Columbus to lunch, the talk was not merely about grains or sheep, as it might have been in Milan, or Lyons, or London, but about the ocean and what lay beyond it.

Strategic motives also lay behind Prince Henry's expeditions. By the middle of the fourteenth century the Ottoman Turks, hostile to Christianity, had cut the ancient European overland trade routes to India, China, and Southeast Asia, which the Crusades had reopened, and had cut them at a time when thirteenth-century travelers like Marco Polo had led Europeans to believe that Asia was the richest, most highly developed, most civilized portion of the Eurasian land mass (or, as it was thought of then, the island of the earth). Trading with China was a dream of Renaissance Europe. Also, the Vatican believed there might be powerful Christian monarchs east of Arabia, or in Africa, like the legendary Prester John, who could open a second front against the Turks.

At first timidly, then with growing confidence, the Portuguese fleets had felt their way down the African coast. Returning sailors would report that they had failed to meet the dragons, the scaly monsters, the quicksand seas of legend. They had found, instead, new sources of spices, ivory and precious metals. In 1473, three years before Columbus was washed up on the beach at Lagos, the Portuguese Lopo Gonçalves had crossed the equator without his ship or the sea bursting into flames as had been feared. The way to the Indies now seemed open. But as the Portuguese continued to explore the west coast of Africa, they were forced to conclude that the continent extended southward much farther than ancient maps had indicated, and that rounding its tip to sail to India might be impossible with the equipment and technology they then possessed. As a direct consequence of this Portuguese failure to round Africa, mariners and bankers alike began considering the only other alternative route to Asia: west across the ocean.[3] But could it be done?

By the time he had reached the age of thirty, Christopher Columbus was convinced that it could.

His early years in Portugal had been promising. He was upward bound, a man in motion, respected, sought; in short, a thoroughly successful immigrant. In 1479, he married the daughter of a Portuguese aristocrat, Doña Felipa Perestrello e Moniz, which gave him access to the Portuguese ruling class and a social standing far above his own origins among the Genoese proletariat. Nearly all his portraits, including the famous one in the Naval Museum of Pegli, near Genoa, show a moon-faced man with a harried, tense expression. They make him appear somehow deskbound, an aging scholar in a musty paper world. But they were based on sketches done late in his life, when he had suffered great reverses and disappointments. In his youth he must have been altogether different: a firebrand — likable, masculine, and spirited — with his brilliant blue eyes, aquiline nose, high cheekbones, freckles, and red hair.

Just how long Columbus spent developing his idea of sailing west across the Atlantic no one knows. But he was not the first man to have conceived it. At some time in the 1480s, he had written to a Florentine physician, Paolo Toscanelli, requesting information on the feasibility of a westward voyage. Along with other humanists in the Florence of Lorenzo the Magnificent, Toscanelli studied and discussed any subject that promised to yield new knowledge. Not surprisingly, geography was a subject of particular interest, and Toscanelli was a capable amateur geographer.

In 1464 (still a dozen years before Columbus swam ashore at Cape St. Vincent), Toscanelli had met the canon of the Cathedral of Lisbon, Fernao Martins, at the bedside of a dying Portuguese cardinal in the Vatican. Toscanelli was there as a physician, Martins as a priest. The two men began talking about geography, Toscanelli asking questions about the latest Portuguese voyages and their results, and telling Martins of his own theories that the Indies could be reached by sailing due west from Portugal. It was a meeting that Martins did not forget. Ten years later, in 1474, he wrote Toscanelli on behalf of the Portuguese Crown, suggesting that the Florentine submit a detailed proposal for a westward crossing to the Indies. In reply, Toscanelli sent Martins a letter stating that the coast of China, by his reckoning, was some five thousand miles west of Portugal, but that, by starting from the Canaries, a vessel could reach the island of Cipango after only about three thousand miles of sailing. This Cipango (Japan), which all Europe knew about from Marco Polo, who in turn had heard about it from the Chinese, was described by Toscanelli as being "most fertile in gold, pearls, and precious stones, and they cover the temples and royal residences with solid gold." [4] In his letter to Martins, Toscanelli also enclosed a chart showing how the voyage could be plotted.

None of this correspondence was secret, since it treated ideas that were being discussed every day. Columbus heard about Toscanelli's chart. Through a Medici representative in Portugal and Spain, Giannetto Berardi, he obtained a written introduction to Toscanelli, who replied by sending him a copy of the letter to Martins and the chart, with a brief covering letter addressed to "Cristóbal Columbo" from "Paul the Physician." (When Columbus wrote back asking Toscanelli for more information, he received a cooler reply, telling him in effect to work out his own solutions.)

The problem — contrary to popular belief even today — was not whether the earth was round. Many people knew that. The Greeks, superb mariners and mathematicians, had known it centuries earlier. Greek triremes had regularly sailed out of the Strait of Gibraltar (the

Pillars of Hercules) and up the Atlantic coast to Cornwall to take aboard cargoes of tin. There are even indications that Greek and Roman mariners had ventured several hundred miles out into the Atlantic but that, finding nothing, they had been forced to turn back. The Greek geographer Strabo, a contemporary of Jesus, wrote that "those who have returned from an attempt to circumnavigate the earth do not say that they have been prevented from continuing their voyage by any opposing continent, for the sea remained perfectly open, but through want of resolution and scarcity of provision." [5]

No, the problem for Columbus was simply that the Atlantic and the Pacific were believed to be one gigantic ocean covering half of the earth's surface. A ship's crew, it was thought, would die of starvation and thirst before it reached land. What Columbus did in his calculations was to shrink the size of that single mighty ocean until crossing it became feasible.

All Renaissance geography was based on the teachings of the Greek mathematician Ptolemy. Using the calculation of degrees worked out by Eratosthenes in the second century B.C. — he had divided the world into 360 degrees each measuring about sixty miles — Ptolemy split the world into two even halves. One half was land, covering 180 degrees and stretching between Iceland, Ireland, and England in the west, then across the Eurasian land mass to the China coast and Japan. The other half was covered by a single mighty ocean. A later cosmographer, Martinus of Tyre, had refigured Ptolemy's calculations, extending the land portion to cover 225 degrees, which left only 135 degrees of ocean to be crossed. These were the figures with which Columbus worked. By shrewdly taking into account Marco Polo's report of the immense size of China, Columbus added another 28 degrees to the total amount of land. He then put Japan 30 degrees closer to Portugal than China. This raised the total amount of land to 283 degrees. And if he sailed from the Canaries, Columbus argued, the total amount of ocean to be navigated would be even further reduced to 68 degrees. The stupendous irony of his calculations is that they were entirely wrong. While Toscanelli had optimistically figured a distance of 3,000 miles between the Canary Islands and Japan, Columbus had even more optimistically squeezed this to a mere 2,400 miles. The actual air distance from the Canaries to Japan is 10,600 miles. [6]

He first tried to sell his set of figures to the Portuguese king, John II, who after a careful examination of the proposal turned it down. But the king had been impressed by Columbus, and when two Portuguese, Dulmo and Estreito, managed to raise funds for an attempt at crossing the Western Ocean in 1487, he gave them his approval. They sailed on the first of March from the Azores, and the Atlantic swallowed them.[7]

In the meantime, Columbus had made a far shorter, and safer, voyage to Palos, the westernmost Spanish port on the Atlantic. He was hoping to present his ideas to the sovereigns of Castile, Ferdinand and Isabella, and to raise capital among the Italian bankers in nearby Seville if necessary. The handsome Isabella, who seems to have felt a certain womanly sympathy for Columbus, referred his proposal to a group of scholars known as the Talavera Commission, since it was headed by Fray Hernando de Talavera, her confessor. Its verdict, which took four and a half years to formulate, was based on conventional European ideas of geography at that time. The two crucial ideas were that a westward voyage to Asia would require three years and that even if Columbus were to manage to reach the antipodes (the land on the other side of the globe from Europe), he would not be able to get back. Also, the commission noted, it was unlikely that valuable lands would be discovered so many years after the Creation.[8]

Though the commission's approach was based on overriding doubt, its central premise was perfectly true. Had there been no American continent, had Columbus been forced to cross 10,600 miles of ocean from the Canaries to Japan, he and his crews would have perished at sea. His ghost ships would have floated aimlessly on that enormous Western Ocean until storms waterlogged and sank them. Or perhaps one, its decks rimed with salt and littered with bleached skeletons, would have washed ashore on some South Sea island, a dreadful, mysterious testament to the folly of dreamers. But Columbus, of course, did not guess at the existence of the American continent. Neither did the commission. At most, there might be undiscovered islands in the vast Western Ocean. No one knew. This is what finally saved the Enterprise of the Indies: no one knew.

Six frustrating, dark years were to pass before Columbus managed to persuade Isabella to furnish him with ships, provisions and crews for the Enterprise. Of all the periods of his adult life, this is the least charted. He was in touch with the Italian community at Seville, and for a while he seems to have resided at Cordova. As far as is known, he did not go to sea in this period. He lived simply. His aristocratic Portuguese wife having died, he found a companion in Beatriz de Harana, the daughter of peasants. Orphaned when still a child, she had been brought up by well-to-do relatives. She lived with him for several years and bore him a son, Ferdinand. Meanwhile, the years were slipping by, the superb athlete's body was growing older. His fiery red hair had turned entirely white. Did he walk on the hillsides above the sea? At the tavern with friends, did he ever get drunk on wine and, lurching down some cobblestone path, roar at the stars in despair? Did he do pushups, or chin-ups, to stay in shape? His biographer, Las Casas, wrote of him in this period of frustration:

He began to sustain a terrible, continued, painful and prolonged battle; a material one of weapons would not have been so sharp and horrendous as that which he had to endure from informing so many people of no understanding, although they presumed to know all about it, and replying patiently to many people who did not know him nor had any respect for his person, receiving insulting speeches which afflicted his soul.[9]

But Columbus had the virtue that so many later Italian immigrants to America would possess in abundance: perseverance in the face of adversity. He studied Latin texts of Marco Polo's book, of Pliny's *Natural History* and of the *Imago Mundi,* a geographical treatise written in the early fifteenth century by Cardinal Pierre d'Ailly, which Columbus heavily underlined and annotated in the margins. The arguments set forth by d'Ailly were those he would present at Court when his chance came around again.

The end of the habitable earth toward the Orient and the end of the habitable earth toward the Occident are near enough, and between them is a small sea.
Between the end of Spain and the beginning of India is no great width. . . . India is near Spain.[10]

Despite his setbacks during these years, Columbus had made one important friend at Court. This was Luis de Santagel, a Spanish Jew who occupied the important position of Keeper of the Privy Purse for Ferdinand. Other Jewish and Italian bankers in Seville had also become interested in the Enterprise, among them Don Isaac Abravanel, who would later be expelled from Spain for refusing baptism, and the Medici representative in Seville, who had already written to Toscanelli on Columbus's behalf, Giannetto Berardi. And now the political winds as well began to shift in Columbus's favor. On the second of January, 1492,

Isabella and Ferdinand rode at the head of their army into Granada, the last Moslem state on the Spanish peninsula to capitulate to the Crown. Columbus, himself a fervent Catholic, marched in the triumphant procession. Surely, now that the Moors had finally been driven from Spain, the sovereigns would turn their attention to the Enterprise and to the race with Portugal for the wealth of the Indies. Hopefully, he requested an audience with Isabella and Ferdinand, only to be told from their own lips that his proposal was definitely and irrevocably rejected.

After years of fruitless effort and hope, Columbus was finished in Spain. Packing his possessions in a pair of saddlebags, he set out on muleback intending to cross the Pyrenees and offer the Enterprise to Charles VIII, king of France. He was already on the road northward from Granada when a royal messenger came galloping up to tell him that the queen had changed her mind. Actually, it had been Santangel who had changed it, suggesting "that he was astonished to see that her Highness, who had always shown a resolute spirit in matters of great pith and consequence, should lack it now for an enterprise of so little risk, yet which could prove of so great service to God and the exaltation of His Church, not to speak of very great increase and glory for her realms and crown." [11] If money was the stumbling block, he and his fellow bankers were prepared to underwrite the cost.

Every schoolboy knows the rest of the story. On the sixth of September, the *Niña, Pinta,* and *Santa María* weighed anchors at San Sebastián, in the Canaries, bound for Japan. To the extreme good fortune of Columbus and his crews, the American continent lay in their path. Thirty days out, the men panicked and asked Columbus to turn back. He agreed to turn back if no land was sighted within the next two or three days. Two days later, on the twelfth of October, at 2 A.M., the cry of *"Tierra! Tierra!"* brought everyone on deck, and by dawn San Salvador lay stretched across the horizon. The Western Ocean had been crossed.

But Columbus's dream of finding Asia was so firmly established in his mind, he had fought the battle of conviction so fervently and with such frustrations, that in four voyages he never realized he was not in Asia. In his eyes, those Caribbean islands were the outer fringes of the Asian mainland. The simple natives he met he called Indians, in the absolute conviction that they were aborigines of the fabled Indies. When he discovered Cuba, Columbus was sure he had reached Japan. He sent his men inland in the fruitless quest for those gold temple roofs so clearly described by Marco Polo.

Only when he explored the delta of the Orinoco during the third voyage, and felt the mighty push of that river against his ships, did doubt enter the admiral's mind. "I believe," he wrote then, "that this is a very great continent, which until today has been unknown." [12] But he changed his mind soon afterwards. No, he was near the Earthly Paradise. No, he changed his mind again, he *was* in India. As his biographer Las Casas noted, "whatever a man strongly desires and has firmly set in his imagination, all that he hears and sees at each step he fancies to be in its favor." [13] But this confusion was perfectly natural considering the extent of new information to be wedged into man's existing concept of the earth. It takes nothing away from Columbus's achievement. He had fought his long battle virtually alone, always a foreigner, an outsider.

Italian immigrants to America would venerate him as their greatest hero. Yet, ironically, they would not recognize themselves in him. He remained a statue on a pedestal, the noble Italian discoverer. They failed to realize that, like themselves, Columbus had started out the son of working-class parents, nearly illiterate. All the rest had been will, personality, vision, and fate.

Four Italian navigators crossed the Atlantic to discover new lands in the late fifteenth and early sixteenth centuries. The first, of course, was Columbus, but the Italian-American heritage includes the other three, all of whom are less well known, and one of whom, John Cabot, would not be identified by many people as an Italian.

Born Giovanni Cabotto, John Cabot anglicized his name when he reached England late in the fifteenth century, at about the same time that Columbus was moving from Portugal to Spain. They may have been born in the same year, 1451, and it is even possible that they had known each other as boys in Genoa.[14] The first record of Giovanni Cabotto appears in 1476, when the Venetian Senate confirmed his citizenship, noting that he had lived in the republic of Venice for fifteen years. From Venice he seems to have gone to Spain, residing at Valencia between 1490 and 1493. He may have met Columbus in Spain; or may have watched him parade his natives and parrots through the thronged streets of Barcelona after returning from his first voyage. Cabot remains, however, a far more shadowy figure than Columbus, partly because no physical description of him survives. The Milanese envoy in London, who knew Cabot, called him "a very good mariner . . . of a fine mind, greatly skilled in navigation." [15] He seems to have been a merchant as well as a ship's captain, which would not have been rare for a business-minded Venetian.

After having tried unsuccessfully to obtain funds from the bankers of Lisbon and Seville for a voyage to the Indies, Cabot went to England, where he made the same proposal to King Henry VII. A report from the Spanish ambassador to Ferdinand and Isabella noted that "a man like Columbus" was proposing "another business like that of the Indies." [16] After Cabot offered to raise the money for this voyage himself, King Henry VII granted him letters patent on the fifth of March, 1496, authorizing "our well beloved John Gabote, citizen of Venice," and his sons, "to sayle to all partes, countreys, and seas of the East, of the West, and of the North, under our banners and ensignes, with five ships." [17]

The five ships never materialized, so he departed from Bristol around the twentieth of May, 1497, with a single vessel, the *Matthew,* which was about the size of Columbus's *Niña.*

Unlike Columbus, who had dipped down to the Canaries before crossing the Atlantic on a sloping, southwesterly course, Cabot struck out due west from Ireland, thereby making the first northern passage since the Vikings. The wind and weather were so good that on June 24 the *Matthew,* with its tiny crew of eighteen, reached land — rugged, inhospitable cliffs ringed by the breaking ocean. As Cabot cautiously sailed the *Matthew* along the coast, he must have been looking for some sign that he had reached Japan. Perhaps, like Columbus, he had taken along a copy of Marco Polo's *Il Milione.* (Years later, exploring the interior of North America, Nicollet would carry with him a Mandarin robe to slip over his jacket and trousers the moment he saw a Chinese official.)[18] Cabot brought the *Matthew* into a large harbor, its shores lined with evergreen forests, and here a boat was lowered and a landing party went ashore. Though the native inhabitants had fled, the crew members found some primitive fishing nets and snares which they took back to their ship as evidence of where they had been. This was to be the only landing Cabot would make, though for a month or so he reconnoitered the coast, turning back when the land rounded away towards the west and the depth of his soundings increased.

What had he discovered? Was it an island, a peninsula, or simply a broad promontory jutting out from the Asian mainland? Reaching Bristol again on the sixth of August, Cabot hurried to London to report his findings to the Court. King Henry VII named the discovery New Isle. But then he changed his mind, and by 1502 he was calling it "the new founde lande," and Newfoundland it has remained.

A Venetian living in London wrote to his brothers in Italy:

The King of England is much pleased. . . . The King has promised that in the spring our countryman shall have ten ships armed to his order, and at his request has conceded him all the prisoners, except such as are confined for high treason, to man his fleet. The King has also given him money wherewith to amuse himself till then, and he is now at Bristol with his wife, who is also Venetian, and with his sons; his name is Zuan Cabot, and he is styled the great admiral.[19]

The much-pleased monarch supplied "our well beloved John Kaboto, Venecian," with not ten but six vessels for the new enterprise, plus crews, stores, and perhaps even colonists. Cabot, reported a contemporary, proposed "to keep along the coast from the place at which he touched, more and more towards the East, until he reaches an island which he calls *Cipango* [Japan], situated in the equinoctial region where he thinks all the species of the world have their origin, as well as the jewels." [20] Cabot actually left with five ships around the beginning of May 1498. One of the ships was forced to put into an Irish port. The rest of the story is best told by Samuel Eliot Morison:

John Cabot and his four ships disappear without a trace. No report of them reached Europe. Anyone may guess whether they capsized and foundered in a black squall, crashed an iceberg at night, or piled up on a rocky coast. One remembers an old Irish proverb, "The waves have some mercy but the rocks have no mercy at all"; and God knows there are plenty of rocks both on and off the North American coast.

Nevertheless, John Cabot's first voyage was the herald and forerunner to the English empire in North America. Like Columbus, he never learned the significance or value of his discoveries.[21]

In Ralph Waldo Emerson's opinion, the third of the Italian navigators, Amerigo Vespucci, was a base crook who had "managed in this lying world to supplant Columbus and baptize half the earth with his dishonest name." [22] Yet some of Vespucci's recent biographers have wondered how his reputation could have been so damaged with the passing years since his contemporaries apparently esteemed him highly. In a letter sent by Columbus to his son Diego, he wrote: "Amerigo Vespucci is on his way to court to see about some matters dealing with navigation. . . . He is a good man. Fate has been unkind to him, as to many others. He has never been compensated as he should have been for his work. But he is motivated by a desire to do everything possible in my behalf. . . ." [23] The letter was written shortly before Columbus's death, when Vespucci had already made two and perhaps three voyages to the New World. So the mystery remains. If Vespucci was dishonest, why should Columbus not have been the first to denounce him?

The Vespuccis were a Florentine family, important enough to have been portrayed in one of Ghirlandaio's frescoes for the Church of All Saints. [24] The fresco depicts Christ being lowered from the cross, and Amerigo appears as a young man standing near the left-hand corner of the painting with a sensuous, somewhat distracted expression. He already looks like a fallen angel, with a narrow but full mouth, dreamy eyes, and a brow fringed with curls. His sister Simonetta was one of the great beauties of the age. Botticelli immortalized her as probably the world's most famous nude, using her as the model for his *Venus;* [25] she stands on a seashell, covering her thighs with her own blonde tresses. When she died tragically young, the casket was left open during her funeral procession so that hundreds of Florentines might view her face for the last time. One of the mourners was Leonardo da Vinci, who drew a sketch of the lovely maiden whom death had taken, and Lorenzo the Magnificent, likening her to a star, wrote a sonnet in her memory. [26]

At the age of twenty-six, Amerigo accompanied his uncle Guido Antonio on a diplomatic mission to Paris. The Vespuccis were often employed by the Medici bankers for delicate negotiations, and during their embassy to the Court of Louis XI they not only transacted business but also reported to Florence on changes of opinion within the French Court. The mission was valuable for Amerigo, since he wrote many of the dispatches himself and thus acquired skill in reporting information clearly and coherently. After his return to Florence, Amerigo was sent to Seville as a representative of the House of Medici. Personable and bright, he became a leading figure in the large Italian colony there. He undoubtedly knew Columbus. As a banker, he was able to learn at first hand how a voyage of exploration is assembled, what its objectives should be, what provisions and how much capital are necessary. He was also able to monitor the activities of other navigators — which led to the charge that he had faked his first voyage in order to claim credit for the discovery of the New World.

This disputed first voyage, Vespucci's defenders say, was necessarily a covert operation. Christopher Columbus had been to the Indies twice. Both times he had returned with the same crude gold trinkets, unlettered natives, and gorgeous parrots. Various members of the Spanish Court — who were familiar with Marco Polo's descriptions of Asia — not unnaturally grew suspicious. According to Amerigo's partisans, this skepticism was shared by King Ferdinand, who gave orders that a fleet should be secretly assembled to check on the admiral's story and to report back on whether it seemed worthwhile to keep investing money, and ships, in this baffling enterprise of the Indies. The Medici banker Giannetto Berardi was put in charge of organizing the secret voyage. When he died unexpectedly, Vespucci completed the preparations. Though his role was to oversee expenses, Vespucci was also, like Toscanelli, a capable amateur geographer, and he asked to be able to accompany the voyage. The request was granted, and when four caravels left Spain on the tenth day of May, 1497, under the overall command of a Spanish captain — if this voyage really did take place — Amerigo was aboard. The caravels, by Amerigo's account, closely followed Columbus's plan of sailing until they reached the Caribbean where, instead of landing at any of the islands, they continued westward to the shores of Costa Rica or Honduras in Central America. Then they coasted along the Gulf of Mexico, rounded Florida, and sailed up the eastern coast of North America perhaps as far as Chesapeake Bay. The voyage lasted seventeen months. When Vespucci returned to Spain, Columbus had already departed on his third voyage.

No one knows today whether Vespucci actually crossed the Atlantic in 1497, or whether he cleverly invented the story of a secret expedition to gain himself greater fame. But he unquestionably did cross the Atlantic some time later — he said it was in May 1499 — and though the fleet was under the command of a Spanish captain, Hojeda, two vessels piloted by Vespucci split off and crossed the Equator, touching the coast of South America on the easternmost bulge of Brazil. The two vessels then coasted northward to rejoin Hojeda, sailing past Venezuela, which received its name from Vespucci. Seeing some crude huts on pilings along the shore, he baptized the coast "little Venice," Venezuela in Florentine dialect.[27]

After landing at Hispaniola, presumably to check on the condition of the Spanish colony there, the fleet returned to Cadiz on the eighth of September, 1500. There is little question that Vespucci did make this second voyage. He wrote frequent letters to his friends in Florence, and his observations of the people and landscapes of South America are far too precise to have been invented. He described in detail, for example, how natives would capture the giant iguana (an animal unknown in Europe), tether it, and then fatten it for roasting. If his dates are accurate, Vespucci was the discoverer of Brazil and the first explorer to have sailed for hundreds of miles along the coast of South America. But Vespucci was no more certain of where he was than Columbus had been. During the 1499–1500 voyage, he still believed he was in Asia. Obviously, the coast of Brazil was not Japan, but he believed it might be the Malay Peninsula — the Golden Chersonese described by Ptolemy.

In 1501–1502, Vespucci made another voyage along the South American coast, this time in the capacity of scientific observer in a Portuguese expedition that ranged far south of the Equator in an effort to find a passage to the Indian Ocean. On his return to Lisbon, Vespucci wrote a famous letter to Florence in which he talked of the lands he had recently explored as a *Mundus Novus,* or New World, because they were inhabited by "a greater multitude of peoples and animals than our Europe, Asia, or Africa." [28]

Here was a radical idea! Christian dogma stated very firmly that God had created the Island of the Earth, the *Orbis Terrarum,* for man's habitation. Now Vespucci was claiming that life existed elsewhere on the globe, in a New World of which the Church was ignorant. Though the letter was intended only for the eyes of a few humanists in Florence, thousands of copies were made and circulated throughout Europe, without Vespucci's knowledge or authorization. Soon, both this letter and another which Vespucci had written to the House of Medici in 1504 were being printed as pamphlets under the titles *Mundus Novus* and *Quatuor Americi Navigationes.* In 1507, still without Vespucci's knowledge, copies of these pamphlets passed into the hands of an obscure German geographer, Martin Waldseemüller, who was preparing a world map. Though he gave credit to Columbus for discovering the islands of the Caribbean, he assigned the name America to the southern portion of the continent, suggesting that it be called "Amerige or America" in honor of its "discoverer Americus, a man of wisdom," who had first perceived that the continent was not part of Asia but a New World which formed a great land barrier running north and south between Europe and Asia. In truth, Vespucci was almost as confused by the new continent as Columbus had been, and he later reversed himself and decided that it was part of Asia after all. But the cartographers did not know this. Perhaps because Waldseemüller's America had a pleasant sound and appearance, the name survived. In 1511, the famous cosmographer Gerardus Mercator published a map with AME lettered across the northern part of the continent and RICA across the southern. The baptism was complete.

In the meantime Vespucci — probably unaware of the effect his letters were having — retired from active navigation to take up the key post of Piloto Mayor of Spain, in charge of approving all transatlantic voyages, of planning them, of compiling maps and charts, and of evaluating information brought back by explorers. He served in this capacity until his death at Seville in February 1512.

In a letter written during his third voyage, Vespucci wrote frankly, "I hope to become famous for centuries if I return safely from this voyage." His wish was strangely granted. The entire continent was named after him. Yet, for whatever reason, his reputation would be so thoroughly destroyed that there is probably not a single statue of Amerigo Vespucci anywhere between the Arctic Circle in northern Canada and Tierra del Fuego at the tip of Argentina.

At the time of Vespucci's death in 1512, Europe's ideas about the New World were still in a turmoil. The debate raged on, whether those "Indies" were really another continent or simply a portion of Asia. And although the debate was finally settled in 1522, when the haggard survivors of Magellan's round-the-world expedition returned to Seville, North America remained unexplored and virtually unknown. Its true discoverer was the last of the four great Italian navigators, Giovanni da Verrazzano.

Though his voyage for the French Crown in 1524 was undertaken a quarter century after Columbus had crossed the Atlantic, Verrazzano remains the first European to have sailed along the eastern coast of America, to have entered New York harbor and rounded Cape Cod.

A fine copperplate engraving done in 1767, more than two centuries after his death, shows a man of military bearing with an expression that combines sternness and sensitivity.[29] The portrait's mood corresponds with the self-portrait that emerges from Verrazzano's prose; otherwise, very little is known about his life. Unlike Columbus, who was a self-made man, Verrazzano was well born. A stately, handsome villa in the Chianti area of Tuscany has been traditionally considered his birthplace in 1485.[30] He undoubtedly received an upper-class education, since his writings reveal the mind and sympathies of a cultured man, but after this Florentine upbringing he virtually disappears for twenty years. He seems to have become a merchant captain, and scraps of information which have survived from the period place him as far east as Cairo and as far west as Newfoundland, where a Jean Verazan accompanied a French expedition. Morison believes that he was sent to Dieppe in his early twenties to begin his mercantile and maritime career. He may have had relatives among the many Italian bankers and merchants living in France.

When Verrazzano was thirty-eight, he was chosen by the French king, Francis I, to lead a voyage to the New World. Francis was a fiery, ambitious monarch, and as he noted sarcastically, he could find no clause in Adam's will stating that the world should be divided between Spain and Portugal. The Florentine bankers in France, who put up a good part of the capital for this voyage, may have recommended Verrazzano as captain. And Francis, who was partial to all things Italian, assented willingly.

Like Cabot, Verrazzano sailed with one vessel — though it was twice the size of the *Matthew* — with a crew of fifty.[31] On the seventeenth of January, 1524, *La Dauphine,* as the ship was called, left the coast of France and began her cold, wintry Atlantic crossing, reaching one of North Carolina's three capes (probably Cape Fear) on the first of March. Verrazzano sailed south for some 150 miles, then turned north and explored the American coastline as far as Maine, bestowing Italian names on the more prominent landmarks. Unlike Columbus, Cabot, and Vespucci, he soon discarded the idea that the land he was exploring might be a part of Asia, though when he noted that the natives on shore were "nimble and great runners," he cautiously compared these qualities with those of the Chinese as described by Marco Polo. In his report to King Francis (a document known as the Cellère "Codex"), he wrote:

My intention on this voyage was to reach Cathay and the extreme eastern coast of Asia, but I did not expect to find such an obstacle of new land as I have found; and if for some reason I did expect to find it, I estimated there would be some strait to get through to the Eastern Ocean [the Pacific]. This was the opinion of all the ancients, who certainly believed that our Western

Ocean was joined to the Eastern Ocean of India without any land in between. . . . Nevertheless, land has been found by modern man which was
unknown to the ancients, another world in respect to the one they knew,
which appears to be larger than our Europe, than Africa, and almost larger
than Asia, if we estimate its size correctly.[32]

Here was a precise, assured report on what Columbus, Cabot, and Vespucci had discovered a quarter century before. Verrazzano also gave a
name to this New World, at least to the North American portion of it.
He called it Francesca, in honor of King Francis. The name vanished,
after appearing on a few maps. Otherwise, we might be known as
Francescans, or Franciscans.

Verrazzano, who may have been a nobleman, was the best educated
of the early explorers, and his accounts of what he saw during this
voyage reveal the North American Indians to have been gentle and
hospitable.[33] The "Codex" contains wonderful (if unfortunately far too
brief) descriptions of the North American coastline as it existed before
Western eyes had seen it. Verrazzano noted "many vines growing wild,
which climb up around the trees." [34] (This was also reported by later explorers as far inland as Ohio, and would seem to confirm the Viking
designation of America as Vinland.) "We found," Verrazzano wrote,
"wild roses, violets, and lilies, and many kinds of herbs and fragrant
flowers different from ours." [35] There were dense woods without roads or
houses except for Indian huts, stretches of tall, wild grass (domestic lawn
grass was introduced later from Europe). His description of New York
harbor has become a classic:

After a hundred leagues we found a very agreeable place between two
small but prominent hills; between them a very wide river, deep at its mouth,
flowed out into the sea; and with the help of the tide, which rises eight feet,
any laden ship could have passed from the sea into the river estuary. Since
we were anchored off the coast and well sheltered, we did not want to run
any risks without knowing anything about the river mouth. So we took a
small boat up this river to land which we found densely populated. The people were almost the same (as the Indians previously seen), dressed in birds'
feathers of various colors, and they came towards us joyfully, uttering loud
cries of wonderment, and showing us the safest place to beach the boat. We
went up this river for about half a league, where we saw that it formed a
beautiful lake [New York harbor], about three leagues in circumference.
About thirty of their small boats ran to and fro across the lake with innumerable people aboard who were crossing from one side to the other to see us.
Suddenly, as often happens in sailing, a violent unfavorable wind blew in from

the sea, and we were forced to return to the ship, leaving the land with much regret on account of its favorable conditions and beauty; we think it is not without some properties of value, since all the hills showed signs of minerals. . . .[36]

After heading up the coast, Verrazzano reported, "We discovered a triangular-shaped island, ten leagues from the mainland, similar in size to the island of Rhodes." [37] Though it was baptized Aloysia in honor of the king's mother, it remained Rode Island to early navigators, then Rhode Island, and finally the name was applied to the whole state. When *La Dauphine* made anchorage off the island, Indians rowed out to meet the ship in their canoes, and Verrazzano's description of them remains the least egocentric and the least condescending view of native life written by any European of the time:

These people are the most beautiful and have the most civil customs that we have found on this voyage. They are taller than we are; they are a bronze color, some tending more towards whiteness, others to a tawny color; the face is clear-cut; the hair is long and black, and they take great pains to decorate it; the eyes are black and alert, and their manner is sweet and gentle, very like the manner of the ancients. I shall not speak to Your Majesty of the other parts of the body, since they all have the proportions belonging to any well-built man. Their women are just as shapely and beautiful; very gracious, of attractive manner and pleasant appearance. . . . They do not value gold because of its color; they think it the most worthless of all, and rate blue and red above all other colors. The things we gave them that they prized the most were little bells, blue crystals, and other trinkets to put in the ear or around the neck. They did not appreciate cloth of silk and gold, nor even of any other kind, nor did they care to have them; the same was true for metals like steel and iron, for many times when we showed them some of our arms, they did not admire them, nor ask for them, but merely examined the workmanship. They did the same with mirrors; they would look at them quickly, and then refuse them, laughing. They are very generous and give away all they have. We made great friends with them. . . .[38]

La Dauphine remained at anchor fifteen days, while her crew rested and Verrazzano and his officers explored the countryside: "We frequently went about fifteen miles into the interior, and found it as pleasant as I can possibly describe and suitable for every kind of cultivation — grain, wine, or oil. For there the fields extend for 25 to 35 leagues; they are open and free of any obstacles or trees, and so fertile that any kind of seed would produce excellent crops." [39] Thus appear the first descriptions of what would become the United States of America.

Under sail again, *La Dauphine* coasted northward past Cape Cod, which Verrazzano named Cape Pallavicini in honor of an Italian general fighting in King Francis's army, and then continued "down east" along the coast of Maine, where the startled mariners encountered Indians who were wary, hostile, and rude, the braves showing their naked buttocks and howling with laughter. Turning eastward, past Nova Scotia, Verrazzano made one more anchorage at Newfoundland, which he noted had been "in times past discovered by the British." [40] Then *La Dauphine* recrossed the Atlantic and entered the harbor at Dieppe on the eighth of July, 1524.

Verrazzano set out on a new voyage three years later, this time with four ships. But one of them was separated in a storm and the sailors aboard two of the others mutinied and demanded to return to France. Holding firm, Verrazzano took his fleet across the Atlantic to the coast of Brazil, picking up a cargo of wood * before returning to Dieppe in the fall. He left France again on a third Atlantic voyage in the spring of the following year, 1528, with two or three vessels. The fleet reached Florida, then sailed down into the Caribbean, following the chain of the Lesser Antilles.

While Verrazzano's flagship, *La Flamengue*, rode at anchor off one of the islands, he approached the shore in a small boat. As its crew maneuvered the boat to avoid being caught in the surf, Verrazzano went over the side and swam or waded to shore. But the natives were not the gentle people that Verrazzano had found in New York and Newport harbors. He was struck from behind, killed, and then cut up and roasted on the beach while his crew, which included his brother Girolamo, looked on in horror, unable to save him.

Although these four Italians were the discoverers of America, not a single one of them had sailed from an Italian port, or sailed under the flag of any of the Italian maritime states — Genoa, Naples, or Venice.

Their voyages, nevertheless, form a logical climax of the Italian Renaissance. The spirit of discovery that motivated Italian scientists and artists during the Renaissance, also led Columbus and the other three Italian navigators across the Atlantic. By a strange coincidence, on that very same night of October 12, 1492, as the shout of *"Tierra!"* brought Columbus's seamen racing to the rail, and America was discovered, one

---

* Brazilian wood, which provided extracts for making dyes, was already in demand among French textile manufacturers.

of the greatest Renaissance masters, Piero della Francesca, died in Arezzo, in poverty, in a room he had not been able to see for many years. He was an old man, past ninety, a victim of the cruelest fate that can strike an artist — he, a painter, had become totally blind at the peak of his creative genius. Though he had been a brilliant mathematician in his youth, and an innovative painter whose use of perspective revolutionized Italian art, the feeling of stillness and of ancient ceremony in his frescoes represent the Renaissance of a generation or two before Columbus. Piero's world seems eternal, his time motionless. The graceful, somber figures of his paintings suggest a world that is closed, that leads backwards to the moment of Christ's birth in the manger at Bethlehem. All that is worth revealing has been revealed before. Men repeat reality. The more they advance, the more they approach the past.

The Renaissance genius who was Columbus's contemporary and who personified the desire for discovery was Leonardo da Vinci. His notebooks almost creak with motion: flying machines flap, gears whirl, pulleys pull, undersea craft scuttle along river bottoms and harbors, tanks clank, and the human body strains its muscles and nerves. It is no coincidence that Leonardo and Columbus were Italians of the same age. Though they never met, they resemble one another in their passion for the future.

In every field except one, the Italians of the Renaissance made the epochal discoveries that ushered in modern history. Their one weakness was politics. Here, their energies were fragmented. Had there been a powerful unifying pope in Rome instead of the Spanish Borgia, Alexander VI, and had such a leader managed to bring together Italy's quarreling states as France and England had been unified, as Spain was being unified under Ferdinand and Isabella, the history of the United States might have been different. The Italian navigators might then have sailed under their own national flag. There would probably have been Italian colonies in that New World discovered by Italians. It is almost too fanciful to conceive what an Italian America would have been like: an America of stone bell towers and thronged village squares, of grape arbors and *signorine,* and Bostonian doormen bowing from the waist and crying out, *"Buon giorno, signor Principe";* and yes, an America perhaps of greater factionalism. Would such colonies have survived the inevitable Protestant, Anglo-Saxon onslaught? Who can say?

Instead, a disaster struck Italy whose unfolding would take almost half a century, changing Italy radically. The consequences of that disaster would rumble on through Italian history into modern times, until finally the most humble, the most disadvantaged peasants would flee the country of their birth, refugees from a world that had not changed.

2

The Fall of the Renaissance

AS THE PROSPEROUS BURGHERS of Italian cities and towns rang in the New Year with dancing, banquets and plentiful wine, 1494 promised a continuation of the good times that seemed to have settled permanently over the peninsula. True, there had been wars over the past half century, but they were minor and localized. In 1492, the most capable of the Renaissance princes, Lorenzo de Medici, called the Magnificent, had died in Florence, but there seemed no lack of astute, forceful leaders to maintain the balance of power between jealous city-states. Commerce, science, and art flourished. In Milan, Leonardo da Vinci was just starting work on a fresco of the Last Supper. Just the previous year Columbus had returned from the discovery of land across the Western Ocean. Italy and Italians were the wonder of the world. As the historian Francesco Guicciardini wrote a generation later, "Italy had never enjoyed such prosperity, or known so favorable a situation as that in which it found itself so securely at rest in the year of our Christian salvation, 1490, and the years immediately before and after." [1]

As that new year of 1494 dawned, a force was gathering across the Alps that would shatter the Renaissance and bring it down in ruin. Its fall would affect not only the upper- and middle-class Italians of the brilliant cities, but also that vast community of urban poor and peasants who, in time, would find no other alternative to their plight than immigration. In their exodus, they would leave behind a country whose Renaissance had been stillborn for them, the distant glory of an Italy far from the reality of their poor villages and poor farms, of their hunger and their children's hunger and illiteracy.

The invader of Italy, and the agent of ruin for the Italian Renaissance, Charles VIII, had been a pleasant, round-faced and not overly bright young man of twenty-two when his father's death had placed him on the throne of France. This was the monarch to whom Columbus had planned to offer the enterprise of the Indies when he had set out on muleback from Cordova, disgusted with Spain and its sovereigns. But Charles had other and more ancient dreams. And on the eighth of September, 1494, with the flower of French knighthood riding behind him, he crossed the Alps into Italy. In vain, Pope Alexander VI issued a bull of excommunication to bar his path. Charles smiled. No one but that obstinate and corrupt old man had sought to check his ambitions. No one but Rodrigo Borgia, the corrupt Borgia Pope Alexander VI, whose vices were becoming the scandal of Christendom.

Charles's first objective was Milan. In the towns of the Po Valley, nervous Lombard tradesmen cheered from their windows as King Charles serenely rode past. The duke of Milan, known as the Moor because of his dark complexion, rode out to offer Charles the keys to the city (he would die a lingering death in a French dungeon years later). As Charles headed south from Milan, Piero de Medici rode out to the borders of Tuscany to surrender in person the fortresses of Sarzana and Pietrasanta which might have checked the French army. Charles smiled and returned the cheers of the Tuscans. He was marching on Naples, not Florence.

A half dozen voices had called him to Italy. The hollow voice of Alexander's predecessor, Sixtus IV, inviting Charles's father to seize the thrones of Naples and Sicily on the basis of an ancient claim granted to the Duke of Anjou in 1266. The sly voice of Alexander's enemy, Cardinal Giuliano della Rovere (the future Pope Julius II), begging Charles to invade Italy and depose the Borgia pope. The shrill voice of Savonarola, struggling with the Medici for the soul of Florence and asking Charles to aid him. The voices of the Moor, of the Venetian senate.[2] And, finally, the deepest voice of all, the mystical voice within Charles himself, the voice of his dream that he should conquer Naples and Sicily because in possessing them he would possess the Holy Crusader's Crown of Jerusalem, that mirage from the time of the Norman knights of Sicily, Roger and Tancred. All Italy seemed to be calling Charles to a still-undefined heroic destiny; he smiled at the peasants who stopped forking hay at his progress — the fleur de lys banners rolling in the sunlight, the mounted knights, the dream of Jerusalem resurrected.

Charles adored Naples. If men were not yet saying, "see Naples and die," the custom should have begun with this dreamy French king. While his staff efficiently plundered banks of their deposits and palazzi of their works of art, Charles, like any enthralled tourist, went to Pompeii and Capri, Positano and Ravello, looked at ancient friezes and contemporary Renaissance canvases, sought out Italian painters to take back to France and Italian gardeners for his beloved chateau at Amboise. It was not Charles who died (at least not at once), but his dream of Holy Jerusalem did, obliterated by profane Naples.

But now the Italian princes, still distracted from reality by their past quarrels, at last sensed the danger. If Charles had been able to invade Italy with such impunity, who might follow? It was too late to recruit and train a national army — an Italian army. War in Italy during the Renaissance, like everything else, had been refined into an art. Armies were small, led by shrewd and sometimes treacherous *condottieri* whose campaigns were delayed by truces and last-minute changes of alliance, whose cannons often used stone rather than iron balls so as not to damage the beautiful castles they besieged. These delicate armies were no match for the national army that Charles had brought into Italy — nor for the Swiss and German pikemen who could be hired by the tens of thousands, and who were ruthless in battle. But there was no time left. A secret pact was signed in the doge's bedchamber in Venice on the thirty-first of March, 1495, appointing the marquis of Mantua commander of all the private horse and troop that could be mustered together.[3] It was a fighting machine whose gears did not mesh. And yet, as all those bands of Renaissance warriors came together and their armor and many-colored pennants shone in the sun, it was a flash of nationalism that had not been seen in Italy since Roman times.

Charles, at last jolted out of his dreams, was retreating back up the peninsula. Mantua could select the place and time of combat. He had forty thousand men to Charles's ten thousand, and he was on home ground. He waited for Charles at Fornovo, near Parma, and at midmorning threw his disorganized units at the French across a river too deep to wade easily, so that some of the Italian horsemen were drowned, some cut down as they tried to scramble up the opposite bank. Mantua himself fought unsparingly, as did Charles, the French knights, the

Swiss, various *condottieri*. Though Charles lost his wagons piled with Italian art and provisions, he was able to extricate his battered army from Italy and march it back across the Alps. In terms of prestige, the victory was his. More important, it telegraphed to every nation in Europe the fact that the Renaissance states of Italy were fatally weak and disunited.

Charles did not reinvade. He was preparing to, but as he ran out to the tennis court at Amboise he struck his head on a low doorway and died.[4] But there was no lack of candidates now for the conquest of Italy. The armies of France and Spain split up the kingdom of Naples, until they began quarreling among themselves. The quarrel degenerated into a personal rivalry between the two strongest monarchs on the European continent. One was Francis I (for whom Verrazzano had named Francesca). As a young man he had been considered a candidate for Holy Roman Emperor as well as the king of France. But that office had gone to another youthful sovereign, the Habsburg Charles V. A fortunate succession had made Charles V the king of Spain as well as Austria, and he also ruled the Netherlands, much of Germany, and parts of eastern Europe and of Italy. Their rivalry might have been fought out almost anywhere on the continent. But since Italy's weakness had been revealed at Fornovo, Italy became the battlefield.

The Italian wars lasted thirty-six years — over a quarter century — during which the entire peninsula was devastated and impoverished. Armies would meet in furious combat that might last, as it did at Marignano, two entire days from morning until midnight. Thirty thousand casualties were counted in that one battle. Spanish, French, Swiss, German and Italian soldiers and mercenaries looted the cities. Banks failed, businesses were ruined. The countryside was plundered and depopulated. People died of hunger, and plague. But no single event stands out so clearly as a symbol of the horrors of those decades as the sack of Rome.

It occurred near the end of the Italian wars, when the combatants themselves were exhausted and brutalized. A huge Imperial army went out of control. From its base in the Po Valley, it lurched down the peninsula toward the Eternal City. Its commander, the constable de Bourbon, was unable to exert any real control over this plundering horde of Germans, Spaniards, and Italians. As the Imperial army approached Rome, the horrified pope, Clement VII, tried to buy off its attack. This had sometimes worked in earlier centuries when barbarians had been at the gates of Rome, but it did not work now. And so on a lovely, sunlit morning in May 1527, as an ashen Clement hurried from chapel into a secret passageway that would take him to the fortress of Castel Sant' Angelo, the first scaling ladders thudded against the lightly defended walls of the city and the Imperial rabble began to pour into the capital of Christendom they were sworn to serve and defend.

On Holy Thursday of that year, 1527, as Pope Clement had blessed the crowd assembled at St. Peter's square, a fanatic had climbed up onto the statue of St. Paul and screamed, "Thou bastard of Sodom! For thy sins Rome shall be destroyed." [5] Now, as Clement watched helplessly from the safety of his fortress, scenes of an earthly Hell were enacted in the streets below. Homes were smashed and looted, people tortured. Churches were plundered and burned. Cardinals were stripped naked and tied onto the backs of mules, led around the city by their tormentors. The Tiber conveyed to sea the bodies of girls and women who had committed suicide after being raped. Inside St. Peter's itself, German Lutherans slaughtered the hundreds of Roman families and priests who had sought sanctuary there. When he closed his eyes at night, Clement saw the blood washing across those marble floors. *Quare de vulva audixisti me?* he cried to God in his anguish. *Qui utinam consumptus essem, ne oculus videret.* [6] * For seven months he remained in his stone ark as the floodwaters of butchery rose over Italy, and the Catholic world disintegrated.

After Rome, Florence was besieged — a siege which dragged on for eight months while Michelangelo, among others, labored to fortify and patch the city walls. The sacrifices of the Florentine people were in vain, since they were betrayed by the very general they had hired to organize their defense. (Machiavelli had warned them that mercenary soldiers were unreliable; but only in retrospect did he stand out as a great political thinker, and most Florentines had not even heard of him in his own lifetime.) The same horde that had pillaged Rome now went to work on Florence, though there the pickings were leaner — a dead cat brought $15 towards the end of the siege. [7] By the time the Treaty of Cambrai put an end to the bloodshed in Italy, nearly every major city and town had been ravaged at least once. The outstanding exception was Venice, which at the outset of the wars had faced a huge coalition that included Spain, France, the Holy Roman Empire, the

---

* "Why did you take me from the womb? Oh, I should have been destroyed before a single human eye saw me."

papacy, Milan and Ferrara. But while the soldiers of the Venetian army died with stubborn courage to defend the approaches to the lagoon, her able diplomats had been able to detach the members of the coalition one by one like so many leaves from an artichoke until finally there were none left and Venice was spared. Only in that magical city did the Renaissance linger through the sixteenth century, as artists like Titian and Veronese painted its sunset colors. Elsewhere Italy was gray, exhausted, ruled by dull and repressive tyrants.

"If the Lord had not put discord between France and Spain, where should we be?" [8] Alexander VI had joked early in the Italian wars. But the humor was black, and Alexander would die before he could see the full consequence of this "discord": Spain won the contest in Italy, and with the Spanish viceroys and their garrisons came the Inquisition. In a land that had blazed with the freedom to think, to question and explore, rigid controls descended over the people and dissent was suppressed by force. The visionary philosopher Giordano Bruno was burned at the stake in Rome. Galileo was threatened with torture and forced to deny his work. Italy became a closed society, entering a period of eclipse and stagnation that lasted for over two hundred years. As a result, very few Italians would follow the great navigators into that larger world beyond the Strait of Gibraltar until the mass departure of the immigrants in the late nineteenth century. And those Italians would enter the Atlantic not as proud captains on the decks of their ships, but as steerage passengers crowded together below decks.

3

Tonti and Mazzei

FOR THREE CENTURIES after Columbus, the New World remained *terra incognita* to Italians. Except for a few skilled Venetian laborers who were shipped over to the colonies to tend silkworms or blow glass, there were virtually no Italians in America. Only two names stand out: Tonti in the seventeenth century, Mazzei in the eighteenth. Both are difficult subjects to write about.

The first, Enrico Tonti, who came to America by way of French Canada, was almost unbelievably brave, a genuine hero. But he was so self-effacing, and wrote so little about himself, that he remains a shadow — a magnificent explorer and settler who made the first descent of the Mississippi with La Salle, but a shadow all the same.

The doyen of nineteenth-century American historians, Francis Parkman, sensed uneasily that Tonti was destined to be neglected. Having called him "that brave, loyal, and generous man," Parkman made an effort to save the Italian explorer from oblivion by adding, "there are very few names in French-American history mentioned with such unanimity of praise as that of Henry de Tonti." [1] Today, probably not more than a few thousand Americans have ever heard of Enrico Tonti. This, in brief, is his story.

On a gusty, chilly December afternoon in 1679, a party of about twenty men walked single file along a trail above the St. Lawrence River. Several of the men struggled under the weight of fully loaded birchbark canoes. A few of them were Indians, the rest French trappers. At the head of the column walked the French explorer Robert Cavelier, the sieur de La Salle. Behind him came a slender, even-featured Italian with a terrible deformity. In place of his right hand was a claw, semiarticulated, skillfully crafted out of brass. Once he had kept it concealed beneath a glove but now it shone in the hard winter light.

In Paris, the previous winter, La Salle had been virtually forced to accept this disabled war veteran as his second-in-command. To gain approval for his plans, La Salle had needed the support at Versailles of the powerful prince of Conti. And Conti had taken under his wing a tragic family of Italians of whom Enrico Tonti was the older son.

Tonti had been born in the midst of the greatest popular insurrection against foreign tyranny that Italy experienced in the seventeenth century. A fruit tax levied in Naples by the Spanish viceroy served as a pretext for the revolt. Fruit vendors overturned their carts on the seventh of July, 1647, while the teeming populace of the *bassi,* the Naples slums, poured into the streets with homemade weapons in their hands. Men came to Lorenzo Tonti, a respected young banker. Would he aid the revolt? He sympathized, but preferred to wait. The city was now controlled by the mob, its leader a barefoot young fisherman from Amalfi, Tomaso Aniello (or as he was called, Masaniello). As fiery as he was unstable, Masaniello went to negotiate with the viceroy stripped to the waist, a huge medallion of the Madonna swinging over his tanned chest. The next morning he was foaming at the mouth, in delirium, screaming out that the wine which had been served him by the viceroy's liveried servants had been drugged. Six days later he was dead, cornered and stabbed in the shadow of the cathedral by a dozen thugs in the viceroy's pay, who dumped his bloody corpse in the sewer and brought his decapitated head to their master.

All the fisherman had demanded was a lowering of taxes and an end to underweight bread loaves — the humble demands of the poor. But with Masaniello's murder the revolt passed into the hands of the middle class. Now Lorenzo Tonti came forth, one of the founders and chief officers of the republic of Naples, which sought as its aims the expulsion of the hated Spanish and self-rule. Lorenzo Tonti was dispatched to the key seaport of Gaeta halfway between Naples and Rome to serve as its governor and to hold it for the revolution. It was a difficult moment for him. His young, aristocratic wife was over eight months pregnant with their first child; but she made the journey, and at Gaeta, in 1647, Enrico Tonti was born.

Though the people of Naples repulsed a Spanish invasion in two days of savage street fighting, the republic, betrayed by one of its leaders, collapsed in April 1648. A death warrant was issued for Lorenzo Tonti, but he was able to flee Neapolitan territory with his wife and infant son. After being sheltered by liberal friends, the Tontis crossed the Alps in 1650 and made their way to Paris. They had lost everything, but they were still young enough to make a new start, and in France they could count on the support of a powerful minister. Louis XIV was still a twelve-year-old boy, and his Court was dominated by the brilliant, Italian-born Cardinal Giulio Mazarini (Mazarin). A supporter of the Neapolitan republic, Mazarin quickly found a post for the destitute republican exile. Lorenzo Tonti, moreover, was an innovative and resourceful banker. A series of inconclusive wars had depleted the French treasury, and the people were already overtaxed. Put to work on this problem, Lorenzo invented one of the world's first life insurance programs — still called the Tontine in his honor. Shares were issued by the state to subscribers grouped into classes according to their age; when they died, the interest on the principal went to their heirs.

Enrico Tonti grew up with a sense of apartness. He was Italian, the son of an ex-revolutionary who was now a high official at Court. Dark-eyed, slightly built, the boy possessed an inner toughness that belied his rather delicate looks. In 1668, he enrolled in the army as a cadet, and the following year he was transferred to the rapidly expanding French navy. But then disaster struck the family. His father, the victim of intrigues at Court, was imprisoned in the Bastille; he would languish there for eleven years and die penniless while Tontines raised millions for the French Crown. (The great Tontine of 1789 in England brought in over a million pounds for the government of George III, and other Tontines were held regularly throughout Europe and even in the American colonies.)

As a naval officer, Enrico Tonti saw action in the Sicilian wars between France and Spain that roiled the waters of the Mediterranean for nearly a decade. He was promoted to captain. But in a battle against a stronger Spanish force off Messina, a grenade blew off his right hand and he was captured. After the torment of amputation and imprisonment in Sicily, he was traded in a prisoner exchange and allowed to go home. But the return to Paris was a melancholy one. His father was in the Bastille, the family desperately poor. He himself was disfigured. Then came the meeting with La Salle and the chance to go to New France.

At first, La Salle was skeptical. How could a one-handed man paddle a canoe, let alone carry it, fight off a homicidal Indian, survive alone in the forest when he was lost or betrayed by his men? He, La Salle, had done all these things. He had been on the waters and in the forests of North America a dozen years, and he knew how punishing the wilderness could be. But the Prince of Conti pressed him and finally La Salle agreed.

In a few weeks, he was writing the Prince, "I cannot overstate my joy in having Tonti with me . . . you could not have believed him capable of doing things for which a strong constitution, a knowledge of the country, and the free use of two arms seem absolutely necessary . . . his energy and ability make him capable of anything. . . ." [2] It was unusually warm praise from La Salle. Though a natural leader able to take discouraged men through any kind of hardship, he was also harsh, demanding, and unforgiving. The same men he marched with now would try to poison him. A few years earlier another party of Indians and Frenchmen had abandoned him in midwinter in the Ohio River Valley, hoping he would die. But La Salle had made it back from below the falls at Louisville to the northern tip of Lake Michigan, alone, hungry, surviving on sheer endurance and the nine Indian languages he had taught himself. Nine languages? Nine lives. Thank God he now had a lieutenant who was dependable and loyal.

Enrico Tonti — or as the French called him, Henri de Tonti — had received his first fitness report. The second would be composed in five seconds at Versailles by *le grand roi,* Louis the Great, Louis XIV. But that was years away.

For Tonti, everything about the American wilderness was unfamiliar. Now the party reached the vast wind-whipped lake at the head of the St. Lawrence, and started across it, hugging the solemn evergreen bluffs to escape the wind. His men watched, fascinated, as Tonti took a paddle in his good left hand and laid its handle into the brass claw. All day the paddles descended, the long bark canoes spurting forward, riding low, loaded with clothing, with blankets against the cold at night, with knives, pistols and rifles, powder and lead to pour new balls for the firearms, with paper, quill pens and candles, with tools and a disassembled forge; with hard bread and bacon and a little blessed brandy.³ In the late afternoon the canoes were pulled ashore and the men cooked supper, seasoning their boiled cornmeal with chunks of fish or game. On clear nights they would simply lie down under the stars, covering themselves with blankets. When it rained they stripped bark from the trees and laid it over a frame of sticks to make a shelter. Before sleep there would be a little brandy and tobacco, prayers, sometimes a fight that La Salle or Tonti would have to break up; occasionally some Indian women, or an all-night vigil against Indian attack.

In early January 1680, they reached the far end of the lake, laboriously carrying all their stores and equipment up winding trails past the newly discovered Niagara Falls. The Senecas, part of the five-nation confederacy of the Iroquois, had worshiped their spirits at these falls for centuries. Now Seneca warriors would emerge quietly from the forest to look on suspiciously as Tonti established a camp and a small shipyard near the head of the Niagara River. La Salle had rushed back to Montreal to pay off the most pressing of his creditors and to get new supplies. He had left the Italian in charge of building a sixty-ton, two-masted warship, the first sailing vessel on the Great Lakes. Tonti set the men to work felling trees.

They were restive at first, querulous, half of them reporting sick. The winter was bitterly cold, their camp desolate. A drunken Indian had staggered out of the forest brandishing a knife, to be repulsed by the blacksmith wielding a red-hot iron bar. For days, the men lived in fear of an Indian attack. But they found Tonti patient and just, a more humane commander than the sieur de la Salle, and before a month was out they were following his orders willingly.

By spring, the warship had taken form. In early summer — with no sign of La Salle — they proudly launched it into the river, stepping its masts and setting up its rigging and five cannon. On its stemhead their skilled French carpenter carved a griffin.⁴ When La Salle finally returned late in the summer he found the vessel riding at anchor. After a festive christening — with hundreds of Senecas watching from the edge of the forest — the *Griffin* caught a fair wind and began its crossing of the Great Lakes.

The vessel was pivotal to La Salle's plans. It would pick up furs at trading posts along the Great Lakes, taking the precious cargo back to Fort Niagara for transshipment to Montreal. La Salle and Tonti would build a second vessel to navigate the Mississippi as far as the Gulf of Mexico; furs would be shipped from there directly to France. With the capital raised from their fur trading operations, they would build a network of forts along the rivers of the middle west. These forts would open up trade and draw French settlers to the area. What they hoped to establish was a sort of frontier Maginot line that would keep the English colonies penned up east of the Alleghenies and challenge Spain's control of Mexico and the southwest. This was the plan La Salle had presented to Louis XIV's ministers at Versailles. Its ultimate aim was to pry New France loose from the ice-rimmed St. Lawrence and send it gliding down into the green, fertile, river-rich interior of the North American continent.

They endured a harsh winter along Lake Michigan, sending the *Griffin* back across the lakes with its first cargo of furs. The party split up, one group under La Salle, the other under Tonti. Both groups traveled overland under harassment from Indians, half starved. At one point, when Tonti set out alone to find help, his canoe overturned on Lake Michigan and he barely made it to shore, holding his brass hand up above the churning waves. For three days he subsisted on acorns. But he rejoined his men and they finally straggled into the outpost at St. Joseph, nearly two months overdue.[5]

In early December 1680, the combined party ascended the St. Joseph River, near the site of Chicago, carrying their loaded canoes. They began crossing icy, swampy land in what is now northern Indiana and Illinois. The marshes of the upper middle west have long since been drained. But when La Salle and Tonti crossed these plains they were filled with water up to the armpits.[6] To their relief, the explorers soon found a tributary of the Illinois River deep enough to float their canoes, then the Illinois itself.

A few miles below the present site of Peoria, La Salle and Tonti camped while their men built a fort that would serve as a jumping-off point for the exploration of the Mississippi basin. Its sardonic name, Fort Heartbreak (Crevecoeur in French) was probably a spontaneous choice on the part of the men who had been chosen to remain there under Tonti's command. The Italian would supervise the construction of *Griffin*'s sister ship, intended for the Mississippi, while La Salle again returned to Canada to raise fresh capital and supplies.

The little fort was built on a low knoll, with a deep ravine on either side and a marsh in front. The plains stretched away on all sides, with only the river to break their monotony. A log palisade about twenty-five feet high formed the outer wall of the fort. The men had their bunkhouse against one side. The priests' cabin was set against the third corner, the magazine and tool shop against the fourth.[7] Tonti lived in a tent pitched at the center of the fort, and when he shut his eyes at night to sleep it was with the trust that his men would not mutiny and kill him. This life was now his destiny and he accepted it, dreaming, as La Salle had dreamed, of the great river rolling southward towards the Gulf of Mexico, of a new empire, of future cities that would bear their names.

As the weeks passed, and work was begun on the new vessel, the men at Fort Heartbreak edged closer and closer to mutiny. They were lonely, discouraged, and afraid that any night an Indian attack would wipe out the little fort and its garrison. Tonti was barely able to control them. When two French voyageurs arrived with the news that the *Griffin* had sunk on Lake Michigan, that La Salle was hopelessly ruined and that none of them would ever be paid, nothing could prevent the mutiny.[8] They bore Tonti no ill will, so they waited until he went out to check a fortified point along the river and then destroyed the fort, stealing its provisions and carving into a plank on the side of the half-completed vessel, "*Nous sommes toutes sauvages.*" Returning to view that scene of desolation, Tonti dispatched two loyal messengers to alert La Salle. With his one remaining workman and two friars, he took shelter in a nearby Illinois Indian town. It was a big settlement of more than seven thousand inhabitants, and Tonti hoped to remain there until La Salle's return. He had managed to salvage the precious forge and other tools; perhaps the ship could still be built.

But now the Iroquois intervened.

Years later, walking along a deserted Louisiana beach, Tonti would remember a belt of white seashells, himself running across the prairie waving it, the bullets, the fear, the knife point driving straight at his pounding heart. He had nearly been killed three times in three days. But he had repaid the Iroquois eventually; *nous sommes toutes sauvages.*

The Indians of the Iroquois League had occupied much of the area of New York State and the lower Great Lakes. But the white man's expansion, his constant tree-felling and building and his eagerness to sell Indians whiskey, had disrupted the Iroquois' ecology and ravaged their culture. They drifted westward like a swarm of angry bees, slaughtering as they went.

They had already committed genocide on the Hurons, Neutrals, and

Eries, and devastated the Canadian Algonquins. Now they were moving against the Illinois, one of the largest American Algonquin tribes.

In their panic the Illinois mobbed Tonti, charging him with having engineered the Iroquois attack. As he tried to reason with them in their language, they seized the irreplaceable forge and the other tools and hurled them into the river. Tonti and his three companions were now prisoners. "All night long fires blazed along the shore. The excited warriors greased their bodies, painted their faces, befeathered their heads, sang their war songs, danced, stamped, yelled, and brandished their hatchets, to work up the courage to face the crisis. The morning came, and with it came the Iroquois." [9]

The battle was fought with rifles in open prairie across the river from the town. As the Illinois braves began to fall back towards the river, Tonti realized that the only way to save them from massacre was to negotiate a battlefield truce. The Iroquois were still officially at peace with France. Tonti would intervene, in the name of Louis XIV. He picked up a wampum belt of seashells as a peace symbol and, waving it over his head, ran towards the Iroquois lines. The Iroquois, taking him for an Indian, concentrated their fire on him but missed. He was surrounded and captured. In the fierce excitement an Iroquois brave stabbed at his heart, but the point of the knife glanced against a rib and he was only gashed. "Tonti, breathless, and bleeding at the mouth with the force of the blow he had received, found words to declare that the Illinois were under the protection of the King and the Governor of Canada, and to demand that they should be left in peace." [10]

But at that moment the Illinois launched a counterattack, and some of the Iroquois, enraged by what they felt was Tonti's duplicity, wanted to see him tortured to death on the spot. With a Seneca chief urging that Tonti should be burned alive, "I was never," he wrote, "in such perplexity, since at that moment there was an Iroquois behind me with a knife in his hand, lifting my hair as if he was going to scalp me. I thought it was all over with me, and that my best hope was they would knock me on the head instead of burning me, as I thought they would do." [11]

But the Iroquois, perhaps in awe of Tonti's gleaming brass hand, which looked like a piece of powerful *medicine*, and dubious about killing a friend of the French governor, Count Frontenac, whom they admired, kept Tonti and his two friars as hostages while they occupied the Illinois town. Three days later, at a ceremony with drums and chanting, the Iroquois chiefs ordered Tonti to leave the area and made him a traditional gift of six packs of beaver skins. But since the Iroquois would not promise to leave their Illinois victims in peace, Tonti contemptuously kicked the beaver skins aside. "The chiefs, in a rage, rose and drove him from the lodge. [He and the friars] withdrew to their hut, where they stood all night on the watch, expecting an attack and resolved to sell their lives dearly. At daybreak, the chiefs ordered them to begone." [12] The Iroquois then massacred the Illinois, tying the women to posts and torturing them to death, and, it is said, eating the small children.

Tonti safely passed the site of Chicago and worked his way up the shore of Lake Michigan trying to reach Green Bay where there was a Jesuit post. One of his friars, the sixty-five-year-old Father Ribourde, wandered into a grove of trees one day to mediate with his breviary and was ambushed and scalped. The other nearly died from eating a piece of leather; it was midwinter and they were starving. At an abandoned Indian village they found some frozen corn and squashes in the fields, and, a little later, an old canoe which they were able to patch up and embark with on the lake. "But we were stopped by the wind for a week," Tonti recorded, "which forced us to consume the few provisions we had gathered together. We had nothing else to eat. At last we held a meeting to see what we should do, and . . . decided to return to the Indian village, so that at least we could die warm." [13] Tonti was ill, his legs swollen from cold and malnutrition, and the friar, Father Membre, was half dead. But on the fourth of December, friendly Indians saw their fire and led them to a village where they were fed and looked after.

In May 1681, Tonti and La Salle were finally reunited in northern Michigan — more than a year after they had crossed Lake Michigan so confidently in the *Griffin* singing French sea chanties and firing off broadsides to announce their arrival at each trading post. All their plans had gone awry. The *Griffin* was on the bottom of Lake Michigan. The other ship, half completed, was now a nest for spiders and rattlesnakes. La Salle was tens of thousands of francs in debt. Tonti had never been paid. But they were alive and, *hélas!*, they would try again.

The key to their project was still the Mississippi, which no European had ever navigated to its mouth. When La Salle had first come to Canada, some fifteen years before, Frenchmen in the colony believed the Mississippi emptied into the Gulf of California. Though Indians had corrected this mistaken notion by their accounts of *"le grande rivière,"* the Great River, it remained unexplored. La Salle and Tonti resolved to navigate it to its mouth, then return to found a colony, build forts — to resurrect La Salle's original plan.

But first they had to raise funds, so they passed the spring going from one outpost to the other, buying up furs. In Canada they would sell the furs to bankroll their new Mississippi expedition. In beautiful early summer weather, they brought their little fleet of low-riding, laden canoes down through Lakes Huron and Erie, to Fort Niagara. There the canoes were lifted out of the water and carried down the winding trails beside the falls to the mouth of the Niagara. Then came the final leg in the thousand-mile journey back to Montreal — the crossing of Lake Ontario.

It was over a year since Enrico Tonti had seen that lake, crossing it then in the other direction, westward. He had endured hunger, privation, betrayal, bloodshed. He had also proved himself in the hardest environment a man could desire. The Indians, respecting him, had begun to call him *bras de fer,* the iron-handed man.

Snow whipped across the frozen landscape, dark at midday, as nearly a hundred people — Frenchmen, Indians, a dozen Indian squaws and even a few children — bent their faces against the fury of the storm and dragged behind them canoes that had been mounted on sledlike runners. They were just south of the future site of Chicago, and they had left Lake Michigan behind, bound for the Illinois. It was the day before Christmas 1681, and the start of La Salle and Tonti's expedition to the Gulf of Mexico.

It was a queer group, with women, children, even a nursing infant, and perhaps this brought it luck. There would be no stopping this time to build forts on the Illinois, to set up a shipyard and assemble a vessel. La Salle and Tonti had decided to stick to canoes, as the Indians had always done, and to keep moving. Down the cold, leafless banks of the Illinois the flotilla of canoes glided, past the ruins of Fort Heartbreak and the rotting ship. On the sixth of February, "they issued on the majestic bosom of the Mississippi." [14]

After a rest — the river still churning with broken-up ice — the explorers began their southward journey. Below the Chickasaw Bluffs they ran into fog so thick that neither shore was visible, but the worst of the winter cold and ice was over. Near the mouth of a large river that for many years was called the Riviere de Tonti, or Tonti's River (and is now called the Arkansas), they met the Arkansas Indians who received them much as the Iroquois of New York had received Verrazzano. The good-hearted Father Membre praised "these savages, who are gay, civil, and free hearted. . . . They are so well formed that we were lost in admiration of their beauty. We did not lose the value of a pin while we were among them." [15]

After formally taking possession of the Arkansas territory for Louis XIV in one of those solemn affairs, full of raised crosses, hymns, benedictions, volleys of musket fire and shouts of *"Vive le Roi!,"* which "their hosts would have liked less, if they had understood it better," [16] the explorers continued downriver. Their trials were behind them now. The voyage was becoming sweeter, gentler. There were moments of tranquil beauty, as the canoes drifted on the placid, copper- and flame-colored surface of the water at sunset, deer and buffalo drinking at the water's edge, flights of birds in the sky. At times hundreds of squirrels would swim out to meet the canoes, and the little animals would climb fearlessly up the paddles and run and jump around.

The explorers began to find, kill, and eat alligators. On one of the last days of the voyage, Tonti, reconnoitering a tributary of the Mississippi, spotted a canoe with a single Indian in it. He began to follow it, curious, when more than a hundred warriors appeared on the riverbank, drawing back their bows. But Tonti waved to them and they held up hands, joining them in a gesture of friendship. Tonti wrote, "I, who had but one hand, told our men to do the same thing." [17]

They were reaching their journey's end. In Parkman's words,

On the sixth of April, the river divided itself into three broad channels. La Salle followed that of the west, and d'Autray that of the east, while Tonti took the middle passage. As he drifted down the turbid current, between low and marshy shores, the brackish water changed to brine, and the breeze grew fresh with the salt breath of the sea. Then the broad bosom of the great Gulf opened on his sight, tossing its restless billows, limitless, voiceless, lonely as when born of chaos, without a sail, without a sign of life.[18]

At a spot near the mouth of the river, a column was driven into dry ground bearing the arms of France and the inscription:

LOUIS LE GRAND, ROI DE FRANCE ET DE
NAVARRE, REGNE; LE NEUVIEME AVRIL,
1682

Years later, Tonti would find the column knocked down by floodwaters and would move it to higher ground.

In the formal document taking possession of Louisiana, which then comprised half of the United States, the Italian's name appears just below that of La Salle. But the king of France was not interested in the vast territory which now bore his name. An enemy of La Salle's had become governor of Canada. This man, Le Febvre de La Barre, was already writing reports to France in which he claimed that La Salle and Tonti had failed to pay their debts, and were reckless adventurers who would involve the colony in a war with the Iroquois. Louis the Great replied to La Barre, "I am convinced like you, that the discovery of the sieur de La Salle is very useless, and that such enterprises ought to be prevented in the future." [19]

From here on the story becomes a chronicle of hopeless disaster. At first, La Salle and Tonti's plans seemed to be fructifying. On a high bluff not far from the site of Fort Crevecoeur, they built a more powerful outpost called Fort St. Louis of the Illinois. Tonti, in command for several years, was able to repulse an Iroquois attack and to induce about twenty thousand Illinois Indians, loyal to France, to settle around the fort. Large-scale fur trading operations were begun, to generate capital. Meanwhile, La Salle returned to France where he was able to convince Louis XIV, temporarily at least, of the importance to France of the Louisiana territory. A large expedition was assembled to cross the Atlantic and found a French colony at the mouth of the Mississippi. With over two hundred skilled workmen and their families aboard, and led by a thirty-six-gun warship, the fleet sailed in 1684. But in the Caribbean, the vessels somehow blundered off course; exasperated, La Salle led his colonists ashore on the swampy, arid Texas coast, near the present site of Matagorda Bay. It was a suicidal mistake. Fever, hunger, and rattlesnake bites decimated the settlers. They were hundreds of miles from the Mississippi, amidst hostile Indians. After storms sank their last two ships, they were trapped.

Voyaging up to the Jesuit posts along Lake Michigan, Tonti learned early in 1685 that La Salle was in trouble. The reports, originating within the French navy, were vague and fragmentary. But Tonti at once mounted a rescue operation at his own cost, reaching the gulf by canoe. There he found no trace of La Salle, and even the Indians of the region reported no news of French colonists. Bewildered, Tonti ascended the Mississippi again. Returning to his headquarters at Fort St. Louis of the Illinois, he found a summons from the governor of Canada to return to Montreal and serve in a punitive war against the Senecas. This took him to upper New York State, where, as commander of the lead column, he fought a day-long battle against Seneca warriors, and burned some huts and fields. It was a stupid, fruitless campaign, which he had opposed from the start, and it was with relief that he returned to the Illinois forts, only to learn from passing Indians that La Salle had been shot to death by his own men in eastern Texas, while trying to find the Mississippi. "Such was the end of one of the great men of the age," Tonti wrote in a letter to France.[20]

Tonti now assembled another rescue party to try to save the few colonists who might still be alive somewhere in eastern Texas. With five Frenchmen and an Indian, he descended the Mississippi to the gulf, setting out on horseback for the Texas desert. But at the Red River three of the Frenchmen and the Indian deserted. Then friendly Indians advised Tonti that the last colonists had been put to death by another tribe a few months before. So his effort had been useless. He turned back towards the Mississippi with his two remaining men when the equivalent of a monsoon struck — rain pouring out of the sky day and night, the water rising over wild, uncultivated fields to form a lake hundreds of square miles in area, driving away or drowning game and giving no shelter to the weary rescuers. Tonti and his two men were able to sleep two nights on a flood-created island where they caught and roasted a bear, and built a raft. After that they slept only fitfully on the raft, or cradled in the branches of trees like animals. "I never suffered so much in my life as during this journey," Tonti wrote. He had never been given to complaining, but now he sensed that his sacrifices were becoming pointless.

The story of Enrico Tonti ends like this, badly and bitterly. After La Salle's death, he had expected recognition from the French Court as La Salle's successor in North America. His was a long record of service in the cause of France. The ghastly wound suffered in the Sicilian wars against Spain. The wound over his heart on the Illinois plain. The hunger. The hardships. Twenty thousand Indians settled in the vicinity of Fort St. Louis of the Illinois, in a confederacy loyal to France. Eight years of faithful service to the sieur de La Salle without once being paid, surviving only through his modest fur trading operations. In return, he was dismissed at Versailles in one sentence as "the Italian." Perhaps his father's transgressions, whatever they had been, still lived in the long memories of Louis's ministers. Or perhaps Louis's concentration was wholly absorbed by the War of the Grand Alliance. Though Tonti petitioned for a grant to the Arkansas country, which La Salle had promised him in lieu of his back pay and loans, amounting to more than twenty thousand francs, the king ignored even this appeal.

In 1693, Tonti wrote a narrative of his voyages in America and sent it to Versailles with a proposal that he be allowed to build a fleet of vessels to sail between the upper Mississippi and France. It was a last-ditch effort to revive the old dream of shifting the focus of New France from Canada to the American middle west. But its one consequence was to promote the expedition which sailed in October 1698, under the command of Admiral Pierre La Moyen d'Iberville, to found the city of New Orleans. This had been La Salle's dream, and Tonti's. "I could have felt some jealousy at seeing another in a country where I had a right to hope for everything," [21] Tonti wrote. But, loyally, he made his fifth and sixth trips down the Mississippi to serve d'Iberville as an adviser, settling finally in Mobile, Alabama, where he married an Indian woman. In 1704, a French ship called the *Pelican* arrived in Mobile with a cargo of marriageable damsels. It also carried yellow fever germs. Enrico Tonti died in the epidemic of September 1704.[22]

It would be hard to find a sharper contrast to the manly, self-sacrificing figure of Enrico Tonti than Filippo Mazzei, who was facile and bright, something of a butterfly. Yet in his own fashion Mazzei was probably as representative an explorer in the late eighteenth century as Tonti had been a hundred years earlier. What he explored was the social order, and he managed to involve himself in both the American and the French revolutions and to act as a diplomatic agent for the liberal king of Poland, Stanislaus II. At the close of a long, eventful life, he wrote his *Memoirs,* one of the more interesting Italian documents of the era.

Mazzei was born on Christmas Day 1730, in Poggio a Caiano, a hill town ten miles from Florence. By the time he was three his mother had aptly nicknamed him *il fastidio,* the pest! In describing his youth, Mazzei drew a sketch of provincial Italian life in the eighteenth century: "Among the few landholders of Poggio a Caiano were the three Sgrilli brothers, who never seemed to have anything to do. I respected their station as the noblest on earth. . . ." [23] The wife of one of these Sgrilli brothers was "a Coccolini from Pisa, haughty and spoiled," who would grow sulky "if she did not have someone to offer her his arm on the way to the chapel, which was no more than a hundred feet from her home." [24] At sixteen, Mazzei fell in love with one of her daughters, who was two years older "but in the art of love . . . at least two centuries older." [25] He was forced to break off the affair in order to start medical studies in Florence, and was probably fortunate to have escaped Poggio a Caiano when he did.

He was a mediocre student but an attractive, lively young man. Ardent, with glowing black eyes and delicate features, he consoled himself for the loss of his "tigress" back home by making love to the married women of Florence, one of them the delicious seventeen-year-old wife of a surgeon. He even managed to seduce his landlord's daughter, though she slept in the same room as her parents. One night, after lovemaking, he fell asleep and woke up in the girl's bed, in broad daylight. "Had I seen her parents open their eyes, I should have gone to their bed at once and said, 'Keep still for your sake and for your daughter's honor, for I have a greater right to her than you; she is my wife.' " [26] But the parents slept on.

Mazzei did not graduate from medical school because of a clash with the ecclesiastical authorities which landed him before the Inquisition. He was forced to back down "with great circumspection. I went forward one step and backward two steps; then I went a half step forward and a whole one backward. I spent a good hour going forward and backward. Finally, I confessed myself beaten, and [the Inquisitor] was exultant as if he had made a great conquest." [27] The rector of the university, however, did furnish Mazzei with a certificate enabling him to practice medicine outside of Italy. It was a valuable document. At that time, Italian medicine was considered the most advanced in the world.

For a while, Mazzei worked as a surgeon's assistant in the Tuscan seaport of Leghorn, thinking of shipping out to South America by way of Spain or Portugal. He became friendly with the Jewish community in Leghorn, which included many of the city's doctors. An enemy of all forms of prejudice, Mazzei had already provoked a street brawl by going to the aid of an elderly Jew who was being abused by a bully. "I was so irritated that I unsheathed my sword and paid [the bully] back with a few good blows, threatening to have him punished even more severely." [28]

One of the Jewish doctors of Leghorn, whom Mazzei identifies only as Salinas, had practiced for many years in Asia Minor and now wished to return there. He offered Mazzei a three-year post as his assistant in the ancient city of Smyrna, on the west coast of Turkey. It was just the kind of opportunity to see the world that Mazzei was seeking, and in August 1752, he and the surgeon set out for Constantinople by way of Vienna. After leaving Austrian territory, they crossed the wild, snow-bound country of the Carpathian Alps. Salinas, ailing, lay strapped on a horse-drawn litter while Mazzei rode beside him. They were accompanied by Turkish soldiers, the Janizaries, who at night slept on the floor of their room, stretched across the threshold. "To allay any fears we might have, they said, as these soldiers always do to travellers in their care, 'no one can harm you unless they first pass over our bodies.' " [29]

The travelers reached Constantinople safely, and remained there several months practicing medicine. It was a city that fascinated the youthful Mazzei. He experienced a fifty-course dinner at the house of an important government official, and the flirtations of veiled women. The sultan's niece saw him on the beach one day and offered to buy him, an honor that Mazzei recorded without comment. At Smyrna, however, he quickly seems to have become bored and restless in an atmosphere nearly as parochial as that of Poggio a Caiano. There was no Florence nearby to distract him, since Constantinople was a three-day journey by ship. Mazzei stayed with Salinas the full three years and could have stayed longer. "But I felt too restricted in that country and I wanted to see other lands and peoples." In December 1755, he sailed as a ship's doctor aboard a British vessel at a salary of five guineas a month plus "a good share of any booty that might be taken." [30]

But the voyage was uneventful, and at the beginning of March 1756, Mazzei was in London. His first act was to rescue some foreign seamen, among them four Italians, who had been impressed into the British navy. This custom of impressing seamen made him wonder if England was truly the home of liberty, and he secured a seat at the trial of Lord Ferrers, a Peer of the Realm who had shot to death an employee. Ferrers was convicted and hanged, and Mazzei wrote admiringly: "Considering that in many of the states of Europe, if a great lord had committed a similar crime, he would merely have been relegated to one of his country estates for a while, I was forced to admit that in England personal liberty was more solidly established than in other countries." For this reason, he added, "I decided to stay in England and later I rented a house." [31]

For a time, he gave Italian lessons to pay the rent (as cultured but insolvent Italians would do in America a century later). Though he also audited some classes in anatomy, Mazzei seems to have abandoned medicine as a profession; perhaps some incident at Smyrna had left him wary of exposing himself to charges of malpractice. In need of an income, Mazzei became a dealer in Tuscan wines. Vain, he was mortified by the idea that Florentines in London, or his well-born English friends, should catch him writing out a sales slip or uncorking flasks. He had given himself airs, and was now painfully vulnerable to ridicule. "I did not wish to lay myself open to being called Filippo the Shopkeeper instead of Filippo Mazzei, if I ever went back to my native land." [32] His shop, therefore, went under the name of Martini & Company; it sold wine, olive oil, cheese, silk, and candied fruits from Genoa. He was prosperous enough, however, to be able to live comfortably on New Bond Street, where he also apparently maintained a mistress — a widow — and her child. His social life was rich and deeply important to him, since he would have more willingly gone without food than the conversation of cultured men. His friends in London included Count Caracciolo, the envoy from Naples, and a great many English aristocrats.

Returning to Florence to visit his mother, Mazzei was denounced to the Inquisition on the charge of having smuggled a trunkful of subversive books into Tuscany, including the works of Rousseau and Voltaire, "for the purpose of infecting all of Italy." [33] Without a hearing, or even the possibility of knowing who his accuser was, he was given four days to leave Florentine territory. After complying, Mazzei rallied enough support from the British envoy to Tuscany, Sir Horace Mann, and from his friends in England to return to Florence. He was thirty-five years old, a man of the world, and an English citizen. He would not be cowed. "In less than a year," he reported proudly, "I had said and written so much that the evil tribunal was totally abolished in Tuscany." [34] An exaggeration, yes. But there was something grand in Mazzei's scorn for any form of bigotry and tyranny.

Returning to London in April 1676, after an absence of two years, he became Filippo the shopkeeper again, opening a larger shop in the Haymarket area. He had virtually entrusted the business to an efficient young Scot, and he was free to pursue the social events and the *conversazioni* he so adored. But he was also restless again.

"At this time I received a letter from Florence, from . . . the Director of the Museum, asking me to secure two Franklin stoves on orders from the Grand Duke Leopold. Since [Benjamin] Franklin was in London as agent for the colony of Pennsylvania, I went directly to him." [35] They walked the streets of London searching for an exact replica of Franklin's stove, and, not finding it, had two stoves made by a London artisan. "I struck up a friendship with Franklin and, through him, with various other persons from the colonies. . . ." [36] As a youth in Leghorn, Mazzei had considered going to South America. Now he was thinking seriously of emigrating to one of the American colonies. Through a mutual friend, he began to correspond with a Virginia landowner who had taught himself Italian, Thomas Jefferson, and he frequented the homes of Virginians in London.

When Mazzei reached England fifteen years before, he had been deeply impressed by the Ferrers trial. Now another trial had a similar but opposite effect on him. This was the Wilkes case. Elected to Parliament from Middlesex (which included London), Wilkes had challenged the most powerful man in England at the time, the despotic Earl of Bute. As Mazzei explains,

When the new parliament met, Wilkes' election was declared void. In this manner, a death blow was given to the solid and sacrosanct basic law of a free country, namely, complete liberty in the election of representatives of the people. There can be no constitution, or at least the constitution cannot have any solid foundation, if men elected to exercise the usual functions of lawmakers for a given period can arrogate to themselves the right to annul or alter a basic law.[37]

Mazzei was a peculiarly modern man in his sensitivity to the repressive power of government. The Wilkes case, though he was in no way personally involved, made him decide to leave England.

In his conversations with his American friends, and in letters to and from Jefferson, Mazzei began to explore the idea of founding an experimental farm in Virginia, where he could introduce Italian vines and seeds. Adams and Jefferson were enthusiastic and promised their support. In three months, Mazzei closed out his London shop, helping his faithful Scot to establish himself in business. There remained the veiled relationship with Mrs. Martin, the widow who Mazzei had taken in, and her daughter. "My friends advised me to take Mrs. Martin and her daughter with me," he wrote "not only for my own sake but also for the girl's, for she was likely to make a better marriage in Virginia than in London." [38] It seems almost certain that Mazzei and Mrs. Martin were lovers, though he never clarified this.

The experimental farm in Virginia was shaping up as a major under-taking. Mazzei would be a gentleman farmer and something of an agronomist, just as he had been something of a surgeon. With the two women, he returned to Tuscany to buy seeds, cuttings, tools, and to recruit ten peasants willing to settle in America. "When I had everything ready . . . I could not find the group of ten farmers who were to accompany me. A certain Masi . . . had told the man who had procured me the other nine that in America the stars fall from the sky and burn the laborers in the fields." The annoyed Mazzei had to find himself another ten field hands willing to emigrate to America. The Grand Duke Leopold of Tuscany, he related, "laughed somewhat at the tale of the falling stars." [39]

Mazzei, the women, and his little band of colonists sailed from Leghorn on September 2, 1773. The sea was calm during the two-month crossing, but "the uncomfortable heat towards the end of October bothered my peasants not a little. I had told them the stupid and ridiculous reason for which the others had not come, and they began to fear the falling stars. I did my best to comfort them and assured them that they would soon find it even colder than they wished." [40] Soon the ship entered the James River, disembarking the Mazzei party some four miles from Williamsburg. Among the leading men of the colony who courteously came to greet the Italians was George Washington.

To pay for the property he intended to buy in Virginia, Mazzei had contracted to ship American grain back to Tuscany. He now purchased a good brig of 170 or 180 tons and found a personable young American captain to sail her to Leghorn. Having seen the vessel underway, the Italian was invited to spend two or three days at Monticello. "Mr. Jefferson was thirty two years old, that is, eleven years younger than I. He had married a widow, twenty three years of age, and they had a little girl only a few months old. We arrived in the evening, and the following morning, while the others were still asleep, Jefferson and I went to take a walk in the neighborhood." [41] The Virginian showed Mazzei a four-hundred-acre tract adjacent to Monticello that was up for sale, and offered to add two thousand acres of his own. This was to be Mazzei's experimental farm, which they named Colle. Mazzei had established himself in America at a remarkable time, and in a remarkable place, with Jefferson as his friend and next-door neighbor.

To Mazzei's credit, he contributed wholeheartedly to the American Revolution, taking bold risks. A few months after his arrival, he was

writing articles for John Pinckney's *Virginia Gazette,* which he signed
Furioso. When British troops landed on the Virginia coast, Mazzei, with
two of his men, enlisted in the militia and marched off to a battle that
miscarried because "the British, on hearing that [our] men were coming
from all parts of the colonies to meet their new guests, had thought it
best to embark again and thus avoid the ceremony. This information was
given to us by Patrick Henry . . . who has no superior in eloquence and
patriotism." [42] On that same march, Mazzei also met the two Madison
brothers; James, the future President, was then twenty-two years old.
Later in the war, a British cavalry force led by the turncoat Benedict
Arnold raided Colle, destroying Mazzei's papers and many of his possessions. And in 1779, when Mazzei was appointed Virginia's agent in
Europe, he was intercepted at sea by a British man-o'-war and risked
imprisonment in the Tower of London or the death penalty.

But, beyond risk-taking, Mazzei contributed his ideas at a moment
when American opinion was crystallizing into resistance, and when the
best American minds were searching for fresh solutions to the problem
of a just government. It was Jefferson who had suggested, early in 1775,
that Mazzei write a series of articles examining the philosophical
grounds for a revolution against England. Jefferson translated some of
these articles from the Italian and corrected and edited others which
Mazzei wrote in English. The two men spent hours together discussing
forms of government, and though Mazzei tended to magnify the impact
of his ideas, he probably did have some influence on the thinking of the
men who would create the American government.

In his writings, Mazzei hammered out his belief that equality had to
be the cornerstone of American democracy. "A truly republican form of
government cannot exist except where all men — from the very rich to
the very poor — are perfectly equal in their natural rights." And again:
"When certain privileges are exercised by a portion of the inhabitants
and denied to others, it is vain to hope for the establishment of a liberal
and permanent government, unless the favored citizens are willing to
relinquish their privileges and stand on a footing of perfect equality
with the rest of the inhabitants." [43] Though Mazzei was a pamphleteer
rather than a social philosopher, his insistence on equality may have
influenced Jefferson directly. In an article translated by Jefferson, Mazzei
had written, "All men are by nature equally free and independent." It
may have been the seed for Jefferson's "All men are created equal." At

any rate, Jefferson sent Mazzei one of the first copies of the Declaration of Independence.

Buoyed by the excitement of those years, Mazzei was able to endure a series of disappointments and one major disaster — his marriage to the French-born, shrewish Mrs. Martin. In Puritan America, keeping a mistress who moreover had an adolescent daughter was regarded as standing with both feet firmly in the pit. Mazzei's friends had advised him bluntly: "if we continued to live together, the young girl would never be able to find a husband." [44] Mazzei and Mrs. Martin were married a few months after their arrival in Virginia. It was a dreadful marriage, and their loud and vengeful public feuds alienated many of Mazzei's new American friends. This of course infuriated him, and he was to spend the next decade vainly trying to keep the Atlantic Ocean between himself and Signora Mazzei. Jefferson noted mordantly that Mazzei was willing to grant her "three quarters of the world of elbow room, on condition she would leave him quiet in the fourth." [45]

The experimental farm that Mazzei had established at Colle failed. It was not really his fault. He had carefully selected Italian seeds to transplant in Virginia, including summer wheat and fifty-day maize (which his neighbors, he noted proudly, called Mazzei's corn), fruit pits, various seedlings, and vine cuttings. He had formed a company and sold shares to Jefferson, Washington, Adams, and even the British governor, Lord Dunmore, whom he despised. Land had been cleared and, in the spring of 1775, the busy Mazzei and his men had planted, only to see their labor reduced to nothing when

something occurred which I was told had not happened before within memory of man . . . a frost, caused by a northwest wind, ruined the corn and wheat just above the ground, froze the small oak and the other young trees, and caused all the other trees to shed their leaves, which did not bud again until the following year. It was horrible to see the woods entirely stripped of leaves in summer, as if it had been midwinter. [46]

Then the war intruded and Mazzei's farm, like many others in Virginia, was neglected.

By the end of 1778, Mazzei was hoping Congress would send him to Europe as a consul to arrange loans for the United States, and he was eager to wipe the mud off his fingers and leave agriculture to others. With Jefferson's assistance, he was able to sell Colle to Baron Riedesel, a Hessian general who had been captured with his troops at Saratoga and was now *hors de combat*. (The baroness, as attractive as Mrs. Mazzei was unbearable, delighted the local Virginia gentry, including Jefferson.) All of Mazzei's men but one chose to remain in Virginia. They had gotten over their fear of falling stars and wanted to be Americans.

Mazzei was unable to secure a consular post, as he had hoped, but Jefferson managed to have him appointed Virginia's agent in Europe, charged particularly with obtaining a loan from the Grand Duke of Tuscany. In June 1779, Mazzei, with his wife and daughter, boarded the brig *Johnston*. It was still wartime on the high seas, however, and when the brig was thirty miles off the Virginia coast it was intercepted by a British corsair. Fortunately, Mazzei had taken precautions. "I had a little memorandum book in which I wrote down all matters I had to attend to in various parts of Europe, and all the words had been abbreviated in such a way that no one else could have deciphered them. I used the same method for the credentials and instructions, which I put into a little bag with some lead, to make sure they would not fall into the enemy's hands." [47] When the British corsair drew alongside, Mazzei dropped the bag into the ocean without being spotted. Even so, he and his family were held for three months in New York City, which was then in British hands.

In New York, with typical Mazzei aplomb, he became friendly with General Patterson, the British commander, by whom he was received "as if we had been childhood friends." [48] A code of chivalry prevailed between gentlemen; Mazzei and his family were transferred to Long Island to endure their detainment in an area where all the inhabitants were patriots. Three months later the Mazzeis reached Cork, Ireland. But they had to be extremely cautious. Mazzei was still a British citizen and liable to prosecution for treason. After being sheltered by Irish people friendly to the American cause, the family was smuggled aboard a Portuguese ship in the middle of the night, just as it was lifting anchor. The ship was bound for the mouth of the Loire River, in France, but nearly sank in a violent coastal storm. Its fearful, seasick passengers finally disembarked at an island off the French coast.

As it turned out, Mazzei's European mission hardly compensated for the voyage. In Paris, Franklin disapproved of it and took his time in forwarding instructions to the "agent." The Grand Duke Leopold of Tuscany, from whom Mazzei had hoped to negotiate a loan for the United States, proved coolly unreceptive, though Mazzei had shipped him a deer and a rattlesnake from the New World. Vainly, Mazzei waited for a duplicate of his official commission from the state of Virginia, having thrown the original overboard when the *Johnston* had been boarded. Just as he had been an amateur physician and merchant and agronomist, it appeared that he was now fated to become an amateur diplomat. But it was not altogether a bad role for him. It gave him a chance to mingle with the titled people he admired (despite his republicanism) and to indulge in his favorite and most successful activity, conversation. The time was passing when he might have made history. Now, he would discuss it, write about it, perhaps — he still hoped — influence it a little.

There remained one more trip to America, his last. Mazzei's stepdaughter had married well after all. The young man was a French count, though penniless. Mazzei offered to help the newlyweds establish themselves in Virginia. He returned to Colle, finding it deserted and half in ruins. Monticello depressed him also, since Jefferson's wife had died there the previous year. Jefferson himself was sailing to France, where he was to replace Franklin as American ambassador. Mazzei had never been paid for his services as Virginia's agent, however unfruitful, and he had counted on the aid of his now-famous sponsor to remind the government in Richmond of its obligations. He sought out other old friends, including Patrick Henry and James Madison. It was Madison who kindly offered to wind up Mazzei's business affairs in Virginia. Mazzei returned to Europe in 1785, settling in Paris. The French Revolution was less than four years away.

No European had yet written an accurate history of the United States, including the revolutionary war and the founding of the American government. Mazzei set to work. In 1788 he brought out a four-volume *History of the United States and of the North American Continent*. The work had a comparatively brief life. At the time, though, the four volumes were widely read in Europe and served as a source of information about the United States. The *History* may have also earned something for its author, who was again in need of an income.

This problem resolved itself happily when Mazzei was offered the post of secret agent for the king of Poland, Stanislaus II. The word secret was only a convention. Relations between France and Poland having been severed, each court maintained at the other a secret agent who was simply a diplomat without official accreditation. A friend of

Mazzei's named Piattoli had offered to obtain the post for him, and "when Piattoli asked me," Mazzei recorded,

I begged him to come to dine with me at Jefferson's home, for I feared that if I accepted a position in the service of a monarch, I should be incurring the displeasure of my countrymen. Jefferson, however, assured me to the contrary, saying that the King of Poland was better known in America than in Europe, that he was the head of a republic and not a despot, and that he was considered the best citizen in his kingdom.[49]

During the early stages of the French Revolution, as the storm gathered, Mazzei was often on the road between Paris and Versailles. His dispatches to Stanislaus were opinionated, as always, but accurate and reliable. In 1789, no one could have foretold the course of France. Mazzei was partial to Louis, detesting Marie Antoinette and seeing in her the principal cause of the breakdown of authority. It was understandable that he viewed the French Revolution in terms of the American, warning anyone who would listen that in order to achieve what he had once defined as "a liberal and permanent government," the French had to avoid the excesses of revolution, just as the Americans had done. He was one of the founders of the Club of 1789, which had been formed to combat the Jacobin Club (so named because its meetings were originally held in a Jacobin, or Dominican, monastery). "The Jacobin Club," Mazzei wrote, "tended to reduce everything to a state of confusion, while ours sought to establish union and peace. Each of the two societies had domestic and foreign correspondents. I was in charge of our foreign correspondence."[50] He sent copies of the club's newspaper to King Stanislaus, who replied graciously, "I become increasingly convinced that at present your Club brings together those men of France who are most temperate, impartial and wise. . . ."[51] Among those men were Lafayette, Mirabeau, Talleyrand, and Du Pont de Nemours.

But the French Revolution rolled on, growing less temperate, and in December 1791 Mazzei abandoned Paris for Warsaw. He had done his best as a foreigner to guide events in Paris, even writing a pamphlet addressed to "The French People, from a Citizen of the United States." It must have taken some courage, since he records that "those who used to go about the streets selling similar works did not wish to have anything to do with it, for they were afraid of being beaten."[52] As his dispatches to Stanislaus turned more gloomy, the king reproached him gently by quoting Pope's maxim: "In politics, despondency is a sort of treason."[53]

There was little Mazzei could do in Warsaw. He dined frequently with the king, who delighted in conversing with this voluble and out-spoken Italian. Stanislaus II is regarded as a flawed hero in Polish history, a patriot and a genuine liberal who could never bring himself to resist the stronger monarchs like Catherine the Great of Russia and William of Prussia who between them destroyed Poland's independence. A charming man, the king was particularly gracious to foreigners he liked. (To surprise a mistress arriving from Paris, he had the royal carpenters prepare an exact replica of the lady's Parisian apartment; even the book she was reading on the night table was turned to the correct page.) There were only nine homes in which the king could be suitably entertained, and when Mazzei had visited each of them several times he felt he should take his leave and return to Italy. The political situation was deteriorating, and the spectre of the Second Partitioning was already hanging over Poland (it occurred in 1793).

Mazzei arrived in Pisa in August 1792. It was his home for the next twenty-four years, save for a journey to St. Petersburg in 1802, at the age of seventy-two, to collect some money still owed him by the Polish Crown. He was already at an age when most men became grandfathers, but in 1796, as rash as ever, he married a sixteen-year-old girl. He himself was sixty-six. The demands of this union were perhaps too much for Mazzei's mental equilibrium. In 1795, his friend Jefferson wrote him a letter openly describing the struggle between the Federalists, led by Hamilton and John Adams, and the Republicans. "The aspect of our politics has wonderfully changed since you left us," he informed Mazzei sarcastically.

In place of that noble love of liberty and republican government which carried us triumphantly through the war, an Anglican, monarchial and aristocratic party has sprung up, whose avowed object is to draw over us the substance as they have already done the forms of the British government. It would give you a fever if I were to name to you the apostates who have gone over to these heresies, men who were Samsons in the field and Solomons in the council. . . .[54]

In an act of folly, Mazzei translated the letter and gave it to an Italian newspaper. Perhaps he hungered to prove to his young bride that his boasts were true, that the great did confide their thoughts to him. Probably, he was no longer fully in command of his faculties. The Mazzei Letter, as it came to be called, has left him with the reputation of an idiot — which he was not. It nearly wrecked Jefferson's political career, and it helped destroy the last lingering bonds of friendship between Jefferson and Washington. Newspapers such as the New York *Herald* attacked Jefferson for circulating "abominable falsehoods" throughout Europe. And when Jefferson became a candidate for the presidency, the unfortunate letter was dredged up all over again.

To his great credit Jefferson never reproached Mazzei, nor did he break off their correspondence, though Jefferson's subsequent letters were bland and businesslike. As vice president, Jefferson thoughtfully arranged for the designer of the new capitol at Washington, D.C., Benjamin Latrobe, to contact Mazzei and ask him to sound out the finest Italian sculptor of the century, Canova, to work on the capitol. Canova was busy with other assignments, and Mazzei found two lesser-known sculptors instead. He was grateful to be of service, and wrote to Jefferson: "I thank you for it with all my heart, for I know that it is through you that I have the honor and privilege of being placed in a position to do something for my dear adopted fatherland." [55]

He died at Pisa on March 19, 1816, at the age of eighty-five.

For all his idealism and intellectual curiosity, Mazzei remained a life-long dilettante. And in this weakness, he reflected his native land at the close of the eighteenth century. Italy had suffered nearly three hundred years of foreign domination. The psychologically crippling condition of being ruled by others, so familiar to all the ex-colonial peoples, had become a way of life in Italy, to the point where Italians tended to be, like Mazzei, gifted amateurs. For the most part, Italy consisted of little agricultural centers like Mazzei's birthplace, Poggio a Caiano, islands of provincialism where the highest aim, and greatest happiness, consisted in having nothing to do. A petty landowner could collect rent from the peasants who actually worked his land, while he and his family enjoyed a comfortable, idle life. This meant that the peasants, though productive, remained ignorant and poor. And the gentry, being largely unproductive though educated, were unable to take responsibility for their society and for the task of changing it. There was, of course, a professional middle class in the cities, capable lawyers, physicians, bankers, scholars, and government officials. But the cities were no longer the centers of economic or political power that they had been during the Renaissance. The real decisions were made at a remote level, by an establishment that was the equivalent of a colonial government. It was composed of Spanish or Austrian princes and their courts, of conservative Italian aristocrats, and high officials of the Church. Few members of this establishment were representative of the Italian people. Either they came from noble families where Spanish, French, or Austrian blood predominated, or they owned vast estates, or they were celibate. Nowhere except in Venice did a parliament exist that could convey even a semblance of the popular will to the ruling elite.

While it would be wrong to view Italy in the eighteenth century in terms of class conflict — foreign visitors were struck by the feeling of harmony, and of a kind of rough equality, that existed between aristocrats, gentry, and peasants — Italy's was, nevertheless, a deteriorating society. If almost everyone today complains of being pressured by too much change, the problem in Italy was too little change, and too little challenge. The tight grip of the Church, foreign rule, and economic stagnation all favored the perpetuation of conventional ideas. In their frustration, many of the most able Italians either became rebels or squandered their energies on pleasure. The love affairs, the fluttering fans, the card games and quadrilles all masked a surfeit of boredom. Among young, educated Italians at the end of the eighteenth century, the mood was one of sharp dissatisfaction. They were familiar with the ideas of the French enlightenment and of the American Revolution, and they wanted a larger role for Italy.

Above all, they wanted to expel their foreign rulers and to govern themselves.

4

Risorgimento

THE MAKING of modern Italy occupied almost a hundred years. The struggle began in the Napoleonic era. It gathered strength in the period of repression that followed the Congress of Vienna, and burst forth at midcentury, in a movement that came to be called the *Risorgimento,* the resurgence or reawakening. The American people were passionately aroused by the events of the Risorgimento, and not only gave shelter to Italian patriots, but made many specific contributions to the cause of Italian independence. That would be reason enough for including a chapter on Italian unification in this book. But there is another reason as well. The Risorgimento, which unified Italy and made Italians the citizens of a modern state, paradoxically also produced another awakening: it hastened the departure of millions of Italians who left this new Italy to become Austrian, Swiss, French, Belgian, Argentine, Chilean, Peruvian, Brazilian — and American. Because of this, the Risorgimento is a vital part of the history of the Italian-Americans.

At first it seemed that Italy would hardly be affected by the upheavals in Paris in 1789 and in the years immediately following. Though many students in the Italian cities were Jacobin sympathizers, and the Italian middle class included a few radicals of the left who welcomed reform even if it meant widespread violence, the peninsula remained firmly in conservative hands. The whole southern portion of the Italian boot, including Sicily, was ruled by a branch of the Spanish Bourbons.* The capital of this backward kingdom of Naples was, of course, Naples itself, though the first Bourbon king, Don Carlos, had built a 1,200-room Versailles-like palace at nearby Caserta.

Most of northern Italy was controlled by Austria. Tuscany was ruled by the Habsburgs, the last Medici having died in 1737. Mazzei's Grand Duke Leopold of Tuscany was in fact a future emperor of Austria. The most vital and progressive of the Italian states, Lombardy, was part of the Habsburg Empire. It was ruled alternately from its capital of Milan, or from Vienna, depending on how political winds were blowing. Venice, which had formerly possessed large territories in the eastern Mediterranean, including Cyprus, and which had always kept somewhat aloof from Italian politics, was now a fading maritime star. Entirely surrounded by Austrian territory, the Venetian state was falling under the economic domination of Vienna.

Only in the northwest corner of Italy, next to France, was there an independent Italian state. This was Piedmont, with its capital in Turin. Its monarchs belonged to the pro-French House of Savoy. Through a series of clever alliances over the course of the eighteenth century, the Savoy kings had extended their control over a good part of Lombardy and over the island of Sardinia. But even Piedmont was a dwarf state compared to the wholly formed nations across the Alps such as France, England, and Austria. Nor did Piedmont in the eighteenth century represent the interests of the rest of Italy; its policy aimed solely at its own expansion.

At the heart of Italy lay the Papal States. From his capital within Rome, the pope ruled much of central Italy — as far east as the Adriatic coast and as far north as Bologna. The administration of this ecclesiastical territory was not remarkably different from that of the other Italian states. The Church owned much of the agricultural land, leasing it out to peasant sharecroppers. This was common practice. In the kingdom of Naples, about half the land was still owned by the Church (though priests represented barely one percent of the population of the kingdom). Even in progressive Lombardy, all of the estates over 250 acres and seventy-five percent of those over 100 acres were owned by the Church or by aristocrats.[1] And while feudalism had been formally abol-

* Southern Italy in this period appears on maps variously as the kingdom of Naples or the kingdom of the Two Sicilies. Though the latter is more accurate, it is also more confusing. In this book, therefore, the Bourbon state will be referred to as the kingdom of Naples.

ished almost everywhere, its forms persisted. A peasant might still pay taxes, sometimes in produce, to a prince or baron rather than to the state; and it was often a prince or baron who decided whether a road should be built, or a bridge repaired, or a new tax levied.

As the revolution in Paris intensified, and Louis XVI and Marie Antoinette were imprisoned, the horrified princes of the Italian states, including the pope, joined the widespread alliance against France. But the allies were repulsed at the battle of Valmy in 1792, and now revolutionary France went on the offensive. A French army was formed (called the Army of Italy) to invade Italy and liberate the Italian people from their conservative rulers. This force, however, barely managed to cross the Alps into Piedmont before its campaign stalled. The numerous pro-Jacobin students in the Italian cities, who had been prepared to celebrate the advent of liberty and equality, resumed turning out underground newspapers and dodging the police. One of them, a descendant of Michelangelo named Filippo Buonarroti, slipped over to Corsica, hoping to interest the French in fomenting Jacobin revolts in the Italian states. One of the people he contacted was an obscure artillery officer, Napoleon Bonaparte.[2] In 1796, Bonaparte was given command of the Army of Italy.

Napoleon was twenty-six. His military background was undistinguished. He had directed the French artillery during the recapture of Toulon from British-aided French royalists and had put down a rebellion in Paris, firing artillery point blank into the mob and killing some six hundred demonstrators. It took him less than a year to subdue northern Italy, smashing one Austrian army after another. "Peoples of Italy!" read his proclamation. "The French army comes to break your chains. The French nation is the friend of all nations; receive us with trust! Your property, your religion, your customs will be respected. We shall wage war like generous enemies, for our only quarrel is with the tyrants who have enslaved you."[3] To the Italian Jacobins, Napoleon seemed the embodiment of a dream. Young, fiery, idealistic — and Italian! To understand this, it is necessary to remember that Corsica had been a Genoese possession for centuries; only in 1769, on the eve of Napoleon's birth, had it come under French control. Napoleon's father was named Carlo, his mother Letizia. Italian names. The family name itself, Buonaparte, was an Italian word meaning the good or better part. (Napoleon changed it to the more French-sounding Bonaparte to further his military career.)

Even Napoleon's features, swarthy and aquiline, seemed to stamp him as an Italian.

At first, Jacobin expectations were fulfilled. In liberated Milan there were joyful demonstrations, liberty trees were planted, and when the women of Milan — among the most beautiful in Europe — looked at the young, romantically tattered French officers, Mars and Venus joined hands and smiled. "If the Milanese were mad with enthusiasm," Stendahl recorded, "the French officers were mad with happiness." [4] It seemed that Italy had found her new Caesar, returned from Gaul, and her destiny.

But Napoleon, of course, was not Italian, despite his origins. Nor was he an idealist. The liberation of Italy, as of all the European states, was part of the revolutionary credo. It was one of Napoleon's objectives in Italy, but not the principal one. He had promised Barras, the French politician who had arranged for him to be appointed commander of the Army of Italy (and who was the former lover of Napoleon's wife, Josephine), twenty million gold francs from Italy to replenish the French treasury. So now, along with liberating Italy, he also had to strip it. When his officials in Lombardy raided workmen's savings banks, the infuriated populace began killing French soldiers in retaliation. Napoleon struck back savagely. Binasco, a town near Milan, was used like Lidice. Its able-bodied men were executed and the town was then burnt to the ground. Hostages were rounded up in the Po Valley and deported to France. Napoleon's civilian staff systematically plundered Italian art. Columns of horse-drawn supply wagons headed back towards the Alps, filled with loot from "liberated" palaces and villas. Hundreds of masterpieces were seized and shipped to the new Parisian museum, the Louvre. Even in the currency of the 1790s, the total value of Italian art taken to France represented several tens of millions of dollars.

Napoleon, meanwhile, raised other revenue by cynically allowing conservative rulers to buy protection from attack. The Duke of Parma avoided "liberty" at the cost of only two million francs, while Pope Pius VII was forced to pay twenty-one million francs — and was betrayed as well. As soon as Napoleon had reached an understanding with the Austrians, moreover, he turned on Italy's sole republic, Venice. Its army could not withstand the vastly more powerful French forces, and on May 14, 1797, the last of the doges voted with his Grand Council to dissolve the state. It was the first time in over a thousand years that a foreign army had entered the lagoon. Soon, the city's famous bronze horses (which the Venetians had seized from Byzantium in 1204) were lowered from their positions above St. Mark's Cathedral and mounted in carts for the trip to Paris. The Venetian navy was appropriated for use in the planned invasion of England.

Now Napoleon swept down the peninsula, knocking kings and grand dukes off their thrones and deposing the elderly Pope Pius VII. The only ruler who remained was Ferdinand, king of Naples, who presided over the most quaint and reactionary court in Europe. His wife was a sister of Marie Antoinette. His prime minister was the English baronet Harold Acton, and one of his principal advisers was the English ambassador Lord Hamilton, whose wife, Emma, was Admiral Nelson's mistress. "The Kings are awake," Ferdinand boasted as he marched on Rome to drive out Napoleon and restore the pope.[5] Delusions of grandeur for Ferdinand, whose ill-equipped army was quickly broken. With his queen and his English advisers and the adulterous Emma, Ferdinand boarded one of Nelson's warships and they all took refuge in Palermo.

But Napoleon had grown tired of Italy. When he left the peninsula to launch his futile Egyptian campaign in 1798, the conservatives mounted a counterattack. It was spearheaded by a Russian general, Alexander Suvarov, an earthy, tough sixty-nine-year-old veteran who had made his reputation in campaigns against the Turks. Suvarov's mixed Russian and Austrian forces pushed the French back across northern Italy, pinning them into a small enclave around Genoa. Warships of the Russian navy, meanwhile, joined Nelson's squadron off the Italian coast. And now the peasants arose.

Just as the middle classes had been generally pro-French, the peasants, with their deep emotional attachment to the Church, and often to their aristocratic dukes and barons, were conservative. It was the peasants, led by their bishops, who wiped out the French garrisons in Piedmont and Tuscany. In the South, Cardinal Fabrizio Ruffo led his "Army of the Faith" in guerilla warfare, slaughtering leftists. British-trained and sometimes British-led bandits marched with these guerillas, who by June 1799 had grown strong enough to assault Naples. With the cry *Viva Maria!* the reactionaries massacred, looted and raped the subjects of King Ferdinand before signing a truce with the besieged republicans, promising them safe conduct to France. This agreement Nelson violated, hanging the liberal Neapolitan admiral Prince Francesco Caracciolo from the yardarm of a warship and executing and imprisoning hundreds of leading republicans.[6]

In the following year, 1800, the scenario was replayed in the opposite direction. Down came Napoleon, crossing the Alps over the Great St. Bernard Pass. Out went the Austrians, beaten at the Battle of Marengo after their general, convinced of victory, had calmly ridden off to supper.[7] Napoleon now partially honored his earlier promises to aid Italian nationalism, joining Piedmont and Lombardy and the western half of Venetia to form the Italian Republic — the first real step towards the unification of Italy since Roman times. A red, white, and green national flag was unfurled, canals and roads were built, feudal laws were rewritten, and ecclesiastical lands expropriated and put up for sale. But the revolutionary era had passed for France, and for Bonaparte. After his coronation as emperor in Paris, Napoleon placed the Iron Crown of Lombardy on his own head in the Milan Cathedral and proclaimed himself king of Italy. To his newly ennobled relatives, Napoleon passed out the Italian states like slices of cake. Some of these relatives, however, like Eugène Beauharnais in Milan, and Joseph Bonaparte and later Joachim Murat in Naples, turned out to be surprisingly good rulers, and the Napoleonic period saw many of Italy's problems dealt with coherently for the first time in centuries.

But Napoleon's defeat in Russia, confirmed at Waterloo, put an abrupt end to progress in Italy. At the Congress of Vienna, Austria's Prince Metternich successfully pressed for the restoration of the Italian states as they had existed before Napoleon. The papal dominions were restored to the pope. Clerical rights were reestablished. The Austrian-controlled police in northern Italy censored newspapers and mail, and jailed liberals. Throughout the peninsula, the clock was turned back to the eighteenth century at a tragically wrong time for Italy.

The Napoleonic era had been both a beginning and an end for Europe — one of the great turning points of history. Only three years separate Napoleon's death at St. Helena from the opening of the first railway line in Britain. Thirty years after Waterloo, when the destiny of the continent had been decided by men moving at the speed of the human footstep, as they had moved since the beginning of time, trains were crossing the fields of Belgium and northern France at fifty miles an hour. The acceleration of history had begun. Mills and factories were being built, cities were growing. Though this change had its negative effects in the exploitation of workingmen and the rape of nature, it was Europe's natural experience in the nineteenth century. Italy, again divided and again misruled, remained outside this experience, a pastoral still life filled with lovely and melancholy ruins.

In 1846, an old and backward-looking pope died, and hope again swept the peninsula. Would a liberal be chosen? Would he emerge as a leader of Italian independence?

As the balloting in the June 1846 Conclave moved towards a decision, little-known Cardinal Mastai-Ferretti collapsed from emotional strain. He was being elected to the papacy, an honor he had not sought and did not seem to want. "Oh God! I am Thy unworthy servant," he cried, when informed of the Conclave's decision.[8] He took the name of Pius IX.

From the moment the Roman crowd saw him give his first blessing from the balcony at St. Peter's, Pius IX — or *Pio Nono,* as the Italians called him — was a popular hero. Mild, self-effacing, with a wry humor, he possessed an aura of goodwill and calm which captivated everyone. It seemed that a new era had begun. His predecessor, Gregory XVI, had been a dour old man who had prohibited the building of railroads in the Papal States because they might disturb the faith. "There is a storm in the air," he warned on his deathbed, "Revolutions will soon break out." [9] But from the moment of his elevation, Pio Nono seemed to dispel this gloomy forecast. Calmly, he began instituting long-range reforms in the creaky, inefficient administration of the Papal States. Commissions were appointed to study the overhaul of civil and penal laws, the building of railroads, and the modernization of agriculture.

Though these reforms were cautiously broached, the restive Italian people took them as a sign that Pio Nono sympathized with the liberals, and even that he would lead Italy from its bondage. This view was echoed by the American secretary of state, James Buchanan, who saw only hope in Pius's elevation. "Firm, without being rash; liberal, without proceeding to such extremes as might endanger the success of his glorious mission, he seems to be an instrument destined by Providence to accomplish the political regeneration of his country." [10]

But Pio Nono had raised expectations he could not fulfill. The crowd looked on him as a political hero. "*Viva Pio Nono, solo! solo!* [11] they roared as he blessed them, and their chants cut him to the heart. He was the Holy Father of all Catholics — including the Austrians — not a redeemer of Italian liberty. An absolute ruler in the Papal States, he could not be the champion of republicanism elsewhere. The conservatives were already hostile to him. To Metternich, his elevation had been "the greatest misfortune of the age." [12] Soon Pius lost the support and the goodwill of the liberals. In an increasingly polarized situation, he became the man in the middle who satisfied no one.

This polarization, moreover, was occurring throughout Europe. The American and French revolutions had represented, in part at least, a rebellion against the tyranny of kings. Now, fifty years later, here was Europe ruled by a motley collection of kings and emperors who took little note of public opinion. For years, European men of letters had predicted a new wave of revolutions that would overthrow these obtuse monarchies.

Minor upheavals occurred in 1821 and 1830. But those were mere throat-clearings for what followed. Addressing a banquet in 1847, the French poet and deputy Alphonse de Lamartine promised his fellow citizens: "after having had the revolution of freedom and the counter-revolution of glory, you will have the revolution of public conscience and the revolution of contempt." [13] His striking phrase, "the revolution of contempt," expressed perfectly what European liberals felt towards their governments, which were clumsy, repressive, and, yes, contemptuous. The great storm which Pope Gregory had foreseen and Pope Pius had been unable to prevent broke out in 1848.

The overture was played in Sicily, shortly after New Year's Day. A popular insurrection against King Ferdinand of Naples (also known as *Re Bomba,* or King Bomb, because of his frequent use of artillery against the people) began in Palermo and spread to the rest of the island. By early February the Bourbons had been chased from Sicily and a republic had been proclaimed. The same revolutionary agitation, spreading into the mainland portion of the kingdom of Naples, forced King Bomb to grant a constitution.

On February 23, France's King Louis Philippe found it necessary to call out the National Guard to control the Paris mobs. Barricades went up at key intersections and by evening fifty-two people had been shot down by guardsmen. Now arms were seized by the people and fresh barricades built by torchlight. The following morning, Paris bristled with 1,512 barricades, some as high as three- or four-story buildings.[14] The king fled into exile, his palace invaded by a mob which put out a For Rent sign and smashed twenty-three thousand pieces of glassware.[15] Three weeks later, the conservative Frederick William IV of Prussia was besieged in his palace in Berlin. From Berlin, the rebellion spread to nearly all the thirty-odd states that made up Germany. The immense

Habsburg Empire, with its capital in Vienna, erupted in mid-March. As in Paris and Berlin, troops fired into crowds of students and workers. By evening the mood of the Viennese was so vengeful that Prince Metternich, handing in his resignation, was told that the government was no longer able to guarantee his safety; with a loan from the Rothschilds, he left the city in a cab and rode out the revolution in England, watching the disintegration of the Europe he had constructed so skillfully thirty-five years before.[16]

With the Austrian capital in the hands of revolutionary students, the pieces of the Habsburg Empire began dropping off. The liberals in Hungary, led by Kossuth, proclaimed democracy and Hungarian independence. And now the Italian provinces arose.

The Habsburgs' man in Italy was the eighty-one-year-old field marshal, Count Joseph Radetsky. He had retired from active duty almost twenty years before, having been one of the Austrian generals who had finally beaten Napoleon at Leipzig. But in 1834 the emperor had called him out of retirement to control the restless provinces of Lombardy and Venetia, where Napoleon's reforms had made the professional class, and even part of the aristocracy, long for that revolution of contempt later defined by Lamartine. All northern Italy was alive with secret societies like the *carbonari*, whose name was inspired by coal which was black on the outside but glowed red-hot within. The Austrian prisons in northern Italy were soon full of *carbonari* and other Italian revolutionaries.

As Austrian viceroy, Radetsky was fatherly, firm, and benign. Three days of bloodshed, he believed, would cow the Italians into thirty years of peace. But he tried to avoid even those three days, and it was said that while Austrian soldiers walked the streets of Milan at night at their own risk, he could ride in an open carriage without hearing himself insulted. A cordial old gentleman, adored by his soldiers and vigorous enough to have fathered an illegitimate child at age seventy-nine, he virtually held together the Habsburg Empire in that critical summer of 1848 by convincing the emperor and his frightened court not to give way, not to grant independence to Hungary or to the Italian provinces.

But first the Italians chased him out. They gave him five, not three, days of bloodshed — the Five Glorious Days of Milan. As students built barricades out of everything from grand pianos to paving stones, their girl friends hurled boiling water down on the Austrian cavalry trying to maneuver through the vacant, barricaded streets. For five days and nights guerilla warfare raged while Radetsky tried to regain control.

Finally he abandoned the city altogether, marching his army eastward to the four powerful, close-set fortresses known as the Quadrilateral, which guarded the mouth of the Brenner Pass. The Brenner was Austria's door to the plains of northern Italy, and as long as Radetsky held the fortress of the Quadrilateral he could always return.

The news from Milan was hailed throughout Italy. Venice joined the struggle. King Charles Albert of Piedmont marched his army across the Po River into neighboring Lombardy to help fight the Austrians. It seemed that the unification of Italy might be at hand. Even the cautious, apprehensive Pius IX blessed twelve thousand volunteers who left Rome to fight Radetsky. As the New York *Evening Post* commented: "This is a most solemn moment for the Italians. May God bless their hearts and arms, and may they attain their long cherished desire — the independence and unity of their country." [17]

Though there were still only a few thousand persons of Italian origin in the United States, public opinion in America was overwhelmingly on the side of the rebels in Italy and elsewhere on the continent. When Congressman John D. Cummins of Ohio introduced a resolution in the House expressing sympathy for the Italian cause, it passed easily. At meetings held throughout the United States, resolutions were read in favor of Italian liberty. One adopted in Washington on March 28 was typical: "That we hail with delight and satisfaction the glorious struggle which the Italian people are making to free themselves from the despotism of a foreign power." [18] The noisy, festive rally held in New York on April 3 in favor of Italian liberty was described as one of the biggest in the city's history.

As news of this unexpected support reached Italy, it touched off demonstrations at every American consulate. The New York *Herald*'s Italian correspondent reported: "Everywhere Americans were declared to be brothers and friends. Thanks were rendered, gratitude was manifested, and every American was received with enthusiasm." [19] Crowds in Genoa held a torchlight procession in front of the American consulate, hailing the consul, the American eagle, and the memory of George Washington. In Venice, after the city's revolt, one of the first acts of the populace was to march on the American consulate shouting "Long live the United States. Long live our sister Republic." When someone asked the city's revolutionary leader, Daniel Manin, whether he wanted to be doge, he replied, "No, my aim is far higher. It is so high I hardly dare tell it to myself — George Washington." [20] A lawyer descended from an old Italian Jewish family, Manin sent an eloquent message to the American government. "We have much to learn from you," it said in closing, "and though we are your elders in civilization, we are not embarrassed to acknowledge it. We have no other ambition than to live in the enjoyment of peace and liberty, to recover the heritage of our ancestors, and to contribute, in some degree, to the infinite development of the human spirit." [21]

This was not a plea for aid. The Venetians knew, as other Italians did, that the American government would remain aloof from European politics. But the warmth of the support they received from across the Atlantic during those turbulent months helped to spread the fame of America as a citadel of freedom. This concept would permeate even the remote villages of Calabria and the interior of Sicily, and would act, ultimately, as one of the motives for emigration to North America.

At the end of May, Radetsky brought his rested, reinforced army out of the Quadrilateral. He moved towards Venice first, bringing most of the province (though not the city) under Austrian control again. Then he turned around and headed west for Milan. He struck quickly, as his old foe Napoleon had taught him to do. To gain the element of surprise, the eighty-one-year-old field marshal had his soldiers wrap their boots, the horses' hooves, and the wheels of their artillery carriages with cloth[22] and moved his army by night. At dawn, the white-coated Austrians would emerge from the mists of the Po Valley to occupy yet another town. The decisive battle took place at Custozza, on the shores of Lake Garda, under a broiling July sun. The Piedmontese army, with its Milanese and other allies, was shattered. A few days later Radetsky was back in Milan.

The defeat at Custozza had the effect of driving Italy's surviving republican governments farther to the left. Venice held out. In Turin, leftists agitated for another battle against Radetsky. But the gravest consequences were felt in Rome, where one of the conservative leaders of the papal government was assassinated. After papal guards had been forced to fire on a crowd of demonstrators outside the Vatican, Pius IX made an ignominious exit from Rome concealed in the Austrian ambassador's carriage. He took refuge in the kingdom of Naples, a despised figure now to many Italians, though by no means powerless. The government of the Papal States was overthrown and a republic proclaimed which the distraught Pius called "abominable, monstrous, illegal, impious, absurd, sacrilegious, and outrageous to every law, human and divine." [23]

The new Republican Assembly in Rome did two things. It drafted a far-reaching program of social reform, and it telegraphed Giuseppe Mazzini in Florence: *Roma Reppublica Venite.*

The two great heroes of Italian liberty, Mazzini and Giuseppe Garibaldi, were both born during the Napoleonic era: Mazzini, a doctor's son, in Genoa in 1805; and Garibaldi, a fisherman's son, two years later at Nice, which was still Italian then and called Nizza. Both would spend long periods of their lives in exile.

For a man who was considered a terrifying revolutionary by the Austrian police in his own time, Mazzini appears remarkably mild. He was a middle-class reformer and a passionate nationalist. Our century would hardly find his ideas radical. Called "the most dangerous man in Europe" by no less an authority than Metternich, Mazzini's crime was to have founded a secret society called *Giovine Italia,* Young Italy. His movement spread to other countries in Europe, where ardent student nationalists formed Young Germany, Young Hungary, Young Ireland. "It made him sick to see men forced to think in one way and act in another, bending to power which they hated and despised. He wanted men to become apostles, 'fragments of the living truth,' and because he made his followers feel that they were just that, he won the sort of devotion against which police power is helpless." [24] Though physically delicate, slim, short, artistic-looking — "beautiful and mercurial and fierce" as his friend Carlyle described him — Mazzini could be tough and coolheaded. When arrested the first time by Austrian police in 1831, he was carrying rifle bullets, a coded letter, a history of the Paris revolt of 1830, the text of a secret oath of Young Italy, and a sword cane.[25] He managed to get rid of all these incriminating objects before they could be used to convict him. A few years later, when he had gone into exile in Marseilles and was being sought by the French police, he put on the uniform of a National Guardsman and walked past police agents while they arrested someone else. In Marseilles during this period, he and fellow nationalists edited a paper which they shipped to Italy in marked barrels of pumice stone and pitch. "Across the border other friends took care to buy the marked barrels, and they distributed Mazzini's propaganda far and wide." [26]

A young Italian widow, Giuditta Sidoli, had become his mistress in

France. He remained faithful to her for years though she returned to Italy and to her children while he took refuge in England, having been hounded out of France and then out of Switzerland by the police. In London, he organized a school for Italian workers and their children, acted as leader of the numerous Italian political exiles in Britain, some of whom arrived there to join him, and wrote to revolutionaries throughout the continent. He knew that the police in most countries steamed open his letters, but when he discovered that his love letters to Giuditta were being steamed open and read by the British government as well, there was a scandal in Parliament that established the inviolability of the mails in England.[27]

Mazzini also encouraged Garibaldi and made his exploits in South America known in Italy and throughout the rest of Europe.

As a fisherman's son, Garibaldi had grown up near the sea, and he would spend much of his life aboard ships. At the age of seventeen he sailed to the Black Sea aboard a merchant vessel. This was an adventure, but a journey to Rome with his father the following year moved him and influenced him far more profoundly. "The Rome that I beheld with the eyes of my youthful imagination," he wrote in his *Memoirs,* "was the Rome of the future — the Rome that I never despaired of even when I was shipwrecked, dying, banished to the furthest depths of the American forests — the dominant thought and inspiration of my whole life." [28]

For several years, Garibaldi sailed around the Mediterranean, and then to South America. During these voyages, he heard older shipmates talking about Italy. One day, a sailor asked, "What do you mean? What *is* Italy?" And when another replied, "I mean the new Italy . . . United Italy, the Italy of all Italians," [29] Garibaldi said he knew how Columbus must have felt when he heard the cry of land. Already exposed to the progressive ideas of the French Saint-Simonians, Garibaldi joined Young Italy in 1833. The organization told him to enroll in the Royal Piedmontese Navy, which he did, and to organize a rebellion among his fellow sailors. In the navy's eyes this amounted to mutiny, and in 1834 Garibaldi was sentenced to death — but he had already fled to Marseilles.

The following year he was in South America, embarking on an amazing twelve-year career as a guerilla fighter. The southern part of Brazil had proclaimed its independence, calling itself Rio Grande do Sul, and a republican government had been established. At first Garibaldi fought on the sea, as captain of a small warship he had named the *Mazzini*.* Later he shifted to guerilla warfare on land, in Brazil, and then in Uruguay. While trying to outfit his men in Montevideo, he bought a supply of smocklike red shirts intended for local slaughterhouse workers, who liked the deep red color because it camouflaged the animals' blood. This was the origin of Garibaldi's famed red shirt uniform.

At first, he had commanded a ragged force of Europeans, South Americans, and black slaves who had escaped or been liberated. But as Garibaldi's fame spread, a growing number of Italian exiles joined him. With them, he formed an army he called the Italian Legion. For five years, the legion helped defend the capital of Uruguay, Montevideo, from the forces of the Argentinian dictator Juan Manuel Rosas. Garibaldi fought on every kind of terrain, growing to love the strong, violent landscapes of jungle and pampas, the sudden raids on horseback followed by escape up twisting mountain trails. In the course of those twelve years he was shipwrecked, ambushed, shot through the neck, captured, imprisoned, and strung up by the wrists to make him talk.[30] A charismatic man, with a grave, profoundly masculine face dominated by a high-bridged nose, and brownish-red hair flowing to his shoulders, he was adored by his soldiers and by Anita, the woman who shared his adventures and bore his children.

He had first seen Anita through a telescope from the deck of the *Mazzini*. It was a moment of deep loneliness and depression, and the sight of her transformed him. "I needed a human heart to love me," he recorded dramatically in his *Memoirs*. A boat was lowered and he was rowed ashore. He found a small, big-breasted, fierce mulatto woman of mixed Portuguese and black descent. It seems that she was married, and her husband may have been present when Garibaldi came ashore to find her. But when the Italian said to her, "I must have you," Anita stood up and followed him. She fought beside him, cursed his men when they rebelled or lost heart, slept with him in the open under the stars.[31] In 1842, believing that her first husband might be dead, they were married and the following year she was pregnant with the first of four children. Even then she continued to fight beside him, nursing one baby from the saddle when they were being pursued through jungle trails by an enemy force.

By the late 1840s, Garibaldi's self-imposed mission in South America

* It was one of the two vessels in Rio Grande do Sul's fleet. The other was commanded by a United States citizen, John Griggs.

had come to an end. There was talk of impending revolutions in Europe, and the men of the Italian Legion were anxious to join in any insurrections that might break out in Italy. By an extraordinary coincidence, Garibaldi, Anita, their children, and about sixty members of the legion embarked on a ship called the *Speranza* (Hope) in March 1848, bound for Marseilles. It was only when the vessel put in at a Spanish port after crossing the Atlantic that they learned of the tremendous revolutions which had actually occurred throughout Europe. Using one of their red shirts, a bedsheet, and the lining from a green waistcoat to make a tricolor Italian flag, they sailed exuberantly for home.

When he received the Assembly's telegram summoning him to Rome, Mazzini went. He entered the city one evening in March 1849, "with a deep sense of awe, almost of worship. . . . I had journeyed towards the Sacred City with a heart sick unto death from the defeat of Lombardy, the new deceptions I had met with in Tuscany, and the dismemberment of our republican party over the whole of Italy. Yet . . . as I passed [into Rome] . . . I felt an electric thrill run through me — a spring of new life." [32] Though he had never governed anything in his life other than *Giovine Italia*, Mazzini accepted the leadership of the Republican Assembly.* He occupied a single room in the Pope's Palace, surviving on an ascetic diet of bread and raisins.

Other members of the new government were almost as inexperienced. The minister of war was a naturalized American citizen who had been a resident of New York since 1834, earning his living as a commission merchant with offices at 47 Pearl Street. Born near Genoa in 1797, Giuseppe Avezzana had become a cadet in the Piedmontese army, participating in the brief, unsuccessful republican uprising of 1821 in Piedmont. Condemned to death in absentia, he had fled to Spain, fought there, and had then gone to Mexico where he had taken part in the Mexican Civil War. But in 1834, weary of bloodshed and battle, he had moved to New York, marrying an American girl and settling down to a conventional middle-class existence as a wholesaler of Italian dry goods.[33] In November 1847, he helped organize a rally at the Broadway Tabernacle honoring, ironically, Pio Nono's reforms. Late in 1848, Avezzana returned to Italy, where he was appointed a colonel in the National Guard at Genoa. From there he went to Rome aboard an American ship, and was promoted to general. The Republican Assem-

* He was officially one of three triumvirs.

bly, fascinated by his heterogeneous military experience, then appointed this Italian-American its minister of war and marine. He would prove to be one of the most capable men in the government.

Garibaldi had brought a thousand of his followers to Rome (a number that would remain magic for him). They were quartered in a former convent. His Italian Legion enrolled a great number of Roman volunteers, including expatriate artists from most of the countries of Europe. With his twelve years of experience in South America, and his calm, rather distant but courteous manner, Garibaldi dominated Rome by the force of his personality. "I shall never forget that day when I saw him on his beautiful white horse," wrote a young artist who enrolled in the legion. "I could not resist him. I went after him. Thousands did likewise. He had only to show himself. . . ." [34] Though Avezzana had appointed him a general, Garibaldi was not given official command of the Republic's army. He was not a Roman, for one thing. Also, he was a veteran guerilla fighter, and it was thought that regular troops might resent that. But his Italian Legion formed the backbone of Rome's defense.

From his sanctuary at Gaeta (Enrico Tonti's birthplace) Pius IX had called on all Catholic nations to crush the Republic and restore him. In Vienna, the emperor had returned to power and the revolutionary students had either been jailed or exiled. The Austrians would have been honored to come to the aid of the Holy Father, but they were still busy mopping up the vestiges of the revolution in Hungary and in northern Italy. To the utter amazement of the Romans, who had naively believed that their one ally in Europe would be France, their sister Republic, the French now landed an army of eight thousand men under General Charles Oudinot at the port of Civitavecchia less than fifty miles from Rome. The official French motive was sympathy for the pope. The actual motive was a desire to share with Austria in the spoils of the Italian peninsula. Nor were the French alone in this desire. Spain landed five thousand well-armed troops at Gaeta, and King Bomb brought up another sixteen thousand from Naples. Against these forces, Rome had Garibaldi's legion, a scattering of former papal guards, and little else.

The Roman people, as they prepared to withstand the French attack, looked to Garibaldi as their leader. Just his presence in the streets inspired confidence. He was accompanied everywhere by a striking orderly, a gigantic black man from Brazil, Andrea Aguyar. As his uniform,

Aguyar wore a cloak over his red tunic, a beret, blue trousers with green stripes, and carried in his hand a lance decorated near its point with a red streamer.[35] The uniforms of most of Garibaldi's other officers were equally colorful.

Oudinot did not take them seriously. When a small force of Milanese patriots bound for Rome landed among his troops at Civitavecchia in boyish error, the French commander gallantly allowed these *bersaglieri,* as they styled themselves, to complete their journey though he knew they would be joining Garibaldi's forces. "Italians never fight," said the French general complacently.

Though the plight of Pio Nono had turned Catholics in the United States against the Republic, the French intervention was condemned by the majority of Americans. Again, meetings were held and resolutions adopted. After a rally of the Friends of Roman Liberty in New Orleans, the governor of that heavily Catholic city read the following resolution:

That we regard the present struggle of the people of central Italy as the struggle of right and justice against brute force and tyranny in their most odious forms; and that we deeply sympathize with the Roman Republicans in their efforts to rid themselves forever of an oppressive form of government, and to establish for themselves and their posterity free and liberal institutions, in accordance with the spirit of the age and the genius and wants of the Italian people.[36]

The American consul in Rome, Nicholas Browne, was openly sympathetic to the Republic. "So deeply rooted in every American heart is the love of liberty," he had written to Mazzini, "that the nation will at once hail with joy the independence of the Roman Republic long before their diplomatic agents can have time, in due official form, to give expression of the generous sentiments of their constituency." [37] Browne's wording clearly implied recognition of the Republic as the legitimate government of Rome. And this Washington was unprepared to give. Though it was American policy to recognize existing governments, such governments first had to demonstrate the will and the ability to maintain themselves. "I consider the restoration of the Pope highly probable," wrote Secretary of State Buchanan, "if not absolutely certain." [38] Besides, recognition meant alienating American Catholics. Browne was recalled in May 1849, and replaced with Minister Lewis Cass, Jr., who was officially cool towards the Republic.

On April 30, meanwhile, Oudinot had moved on Rome. The French columns marched through a deserted countryside, farmhouse walls plastered accusingly with posters bearing the fifth article of the French constitution: FRANCE RESPECTS FOREIGN NATIONALITIES, HER MIGHT WILL NEVER BE EMPLOYED AGAINST THE LIBERTY OF ANY PEOPLE.[39] An American in Rome, William Wetmore Story, kept a diary of these tumultuous days. The entry for April 30 reads: "Expectations of hourly approach of the French. All the streets deserted, gloomy, and morose, as before some terrible thunderstorm. The women all fled to the houses . . . the shops all shut, with here and there a door half open and revealing the form of a soldier peering out." And he added his own views. "One cannot . . . but be excited and interested in a struggle like this — to expel the most unjustifiable invasion and aggression. But a short year ago France struggled through a bloody revolution for free principles and government . . . and now almost its first political act is the invasion of the only republic in Europe, contrary to its own constitution and to all international rights and laws." [40]

In their resplendent red and blue uniforms, wearing white gloves, the French soldiers approached St. Peter's, confident that the city gates would be opened to them by a grateful populace. They had been told that they were marching to save Rome from an unpopular revolution. But as they neared the walls, gunfire crackled out and French soldiers in the lead columns began crumbling onto the wide, dusty paving stones. The Roman artillery opened up, its rumbling blows drying the throats of people in the city who moved uneasily towards their shuttered windows. The battle raged most of the day, with Garibaldi leading a wild, headlong charge through two ancient villas just outside the walls, his Italian Legion clashing in hand-to-hand combat with the experienced companies of the *20me de Ligne*.[41] By evening, Oudinot's army was straggling back to Civitavecchia, thoroughly defeated.* The previously despised Italian soldiers, as one French officer wrote, had been "as wild as dervishes, clawing at us even with their hands." [42]

A bitter conflict now developed between Garibaldi and Mazzini. A fighter, Garibaldi wanted to follow up the day's victory and, by attacking the numbed French immediately at Civitavecchia, drive them out of Italy. But Mazzini took the statesman's long view. He hoped that the Roman victory would cause a reevaluation in Paris, and that the French government would now comprehend the enthusiasm of the Roman

---

* A good part of the credit for the Roman victory was due to Avezzana, the Italian-American minister of war, who had planned the counterattack.

people for their Republic. His view prevailed, and the French prisoners captured outside the walls of Rome were treated to fettuccine and wine and shown the sights of Rome before being returned to Oudinot. The French commander could not have cared less for the gesture. He was furious, humiliated. To Paris he sent a public message proclaiming victory, a private one requesting more troops and siege cannons.

In Mazzini's eyes, the Roman Republic was not at war with France. It was merely in a "state of defense." But the French government, as Mazzini ought to have foreseen, was not about to tolerate a defeat at the hands of Roman volunteers. "Our military honor is in peril," Oudinot was warned.[43] He was heavily reinforced.

Despite a stomach wound from the April 30 battle against Oudinot's columns, Garibaldi led some two thousand three hundred volunteers out of Rome a few days later. His objective was the eighteen thousand Bourbon troops camped in the Alban Hills just east of the city. It was not a situation where numbers counted, but even so Garibaldi took care to fight a rapid, rapierlike campaign. The decisive battle came at the beautiful hill town of Palestrina, and after the Neapolitan troops had retreated in disorder, the townspeople lit up all the windows and gave the Italian Legion food, wine, and love. At midnight a messenger came galloping down the cobblestoned main street. The French were coming! They were marching on Rome again! The groaning legionnaires were formed into columns for the weary, moonlit tramp back to the Eternal City. It was only a rumor. At dawn they crawled exhausted into their convent and went to sleep.

Four days later, a young diplomat arrived from Paris. For a moment it seemed that Mazzini's policy might work after all. The Romans repeated the diplomat's name, Ferdinand de Lesseps. Their grandchildren would study it in school as the name of the man who had joined the Red Sea to the Mediterranean by cutting a canal through the isthmus of Suez. But his canal-building feats were still in the future. He now desired to join the republics of France and Rome. Personally sympathetic to the Italians, Lesseps told a reporter from the New York *Evening Post*, "We thought Rome in a state of anarchy, but I find it peaceable, and can hear of no one who is desirous of destroying the Republic." [44] He told Paris the same thing, but his government had deceived him from the start. They had sent him to Rome simply to gain time. And while he earnestly negotiated with the gaunt, hollow-eyed Mazzini, French supply vessels were putting in at Civitavecchia to unload troops and the cannon and grappling hooks that Oudinot had requested. Oudinot had sworn a truce with the Roman Republic which was to last until the fourth of June, while Lesseps negotiated. In a betrayal of the truce, his army attacked at dawn on the third.

It was Sunday morning. The sky was just acquiring color when bells began to ring wildly throughout Rome sounding the alarm. Unshaven soldiers, still buttoning their uniforms, came rushing out of their billets. Orderlies on horseback galloped through the streets. Awakened by the din, Roman citizens could hear the cannon booming now up along the massive walls that defended the city near St. Peter's, where the French were again attacking. Now Garibaldi galloped past, riding hard, with the huge black man, Aguyar, and a dozen officers just behind him. "To the walls," Garibaldi shouted. "To the attack. Italians, to the attack." Groups of soldiers ran up the streets leading to the top of the Janiculum Hill, beside St. Peter's. They arrived winded to find that the French had taken the villas. This was a disaster. Though outside the walls of Rome, the villas occupied high ground from which the French could fire on the Roman defenders.

The villas, with their beautiful box gardens and Roman statues, emerging from night, were Garibaldi's great military error, one he would never quite live down.[45] A masterful guerilla leader, he had had little experience in the set battle beyond the bayonet charge, and this, fatally, is what he ordered. As groups of men reached the walls, he threw them into the open ground that rose sloping towards the ancient Corsini villa.

By eight o'clock that morning, the ground was dark with corpses, Italian and French. The villa had been taken several times, lost again. Garibaldi watched the carnage in a sort of daze, unable now to rectify his error. His poncho and hat torn by shrapnel, he led the final charge himself. With him were remnants of the legion, a company of papal guards, and a few *bersaglieri*. At last the Corsini villa was taken, and the French driven off the hill on which it stood. But when the French counterattack came, it was too powerful. Scrambling and dodging bullets, the Italians retreated back to the walls.

The siege of Rome began.

Day and night during those hot July weeks the French cannon thundered and the French troops, crouching behind wood palisades, dug their siege trenches closer to the walls. Margaret Fuller Ossoli, an American woman married to a Roman nobleman, described one battle she had witnessed:

[I]t began at four in the morning and lasted until the last gleam of light. The musket fire was almost intermittent . . . both French and Italians fought with the most obstinate valour. The French could not use their heavy cannon, being always driven away by the legions of Garibaldi . . . when trying to find positions for them. The loss on our side is about three hundred killed and wounded; theirs must be much greater.[46]

Marchioness Fuller Ossoli served as a nurse at the Fate Bene Fratelli hospital, caring for wounded soldiers. "There is scarcely one," she wrote to friends in America, "who is not moved by a noble spirit. Many, especially among the Lombards, are the flower of Italian youth." [47]

Rallies continued to be held in American cities supporting the Republic. On the fourth of July, huge crowds attended a meeting at Independence Square in Philadelphia where the following resolution was passed: "that the conduct of Louis Napoleon, in sending an army of regular soldiers, bearing the name, but without the hearts of Frenchmen, against the Republic of Rome, will forever stamp him in history as the Iscariot of liberty, the Benedict Arnold of the old world." [48]

By the end of July, it was clear that Rome could not hold out. Food supplies were low. The French siege lines were directly beneath the battered walls of Rome.

Two days before the city surrendered, Garibaldi went before the Assembly. He had just come from a battle. There was dirt and blood on his uniform. "*Ovunque noi saremo, sara Roma,*" he told the hushed galleries. "Wherever we are, Rome will be there." To a huge crowd gathered in St. Peter's square at sunset, he said, speaking from the saddle near the steps of the basilica: "I am leaving Rome. Whoever is willing to follow me will be received among my people. I ask nothing of them but a heart filled with love for our country. They will have no pay, no provisions, and no rest. I offer hunger, cold, forced marches, battles, and death." [49]

For all the romantic splendor of that scene, staged in a doomed and besieged city, at sunset, in the most beautiful architectural setting in the world, there was actually little Garibaldi could look forward to but defeat and death. Italy was nearly subjugated. In the spring, King Charles Albert had led the Piedmontese army against Radetsky's superior forces a second time, to suffer another defeat at Novara. All of northern Italy was controlled by Austria except the city of Venice, where Manin's republican government still held out despite an Austrian block-ade. The revolts in southern Italy had long since been put down by King Bomb. Tuscany had come back under Austrian control, and the Inquisition had been reestablished there. Now Rome was going down in defeat. It all seemed another futile repetition of what had happened so many times in the past, the doomed Italian attempt to free their country from foreign rule. Only in retrospect would it become clear that the desperate, drawn-out battle fought by Garibaldi and his supporters in Rome had been so genuinely heroic that its political consequences could not be suppressed.

With his pregnant Anita riding beside him, Garibaldi led his little army with its single artillery piece out of the Porta San Giovanni at dusk. As night fell, his columns disappeared into the hills northwest of Rome. They would march all night to outdistance the inevitable French pur-suit. In central Italy, Garibaldi hoped to raise a new and mighty Italian army. But his agony was just beginning.

About four thousand volunteers had followed him out of Rome. Within two days most had deserted, slipping back to the French-occupied city. Though he must have known this would happen, Gari-baldi cursed these "degenerate descendants of the greatest of all na-tions," his "unwarlike and effeminate countrymen." [50] For a month he led the hard remnants along the mountainous spine of Italy. There would be no Army of Central Italy, he realized. The people in the vil-lages locked their doors and shutters as his little force passed. They betrayed his stragglers. Four armies were pursuing him: the French, the Spaniards who had landed at Gaeta, the Neapolitans, and, most deadly of all, the Austrians. But this was still his kind of warfare. He would change his direction of march during the night, the men groaning and cursing as they pushed their supply carts up steep mountain trails, their wheels clattering suddenly over the cobblestones of some dark, inhos-pitable village. By morning they would be miles away, safe for another twenty-four hours.

As Garibaldi made his way up the Adriatic coast, hoping to reach Venice, the Austrians caught up with the guerilla army. Garibaldi's force was at the foothills of San Marino, the tiny Italian state that had maintained its neutrality for centuries. Up the steep road to San Marino trudged the tired remnants of Garibaldi's legion. Granted temporary sanctuary, they lay down gratefully on the floor of a Capuchin monastery. Garibaldi dissolved the legion. He himself would make a dash for Venice accompanied by a few volunteers. He begged Anita, pregnant and seriously ill, to remain in San Marino. *"Tu vuoi lasciarmi"* ("You want to leave me"), she accused him.[51] He gave in, and that night, under cover of darkness, he made his way through the Austrian lines with about two hundred followers. Anita was with him. Late the following afternoon they reached Cesenatico on the coast. The fishing fleet had just come in, and as Garibaldi's men disarmed the few Austrian sentries in their guardhouse, he rounded up the muttering fishermen and had them prepare their boats again for the sea. At dusk they escaped through the breakers at the mouth of the port, heading for Venice.

But the Austrian fleet intercepted them that night. Only three boats escaped, one containing Garibaldi and the now critically ill Anita, feverish and suffering agonizing spasms of pain in her womb. Before dawn, they put ashore in the flat, marshy lagoon country south of Venice. Already, Austrian troops were fanning out through the area to capture them. Garibaldi carried his barely conscious wife through tall, concealing reeds until he reached a farmhouse where she could be put to bed. That night, helped by local fishermen, he carried her out to a boat. They would try to reach Venice. But one of the fishermen, realizing who Garibaldi was and what the Austrians would do to anyone who aided him, panicked.[52] Garibaldi and Anita were put ashore again. There was a hut near the beach. They spent the night there, Anita in increasing pain. On the evening of the following day she was carried to a farmhouse, where she died. She was twenty-nine years old and six months pregnant.

Garibaldi wept and embraced her body, close to hysteria. But he could not even stay to see her buried. In the morning, with his one remaining companion, he slipped into the dense maritime forest north of Ravenna. Resting among the pines, he made his way out of the forest by night, eluding Austrian patrols to recross the mountains again in the direction of Florence. He was difficult to recognize now. He had shaved off his beard, and suffering had left him haggard. He no longer wore a red shirt and poncho, but peasant's clothes.

One evening, just outside of Florence, he fell asleep at a table in a small inn. A group of Austrian soldiers entered, part of the advance guard of a large force combing the area for him. But the inn was dark. Garibaldi raised his head from his arms and sat listening to their conversation. Then he lit a cigar and calmly smoked it until they left.[53] He and his companion, Culico, stuck to the mountains now, avoiding towns, until they reached the Tuscan coast opposite the island of Elba. A boat took them to Chiavari, a fishing port south of Genoa. This was Piedmontese-controlled territory. Garibaldi had escaped the Austrians. But the Piedmontese government, just launching long-range plans to improve relations with France, was unwilling to shelter an outlaw who had fought the French army. The minister of the interior at Turin wired Genoa: "Send him to America, if he will agree. . . . If he doesn't, arrest him." [54]

Garibaldi went to Nice, where he was allowed twenty-four hours to see his elderly mother and his children. His four-year-old daughter said at once, "Mamma will have told you in Rome how good I was. Where is Mamma?" [55] He could not bring himself to answer her. His two sons were left in the care of cousins, the little girl with friends. He tried to go to Tunis, but was refused entry. He went to Gibraltar, where he was allowed ashore for fifteen days, then sailed across the strait to put up at the home of the Piedmontese consul in Tangier. There he rested for seven months, hunting and fishing, riding along the beach, repairing fishing nets and sails. On June 12, 1850, he left for New York.

5

American Exile

THE NEW YORK that Garibaldi reached on July 29, 1850, aboard the English packet ship *Waterloo,* was still far from being a city of Italians. In the mid-century census taken that year, only 3,045 Italian residents had been counted in the whole of the United States — hardly enough to fill a single town. Though Italian immigrants were already crossing the Atlantic by the thousands, they were bound for the countries of South America, particularly Brazil and Argentina, where they could dwell among other Latin people and where the process of assimilation promised to be smoother and more rapid.

There was neither a tradition of Italian immigration to North America, nor any mechanism to produce it. Italy did not exist as a nation, so that if a citizen of Venice emigrated to Philadelphia, for example, he did so as an Austrian subject, or rather as a poor relation of the Habsburg Empire who could expect very little support from Austrian consular officials in the United States. An Italian immigrant from Naples was a citizen of the kingdom of Naples and could expect, if anything, even less assistance.

By 1850, however, New York was beginning to rival London as a place of exile for Italian patriots. One of the first Italian liberals to settle permanently in New York was Lorenzo da Ponte, a remarkable Venetian who arrived in America in 1805 at the age of fifty-six. After working as a grocer, distiller, bookseller, and Italian teacher, Da Ponte was appointed the first professor of Italian language and literature at Columbia

University. At the age of eighty-five, he was one of the prime movers in the building of the beautiful Italian opera house, among the finest neo-classic structures in the city. He could slip into the private box at his disposal and hear his own verses being sung; in his younger years in Europe, he had written the libretti for three of Mozart's operas, *Don Giovanni, Cosi Fan Tuttè,* and *The Marriage of Figaro.* Da Ponte was ninety when he died.

A number of Italian exiles had come to New York directly from Austrian prisons. In March 1835, the new Austrian Emperor Ferdinand II offered an amnesty to Italian political prisoners interred in the dungeon at Spielberg on the condition that they accept perpetual banishment. These prisoners were *carbonari* or other youthful revolutionaries, most of whom had been in their early twenties at the time of their arrests. Felice Foresti, who would follow Da Ponte as professor of Italian literature at Columbia and who would serve as representative for the Roman Republic in America, had been in Austrian dungeons for eighteen years. A lawyer born in Ferrara in 1789, Foresti had been arrested as a *carbonaro,* and, after a secret trial, sentenced to death. The sentence had been commuted to twenty years of hard imprisonment, and he had spent his first two years at Spielberg in leg irons and chains so heavy he could barely move.[1] Among the others in this same group were Count Frederico Confalonieri and Piero Borsieri, both of whom had passed twelve years in Spielberg.

Most educated Americans were already familiar with the names of these men through the publication of Silvio Pellico's *My Prisons,* an account of the suffering endured by Italian patriots at Spielberg and in other Austrian dungeons. In August 1836, having accepted the offer of amnesty, about twenty such men were put aboard the Imperial Austrian brig *Ussero* in the Adriatic and brought to America under guard. In New York, still technically prisoners, they were received by the Austrian consul who liberated them to American authorities. Though the American press ran articles for months hailing these "Martyrs of Spielberg," most of them found it difficult to adapt themselves to an environment that was wholly new. They had been cut off from the world for years. Most of them had been arrested and tried while students, and even those who had begun practicing a profession had not practiced it for a long time. Beyond that, they had to learn a new language and adapt to new customs. They were not immigrants, but exiles; and as the New York *Times* pointed out in a piece welcoming them to America: "We sincerely trust that these worthy victims of despotism may be able to find a hospitable sympathy in our country until a change for the better in the politics of the European cabinets may afford them an honorable occasion to return to their homeland." [2]

Count Confalonieri, whose admiration for the ideals of American democracy was mingled with distaste for what he felt was a prevalence of "irreligion, immorality, and unbridled greed," returned to Europe in 1837; Borsieri returned in 1839. The rest stayed on, generally living the quiet, rather melancholy lives of political exiles. Some earned a precarious living by teaching Italian at home, though two of them, the Sicilians Pietro Bachi and Luigi Monti, became Harvard professors. Monti also served as American consul to Palermo after 1861.[3]

The most successful exile in this group was Louis Tinelli, a Lombard who earned a law degree in Milan before taking part with Avezzana in the 1821 uprising in Piedmont. He escaped to England, where he aided Mazzini, but after a few years he found it possible to return to his native Lombardy. There he established a silk spinning plant near Lake Como. In August 1833, he was arrested by the Austrian police for pro-Mazzini activities, but before he could be sent to Spielberg the amnesty offer was made and Tinelli, accepting it with a melancholy heart since his wife refused to join him, came to New York aboard the *Ussero*. Helped by American friends, he established mulberry groves and a silk-spinning plant in New Jersey, winning a gold medal from the Institute of American Industry in 1840. Appointed a United States consul to Portugal in 1841, Tinelli rejoined Mazzini in northern Italy at the outbreak of the 1848 revolutions, but after the defeat at Custozza he returned to his consular post. Back in America in 1850, he engaged in manufacturing and opened a law office. During the Civil War, he helped form an Italian regiment in New York, then saw action himself as a colonel in the Union army. (His two sons were also Union officers.) Tinelli died in 1873 and was buried in Brooklyn.[4]

A Neapolitan nobleman, Orazio de Attelis, the marquis of Sant'Angelo, entered the United States from Mexico in 1824. He had already lived an amazing life. Born in 1774, he had served as an officer in Napoleon's army, taking part in the Russian campaign as Murat's aide-de-camp with the rank of general. (Napoleon's officer corps included a good many Italian, and Polish, aristocrats.) After Waterloo, the marquis fled to Spain, where he fought on the side of the liberals in 1821. From there he went into exile, first to Mexico and then to the United States. In New

Orleans, where he quickly became a successful trader, he founded a newspaper, the *Correo Atlantico,* which had editions in various languages. After taking out American citizenship, he moved to New York in the early 1840s. When the revolutions of 1848 broke out in Italy, though he was already in his seventies, the old Neapolitan nobleman returned to the peninsula, hoping to fight with Garibaldi in defense of the Roman Republic. But he fell ill and died in January 1850.[5]

In the early 1840s, a young man reached New York who would become the chief spokesman for many of these exiles as well as for the working-class Italians in the city. G. P. Secchi de Casali had joined the *carbonari* in his native Piacenza at age seventeen. After being hunted by the Austrian police, he had lived by his wits in various European countries and in North Africa before coming to America. He arrived alone, with almost no money and no prospects for a job. In 1849, he became editor of a struggling weekly called *l'Europeo-Americano.* Printed in both Italian and English, it died nine issues later. But Secchi de Casali, pawning his gold watch and his wife's earrings (neither of which he was apparently ever able to redeem),[6] and with $78 in advance subscriptions, brought out *l'Eco d'Italia* in 1849. It lasted half a century, and for a while it even came out as a daily.

The crushed revolutions of 1848 and 1849 in the north of Italy and in Rome brought a new wave of exiles. Being an American citizen, Avezzana, who had become vice president of the Roman Republic as well as its minister of war, was able to reembark for New York with a passport issued to him by Lewis Cass, Jr., bearing — for the sake of caution — the false name of Everett.[7] In New York, like some latter-day Cincinnatus, Avezzana returned to his modest dry goods business. (He would rejoin Garibaldi in 1860 during the final phase of the Risorgimento and take part, as a lieutenant-general, in the Battle of the Volturno; elected a deputy in the newly formed Italian parliament, he died in Rome in 1879.)

American Minister Lewis Cass, Jr., previously criticized for his failure to support the Republic, now proved to be a genuine friend of the Italian people. While the rest of the diplomatic community rode out the siege of Rome at Gaeta in safety, Cass remained at his post in the Eternal City. He kept the ministry open, and kept the stars and stripes flying over all official American buildings in the city.[8] They became places of refuge in the final days of the Republic, when Italians who had served in Garibaldi's legion, or in the republican government, had either to flee

Italy or face arrest and long prison sentences. With Cass's approval, the American vice consul, James E. Freeman, wrote out official-looking certificates of safe conduct to America for anyone who requested asylum.* In this way, hundreds of Italian patriots were saved and many of them made their way to America.

All of the Italian exiles in New York, including of course General Avezzana, were at dockside at the quarantine station on Staten Island when the *Waterloo* arrived. They found themselves moved and saddened when Garibaldi had to be carried ashore "like a bale of goods," [9] half paralyzed by a severe attack of rheumatism. He had still not recovered from the physical and psychological suffering of the previous year. A procession of hired carriages escorted Garibaldi to the Pavilion Hotel, where his solicitous Italian friends held a quiet celebration. Though the New York *Herald* had vowed that Garibaldi would be received with "all the ardor of feeling, warmth of welcome, and republican enthusiasm that so particularly distinguishes the American character," [10] he at once excused himself and asked his Italian friends to cancel the banquets they had organized in his honor. He was ill, he said wearily, but another reason was his desire to avoid controversy in America. Though a man of strong religious feeling, Garibaldi was a virulent priest-hater who had labeled the papacy "the negation of God" (among his milder remarks), and he knew that public tributes in his honor risked touching off counter-demonstrations by Irish Catholics. After a few weeks of quiet convalescence with friends at Hastings-on-Hudson and Yonkers, then at Irving Place in New York, he faded into a rustic existence on Staten Island, where he moved into the house of Antonio Meucci, an immigrant who employed Italians in a small candle factory.

Garibaldi was still tired and withdrawn, and nothing seemed to dispel his melancholy. "Soberly, not to say somberly dressed in a dark blue frock coat with a black scarf round his neck, he would sit in a corner of the room, almost forgotten, rarely speaking." [11] The long days he passed in solitude, often tramping through the woods, hunting, or fishing off the piers. He joined the local volunteer fire brigade and a Masonic lodge.[12] But he was running low on funds. Refused a job by the Post Office Department, he gratefully accepted Meucci's offer to work in his

---

* Mazzini was issued an American passport in the name of George Moore; Garibaldi also had an American passport in his saddlebags when he made his farewell address to the Romans at St. Peter's.

candle factory, and for several months he spent his days "bringing up barrels of tallow for the boiling vat from the old Vanderbilt landing." [13] He was simply one more immigrant laborer who shrugged and spread out his hands when asked a question in English too rapid to comprehend.

Christmas came and passed, and Garibaldi, tired of the heavy work and seeing no prospects of better employment, went along the docks looking for a ship where he could sign on as a common sailor. The sea had been his first profession, and now he longed to return to it. But he was not needed and disconsolately he returned to Meucci's candle works. A few weeks later, however, an old friend arrived in New York and Garibaldi sailed with him on a business trip to South America. He had been in America almost a year and had taken out his first papers; often, towards the end of his life, he would claim to be an American citizen.

In Lima, Peru, Garibaldi's wish to return to the sea was granted. Taking command of an old sailing ship, the *Carmen*, he crossed the Pacific with her. During the next two years he sailed her to Hong Kong and Canton, then down to Australia, back to Peru, around Cape Horn, and up to North America again.[14] Reaching Boston in September 1853, he made a trip to New York to see his friends and to mediate an increasingly bitter dispute between pro-Mazzini Republicans, led by Foresti, and Monarchists, led by Secchi de Casali, who wanted to see Italy unified under the House of Savoy.[15] Then he returned to Boston, where he took command of an American ship, *Commonwealth*, and crossed the Atlantic to England.

He would bide his time and wait for events in Italy to call him back to the peninsula. Another seven years were to pass before he would embark with a thousand men at Quarto, near Genoa, invade Sicily, and thus precipitate the unification of Italy.

The modest immigrant who had sheltered, fed, and employed Garibaldi in New York was something more than a candlestick maker. A photograph taken of Antonio Meucci late in his life shows a man with a small, pinched face supporting an enormous white beard; he seems to have been of medium height and pudgy. The trait which he had in common with so many Italian immigrants was perseverance. Born in Florence of lower-class parents in 1808, Meucci completed only grade school before going to work as a delivery boy, and then as a customs guard on the borders of Tuscany. In his early twenties, just married, he accepted the offer of a job in Havana. He would work at the Italian opera house as a machinist while his wife sewed and repaired costumes. But shortly after the Meuccis arrived in Havana, the Italian opera house burned down and with it went their jobs. Two gruelling, poverty-stricken years followed. At last the young couple scraped together enough money for a passage to New York where they arrived in 1845 with no prospects of work except what they could find among the few Italians already settled in the city. Meucci struggled to set himself up in business. He distributed beer for a while; then he started a piano manufacturing shop, then his candle factory — all this in the space of a few years, a driving and indefatigable man.[16] But it was the experiments carried out in his spare time that he believed would make him world-famous and a millionaire and that turned him, instead, in the minds of many of his Italian friends, into the archetypal immigrant, impotent, swindled, and betrayed in an alien society.

After the destruction of the Italian opera house in Havana, Meucci had found employment as a laborer in a metal-working shop. In the course of electroplating metal surfaces, he had begun carrying out some experiments with electricity and copper wire. He continued these experiments in his house at Clifton, on Staten Island. The year before he sheltered Garibaldi, Meucci discovered, or stumbled across the fact, that copper wire could carry sounds. In that same year, 1849, he constructed a primitive telephone consisting of simple diaphragms placed at both ends of an eight-foot length of copper wire hooked up to a battery. The thing conveyed sounds, though indistinctly. By the time Garibaldi had entered the household in mid-1850, an improved version of this *telettrofono* (as Meucci called it in Italian — telettrophone in English) ran through the house. In his *Memoirs*, Garibaldi noted:

While occupied in manufacturing candles, Meucci never ceased studying his apparatus and carrying on his experiments, in which I assisted him, my heart leaping with joy at the first tests, when Meucci, having run a metal wire between the second floor of the house and the basement, with two cones sealed with membranes attached to the two ends of the wire, worked at perfecting the vibrations of sound and current, which other experimenters later did perfect.[17]

This was twenty-six years before Alexander Graham Bell presented his invention at the Philadelphia Exposition of 1876. At least a half-dozen men in Europe and the United States were groping towards a working telephone during those years. One of them, the German Philip Reis, was also a poor, self-taught man like Meucci. But he had become a well-known researcher, able to report authoritatively in a paper to the Physical Society of Frankfurt that "it has not been possible to reproduce human speech with sufficient clarity because the consonants are for the most part reproduced distinctly but not the vowels. . . ." Both Reis and, later, Bell called their instruments telephones, a logical word derived from the Greek *tele* (meaning far) and *phone* (meaning sound). There was no real logic to the term telettrophone. The fact that Meucci used it for over twenty years, when researchers on both sides of the Atlantic were already talking about telephones, was symbolic of his isolation.

As early as 1860, Meucci had developed what he felt was a satisfactory electromagnetic telephone. Though he tried to keep his invention secret, he talked confidently of being able to lay an underseas cable between New York and Staten Island — if only someone would advance him the capital.[18] He was working on other inventions as well. Perhaps one of them would make him rich, and then he could devote all his time to the telephone. His next moves, however, were revealingly maladroit. Hoping to interest the Italian government in his *telettrofono*, Meucci gave a full description of the unpatented invention to an Italian friend who was returning to Naples. Naples was one of the most reactionary capitals in Europe and hardly a promising choice. The friend, Enrico Bandelari, presented Meucci's papers to the director of the Post Office Department, who dismissed the talking telegraph as a pipe dream and Meucci, this *immigrant*, as a crank. On October 13, 1865, a full description of the still-unpatented invention was printed in *l'Eco d'Italia*, probably because Meucci was trying to raise capital among New York Italians. In this he was only fitfully successful. He would receive meager sums from a succession of investors.

Finally, a friend introduced Meucci to an able patent lawyer, Thomas B. Stetson, who helped the Italian obtain a caveat from the United States Patent Office on the basis of a rather vague description of his invention accompanied by a drawing of two men using a telephone, which an Italian artist in New York, Nastori Corradi, had prepared to Meucci's specifications. The date of the caveat was December 23, 1871 — still five years before Bell's patent.

Meucci's business affairs had been going badly. Now fate intervened and he was ruined. He was aboard the Staten Island ferry *Westerfield* when its boiler exploded — one of the greatest disasters of the era, in which over a hundred passengers were killed.[19] Meucci narrowly missed being one of the fatalities, having received a piece of shrapnel in his abdomen. By the time his long convalescence ended he was on relief. Meucci's wife took all his telettrophones and batteries and wire and sold the lot to the local junkman for six dollars. This was not in itself an irredeemable loss. Meucci had kept very complete notebooks of all his inventions, and he was able to reconstruct his telephones. But the accident, and his wife's impatient gesture, slowed him down. His financial condition now made it even harder for him to come into contact with people who could understand his invention and encourage him. As an immigrant, he was already cut off. As an immigrant on relief, he was lost.

As soon as Meucci had recovered from the wound (he was bedridden for over six months), with the aid of an Italian friend he approached the president of the American District Telegraph Company in New York, Edward B. Grant, requesting that his invention be tested using the company's facilities. Meucci gave Grant a detailed description of his telephone in a memorandum of a dozen or so pages (the invention was now protected by a caveat). Grant glanced at the memorandum, which was probably written in mangled English, and turned the matter over to an assistant, George F. Durant, who later testified in court that Meucci and his friend Bertolino

called repeatedly, at intervals of perhaps two weeks or a month. And I told Mr. Grant that I didn't see anything in the papers at all; that I thought the man was a crank, although when they came I treated them very politely and I told them I had been pressed for time and had not given the matter any attention. After they called several times, Mr. Grant suggested that I had better hand the papers back to them, which I did, and was very glad to get rid of them.[20]

Meucci, however, swore that his memorandum was never returned.

Events now began to move swiftly. Stetson, who appears to have genuinely believed in Meucci's invention, strongly urged him to take out a patent. The cost of preparing the necessary documents, Stetson informed him, was $250. Meucci was unable to raise the sum, and had to settle for renewing the caveat in 1872 and 1873, both times borrowing the necessary $10 from a friend. But in 1874 he was unable to afford even the $10, and the caveat lapsed. (The fact that no copy of this caveat could later be found in the files of the U.S. Patent Office would be cited by Meucci's supporters as evidence that his invention had been stolen.) Partly on Stetson's advice, Meucci shifted his efforts to other inventions, which included candle molds, a new formula for glue, a hygrometer, and a formula for effervescent drinks. It was felt that investors might be more interested in backing these relatively simpler products.

Two years later, on February 14, 1876, Alexander Graham Bell applied for his patent. By a peculiar coincidence, another American scientist, Elisha Gray, applied for virtually the same patent two hours later.

After Bell's triumph at Philadelphia, where the emperor of Brazil uttered his famous line, "My God, it speaks!" — turning Bell's invention into the wonder of the day — an embittered Meucci insisted that he had been the original inventor of the telephone and pointed to his caveat of 1871 as evidence. Edison had by then entered the field with a functioning telephone of his own, and a high-powered financial battle had developed between a half-dozen companies seeking domination of what promised to be an extraordinarily lucrative business. In fact, the Bell patent would prove to be the single most remunerative invention of the age, if not of all time. The New York-based Globe Telephone Company, seeking to check the Bell Company's expansion, announced in 1885 that it had secured title to Meucci's invention and declared its intent to manufacture a Meucci telephone without infringing on Bell's patent. Two months later the Bell Company sued, and in 1885 the trial opened at the United States Circuit Court for the Southern District of New York.

The trial lasted two years. Though the Bell Company's lawyers and a number of its witnesses sought to establish that Meucci's invention had merely been a childlike string telephone, or "lover's telephone," employing wire to transmit sounds mechanically, without electricity, the descriptions of Meucci's apparatus in 1850 left by Garibaldi and others who had seen it made it clear that Meucci had employed electric current. As evidence, Meucci presented in court the drawings he had made of his experimental telephones from the notebooks he had rigorously kept over the years. (He could not, unfortunately, produce the working models, since his wife had sold those to the junkman.) He testified that he had first conceived the idea of an electromagnetic telephone in 1849, that "prior to December, 1871, I tried to keep my invention a secret, talked mostly to my wife through it, and a few friends. After I received my caveat, I never made a secret of my invention, have told many people about it, and talked with numerous persons through it. After I received my caveat, some reporters came to see me. I told them about it, and a description of it was published in some paper in New York. . . ." [21]

But what spoiled Meucci's attempts to establish his priority was the caveat itself, which made little sense and barely conveyed the idea of an electromagnetic telephone. Stetson testified that he had devoted only a half hour to its preparation and that, having to correct Meucci's English, he had also thoroughly rewritten the descriptive parts in the light of his own understanding of the invention. As he testified, "It is never practicable to be absolutely certain that one understands another fully; in this case, I am quite sure that I did not understand the invention. What I did understand I put into such shape as I thought was proper for a caveat." He maintained that, despite his rewrites and additions, "the caveat . . . is proof positive that Mr. Meucci had at that time the idea of communicating spoken words by the aid of electricity." [22] The Bell Company's witnesses, however, included engineers from such institutions as MIT, and they challenged both the caveat and Meucci's primitive knowledge of electrical science. This testimony decided the issue, and on July 19, 1887, Judge Wallace ruled in favor of the Bell Telephone Company. In his decision, he said that

the proofs failed to show that [Meucci] had reached any practical result beyond that of conveying speech mechanically by means of a wire telephone. He doubtless employed a metallic conductor as a medium for conveying sound, and supposed that by electrifying the apparatus or the operator he could obtain a better result. . . . It is idle to contend that an inventor having such conceptions could at that time have been the inventor of the Bell telephone.[23]

The case was then appealed to the Supreme Court. A hearing was set in Washington during the term of October 1891, but by then the Globe Telephone Company had abandoned the case. Meucci had died in 1889. He was buried at the expense of the Italian government, perhaps the only time this particular honor had been extended to an American citizen. All of New York's newspapers carried long obituaries of the immigrant whose later years had been spent on relief. As the New York *Herald* wrote, he had died "in the full belief of the priority of his claim as the inventor of the telephone which, during the interval of his sickness, he declared must be recognized sooner or later." Without Meucci's presence as a witness, the appeal, shaky enough at best, was doomed. Also, the Bell organization had grown so powerful by that time that it seemed hopeless to challenge its dominant position.

Did Meucci invent the telephone? Probably not. But to do Meucci justice, he was neither a crank nor a fraud. An entry in one of his note-books, dated August 17, 1870, six years before Bell's patent, describes his cognition at that time of a telephone receiver.

Fabric of cotton, flax, silk, saturated with starch very thick, and the starch dissolved in a solution of nitrate of silver and then paraffin has given a good diaphragm, only to use this quality of membrance it is necessary to put in the center a small disk of iron or platinum metallic iron, in order that it can [missing] on the center of the bobbin and communicate the electricity in its vibration with the sound of the word [24]

Though Meucci's English is rough, these notes make one point clear. He had been experimenting since 1849 with an electromagnetic telephone, not with the purely mechanical transmission of sounds as was claimed in the Bell-Globe trial. It is quite possible that if Meucci had not been an immigrant, a business failure, a casualty of the *Westerfield* disaster, a man unable to express himself coherently in English, and above all a man ignorant of the advances being made in electrical science in profes-sional laboratories, he might have been able to perfect his telephone several years before Bell, Gray, and Edison — or if not perfect it en-tirely, to have gained recognition as a legitimate pioneer who had made valuable strides towards one of the basic inventions in history.

In 1923, Italian-Americans raised funds by subscription to erect a monument to Meucci at Rosebank, Staten Island.

The decade preceding the Civil War, from 1850 to 1860, was the last in which the Italian-American community would look more towards the past, in Europe, than to the future in America. The community was still very small. In 1852, for example, 351 Italians had entered the United States, though two years later there was a sudden leap to 1,263. For the rest of the decade the figure hovered around 1,000 a year. The census of 1860 still found only 10,000 Italian-born residents and their children in America, a tiny minority in a population of twenty-eight million. Most of these Italians were from the north of Italy. Many were middle class. They were not particularly anxious to be assimilated, and their great dream remained to return to a free, united Italy. This was true even among people who had taken out American citizenship. The columns of Secchi de Casali's *l'Eco d'Italia* were filled mainly with political news from Italy and other European countries. The paper also printed short stories and poems in Italian written by members of the New York com-munity. Its very name, "the echo of Italy," was redolent with nostalgia.

For the poor, America was a more immediate reality. Though they lived in tiny Italian enclaves in the slums of New York, of Boston and Philadelphia, among themselves they were people of utterly diverse origins. A Tuscan could hardly abide the Neapolitans. The Sicilians were a people apart. (After creating the world, Sicilians said, God had created the Straits of Messina to separate men from madmen.) Poor Italians in America before the Civil War were generally street people: plaster statuette vendors from Lucca, organ-grinders from Naples who filled the avenues of New York and other cities with their sad, metallic tunes, shoeshine "boys" from Palermo. They occasionally helped one another and more often preyed off one another. Italian immigrants were already being exploited by other Italians, the *padroni,* or bosses, who offered jobs, protection, and lodging in return for a part of the immigrant's pay. Children were particularly easy targets for exploitation, forced to wander the streets playing violins or hand organs, their earnings going to a *padrone* who, as Secchi de Casali wrote, mistreated "the little white slaves, giving them in turn bad food, inhuman treatment, ragged clothes and not a particle of education." [25] But these problems were still in their embryonic stages, and Americans were not aware of them just as they were not aware of the few Italians in their midst. No cause except abolition had so stirred the American people in the years immediately before and after 1850 as the struggle for independence in Italy, and when most Americans thought of Italians, they still thought of republican heroes and reactionary tyrants, rather than of the few Italians they could see around them.

The pope's return to Rome in April 1850, under the protection of French arms, had touched off a new wave of mass protests in America. When the embittered pontiff had ridden through the sullen streets of his capital, he had found church walls lettered with the following double-column manifesto:

Death to	Pius IX
Mazzini	is in our hearts.
The Republic is	The best form of government
The worst government	is that of the priests.
Down with	The power of the priests
The rule of the people	is eternal.[26]

Jeered by his contemptuous subjects, who called him *Porco Pio Nono* (Pig Pius IX), the pontiff gave his tacit consent to a crackdown in the

Papal States, which resulted in some 58,523 political arrests between 1852 and 1854. American Minister Lewis Cass, Jr., wrote to Horace Greeley in 1853 that "supported by France and Austria, the government is . . . cruel in the extreme. What with fines, imprisonments, expulsions, etc., scarcely a family high or low has not been subjected . . . to some severe punishment for participation, no matter how slight or indirect, in the revolutionary proceedings of 1848." [27] A militant Catholic vigilante group, the *sanfedisti,* killed and tortured suspected liberals with impunity. Each member was obliged to swear an oath which affirmed in part:

I swear to remain firm in the defense of the sacred cause which I have embraced; to spare no individual of the infamous sect of liberals, whatever be his birth, his parentage, his position; to take no pity on the tears of infants or the aged, but to shed to the last drop the blood of the infamous liberals, whatever be their sex or age. Finally, I swear an implacable hatred to all the enemies of our Catholic and Roman faith, the only true religion.[28]

The American press reported at length on the repressions being carried out in the Papal States, and on the condition of prisons there. The *Daily Evening Transcript* in Boston expressed a widely held feeling of indignation: "We are inclined to attribute these monstrous barbarities no less to the inherent vices of an ecclesiastical regime than to the deliberate emotions of tyranny and malice, for it is impossible to doubt that what was always bad in the Roman States has now become much worse under the aggravation of rebellion and the temptations of impunity." [29] The transgressions of Pius IX as a temporal ruler were to have profound political effects in the United States.

The arrival of poor immigrants from Europe, a phenomenon that gathered headway in the 1830s, caused a reaction in America known as the nativist movement. The United States, of course, had been a country of immigrants all along. But the early immigrants had enjoyed a common Puritan and Anglo-Saxon background, and also, to a considerable extent, a background of militant middle-class liberalism. As the *Federalist Papers* noted, "Providence has been pleased to give this one connected country to one united people — a people descended from the same ancestors speaking the same language, professing the same religion, attached to the same principles of government. . . ." [30] The descendants of these earlier Puritan settlers now saw a threat in the mass influx of foreign laborers from a dozen different countries. Fifteen million immigrants were to pour into the United States in the half century between 1840 and 1890, and though some were still the ethnic and cultural kinfolk of earlier Americans, the majority *were* different. They were German Forty-Eighters (i.e., refugees of the revolutions of 1848) with proto-Marxist ideas. They were taciturn, socialistic Scandinavians, fiery Hungarians and anarchic Piedmontese. They were bearded Poles and Russians. Above all, they were Irish Catholics.

The fear of Catholicism was deeply rooted in America's Puritan soul. It went back to sixteenth- and seventeenth-century England, where anti-Catholic hysteria was a natural part of a foreign policy that constantly pitted brave English sailors against the swaggering fleets of Spain and France. The threat to Britain of the Spanish Armada had been a Catholic threat. The colonies which English dissidents founded in America, moreover, were forced to struggle for survival against two Catholic empires, the French to the north and the Spanish to the south. And in the struggle against the French in particular, the American colonists had attributed their victory to the superiority of a Protestant democracy over an aristocratic, feudal Catholic empire ruled from Paris by a king and from Rome by the pope. The influx of so many Catholic immigrants, the majority of whom appeared poor, ignorant, and superstitious, revived these barely dormant fears.

Had Pius IX been a truly liberal reformer, he might have dispelled much of the American nativist hostility towards Catholic immigrants. But the repression of democracy in the Papal States and in Italy as a whole helped instead to ignite the powerful anti-Catholic "Know-Nothing" movement of the 1850s — so called because members of a secret nativist group, when questioned about their activities, had replied, "I know nothing." They sought to have only native Americans elected to office, and to impose a twenty-five-year residency requirement for citizenship. This was the era of signs reading, "Man wanted, no Irish need apply," so strong was the prejudice towards Catholic immigrants. The Italians, ironically, were largely exempt from hostility. They were too few. Also, many of them were exiled republicans who were as virulently anti-Papist as any Know-Nothing. In 1853, in fact, Secchi de Casali started an English-language paper, the *Crusader*, whose editorial aims included "incessant war against the system of the Papacy" and "the maintainance of public schools at any sacrifice." The *Crusader* differed from the Know-Nothing penny press, however, by demanding "equal rights to naturalized and native citizens."

The Know-Nothing movement subsided in the late 1850s only because it was overwhelmed by a greater conflict. The nativists themselves were split into Confederate and Union partisans. But they would remain a potent force in American society and, reemerging after the Civil War in other disguises, would lash out at later Italian-American immigrants with particular venom.

6

Oppressa Resurgit

THE CIVIL WAR that tore Americans apart was paradoxically the event that tied the European immigrants to their adopted land. All of a sudden the news from Dublin, or Frankfurt, or Rome became less immediate than the news from Washington or Richmond. The Italian community, though it was smaller and of more recent origin than other immigrant groups, felt this transformation as strongly as the others. Almost every Italian resident of New York or Philadelphia knew some Italian boy who was fighting in one of the two armies, and hundreds of families wrote to, waited for, and sometimes mourned their own sons. The Civil War gave all foreign-born Americans a new kind of visibility, and made them feel wanted. No longer were they merely strange-looking Poles, or Hungarians, or Italians, speaking broken English. Many of the male immigrants were young enough to serve. And they were needed — particularly since a good number of them were veterans of the battlefields of Europe.

Corps of foreign-born volunteers were a feature of the Union army in particular. The German Forty-Eighters were quick to enlist in a brigade of their own commanded by General Franz Sigel, a graduate of the German Military Academy and himself a veteran of the 1848 revolutions. "I fights mit Sigel" became one of the rallying cries of the Union. The Irish, too, formed a brigade which fought under a green flag bearing the golden harp of Ireland. The Irish-Americans, commanded by General

Thomas Francis Meagher, who had been a leading member of the
Mazzini-inspired Young Ireland movement and a revolutionary in 1848,
went into battle with the Gaelic cry, *Faugh a Ballagh!* (It was while
watching this splendid but unlucky Irish Brigade being mowed down at
the battle of Fredericksburg that Robert E. Lee turned to his staff and
said, "It is well that war is so terrible — we should grow too fond of
it.")

Just after the North's declaration of war, *l'Eco d'Italia* proposed that
an Italian Legion be formed to fight in the Union ranks under Italian-
American officers. A recruiting office was opened at 298 Broadway, in
New York. A second Italian regiment known as the Garibaldi Guard
was also being mustered. According to the New York *Herald,* the guard
had attracted "all the organ grinders of the city," whom it portrayed with
rude flippancy as "a hardy and enduring race, familiarized with hardship and exposure." [1] The guard soon consisted of more than organ-
grinders, however, since it absorbed many of the other national units
that had been forming in New York: Hungarians, Swiss, Frenchmen,
Spaniards. Finally absorbing the Italian Legion as well, the guard was
placed under the command of a Hungarian exile, Colonel Fred C.
d'Utassy. The two highest ranking Italians were Lieutenant Colonel
Alexander Repetti, who had fought under Garibaldi, and Lieutenant
Colonel Louis Tinelli. Its men had come from "the glorious fields and
strifes on Italian soil and from others on every beleaguered fortress of
1848," reported the *Herald,* having forgotten its previous remarks about
organ-grinders.[2]

The foreign motif was stressed in the guard's dashing uniform — blue
frock coats with a red undershirt, blue trousers with red piping, and felt
hats ornamented with feathers and green leaves. While this uniform
made the guardsmen conspicuous targets, it gave New Yorkers a magnificent spectacle as the regiment double-timed up Broadway in the
spring of 1861, carrying not only the American flag but also the original
flag carried by Garibaldi through the campaigns of 1848–1849, which
had been presented to the guard at its first full-dress parade by General
Avezzana. After a rocky start which included looting and insubordina-
tion (the exasperated Secchi de Casali called the unit "a band of male-
factors" who had dishonored Garibaldi's name), the guard fought well
throughout the long war and was still in action in the final battles leading to Appomattox. There is a monument to the Garibaldi Guard at

Cemetery Ridge, on the Gettysburg battlefield where the guard had fifteen killed and eighty wounded.

Three Italian-Americans were promoted to the rank of brigadier general in the Union army: Enrico Fardella, Eduardo Ferrero, and Francis Spinola — who had been a New York state senator at the outbreak of the war. Twice wounded while leading a bayonet charge at the Battle of Wapping Heights, Spinola became a celebrated Union hero and was later elected to Congress.*

A dashing Confederate officer in Hood's Texas Brigade was Decimus et Ultimus Barziza, who had received his queer name because his father, a penniless Venetian nobleman married to a Williamsburg belle, already had nine other children at the time of his birth and could not afford more. So the infant son was hopefully christened "Tenth and Last" in Latin. (His Texas friends called him "D.U." or "Bar"; his wife and adopted child called him "Dessie.")

After fighting in the peninsula campaign, where he was wounded and promoted to captain, the youthful Barziza led his men in the battles of Malvern Hill, Freeman's Ford, Thoroughfare Gap, and the Second Manassas, where he was again wounded.[3] Recovering, he led a company at Fredericksburg and then at Gettysburg where, in the struggle for possession of the Little Round Top, Barziza's Texans and Union infantrymen fired at each other at distances no farther than thirty-five yards. "The trees were literally barked and thousands of bullets flew to atoms against the hard rocks," Barziza wrote. "Our line was compelled finally to retire, and left me wounded in the hands of the enemy. I tried to feign dead, but it would not answer, and some time after I was taken to the enemy's rear."[4]

After having been hospitalized in Baltimore, Barziza managed to escape by leaping from the window of a speeding prison train at three

* Abraham Lincoln, who like Jefferson was an Italianophile, offered Garibaldi a commission as a major general in the Union army. Secretary of State William H. Seward wrote to the American minister in Antwerp, instructing him to "proceed at once and enter into communication with the distinguished soldier of Freedom. Say to him that this government believes his services in the present contest for the unity and liberty of the American people, would be exceedingly useful and that therefore they are earnestly desired and invited." Seward offered, apart from a major general's stars, "the hearty welcome of the American people. Tell him that we have abundant resources, and numbers unlimited at our command, and a nation resolved to remain united and free." Sanford relayed the message to Garibaldi's home on the tiny island of Caprera, situated between Sardinia and Corsica. Garibaldi replied that he would be "very happy to serve a country for which I have so much affection and of which I am an adoptive citizen," but that the task of reuniting all of Italy still was uppermost in his plans.

o'clock in the morning as it rolled through the Pennsylvania countryside. In his book of memoirs, he records what followed:

Fortunately, I fell upon a level place, and did not seriously hurt myself. I cannot describe my feelings at this time. I started in a run from the direction of the railroad, and after traveling as well as I could until daybreak, I lay down in the woods and resolved in my mind what was best to be done. . . .

I finally resolved to make my way to the railroad, and trust to fate and fortune. I had not gone far before I saw a town ahead, and thinking and hoping it was Harrisburg, I remembered I had enough money to take me to Philadelphia. Approaching the town, I asked a lad the time of day as an excuse to stop awhile. I then asked him how far they called it to Philadelphia. "Oh Sir," he replied, "I don't know, but it must be a long way, as it is a hundred miles to Harrisburg." At this piece of information, I was exceedingly disturbed, and longed for a little more money. However, I kept on in the town, quite undetermined as to my action. I was cold and hungry, and passing up the streets of the town . . . I espied the sign of a lager beer saloon, and went in, took a drink and a cigar, and very unceremoniously sat down before the stove, and assumed an air of familiarity with a barroom, which is not difficult to do. The proprietor, who was a dutchman, was alone, and soon entered in conversation with me. He told me he was a discharged soldier from some Pennsylvania regiment, and named the campaigns he had passed through. I represented myself as a disabled and discharged soldier from the 2d Massachusetts infantry. We discussed the war prospects, denounced Jeff. Davis and his cabinet, consigned all the rebels to the devil, and took a drink at the host's expense. I made this place my headquarters; learned from the dutchman the fare to Philadelphia, and the hour at which the train came through. I still did not know what town I was in, and, of course, asked nobody. I heard, however, the dutchman mention the *"Globe"* as the paper published in the town, and some hours after, I found a paper lying on the counter of a store and read *"The Huntingdon Globe."* I was then in Huntingdon, but I had never heard of the place before.

I went out in the street, sought a barber-shop, had my hair cut, and got shaved, and proceeded to a jeweler's to sell a large, plain gold ring.

Judging it would look suspicious for a stranger to offer for sale a ring in a small town like this, I had recourse to strategy.

I walked in the shop, stood over the show-glass, and requested the keeper to show me some gutta-percha rings, that I wished to purchase one. He accordingly did so, and I pulled off my ring and let it drop on the glass, and put on the other on the same finger. The jeweler took up my ring, and remarked: "This is a very fine ring." "Yes," said I, "what is it worth?" After examining it, he rejoined, "about four and a half in greenbacks." "What is this worth?" said I, meaning the one I then had on. "Fifty cents," said he. "Well," I remarked, "give me the difference, I had as soon wear a gutta percha as a gold ring." He accordingly handed me over the money, and I left, went to a restaurant and indulged in a plate of oysters, took a drink, puffed a cigar, and felt quite happy.[5]

Catching a train to Philadelphia, then one to New York and then one to Troy, Barziza crossed the border into Canada. From Nova Scotia he took a Canadian vessel to Bermuda, returning to Wilmington, North Carolina, aboard the blockade runner, *Edith*. After the Confederate surrender, Barziza settled in Houston where he worked as a night clerk while studying law. Admitted to the bar in 1866, he became a brilliant criminal lawyer and was elected to two terms in the Texas legislature. During the second term, he missed being elected Speaker by two votes. A description of him at that time depicted him as "black-eyed, black-haired, and of Italian descent; he [is] bright, energetic, eloquent and heterogeneous . . . fiery, impetuous, bold. . . ."[6] During his second term, Barziza and thirty-five other representatives, trying to block what they felt was a land grab by the Texas & Pacific Railway Company, walked out of the chamber, making it impossible for the majority to have a quorum and pass a bill in favor of the railroad. Though the speaker instructed the sergeant at arms to arrest the missing members, Barziza simply resigned along with four other legislators. He never set foot in the House again, dying in Houston in 1882 at the premature age of forty-three.

The most exceptional Italian involved in the Civil War, however, a man who would win the Medal of Honor, have three careers, become closely associated with the moneyed establishment in New York and survive a sensational lawsuit, was the Union cavalryman Luigi Palma di Cesnola.

His full name was Count Emmanuele Pietro Paolo Maria Luigi Palma di Cesnola,[7] in the Spanish manner. The name Palma, in fact, was Spanish, the legacy of an ancestor who had arrived in Italy as a soldier of fortune in the thirteenth century. Di Cesnola means simply "from Cesnola," a castle stronghold in the Italian Alps which the Palmas had received as a feudal grant from their patrons, the House of Savoy. The family crest, a palm flanked by a lion and an eagle, bore the Latin inscription *oppressa resurgit*, "oppressed, he rises again."

Cesnola's parents were an odd, unhappy couple. His father was an impoverished count, a *carbonaro* spinning revolutionary dreams in the Piedmontese capital, Turin. His mother, Countess Eugenia Ricca di Castelvecchio, was a wealthy, conservative woman twenty-six years younger than her husband. A daughter of the vice regent of Sardinia for the House of Savoy, she lived with her children in the countryside. Not surprisingly, Luigi had an unhappy and turbulent childhood. At the age of fifteen, inspired by his father's dream of Italian unity, he enlisted directly from military school into the Fourth Infantry Regiment of the Royal Army of Piedmont — King Charles Albert's army. He was just in time to take part in the Piedmontese campaign against Radetsky following Milan's Five Glorious Days, and to face Austrian fire a few weeks later at Custozza. By the time the battle of Novara began on March 17, 1849, Cesnola was a sixteen-year-old veteran, a man. Though the battle was an Italian defeat, Cesnola was promoted from corporal to second lieutenant on the field and was later awarded a silver medal for bravery.[8]

Over the next three years, he rose quickly towards a promising army career. He graduated from the Royal Military Academy with a regular commission and, after two years of duty, became aide-de-camp to the lord major general of Piedmont. But a few months later he was forced to retire in disgrace. The cause of the scandal was never clarified. Cesnola later hinted that it involved a woman, and since he was a dashing young officer, tall, with a sturdy body and a handsome, hawk-nosed Mediterranean face worthy of his Iberian ancestor, this may have been quite true. But there was a self-wounding dualism in Cesnola's nature that would emerge again and again. To escape the scandal, he volunteered for the Crimean War. Soon he was aide-de-camp to a Sardinian general fighting with the British army. After the war, Cesnola drifted around Turkey and the Middle East for a while. He was not yet ready to return to Italy. In 1858, he sailed directly from Constantinople to New York.

His first two years in America were unbelievably drab and lonely. He knew no one. His title and his cavalry experience seemed ridiculous affectations in the cheap boarding houses where he lived, bewildered by his helplessness. His English was halting, he had no profession. In Arizona he would have made a fine sheriff, but all he could find to do in New York was to grind out translations and compose music that no one wanted.[9] His was a more genteel but also a heightened version of the immigrant experience. The disorientation. The isolation. The barrier of language and money. The problem of attracting and interesting a woman — so important a source of strength for a young man with no family and no deep friendships. The lower-class immigrants embraced one another in self-defense, formed tenement neighborhoods that were like hilltop villages, ate sausages and *ravioli*, played bocce, read *l'Eco d'Italia*, confessed to an Italian priest when they could find one, played card games like *briscola* and *scopa*. But Cesnola was outside their circle. He was a count and a gentleman. He could have returned to Italy, but he hung on in New York, grimly. It was a period of his life he rarely mentioned.

In 1859, still facing a vague and diminished future, he began to give Italian and French lessons. Most of his students were leisured, well-to-do young women, and a year later one of them fell in love with this errant Piedmontese cavalier. She was Mary Reid, a vivacious, thirty-year-old New Yorker whose father had died recently and left her an inheritance. Mary's mother and her society friends pleaded with her to give up the penniless Italian, who seemed to them a classic fortune hunter, but she was determined not to lose him. Cesnola told her frankly that he was not in love with her, but that he could offer her "the greatest affection," which he believed was the best foundation for a marriage. They were married on June 11, 1861, two months after the outbreak of the Civil War.

To resolve his financial problems, and to prepare the way for a commission in the Union forces, Cesnola opened a private military academy at the Hotel St. Germaine on the then-fashionable corner of 22nd and Broadway.[10] For a fee of $100, payable in advance, New Yorkers were given a cram course in the martial arts. As they sat astride barrels mounted on wood frames, their aristocratic and magnetic instructor, who could talk intimately about the famous Charge of the Light Brigade, enlightened them on cavalry tactics. Infantry and artillery were covered as well. Within six months, Cesnola had graduated over seven hundred future officers.[11] His effort was not unrewarded. Having made a small but gratifying profit, he settled with the hotel and joined the Union army himself. Though he was only twenty-eight, and still an Italian citizen, he received a commission as major, with an immediate promotion to lieutenant colonel, in the Eleventh New York Cavalry then mustering on Staten Island.

Bold, headstrong, sure of what he wanted, Cesnola was a hero to his men but a problem to his superiors. Four months after entering active service with the Eleventh Cavalry, he resigned out of contempt for his commander who a few days later had Cesnola arrested for trying to take the men with him. The charge was interfering with the regiment in a way "calculated to produce a mutiny." But anonymous letters soon began reaching the War Department praising Cesnola and berating his superior as "an old robber who without military talent or skill has assumed the title and position of Col. to make money." [12] The letters had been written by men in the unit. Cesnola fumed for a week in Washington's Old Capitol Prison, writing letters of his own to the Union commander, General George B. McClellan, asking that he be allowed to serve either under McClellan or the German Forty-Eighter General Sigel, whom Cesnola admired. Furthermore, he wanted to be either "chief of staff or colonel of a cavalry regiment." He would not accept another post as lieutenant colonel.

Perhaps because officers with experience in the Crimean War were rare in the Union cavalry, or because he knew his own mind, Cesnola was released from prison and appointed commander of the Fourth Regiment of New York State's Voluntary Cavalry. He would make it one of the finest regiments of cavalry in the Civil War. But first he had to recruit men. He opened two offices in New York City, one at his own expense, the other paid for by the state of New York. By the end of November 1862, the Fourth was in action in Virginia. Its daring, brash commander was now one of the most highly respected cavalrymen in the Union forces. He had been put in command of three other cavalry regiments as well: Connecticut's First, the New York Ninth, and the Ohio Sixth.

The Union cavalry had been badly outclassed in the early months of the war. Whether farmboy or plantation owner, the Southerner rode horses every day. In the north, particularly in the cities, horseback riding was becoming a pastime, not a necessity. Many a northern lad could not ride. But by the end of 1862, when Cesnola received his command, Union cavalrymen were beginning to acquire confidence. Cesnola led his regiments into action in the Shenandoah Valley against Jeb Stuart's gray-uniformed horsemen, the Confederacy's finest cavalry forces. It was in these skirmishes — and battles — that the Union cavalry found itself.

Colonel Cesnola was well on his way to a brigadier general's star. He had been put in command of a brigade of five cavalry regiments: the Maryland First, the New York Fourth and Ninth, the Ohio Sixth, and the Pennsylvania Seventeenth. But on February 2, 1863, Cesnola was dishonorably dismissed from the Union army by Secretary of War Stanton, in the name of President Lincoln. Cesnola had shipped six Remington pistols and their holsters to his wife in New York in a box containing some clothes as well. The box had been detained at the Adams Express Company in Washington, where an officer had examined it and reported to the provost marshal's office that it contained stolen government property.[13] The affair bore a depressing similarity to Cesnola's wrecked career in the Piedmontese army. The high courage. The great promise. The destructive scandal. *Oppressa resurgit.* How desperately Cesnola fought to rise again and to acquit himself this second time! He argued that the pistols had been destined for guards at his induction camp on Staten Island, where new companies were being mustered for his regiments. The guards were needed to protect the camp from bounty hunters. He insisted that one of his officers in New York, Major August Pryun, had been instructed to pick up the pistols at the Cesnola home. He pointed out that the pistols were New York State property and not Federal property. He even possessed a receipt for the pistols from the New York State arsenal. He was being humiliated and degraded. "Without a hearing, without a reason, I have been a week ago publicly disgraced by your order," [14] he complained to Stanton. And in fact it did seem odd that a brave and energetic cavalry commander (this was never disputed) should be dismissed over the shipment of six Remington pistols to his wife, who was not after all Annie Oakley. Had he clashed with a superior again, stepped on too many toes?

But he was not a man to accept a reversal or a dishonor meekly. On March 3, 1863, his dismissal was revoked. He returned to the Fourth cavalry as a colonel, but no longer as brigade commander. It was a painful situation. As Elizabeth McFadden wrote, "He was to yearn and struggle from then on for a restoration of the full brigade to his authority." [15] He was depressed for other reasons as well. The Fourth Cavalry Regiment again lacked horses. "This & thousand other wrong things dishearten me," he wrote despondently, "that I shall not be able to stand great [sic] deal longer this life of humiliation, never revenged, and injustice." [16]

But action was now frequent and intense. At Kelly's Ford, the skirmishes between Confederate and Union cavalry rose to the level of pitched battles. For the first time in the war, Jeb Stuart's Virginia cavalry was beaten with heavy losses. Soon afterwards, the Union commander, General "Fighting Joe" Hooker, sent the Union cavalry on a massive raid into southern Virginia. The raid destroyed railroad lines,

depots, canal locks and grain warehouses, and penetrated the outer de-
fenses of the Confederate capital, Richmond.

On June 9, at Brandy Station, the Confederate and Union cavalries
met in the single greatest cavalry battle of the Civil War — hand-to-
hand combat on horseback with pistols and sabers, in which Cesnola
took part at the head of his regiment, helping to forge a Union victory.
Now Lee was moving northward towards the Pennsylvania border and
the two cavalry forces drifted with him. On June 17, three weeks before
Gettysburg, Jeb Stuart's horsemen and the Fourth New York cavalry
met at Aldie, Virginia. Cesnola, in the course of deploying his men, so
infuriated a Union infantry general that his sword was taken from him
and he was placed under arrest. The Fourth galloped on its first charge
without him.

When the regiment was driven back by Confederate artillery, one of
Cesnola's men rode back and begged the colonel to lead them. He was
under arrest, but nothing could restrain him. Unarmed, he leaped on his
horse and led the regiment against the Confederate cannon. This gallant
charge so moved the Union cavalry commander, Brigadier General
L. G. Estes, that when the Fourth galloped back to camp, Cesnola was
immediately released from arrest and Estes rode over and handed his
own sword to the Italian.

Cesnola, fired up, led the Fourth to another charge. It would be his
last for many months. For hours, until Confederate soldiers returned
after sundown to collect their dead and wounded, and found him, he
lay under his dead horse with a bullet wound in his arm and a saber cut
on the crown of his head.[17]

The prison where he spent the next ten months, Libby, in Richmond,
was one of the worst in the Confederacy — some twelve hundred Union
officers crammed into six bare rooms, in what had formerly been a
tobacco warehouse.[18] Though wounded, Cesnola was a tough-minded
and intransigent prisoner, whose continual demands of better treatment
for the Union enlisted men imprisoned at nearby Belle Isle caused the
Confederate prisoner-exchange commissioner, Robert Ould, angrily to
delay Cesnola's release as long as possible. But Mary Reid Cesnola
pulled strings in Washington. The men of the New York Fourth petitioned for Cesnola's release in a special appeal. He was finally exchanged
on May 21, 1864. After a brief reunion in New York with Mary and
their first-born daughter, Eugenia Gabriella, he was back in the war,
"moodily in charge of 6,000 dismounted cavalrymen and 3,000 Rebel

prisoners in a camp at Belle Plain." [19] Some of those dismounted cavalry-men were the troopers of his New York Fourth, who had welcomed him back "as they would their own father." [20] Going over the head of his superior, Major General T. A. Torbert, Cesnola ordered Torbert's quartermaster to produce horses for the Fourth at once, and "in 24 hours I had my dear old regiment completely mounted & equipped and I did not allow one single horse to be given to any other Regiment until I had the 4th New York Cav. completely mounted." [21] It was the old Cesnola, lavishing attention on his men and irritating his superiors.

Soon, the Fourth was raiding Confederate territory again. The regiment took fifty-one casualties in two hours of fighting and lived off the land. Cesnola was sickened by scenes of looting and violence against civilians when "my Lt. Col. & myself were . . . obliged to draw our revolvers after using without effect our sabers, not against the men of my regiment (thank God) but against others." [22] His courage, and ability to remain calm and effective under pressure, were proven again a few days later. A Union attack had miscarried, broken up by a force of about forty thousand Confederates. The Fourth Cavalry was cut off. The Union commander, General Sheridan, gave it up for lost. "But to the surprise of everybody," Cesnola later wrote proudly, "I struck the rear of Malvern Hill and formed a line of battle with my little regiment 217 men strong, charged the rebels and cut my way to Deep Bottom without losing a man except those who were killed. I even brought away my wounded." [23]

The Fourth Cavalry had almost finished its term of enlistment, and this was to be Cesnola's last major engagement. He was mustered out on September 4, 1864, a thirty-four-year-old cavalry veteran whose contentiousness and lack of political skill had probably robbed him of at least one general's star. (More than twenty years would elapse before his heroism at Aldie was recognized, and he was awarded the Congressional Medal of Honor.)

With nothing to do in New York and already worried about his future, Cesnola tried to reenter the Union army as a division or brigade commander, but the war was almost over. Cesnola joined the thousands of office hunters swarming around the White House after Lincoln's reelection. Though he had forcefully backed Lincoln's rival in the election, General McClellan, Cesnola was apparently received at the White House on April 12, 1865, two days before the President's assassination. Cesnola later swore that in the presence of New York Senator Ira Harris,[24]

President Lincoln awarded him the brevet rank of brigadier general and approved Cesnola's request to be appointed American consul somewhere in Europe.

Though no record of the appointment, or of the award of rank, has ever been found among Lincoln's papers, Cesnola did indeed receive a consular post. After some twenty days of nervously pacing the corridors of the State Department, Cesnola was received by Secretary of State Seward (who had barely escaped being knifed to death by an accomplice of Booth's). Cesnola was appointed consul to Cyprus. He had hoped for a post in Italy, but having borrowed heavily from friends in New York he had little choice. One problem remained. He was not an American citizen. This was rectified in New York on August 16, 1865, Cesnola giving his occupation as soldier. On September 25, he sailed for Genoa with his wife and baby daughter.

It was his first visit home since the scandal when he had been forced to resign from the Piedmontese army and to exile himself to the Crimea and then to New York. Now he was returning as a cavalry hero from the noble Lincoln's army, with a New York society wife. King Victor Emmanuel received this prodigal son at the Royal Palace in Turin and decorated him with a medal, while at Rivarolo Canavese, where Cesnola's mother had her country home, the townspeople surrounded the Cesnola carriage to gawk and cheer. *Oppressa resurgit.* The "General," as he now styled himself, his commanding expression rendered even more virile by a drooping black moustache, could not have felt prouder.

The Cesnolas first saw Cyprus on Christmas Day 1865. Because of rough seas, their ship had to anchor more than a mile offshore in the Bay of Larnaca. The town of Larnaca, where the foreign consulates were located, "looked the very picture of desolation," Cesnola wrote. His instinct (and his wife's) was "not to land on such a forlorn-looking island." [25] A lighter took them to shallow water, where Turkish boatmen carried the new consul ashore.

The island of Cyprus, third largest in the Mediterranean after Sicily and Sardinia, was administered by the Turks who had captured it from the Venetians. It was hardly less primitive in the late nineteenth century than when St. Paul had visited it to preach to the Gentiles in A.D. 46. There was almost no industry. The rich, volcanic soil was terraced into vineyards shaded with olive trees. Cedar, cypress, and eucalyptus trees

grew beside ancient roads. It was a beautiful and sleepy island where
the duties of a consul were light except in moments of Greco-Turkish
tension. Several members of the diplomatic community, however, were
busy supervising crews of native diggers in a gigantic game of archeology. Rarely had any hobby been so passionately absorbing, and at the
same time so profitable. The leading European museums and private
collectors were avidly buying antiquities, and all over the Mediterranean,
in dusty, out-of-the-way places, affluent amateurs were exposing the
contents of ancient tombs, or, in some cases, even ancient cities. (The
great German amateur Heinrich Schliemann was already at work in
Asia Minor locating the site of Troy.) The chief of the British mission
to Cyprus, R. Hamilton Lang, had been the preeminent archeologist on
the island before Cesnola's arrival, but he soon yielded to the forceful
Piedmontese.

Cesnola began hiring workmen to dig for him in "a mere amateur way"
in 1866.[26] But by the following year he was devoting most of his time
and prodigious energies to it, studying the ancient history of the eastern
Mediterranean, and Cyprus in particular, and often camping out with
his diggers. Now and then, a worsening of the perennial crisis between
the Greeks and Turks would bring him racing back to his consular duties.
(He was also acting as consul for Russia, Greece, and one other power he
never specified.) But he would presently return to his army of diggers,
watching them unearth another tomb to pluck out the delicate little
gold filigree necklaces, the chalices, the pottery statuettes which had
been placed beside corpses centuries before, to accompany the deceased
to the underworld.

Though the techniques employed by his diggers were crude, Cesnola
seems to have accepted them as the standard of the day. Often, statues
pried out of the earth with iron crowbars would lose fingers, a nose, an
ear. Or they would be damaged in being conveyed to the courtyard of
the consulate at Larnaca on the floor of primitive, ox-drawn carts or
strapped on the back of camels which, Cesnola noted, had the nasty
habit of lying down abruptly.[27]

Though engrossing, archeology was also an expensive hobby. The
workmen had to be paid. Turkish officials often had to be bribed. As
Cesnola ran through his own meager savings, and then those of his wife,
he began to feel that the necklaces, cups, and statues his crews were
digging up were "as thoroughly my property as anything could ever be
the property of anyone."[28] By the end of his first two years in Cyprus

his "property" was beginning to run to thousands of pieces, and he was becoming recognized as the authority on ancient Cypriot culture. Earlier, he had vainly hoped that he might be transferred to some more "civilized" post. Now, despite his wife's boredom at Larnaca, he had become passionately involved with Cyprus.

Early in 1870, diggers working for him at a site near the ancient settlement of Golgos uncovered an enormous head of solid limestone. It was a deeply impressive find even to the illiterate diggers — the vast head with its staring eyes and curling beard — and at once the population of several nearby villages descended on the site with spades and pickaxes. Every peasant on Cyprus by then knew the potential value of antiquities, though most of the pieces were torn from the graves of their remote ancestors. They yearned to hack away at the suddenly fertile ground.

It was after midnight when Cesnola, asleep in his villa at Larnaca, was awakened by shouts in the courtyard outside. Two messengers, sent to alert him, were bickering between themselves. The chief of police at Golgos, they informed him, was claiming the massive head, and any other pieces found on the site, for the Sultan in Constantinople.[29] The old cavalryman jumped on his mule and spurred the unfortunate beast in a flat-out charge for Golgos — the mule's belly scraping the ground, as Cesnola later told it.[30] Other mule riders, galloping towards him in the darkness, turned out to be peasants sneaking off to alert the other European consuls in hopes of earning some claim money. When Cesnola arrived at the site, he saw more than a hundred men milling about the dig, bickering among themselves as their women looked on and children ran in yelping packs in and out of the firelight. A pair of Turkish policemen were guarding the head, and a few other pieces of sculpture discovered with it. "I at once rode towards them, dismounted, and ordered one of them to take my foaming animal in charge and walk it about, which he did without question. I then called the other . . . and motioned him to disperse the crowd and clear a space around the sculptures. He obeyed as promptly as his companion and these steps had due effect upon the peasants."[31]

Under Cesnola's supervision, the sculptures were lifted into ox-drawn carts and borne to Larnaca. He confessed later "that I rather captured than discovered these stone treasures."[32] But this martial feat nonetheless had the effect of adding value to his collection, and to his reputation as an archeologist. He was now virtually monopolizing the digging at Cyprus. Though the Turkish authorities at Constantinople were becoming restive in view of the number of pieces Cesnola was unearthing or buying, Ottoman officials were notoriously corruptible, and Cesnola, his experience in dealing with the Turks dating back to his Crimean War days, had taken pains to come to terms with the Turkish governor on the island and to befriend or bribe lesser luminaries. His problem now was not so much moving his antiquities as selling them. His approach in this, as in everything else, was daring.

As early as 1869, the Paris firm of Rollin & Feuardent had advanced Cesnola some money to cover expenses and had sold a few pieces of his at auction. Word of Cesnola's finds was beginning to circulate among the major European museums. In the same year, the highly respected Dr. Carl Friederichs of the Royal Berlin Museum visited Cesnola at Cyprus, carefully selecting a few of his best pieces.[33] This attention was flattering, but it posed a major question for the consul-archeologist. If he allowed museum curators to come and nibble away at his collection, taking the rarest and most valuable items, he would soon be left with tons of unrelated stone, glass, and metal objects that no one would want. This problem became suddenly acute in the spring of 1870, when he was advised by the State Department that the consulate might be closed down. Cesnola anxiously wrote to Washington, and to his influential New York friends, explaining that he had invested some $20,000 of his own money in the excavations, and that he would be "ruined" if he were forced to leave the island now. When the reply came back, reassuring him that his term would be extended for several years, Cesnola was able to turn his attention to negotiating with the European museums on his own terms.

Russia's Hermitage dispatched a capable young art scholar to Cyprus, Johannes Doell, who arrived with a pretty mistress.[34] Doell and his lady were guests of the Cesnolas for several weeks as the Russian scholar inspected and catalogued the thousands of pieces assembled at Larnaca. Cesnola was gambling now, and for high stakes. He asked $60,000 from the Hermitage, with the understanding that his antiquities would be displayed as the Cesnola Collection, "a little vanity," he wrote, "to repay me for all the work I've done." [35] He was simultaneously negotiating with the Louvre, and asking even more — $80,000 for the collection.

But the outbreak of the Franco-Prussian War and its disastrous consequences for France scuttled the negotiations, while the Hermitage — apparently on the advice of Dr. Friederichs in Berlin — also decided not to buy.

This unexpected double blow suddenly confronted Cesnola with ruin. He was still on Cyprus, surrounded by a mountain of antiquities being eyed covetously by the curators of the new Ottoman Museum in Constantinople, and his debts were growing. Mary Reid Cesnola, moreover, was thoroughly sick of the island and anxious to return to civilization.

Cesnola, now seriously worried, still hoped to sell the collection elsewhere in Europe, or even in America. Failing that, he could sell off the pieces individually. But he had to hurry, or the Turkish government could simply appropriate the huge collection. With his customary boldness, Cesnola urgently requested that Washington send two warships to haul his treasures to safety. Though the secretary of the navy replied that he would in fact send a warship, Cesnola's time was running out. He chartered a schooner and was preparing to load it with his treasures when an order arrived from Constantinople prohibiting the export of a single piece. To make sure the order would be complied with, a Turkish warship anchored in the Bay of Larnaca, its cannon trained ominously on the Cesnola residence. Cesnola read the Turkish document with considerable anguish until his native assistant suggested a way around it. The document specifically prohibited the American consul from exporting the antiquities, without mentioning him by name. Cesnola simply shipped out his collection in his capacity as Russian consul. As for the Turkish warship, it sailed away, its commander unwilling to risk offending the Russian government by intercepting the antiquities on the high seas.

Cesnola shipped the antiquities to England. He took another gamble now, signing a contract with the Paris firm of Rollin & Feuardent. They advanced him money to cover his shipping costs and some of his other expenses. If, however, Cesnola was unable to sell his collection by the end of the year, it would pass entirely to Rollin & Feuardent and they would auction it off piece by piece. He had only a few months in which to conclude an agreement, and selling a collection of that sort rapidly was difficult. The pieces had to be tapped and scraped by experts, scholars had to be consulted, boards of trustees had to make their considered decisions. Cesnola had managed to interest the British Museum in buying the collection, but his chief hope now rested with a museum that had not yet even been built.

The July issue of *Harper's New Monthly Magazine,* one of the most elegant American periodicals of the era, had contained a fifteen-page article on Cesnola's Cyprus finds. Prepared by Cesnola himself and by a faithful New York friend, Hiram Hitchcock,[36] the piece had been shrewdly designed to appeal to the trustees of the newly founded Metropolitan Museum of Art in New York. It dwelt on Cesnola's superb war record as a Union cavalry commander before establishing him as the man who had drawn back the veil on the ancient history of Cyprus to reveal the existence of a cultural bridge between the civilizations of Egypt and Greece. "The importance of General Di Cesnola's discoveries on the island of Cyprus and the archeological and artistic value of the collection," *Harper's* announced, "can hardly be overestimated." [37]

As Cesnola had hoped, the Metropolitan's trustees did respond to the article. They asked banker Junius Spencer Morgan, then in London, to call on Cesnola and view the collection. When Morgan reported back with cautious approval, the Metropolitan's president, John Taylor Johnson, offered $50,000 of his own money for the entire collection in the expectation of getting at least some of it back from gifts or from funds raised by subscription. Morgan and Cesnola signed a contract at the end of November which stipulated that he would receive $20,000 at once, another $15,000 within a year, and the final $15,000 within two years. Cesnola was not disposed to quibble. A month longer, and the collection would have passed into the hands of Rollin & Feuardent. The "Russian consul" had won his gamble. It was important, though, Cesnola wrote Johnson, that the collection be properly classified and arranged for viewing. He himself was the logical person to do this, since he had found the pieces and possessed three hundred pages of notes on them, and he was fortunately available.[38]

When the British luxury steamer *Java* sailed from Southampton on the day after Christmas 1872, the Cesnolas were among the 142 coddled Victorians enjoying the all first-class service.[39] It was a far cry from the moment almost precisely seven years before when a Turkish lighter, dancing on the rough waves in the Bay of Larnaca, had carried the anxious new American consul and his grumpy, pregnant wife towards the miserable-looking beach. For Mary Reid Cesnola, there was the joy of returning to her beloved New York. For the "General," the deep, bitter pleasure of newly acquired wealth. "How God is good towards me," he wrote frankly. "I was cast away by my wife's relations, because *I was poor.* Very soon, I shall be *richer* than all of them *together.*" [40] The *Java* docked on January 11, 1873, as Mary Cesnola's relatives and friends waited to embrace her. An American diplomat was returning home, mission accomplished. His precious antiquities were arriving in five separate vessels to lessen the risk of loss.

With his family comfortably settled in a brownstone, Cesnola reported to the State Department where, to his surprise, he was offered a post at Constantinople. But he was now too deeply involved in archeology, and he declined it. Back in New York, Cesnola began the task of sorting, cataloguing, and repairing his antiquities. Nearly a third of the statues were broken, and there were several thousand stone fragments lumped together in cases, which had to be sorted and reunited with their original torsos.[41] The museum had agreed to pay him a salary of $500 a month during this work of restoration, which Cesnola estimated might take as long as a year. This sum also covered Cesnola's expenses in preparing the antiquities for a show to be held at the museum's temporary home, the Douglas Mansion on West 14th Street.

With the aid of a German cabinetmaker named Theodore Gehlen and several other assistants, Cesnola set to work.[42] The collection had arrived from England in 270 gigantic cases. The pieces had to be laid out and sorted. For days, the basement of the Douglas Mansion looked like the aftermath of an explosion rendered in plaster, with hundreds of torsos lying on the floor. Heads, noses, arms, fingers and feet lay scattered about. The jewelry and the ancient glass had arrived intact, fortunately. Only the statues had to be repaired. Cesnola was not an art scholar, nor was he a trained archeologist. His goal in repairing the statues was to make them look their best. He and Gehlen labored so hard at this massive job of restoration that it was finished in a breathtaking two and a half months. In his first assignment for the museum, Cesnola had been careful not to take advantage of the agreement assuring him of $500 a month until the work of restoration was finished. He had worked fourteen- and sixteen-hour days down in the basement. The trustees would remember.

The show opened in March 1873. It was a huge critical success, and attracted visitors from all over America. "Around his treasures walked the famous general moving among them as among time-tested troops, courteously attentive to the guests, speaking about the great find at Golgos, in short, giving a continual lecture." [43] The reaction from the public and the New York press was so favorable in fact that the trustees made Cesnola a new offer. They would send him back to Cyprus to dig, underwriting his expenses, in return for the right of first refusal to whatever he found. Cesnola was delighted. His work on Cyprus, he felt, was incomplete, and archeology was in his blood. He would take care of the Turkish officials, somehow. And he would challenge the indefatigable hunter of Troy, Heinrich Schliemann, to a personal duel to see which of them would become the greatest archeologist of the nineteenth century. By the end of 1872, the methodical Schliemann had already uncovered seven successive layers of human remains on his site overlooking the Hellespont. Now, as the Cesnolas arrived in Italy in the fall of 1873, every newspaper in the world carried stories of Schliemann's dramatic find, a stupendous gold treasure from ancient Troy — Priam's Gold it was called. There were gold diadems, a goblet in 23-carat gold, a gold bottle, 8,700 small gold rings, buttons, and ornaments.[44] While Cesnola's wife and daughters settled down for a protracted stay in Rivaroso Cavanese, his mother's home, Cesnola rushed back to Cyprus.

His native diggers were overjoyed to see their "General" again — though their mood would change. His arrival meant work, and money. Cesnola now organized the digging on an almost lavish scale, with armed Turkish guards protecting his sites from marauding peasants while his crews dug for an archeological wonder, or a treasure, to match Schliemann's Troy.

Cesnola had barely settled down to a systematic rhythm of excavation when he received a numbing message from the trustees of the Metropolitan. Owing to the collapse of the stock market that year, they were regretfully forced to let Cesnola's contract drop. He did not despair. Using what was left of the $50,000 he had received from the museum, he kept his diggers busy at a site on the southern coast, near Amanthus, where they uncovered an enormous marble sarcophagus which took them ten hours to raise out of the ground and to lift onto a cart designed to hold it. It was night when the valuable sarcophagus was finally loaded onto a boat for the sea journey to Larnaca.[45]

With his men, Cesnola rode along the coast the rest of the night, determined to press his search to other sites. At dawn, as a servant cooked breakfast for him over a campfire, he sat in a campaign chair examining, through a pair of binoculars, a bluff about two to three hundred feet high. The ancient city of Curium had once stood on that bluff, and as he gazed at it Cesnola was moved by a mysterious sense of cognition — what parapsychology would term a remarkably accurate hunch.

Cesnola went over the site very carefully, no longer the stumbling amateur but an archeologist now with ten years of experience. Other archeologists had tested the Curium site superficially without finding anything much. But as Cesnola directed the work of his diggers, a pebbled red, brown, white and blue mosaic floor emerged and, from previously unopened tombs, a shower of bronze, silver, and gold jewelry. Beneath the mosaic floor "I discovered a gallery excavated in the rock, eleven feet four inches long, four feet ten inches wide, and scarcely four feet high." [46] At the end of this gallery was an "oven-shaped cavity" from which Cesnola's men removed some three thousand baskets of earth, only to discover that the "cavity" was connected by a passage to a second, similar chamber. There were to be four chambers in all. When only a foot and a half of earth remained on the floor of the first chamber, Cesnola poked it with his measuring stick and struck "something hard," which turned out to be a gold bracelet with several other gold ornaments around it. When his diggers had removed most of the earth from the remaining chambers, Cesnola dismissed them. There was no room for them all in that cramped space, for one thing, and he did not fully trust them for another. (At the end of each day Schliemann had searched every one of his diggers, a humiliating practice that Cesnola avoided.) With only his foreman, and a servant to hold a lantern over their heads, Cesnola spent weeks in those chambers twenty feet underground, sifting earth while scores of gold objects — bracelets, rings, earrings, beads — slid into their hands. Two of the bracelets, made of solid gold, weighed three pounds each and bore the inscription of an ancient king, Eteander. What the four chambers represented, Cesnola speculated, was the treasure vault of a royal temple.

He had discovered the Treasure of Curium.

The trustees of the Metropolitan could have ignored the giant sarcophagus, or another giant head. But they could not ignore the excitement surrounding a vein of ancient gold. Cesnola now began a second campaign to sell them this new collection. In a letter, he explained that the 7,161 objects in this collection were worth more than the previous one. "Its character . . . is different from the other; for while that in New York is poor in gold, precious stones, silver, bronze, and alabaster, and rich in heavy bulky stone sculptures, this collection is just the opposite, being very rich in what the other is poor; and not deficient in what the other is rich." [47] He was a superb salesman. And to cap his sales effort, he was writing a book describing the ancient history of Cyprus and the story of his discoveries on the island.

Time was again a factor. The Turkish authorities were angry, and their concern was beginning to be shared by middle-class Cypriots who realized now that it was their heritage which was being shipped away to distant museums. Cesnola's diggers were stoned, and had to suspend work. Beleaguered in Larnaca, Cesnola again tried to get a United States warship to anchor in the bay and pick up his new collection, but none came. He was forced to ship out the cases himself.

Reunited with his family in Italy, he labored to finish the manuscript of his book and tried to plot his next moves. Though he felt that he might be able to sell his new collection for as much as $100,000, this still did not represent long-term security. He was nearly forty. His career as a cavalry officer was finished. It seemed unlikely that he could return to Cyprus and continue his archeological work there. The consular post he might have had at Constantinople had passed into the hands of a younger man. He suggested to his friend Hitchcock that the Metropolitan appoint him superintendent for life. That was the kind of stable, secure position he was seeking.

Just before Christmas 1876, the Metropolitan's trustees offered $60,000 for the new collection, and Hitchcock reported that they were inclined to offer him the post of director. Would they pay shipping costs for the new material, he queried? They would. He cabled back: "All right! Three hearty cheers for our dear New York Museum." [48]

His career as an archeologist was over. In eleven years on Cyprus, he had identified the sites of sixteen ancient cities, excavated fifteen temples and 60,932 tombs, and collected 35,573 objects — over 2,000 statues, over 14,000 pottery vases, nearly 4,000 glass objects. [49] These great numbers calmed and reassured him. As the *Britannic* crossed the Atlantic bound for New York in the spring of 1877, he could be observed pacing the first-class deck, erect, somewhat portly, his expression rendered more fierce by his almost Asiatic walrus moustache and his dark, piercing gaze magnified behind pince-nez. With Schliemann, he now shared the reputation of having been the greatest amateur archeologist of the age.

On his arrival in May, he was named secretary of the Metropolitan. The position was without salary, but Cesnola realized he would have to bide his time while the museum's permanent home was rising in Central Park off Fifth Avenue, a dumpy, red-brick building still lacking its present neoclassic façade. Cesnola, meanwhile, bought a four-story brownstone on 57th Street for his family, a place where his wife could entertain after so many years of living out of trunks. On May 15, 1879, he was appointed the Metropolitan Museum of Art's first director, starting at a salary of $5,000 a year. [50] More important, the post was permanent.

From the day when he assumed the directorship, Cesnola worked at supervising the move to the museum's new home in Central Park. The new museum would not only exhibit his collection, but would bear the stamp of his taste for many years to come.

It took a year exactly to prepare for the opening on March 30, 1880. "Even before noon, guests arrived. A solid line of carriages — landaus, clarences, coupes, and liveried hacks — stretched south down the graveled Fifth Avenue as far as one could see. They halted there, the horses stomping and whinnying in fret, until the doors opened at 3 p.m." [51] Three thousand five hundred guests had been invited, including the President of the United States, Rutherford B. Hayes. The keynote speaker was Joseph C. Choate, a Harvard graduate and lawyer whose famous wit was aimed that afternoon squarely at the industrial tycoons on whom the museum was counting for its growth.

"Probably no age and no city," Choate reminded them, "has ever seen such gigantic fortunes accumulated out of nothing as have been piled up here within the last five years. They have been made out of this city and out of this toiling people." He offered the services of the trustees in relieving

these distended and apoplectic pockets. Think of it, ye millionaires of many markets, what glory may yet be yours, if you only listen to our advice and convert pork into porcelain, grain and produce into priceless pottery, the rude ores of commerce into sculptured marble, and railroad shares and mining stock — things which perish without the using and which in the next financial panic shall surely shrivel like parched scrolls — into the glorified canvasses of the world's masters, that shall adorn these walls for centuries.[52]

When Choate had finished, to thunderous applause, President Hayes stood up and in a single sentence declared the museum open.[53] Then the President was taken on a tour by the proud Cesnola, whose antiquities from Cyprus were prominently displayed in the main exhibition hall.

Art was a justifiable interest in Victorian America if it was socially useful, and in its early years the Metropolitan's trustees stressed this didactic mission. "The basis and justification for the museum's existence lay in its educational role. The accumulation of masterpieces was specifically ruled out (such an endeavor being considered impossible in any case), and the trustees, at least in their public statements, placed their profound trust in art conceived as a 'department of knowledge.' " [54] This vision raised no conflict in Cesnola's mind. He seconded it willingly.

His own interest in art was not primarily aesthetic. As a nobleman born into a rigid European class system, he could perfectly well see himself as a dispenser of enlightenment to the common folk. In the annual report of 1882, which summed up the accomplishments of the museum from its first days at the Douglas Mansion, Cesnola observed that "The Metropolitan Museum of Art has already paid. It has paid during the past six years many hundred thousand dollars into the hands of workmen, women, and children in decorative employments unknown a few years ago. . . ." [55] This was putting it in terms that any tycoon could appreciate. But such an attitude, to be effective, depended largely on the rectitude of its sponsors. Unfortunately, a major scandal now enveloped the new director.

An article had quietly appeared in the August 1880 issue of *Art Amateur,* charging that a number of Cesnola's pieces now on display at the Metropolitan had undergone "certain deceptive and unintelligent restorations." It was signed by Gaston Feuardent, the dapper New York representative of the firm of Rollin & Feuardent which had handled some of Cesnola's first pieces from Cyprus, which had advanced him money, and which had held an option on his first collection. The author questioned in particular a small limestone statue of a woman holding a mirror in her left hand. The mirror, he claimed, had not been present when he had studied the piece in London in 1872 and again in New York six years later. It had been added to the statuette, he implied, in order to change it into an Aphrodite and thus raise its value. "To endeavor to increase interest in a collection by deceptive alterations or restorations," Feuardent said bluntly, "can only be called a miscalculation, a profanation or a fraud." [56] Moreover, said Feuardent, European museums that had carefully checked the Cesnola collections had been "quite unanimous in declining to purchase." His broadside struck not only Cesnola but the trustees as well.

The article might have passed unobserved. But the New York press was struggling with a bad case of the summer doldrums, and the Feuardent article was better than news. It was a scandal that could be strung out for days. When the stories appeared, Cesnola was enjoying a blissful rest and a treatment for rheumatism at Richfield Springs, New York. Two of the trustees who happened to be in the city tried to soften the blow by advising Cesnola to "take it coolly, bathe, and be patient." Their director nearly leapt out of the mineral baths in his fury. To the New

York *Post* he raged that he had been slandered by a "mere dealer," whose knowledge of archeology came from "cleaning old coins in the back room of an antiquity shop in Paris." [57] But unfortunately for the "General," Feuardent was a respected antiquarian and a member of the American Numismatic and Archeological Society. As Feuardent broadened his charges to include other pieces from Golgos, a number of the most authoritative newspapers and magazines, including the *Times,* took his charges seriously enough to call for an impartial investigation. Vainly the trustees tried to ride out the storm, following Choate's seasoned advice. The tempest only blew more strongly as the weeks passed.

With the indignant director eager to sue his tormentor, and Choate advising caution, the trustees took the safest and most reasonable step. They appointed a panel to examine the charges. Though Feuardent's request to be able to select at least one member was refused, the panel was nonetheless a distinguished body. It was headed by Frederick Augustus Porter Barnard, the retiring president of Columbia, and it included a famous judge, Charles Patrick Daly, and the sculptor John Adams Quincy Ward, a trustee.[58] For several weeks, the panel met to examine each of the controversial pieces. They were set on a table, "mopped and scraped." At the end of January 1881, the panel delivered its report. It completely vindicated Cesnola. The trustees, in a separate report a few weeks later, stated that they had always "known the falsehood of the published charges and have never ceased to entertain the highest confidence in [Cesnola's] devotion and faithfulness. . . ." The New York *Tribune,* in an editorial, labeled the charges "each and all without foundation . . . vulgar in their origin and discreditable in the manner in which they were pushed." [59]

But the matter did not rest there. It was as if Feuardent had discovered something powerfully wrong, something deeply morally offensive to him in the person of Luigi Palma di Cesnola. He derived no motive of profit, or heightened reputation, from his attacks. If anything the opposite. But he could not, would not, leave the director alone.

Soon after the panel had rendered its judgment, Feuardent began circulating cards with drawings of the Cyprus statues before and after "restoration." Statues were shown with different heads or accessories, and each charge was carefully documented using descriptions which had appeared in Hitchcock's article in *Harper's,* in the Doell catalogue, in Cesnola's own book on Cyprus, and in the Metropolitan Museum's photographs on sale to the public. "Mr. Feuardent may deluge this country with these cards but they won't do him any good," [60] Cesnola contemptuously informed reporters. Yet Feuardent persisted, and the controversy again blazed forth. The *Times* called for a new and fuller investigation of Feuardent's charges. "If accepted as proved, or what amounts to the same thing in this case, passed without challenge, it must place Di Cesnola in the category of imposters." [61] The *Times* went on to call Feuardent's accusations "cumulative, convincing . . . apparently unanswerable. . . ." The satirical weeklies and the yellow press were having a picnic. Cesnola was cruelly depicted as a goggle-eyed madman at work in a basement storeroom feverishly assembling broken pieces of statuary. The *Police Gazette* ran an article under the title, "Cesnola's Bogus Antiques. Was a Worthless Collection Palmed off on a Credulous Set of Old Fossils?" [62] By this time, the controversy had drifted into a sensational lawsuit.

Cesnola had wanted to sue Feuardent from the start. He could simply not conceive why a man with his record — as a soldier, as a United States consul, and finally as an archeologist — should be subjected week after week to attack and ridicule. His tone was aggrieved, bewildered. His service to the museum had yielded "only a harvest of *thorns* but no roses; and I am well sick of it." [63] Sue, he insisted. Destroy Feuardent. Expose him. But Choate had held off. It was Feuardent who finally brought suit, charging that he had no other alternative in view of the trustees' failure to hold a "real investigation."

But before the trial opened in October 1883, Cesnola gambled brilliantly — as he had so many times in the past. Two statues attacked by Feuardent, an Aphrodite which he had called "a fraudulent patchwork of unrelated parts" and a Sacrificer, similarly challenged, were taken out of their glass cases and set up in the center of the museum's main hall. The charges against them were clearly stated on cards, and the public — in a step unprecedented for any museum in the world — was invited to use files and chisels, magnifying lenses and chemical solutions, to see if the charges corresponded to reality.[64] Any test was admissible. It was a huge sensation. Laymen and professional sculptors went to work. After they had chipped, sawed, filed and peered for days, not one of Feuardent's charges had been substantiated. The Aphrodite proved to be of one piece, with her original head glued back on by Cesnola. The headless Sacrificer was also acquitted; he had lost his feet, and Cesnola had glued them back on and strengthened the whole with a new base.

The Italian-American press was jubilant. The period of massive Italian immigration had begun, much of it from the South, and Italians were feeling the sting of prejudice. Their one shining representative among the Anglo-Saxon establishment, their symbol of courage and of culture, was General Luigi Palma di Cesnola. The attack on Cesnola had horrified them. But now the "General" had outwitted his accuser, had shown him before thousands of people to be a fool.

The real trial was an anticlimax. The chic scandal of New York when it opened, it dragged on for so long that the jury members began to resemble Cesnola's statues. Feuardent's own credibility had been damaged during the museum's public investigation of the Aphrodite and the Sacrificer, and though Cesnola's methods of restoration were repeatedly questioned, there was no way in which the intrinsic value of the Cyprus pieces could be reduced. And so the attack centered on Cesnola himself, which is perhaps what Feuardent had intended all along. The director, when he took the stand, was subjected to unusually harsh questioning from Feuardent's attorney Francis Bangs, who asked him how he had come by the title of "General."

"I had not a commission, but I had the title."
"How did you get it? Whom did you get it from?"
"Mr. Lincoln."
"How?"
"Before I was sent out as consul to Cyprus."
"How, by mail or otherwise?"
"I received it verbally."
"What is the next lowest grade in the Army to general?"
"Colonel."
"It is lieutenant-general, isn't it?"
"Yes, sir."
"And then major-general?"
"Yes, sir."
"And then brigadier-general?"
"Yes, sir."
"And then colonel?"
"Yes, sir."
"And you go by the name of 'General'?"
"I don't know. I am called that."
"Here is the title-page of your book, which says, 'By General Louis Palma di Cesnola.'"
"I know it is there."
"Do you know of any man in the United States who held the rank of General except Grant, Sherman and yourself?"
"No, sir. I never pretended to know." [65]

Bangs then took to calling his client "General Feuardent." But his witticisms were expended in a dying cause. In a memorandum to the judge, Cesnola offered Feuardent the chance to saw any of the controversial statues into pieces in the courtroom to see if he could prove his charges. Bangs at once declined the offer.[66] Though the bewildered jury met for twenty-eight hours, its verdict was hardly a surprise. Cesnola was acquitted. But his professional reputation had been damaged to the point where it could not be wholly restored by that decision. Whatever Feuardent's intentions had been, and however legitimate his criticism, he had damaged Cesnola horribly. But the cavalier was an old trooper, and he carried on.

He remained a highly effective director, putting in long hours at his office every day and checking into every detail of the museum's operations. The new president of the museum, Henry Gordon Marquand, admired the director and supported him wholeheartedly — a great source of strength and satisfaction for Cesnola. Portly but still erect, beleaguered, hard-working, he was a sympathetic figure. Even the museum guards honored him a little, stiffening to attention as he strode along the marble corridors.[67] Though he was sometimes a trifle imperious even for the trustees, Cesnola possessed the nobleman's egalitarian sense of good manners. He was unfailingly polite to members of the public calling at his office, including a $10-a-year charter member who made an annual visit to the director during which he would ask Cesnola questions about the museum's costs and finances, and operating charter. In 1899 the visits ceased. Two years later the astonished trustees discovered that this man, Jacob S. Rogers of Paterson, New Jersey, had left the museum a sum believed to be in the neighborhood of eight million dollars. A terrible-tempered locomotive manufacturer, Rogers had apparently never hung a valuable painting or drawing in his home.[68] But something about the Metropolitan Museum, or more likely something in Cesnola's manner, had struck him favorably. The will was contested, but after the hearings the museum's share still came to nearly five million dollars. As Calvin Tomkins wrote, "Through merest chance and the quirks of human personality, a respectable but still struggling institution had been transformed into a powerful and independent force in the markets of art."

Cesnola's reign nevertheless continued to be stormy. He was a natural center of controversy. When a plumber in overalls was turned away in 1897, there were banner headlines in the New York papers. SENSITIVE AND REFINED PLUMBER AFFRONTED, one read.[69] Cesnola huffed to reporters that

"We do not want, nor will we permit a person who has been digging in a filthy sewer or working among grease and oil to come in here. . . ." [70] When he exhibited a huge, three-ton bronze piece by an Italian sculptor depicting "a night of orgies" in ancient Rome, the press swarmed all over him. The work was "uncommonly offensive" said the *Times*. Even the *Post,* which had always stood by Cesnola, lamented that "the Metropolitan Museum is in miserable odor" [71] due to mismanagement. Cesnola consoled himself with the thought that future generations would come to appreciate his work. "If I had not this connection continually before me," he wrote to Marquand, "I could not have borne so patiently, as I have done, injustice, contumely, injury, and insult, as varied and cruel as devilish ingenuity could devise — borne them, though the muscles ached for a foe on whom it was possible to avenge the wrong, and the brain reeled at the degradation!" [72]

But there were satisfactions, both professional and personal. No one could deny that the museum, with the contents of those "apoplectic and distended pockets" to which Choate had appealed, was beginning to acquire a significant collection of art. By 1900, the Metropolitan's more valuable works included Vermeer's *Woman with a Water Jug,* Van Dyck's *James Stuart,* a Delacroix, two Manets, Winslow Homer's *Gulf Stream,* a profusion of Greek and Etruscan vases, glass, jewelry and porcelains from the collection of Edward C. Moore, the president of Tiffany & Co., over three thousand musical instruments, and of course Cesnola's own Cyprus collection. Though the importance of Cesnola's Cyprian antiquities was downgraded by later art scholars — the Treasure of Curium was withdrawn to a vault in the Museum basement in 1914 and has never been shown since — Cesnola's best pieces were valuable works of art and are still on prominent display.

Cesnola's personal life was tranquil and warm. Rescued from the social desert of Cyprus, Madame Cesnola, or the Countess Cesnola as she was called, delighted in entertaining her New York friends and the museum's wealthy sponsors at her elegant brownstone on 57th Street. In later years she spent much of her time at the family's seventy-six-acre estate at Mount Kisco, New York. With a staff of eight servants to help her, she made it the center of family life and devoted herself to Catholic charities, helping to found the Cristoforo Colombo Hospital and an Italian orphan asylum. [73]

A heavy-set man now, with a magnificent silvery walrus moustache and white hair, still erect in his bearing, Cesnola received the Congressional

Medal of Honor in 1897. The old cavalryman could not have been more proud. He had bitterly resented Bangs's ridicule of his pretensions to rank at the trial, and starting in 1884, had mounted a campaign through veterans' organizations to have the Senate officially confirm him in the rank of brigadier general. This was found to be legally impossible, since President Lincoln had left no written record of the promotion among his papers. But the documentation that Cesnola had assembled, including an affidavit from General Estes testifying to the Italian's bravery at Aldie, did go before the secretary of war, General Russell A. Alger. Impressed, General Alger referred the matter to Congress, which, after taking into account both Cesnola's heroism at Aldie and at Malvern Hill, awarded him the Congressional Medal of Honor for the action at Aldie.* The citation read:

Di Cesnola, Louis, Colonel, 4th Cavalry — was present in arrest, when seeing his regiment fall back, he rallied his men and accompanied them without arms in a second charge, in recognition of which gallantry he was released from arrest. He continued in action at the head of his regiment until he was desperately wounded and taken prisoner, in action, at Aldie, Va., June 17, 1863.[74]

Other tributes followed. In 1900, the elderly Piedmontese made a last visit to Italy. He was feted at rich provincial banquets where veterans of 1848 lined up to shake his hand. He was awarded an Italian decoration for his accomplishments in America, and the Cesnola ladies were entertained by the queen of Italy. "With all this hobnobbing with high-born people," he wrote back to friends, "I begin to long again to be at home in New York once more and return to my daily *mill grinding & grinding!*" [75]

He was soon back at his enormous oak desk. The restive younger trustees, including Choate, had twice attempted to force his resignation, but he had survived both attempts. He remained at work in the museum until his death in 1904, at the age of seventy-two. He had been the director of the Metropolitan Museum of Art for a quarter of a century, and his funeral at St. Patrick's Cathedral brought together for a rare hour the leaders of the Italian-American community and such mighty figures as the Morgans and Vanderbilts. A grand nineteenth-century Victorian had passed. The memorial resolution adopted by the trustees managed to

---

* It is interesting that Cesnola was still an Italian citizen at the time he performed the feats of valor for which he received the United States's highest decoration. Two other Italian-Americans also won the Medal of Honor during the Civil War: Joseph E. Sova of the Eighth Cavalry and Orlando E. Caruana of the Fifty-first Infantry.

be both sincere and affectionate. It said, in part: "The martial, independent figure of General di Cesnola — somewhat restive in opposition and somewhat impetuous in speech and action, but at all times devoted to his duty . . . will long remain a kindly and grateful memory." [76]

TWO

THE GREAT MIGRATION

The South

TOWARDS THE END of the nineteenth century, the character of Italian immigration to the United States changed. The era of the explorers, of the exiles and of adventurous noblemen like Luigi Palma di Cesnola, had ended. The time of mass immigration had begun.

In 1870, as Italians were completing their unification and making Rome their capital, it was still rare to find an Italian in America. The number of Italian immigrants that year was 2,891. Most of these were professional men, or skilled artisans from north and central Italy.

By 1900, thirty years later, Italian immigration had passed 100,000 a year. It would rapidly rise above 200,000 per year, then 250,000. These new Italian immigrants were chiefly peasants from the south of Italy, and Sicily. Many were illiterate. They were the most disadvantaged and humble white people that other Americans had ever seen. The Italian writer and anti-Fascist patriot Ignazio Silone described the status of these peasants in southern Italy through one of his characters, who related this hierarchy:

> At the head of everything is God, Lord of Heaven.
> After him comes Prince Torlonia, lord of the earth.
> Then come Prince Torlonia's armed guards.
> Then come Prince Torlonia's armed guards' dogs.
> Then, nothing at all. Then nothing at all. Then nothing at all. Then come the peasants. And that's all.

There was little contact, or even a basis for communication, between the earlier community of Italian-Americans and these new immigrants from the South still pursued, in their slum misery, by Prince Torlonia's armed guards' dogs. The Countess Cesnola might do charity work among poor Italians, which was commendable. But well-meant charity could not begin to resolve the magnitude of these immigrants' problems. They would resolve those problems themselves, well or badly, with all the distortions but also with the insights of spirit that arise from the questioning of one's poverty.

The story of where these millions of Italian immigrants came from, why they left, and, to some extent at least, who they are today, forms the second part of this book.

The exodus of southern Italians from their villages at the turn of the twentieth century has no parallel in history. Out of a total population of fourteen million in the South at the time of national unification in 1860–1870, at least five million — *over a third of the population* — had left to seek work overseas by the outbreak of World War I. (In Italy as a whole, over eleven million people, a quarter of the population, emigrated at least once in the thirty-year period between 1881 and 1911.)[1] The land literally hemorrhaged peasants.

Over four million immigrants from southern Italy went to America. Others emigrated to Brazil and Argentina, Tunisia and Algeria, Egypt, France, Germany, Austria-Hungary, the Low Countries, Britain, Canada, Australia, even Turkey and Russia. Still others settled in the new Italian colonies established in North Africa, a colonial empire fashioned so that Italian labor could continue to leave the country without ceasing to be Italian — and a national resource. These peasant immigrants from the villages of southern Italy were not driven away by political, racial, or religious persecution, or by war. They left because many causes had come together at one time to uproot and expel them.

Of these causes, the most dramatic was environmental. While many areas of southern Italy remained green, fertile, and extraordinarily beautiful, in others the surface of the land was coming apart. By the end of the nineteenth century, portions of southern Italy were facing ecological ruin on a scale unmatched even today, except where strip mining has been practiced. The cutting of forests resulted in the earth gradually running off, leaving a surface of rock. Then the rain, driving into the natural fissures within the rock, split it so that landslides followed every heavy rainstorm. The end result of this terrible process were the *marni,* entire hillsides, hundreds, sometimes thousands, of feet high, as bare of vegetation as the surface of the moon. And since many villages in the south of Italy, and Sicily, were built on the tops of hillsides, often the village would remain isolated on the crest of this lunarlike disaster. In places where the earth had not run off entirely, mud slides would occur. Houses toppled and were carried down the slopes. Even large churches were carried away on rivers of mud. All this detritus of clay and loose rock, moreover, slid down to block the mouths of valleys and gullies, allowing stagnant water to form. In these pools of stagnant water, mosquitoes bred.

This ecological chain was not solely the result of mistaken policies or even of neglect. It had been set in motion by forces particular to the history of the Italian South — once-quiescent forces that had gathered momentum in the second half of the nineteenth century until they had acted like the rain driving down into bare limestone rock, swelling its capillaries to the point where entire mountainsides crashed down. The peasants, for centuries, had been like those mountains: solid, elemental, persevering. No one had expected to see them move. But then their own human landscape had cracked under the pressure of misery, and all those people, dressed in black, fragments of a landslide pushing each other along, had come down off their hillsides and, like the victims of disaster that they were, had swarmed to the sea.

The South was founded by immigrants.

Almost nothing is known about the native populations of Sicily and southern Italy except that they were displaced, or absorbed, by the Greeks. Starting around the eighth century B.C., the Greek city-states sent fleets out to found colonies. Lean Greek triremes, not very different in size or shape from the Viking ships, penetrated into the Black Sea and touched all the shores of the Mediterranean. Where the land seemed most fertile, or was still unsettled, the Greeks founded their colonies. Odessa, the Russian port on the Black Sea, began as a Greek colony. So did Marseilles and Nice, in France. So did Naples, which takes its name from the Greek *Neapolis,* meaning "New City." [2] The most important Greek colonies were in southern Italy and in Sicily — the area that the Greeks favored to the extent that they called it *Magna Grecia,* or "Greater Greece." It was a name like New England. It referred to new territories in a wilderness, or virgin, area.

When the Greek fleets scouted the shores of southern Italy, they found that the peninsula north of Naples was already occupied by the powerful Etruscans. They found that the western part of Sicily was already occupied by colonists from Carthage. The Greeks settled the remaining area, which was the lower part of the Italian boot and the eastern coast of Sicily. The first tribe with whom the Greeks came into contact on the Italian mainland was one they called the *Itali*. And it was from that obscure encounter, occurring nearly a thousand years before Christ, that Italy derived its name. Sicily took its name from a tribe called the *Siculi*, whom the Greeks identified as the native residents of the island.

The cities founded by these Greek colonists were seaports. Each had its harbor, its commercial center and market, its theaters, its temples, and its fortified acropolis, which in Greek means "upper town." [3] Some grew to be major cities possessing colonies of their own around the Mediterranean. The city of Tarentum (the present Taranto), built at the mouth of a natural harbor, had a population of about three hundred thousand and founded some twenty-five colonies of its own. Sybaris, also nestling in the arch at the bottom of the Italian boot, dominated the trade between the Greek homeland and northern Italy because the Sybarites built a network of roads leading up the Italian boot to other seaports, including Paestum where magnificent Greek temples still remain. Goods could be transshipped using the Sybarites' road network. By the sixth century B.C., Greek traders and their mercantile fleets were operating virtually all over Europe.

Trade was one reason for the growth of the Greek colonies in southern Italy and Sicily. The other was agriculture. The land had not yet been stripped of its natural wealth. It was covered with lush, beautiful forests, and in spring and summer its fields blazed with wild flowers. "Sicily shimmered with corn fields which were, for an immigrant from stony Greece, the ancient equivalent of the North American prairie provinces." [4] The brilliance of Greek culture, moreover, was reflected in the colonies of southern Italy and Sicily. They had their poets, dramatists, philosophers and scientists. The philosopher Pythagoras lived in Croton, another city on the arch of the Italian boot. Archimedes, the father of mechanics, was a leading citizen of Syracuse, in Sicily — and was Sicilian by birth. During the reign of Dionysius I, from 405 to 367 B.C., Syracuse was probably the leading city of the Hellenic world.

But Sicily, because of its geographical location, was destined to be a constant battleground. To the east was Greek power. To the south, across less than a hundred miles of sea, was Carthage (the present Tunis). And to the north, in the Italian peninsula itself, Roman power was consolidating. In the thirty-eight years under Dionysius, Syracuse fought no less than four wars against Carthage, and these had been preceded by two Carthaginian invasions of Sicily in 409 and 406. A stronger Roman threat followed. Though the Greek general Pyrrhus won two bloody victories* over Roman armies in southern Italy and attempted to lead a Hellenic revival, this was only a brief interlude of relative independence for the Greek city-states before their final decline. After the Romans had defeated Pyrrhus in a third battle at Benevento, they were able to move against Sicily and to challenge Carthage for control of the strategic and agriculturally rich island.

The first Punic war between Rome and Carthage was fought largely in Sicily. Cities were taken and retaken, burned and despoiled. In suing for peace in 241 B.C., Carthage ceded all of western Sicily to Rome. Gradually, Rome extended its grip over the once-powerful Greek cities on the eastern half of the island as well. When a Roman fleet besieged Syracuse in 212 B.C., Archimedes was said to have built a gigantic concave mirror able to concentrate sunlight in a scaring ray. But not even this weapon turned back the Roman invaders. They took the city (Archimedes was killed in the fighting), and with the fall of Syracuse the classical era all but came to an end in southern Italy. Though the people continued to speak and write Greek, and Hellenic influence remained strong, the formerly brilliant city-states of *Magna Grecia* became mere provincial towns in the expanding Roman Republic, and then in the empire.

Despite the vast, unified market for trade that flourished under Roman rule — the first European common market — the Roman era was less favorable for southern Italy and Sicily. The island, in particular, served as Rome's breadbasket, its source of grain. Sicily's economy was organized around huge agricultural estates that were run on slave labor, like the cotton plantations in the American South centuries later. These slaves were not black. They might be Greeks, Persians, Egyptians, Germans, Gauls, or Italians — usually prisoners from Rome's wars and civil wars. With these estates often owned by wealthy absentee landlords, and the slave gangs lashed into submission by brutal overseers, no kind of social stability was possible. Crime, frequent slave rebellions, and civil dis-

---

* While he won his first two battles, Pyrrhus's casualties were so heavy that his ultimate defeat was inevitable, hence the term Pyrrhic victory.

order were the result. Thus, the tradition of rebellion against authority — and of its opposite, a thirst for justice — had already been implanted into the Sicilian, and to some extent the southern Italian, mentality. Neither area became wholly Roman in its culture. The people, speaking mostly Greek, felt that the Romans were foreign rulers.

By the end of the third century after Christ, the Roman Empire had become so vast, and unwieldy, that it could no longer be administered from Rome. It split into two parts. The western empire was ruled first from Rome, then from Milan and Ravenna in the north of Italy. The richer eastern portion was ruled from a succession of cities until the first Christian emperor, Constantine, built his *polis,* or city, of Constantinopolis (our Istanbul), which became its final and enduring capital. The city was also known as Byzantium, just as the eastern Roman Empire was known as the Byzantine Empire. It survived the fall of the western Roman Empire by about a thousand years.

The Gothic and Hunnish barbarians who invaded the crumbling western empire and slashed through Italy, destroying, looting, and raping, inflicted less damage on southern Italy and on Sicily than on the northern portions of the peninsula. But their raids served to accentuate the ethnic differences between northern and southern Italy. The basic racial stock of the northern Italians had included the Etruscans, the Celts, who had occupied much of the Po Valley, and then the Romans. After the fall of Rome, most of northern Italy was occupied by the Nordic Lombards, a people of Germanic origin, who ruled as feudal masters. The prevailing racial influences on northern Italy, therefore, came from across the Alps, from northern and eastern Europe.

The racial origins of southern Italians, on the other hand, were Mediterranean. Greeks, and Arabs from Carthage, had been the original colonists in southern Italy and Sicily. After the fall of Rome, most of southern Italy and Sicily reverted to their previous association with the Greek world. The south of Italy was ruled mostly by Greek-speaking Byzantine knights, or local knights who generally accepted the authority of the Byzantine, or eastern, Empire. Many of the great agricultural estates previously owned by the Romans had passed directly into the hands of these knights or of the Catholic church, the only civil authority to have survived the collapse of the western empire. Such was the origin of the long-lived feudal system of southern Italy in which the Church and the aristocracy owned the best land and leased out little plots to the peasants in exchange for rent or for a portion of their crops.

But now a new foreign threat arose, and Sicily in particular received a new infusion of Arab blood, and culture. Shortly after Mohammed's death in A.D. 632, the Arab Saracens materialized out of the barren heart of the desert to conquer most of the Mediterranean world. From their base in what is now Saudi Arabia, they overran the vast Persian Empire, then the Egyptian. They rode west along the fertile coastline of North Africa, reached Morocco, jumped the Strait of Gibraltar, conquered Spain, and were galloping for Paris when an army of French knights turned them back at Tours in A.D. 732.

The conquest of Egypt had given these Saracens a fleet. Though they used it initially to disrupt the commercial sea lanes between southern Italy and the Byzantine Empire, about a century after the battle of Tours a small force of Saracens crossed from North Africa to Sicily, summoned as allies by an ambitious Byzantine governor.[5] Within fifty years they had conquered the whole island. They were good rulers on the whole. Though they built mosques and introduced the Moslem faith, they were relatively tolerant. Trade flourished. Their chief commercial port was Palermo, which became a thriving city of some three hundred thousand inhabitants at a time when the rest of Europe was sunk in the Dark Ages. At the royal palace in Palermo the Saracens established a famous weaving house, where Italian craftsmen first learned the superb techniques and designs developed in Asia Minor (some of these techniques had come directly from China). It was this Saracen innovation that gave Italy its early lead in European textile manufacturing, and made textiles the chief export item of the Italian city-states during the Renaissance. The Saracens also introduced three basic agricultural crops to Europe by way of Sicily. One was cotton. The second was sugar cane. The third was citrus fruits — lemons and oranges. The famous, lush orange groves of the *Conca d'Oro,* or Golden Shell, behind Palermo, were planted by the Saracens.[6]

But while the Arabs were largely benevolent rulers in Sicily, their presence was disastrous for the southern part of the Italian mainland. They gained control of only part of it. They ruled Bari, and for a while Amalfi was under their influence. But other parts of southern Italy were still under Byzantine control, or under Lombard influence, or the influence of the pope in Rome — these fields of influence often meshing and mingling. Many cities were destroyed in the resulting warfare. And even more were looted by Saracen fleets which now dominated the Mediterranean, and functioned as huge piratical forces responsible to no higher authority.

The word piracy generally calls to mind a ship or two sailing under the Jolly Roger. The Saracen pirate fleets sometimes ran to three or four hundred ships. Once the Saracens had established piracy as virtually the only form of navigation in the Mediterranean, Greeks and Italians also took it up. And since most of the cities and towns in southern Italy had been built as seaports, the effect of piracy on southern Italy was enormous. Any visitor to southern Italy can still see the cylindrical stone towers erected all along the coast as early warning stations, or, in an emergency, places of refuge. The most terrifying aspect of a Saracen attack was that the inhabitants of coastal cities, towns, and villages were seized and dragged aboard ship, to be sold into slavery. When a Saracen fleet occupied Reggio Calabria, seventeen thousand people were kidnapped into slavery.[7] Norman Douglas, visiting a Calabrian village at the turn of the century, was shown a portrait of Sultana, a beautiful local girl of legend who had been captured by Saracen pirates and sold into a harem. She had escaped somehow and made her way back home. Most victims were not that fortunate.

The curse of piracy on the coasts of southern Italy lasted an incredibly long time — about a thousand years, from A.D. 800 to 1800. It was a basic cause of the deterioration of life. The only recourse for people was to flee inland, away from low-lying shores and up to the tops of peaks. And so, like a receding wave, life deserted the once-fertile and flourishing coast. Even major cities were abandoned. When the Saracens raided Taranto, the inhabitants fled to a site farther inland full of grottoes and caverns where they could take temporary shelter. But the pirates remained such a deadly threat that these people never did return to Taranto. They built a village on the hillside above the caves where they had first taken refuge.[8] In thousands of other localities as well, entire populations withdrew to the more easily defensible hilltops. These became the sites of villages built for survival. The houses were crowded together on steep land. Each family lived within shouting distance of its neighbors, the men able to form a defensive force within a few minutes. Only, of course, these villages were not temporary. Today, southern Italy and Sicily are still inhabited mainly by peasants living on hilltop villages. The consequences of this inland and uphill migration were far-reaching.

The fertile agricultural land along the coast, first cultivated by the

Greek colonists, was abandoned. It degenerated into gloomy marshland, breeding mosquitoes. Like a fog that nothing could dispel, malaria settled over the poisoned air of these marshes. The hilltop villages, on the other hand, made a tribal world that was too small to be biologically healthy. Crowding and lack of sanitation were accepted as normal. Four or five people might sleep in one or two rooms, sometimes with their pigs, sheep, chickens, and dogs. Often, the floor in these houses was simply cold, naked earth. The psychological effect of life in a hilltop village on its inhabitants is easily grasped. One's family, and to a lesser extent the village itself, become a fortress against the hostile world "down there." In a society where everyone is poor, and the scope of ambition so limited, power over others becomes the paramount goal. This power was expressed in terms of respect and submission.

By the eleventh century, the Saracens were in full retreat. A formidable band of Christian knights had appeared to drive the infidels from Sicily and from their few outposts on the Italian mainland. These were the Normans, a warrior race of Scandinavian origin (the name Norman was derived from "Northmen") who had seized the western coast of France, still called Normandy after them. In the tenth century, they had set out to capture the two largest islands in Europe, Britain and Sicily. While William the Conqueror subdued Britain at the Battle of Hastings in 1066, a fellow Norman, Count Roger de Hauteville, reached Sicily and occupied Messina. He had been invited to the island by a vengeful Sicilian lord recently driven from power, and this was sufficient pretext for what soon turned into a Norman invasion. After Roger had defeated the Saracen army at Misilmeri, on the outskirts of Palermo, he took their carrier pigeons and soaked them in the blood of dead Arab soldiers, sending this flight of red pigeons back to Palermo to announce the disaster, and the end of Saracen power in the island.

While conquering Sicily, the Normans also fought against various Byzantine and papal forces on the Italian mainland. In 1084, after capturing the Byzantine port of Durazzo on the Adriatic (now a coastal city in Albania), the Norman knight Robert Guiscard sacked Rome. But Pope Gregory VII, and his successor Urban II, both extremely able statesmen, were able to reshape Norman ambitions and turn them against the heathen Arabs and Seljuk Turks in the eastern Mediterranean. The goal of Norman energies now became the liberation of Jerusalem, and for over a century Norman crusaders sailed from Brindisi and from other ports in southern Italy, to wage holy war against the Saracens.

The Normans were the last enlightened conquerors of Sicily, and of southern Italy (though their power was never quite as strong on the mainland). While they obliterated the mosques that the Saracens had built, or converted them into churches, they were not intolerant otherwise. Under their rule a pluralistic culture flourished in Sicily, where the court language was French, where the mass of people still spoke Greek, but where Latin, Arabic, and Hebrew were also recognized as official languages.[9] Arab scholars and mathematicians were attached to the Norman court. Thousands of English and English-Norman knights and their families settled in Sicily during this period, as well as many thousands of Lombards from northern Italy.

The Norman period lasted into the thirteenth century, and culminated with the reign of Frederick II, who was styled *Stupor Mundi* ("Wonder of the World") by his contemporaries. The son of a Norman mother and a German Hohenstaufen father, he was brought up in Palermo. At the age of fourteen he was crowned Holy Roman Emperor. Though his dominions stretched through Europe as far north as the Baltic, he loved Sicily and the mountainous Puglie of southern Italy best. Frederick was a cultured man, the product of Greek, Arab, and European tutors. He had learned Arabic as a boy, and in many of his tastes he remained more Arab than European — he kept a harem, for example, of beautiful women of a dozen nationalities. When the Saracen population in Sicily revolted after a terrible famine in 1212, instead of killing these rebels Frederick had them deported to the Italian mainland. His own soldiers were in part Saracen, and "at his great Apulian stronghold of Lucera he built them a miniature Baghdad complete with mosques."[10] At his court, learned Arabs, Jews, northern Europeans, and Italians wrote, collected and copied ancient Greek manuscripts, and debated science and philosophy. Many of the texts that illuminated Renaissance minds reached Italy through Palermo at this time. Frederick expanded Europe's oldest university, at Salerno, and founded the University of Naples in 1224. He was one of the first men to write verse in the new language of Italian.

Above all, Frederick gave southern Italy, and Sicily, what they would not have for centuries afterwards: the rule of an efficient central government. In northern Europe, nations would soon be emerging from feudalism. In southern Italy the process was reversed. After Frederick, the south of Italy, and Sicily, degenerated into feudalism and poverty.

One reason for this decline was the eclipse of the eastern Mediterranean as a source of trade, of power, and of civilization. Though Constantinople itself — the Greek capital of Byzantium — would not fall until 1453, the eastern or Greek empire had been deteriorating since the twelfth century. The Arab world was disintegrating in much the same way. In both cases, the immediate cause was the emergence of the half-nomadic, half-barbarian Turks who cut the ancient trade routes between Asia and Europe. This was of crucial economic importance to Sicily and southern Italy, which were geographically situated athwart these commercial routes. But there was a more fundamental process at work, in which the focus of European vitality was moving inexorably northward. It would pause for a century, or even a century and a half, in central and northern Italy, then leap the Alps as the Italian Renaissance ended and that of the countries of northern Europe began. At the end of the fifteenth century, the voyages of Columbus and of other European explorers would permanently reduce the Mediterranean from the center of the world's trade, and civilization, which it had been for centuries (China being the other, and largely independent, center), and leave it a commercial backwater.

The South was therefore locked into a pattern that would change only barely with the passing of the centuries. While in northern Europe the accumulation of capital, the discovery of technology, and the breakdown of feudal class barriers would create a large, forward-looking middle class, in southern Europe as a whole, and in the south of Italy and Sicily in particular, the overwhelming majority of the inhabitants — as high as ninety-six or ninety-seven percent — remained peasants, people without any power, isolated in their remote villages, repeating the same cycle of life as the generations that had preceded them. If anything they were poorer, more cruelly and inefficiently administered.

Under medieval feudalism, at least, the feudal lord remained close to his castle, to his fiefdom, and to his subjects. If a peasant were caught stealing, the lord would decide whether or not the man's hand should be cut off. He was the law, and his hired warriors functioned as the police. If a road had to be built or repaired, the feudal lord would decide when the construction would start, how many men would be employed, and so forth. While it was a terribly haphazard form of government (the road might not be built for half a century), it was at least personal. A peasant could go before the lord, plead his case, and perhaps obtain redress. Or in really bad times the peasant could take up arms against his lord.

But with the start of the period of Spanish domination over southern Italy and Sicily in the early sixteenth century, government turned into a potpourri of the old feudal system and a centralized authority in Naples — a central government that was both remote and inefficient. Its only object was to collect taxes and quell rebellion. The aristocratic owners of estates in Sicily, or Calabria, and the Puglie became absentee land-owners. They spent their time in Naples or Palermo, or even in Rome. The estates were usually administered by an agent whose only interest was to squeeze as much rent as possible out of the peasants.

As a result, the *contadini*, or peasants, did not benefit at all from the social and technological revolution occurring only a few hundred miles to the north. Their way of life came to resemble that of North Africa more than that of Europe. They continued to scratch the rocky soil with plows unchanged from those used by the Greek colonists two thousand years earlier. Often a plow was no more than a metal pin attached to a pair of wooden handles, capable of reaching barely half a foot below the surface. The forests were gradually disappearing; the land itself was growing poorer and yielding less. The surface remained filled with light, often lovely. The occasional traveler to southern Italy and Sicily in the seventeenth and eighteenth centuries was dazzled by the lush orange and lemon groves, the incredible green of the region's fields in spring, planted with early beans and corn, the groves of palm trees, the wild flowers growing profusely on hillsides overlooking a turquoise sea. Above all, what the south of Italy possessed was the particular beauty of an old civilization, where everything built by man appears to have achieved a harmony with nature. The beauty could perhaps ameliorate the poverty a little. But the poverty was inexorable. In the end it destroyed even the value of such beauty in the eyes of those who worked the land.

Before emigration, there were only two avenues of escape — or illusions of escape — for the people. One was violence. The land swarmed with bandits, who were sometimes merely criminals and at other times political rebels. A British artist who traveled throughout the kingdom of Naples in the 1770s, Henry Swindburne, reported that no less than four thousand people were killed by bandits every year. The same forests of Calabria and the Puglie where Spartacus had once taken shelter from the Roman armies sent to crush him, were now full of brigands and kidnappers who naturally thrived in periods of disorder. In 1809, during the Napoleonic wars, outlaws in the kingdom of Naples committed thirty-three thousand crimes.[11] The reaction of the authorities was often as cruel. Eighteenth-century visitors to Sicily and southern Italy reported seeing poles mounted outside every village, on which bandits' heads were displayed as a warning to the populace.

This is the account of the execution of a bandit chief named Benincasa:

Betrayed and bound by his followers as he slept in the forest of Cassano, Benincasa was brought to Cosenza, and General Mahnes ordered that both his hands be lopped off and that he be led, thus mutilated, to his home in San Giovanni, and there hanged; a cruel sentence, which the wretch received with a bitter smile. His right hand was cut off and the stump bound, not out of compassion or regard for his life, but in order that all his blood might not flow out of the opened veins, seeing that he was reserved for a more miserable death. Not a cry escaped him, and when he saw that the first operation was over, he voluntarily laid his left hand upon the block and coldly watched the second mutilation, and saw his two amputated hands lying on the ground, which were then tied together by the thumbs and hung round his neck; an awful and piteous spectacle. . . . [Under guard] he arrived at his home, and slept through the following night; on the next day, as the hour of execution approached, he refused the comforts of religion, ascended the gallows neither swiftly nor slowly, and died admired for his brutal intrepidity.[12]

Even among people who were not outlaws, feuds and blood feuds born of the compression of village life deformed their spirit with violence. In *Christ Stopped at Eboli,* Carlo Levi talked with an army lieutenant from southern Italy.

He was, he said, only the link in a chain of hates that went back for generations, a hundred years, two hundred years, or more, perhaps forever. He was bound up in these inherited passions. There was nothing he could do about it except to eat his heart out. Here they had hated each other for centuries and would go on hating, among the same houses, before the same white stones. . . .[13]

This passage introduces the second avenue of escape, which was fantasy. The popular culture of southern Italy, and of Sicily, was permeated with the fantastic. People believed in spirits, in the evil eye, in magic potions, in magic numbers and the properties of numbers, in luck, in fate — above all, in miracles. It would not be difficult to establish a psychological correlation between the powerlessness of the people and their belief in religious miracles, saints who could cure with a touch of their hand, dozens of saints who could fly — one monk able to hover over religious processions like a helicopter, some ten to fifteen feet off the ground. Even the religious processions themselves smacked of the fantastic — parishioners dressed in white smocks, pulling carts on which huge floats had been constructed three or four stories high with dozens of winged angels revolving on mechanically operated disks. All of these fantastic manifestations were, like brigandage, a symbol of frustrated energies.

By the mid-eighteenth century, Naples, the Bourbon capital of southern Italy and of Sicily, had become one of the most densely populated cities in the world, with about four hundred thousand inhabitants. A dreadful famine struck the city in 1764, giving rise to conditions so hideous that the Neapolitan intellectual Genovesi remarked that one could not believe Naples was part of Europe.[14] Among the educated classes, among professional men particularly, the feeling was growing that reforms were not only desperately needed but inevitable. Yet the Bourbon government, and the feudal lords in the countryside, would not budge. As the historian Giuliano Procacci wrote, "Southern society revolved about a vacuum. It was unable to produce from within itself the energies that could have revived it." [15]

As had happened so many times before, forces from outside the South deflected its course. The Napoleonic years saw many reforms started. But these were soon overturned in the Bourbon restoration that followed Waterloo. The situation in the kingdom of Naples remained more or less static up to the mid-nineteenth century, under *Re Bomba*. When the revolutions of 1848–1849 were crushed, it seemed that the chances for social reform in the kingdom of Naples had ended. The Bourbons would continue to rule. Life would go on as before.

By the late 1850s, however, a mechanism had been set in motion by the kingdom of Piedmont's shrewd, far-sighted prime minister, Count Camillo Cavour, that would finally lead to Italian unification and to the overthrow of the Bourbon monarchy in the South. While Cavour convinced the French to intervene in order to help drive the Austrians from northern Italy, Garibaldi suddenly invaded Sicily.

From a beach a few miles south of Genoa, files of men climbed aboard small boats to be rowed out to the two steamships anchored offshore, the *Lombardo* and the *Piemonte*. The wives of some of these men stood on the beach, surrounded by their children — the women graceful in their long, Victorian dresses. Garibaldi had brought together his new force of volunteers for the purpose of invading Bourbon territory and forcing the unification of Italy. It was a small army, only 1,089 strong, composed mainly of young professional men, of lawyers, journalists, civil servants, artists, and even an Oxford scholar.[16] The date was May 5, 1860, and their destination was Sicily.*

Though many of the *Mille* (or the Thousand, as they came to be called) were fearful, or pessimistic about their chances against the vastly larger Bourbon army, their general was serene and confident. He had waited so long, and now events were moving with him.

The previous spring, France had declared war on Austria and French troops had poured into Piedmont to aid in expelling the Austrians from Italy. This intervention had been Cavour's diplomatic masterpiece. He had prepared the ground very carefully, sending Piedmontese regiments and officers (including Cesnola) to fight in the Crimean War beside the English and French, thus placing those relatively liberal governments in debt to tiny Piedmont. Then he had courted Napoleon III — that same Louis Napoleon who had crushed the Roman Republic and who, after assuming dictatorial powers in 1852, had styled himself Emperor Napoleon III of France.† Cavour told the emperor that Italy was bound to be unified sooner or later, and that the unification should be carried out by responsible conservatives like King Victor Emmanuel of Piedmont, rather than by radicals like Mazzini and Garibaldi. He convinced the emperor to help drive the Austrians from northern Italy. Napoleon III led the French army in person, just as Victor Emmanuel personally led the Piedmontese forces. At Magenta (the silk town whose dye works had created the color)[17] they defeated the Austrian army once. At Solferino, near Lake Garda, the Austrians were again beaten in a bloody, day-long battle. But now Napoleon III shortchanged Cavour. He met the young Austrian emperor at Villafranca and the two men sat down and settled Italy's fate between them. Only Lombardy and Parma were added to Piedmont. Austria maintained its control over Venice and reoccupied other parts of northern Italy.

Cavour handed in his resignation in disgust. But six months later, back in office as Prime Minister, he engineered plebiscites in Tuscany and in Emilia (to the north of Tuscany) which were held in March 1860.[18] The

---

* The expedition of the *Mille* was something of a cause in the Anglo-Saxon world. Both Lady Byron and the Duke of Wellington contributed funds. Colonel Colt, an admirer of Garibaldi, sent him a hundred revolvers — the same kind used by cowboys in the West — which the Garibaldini put to good use in Sicily. The first sizable reinforcements to reach Garibaldi in Sicily steamed into the Gulf of Castellamare aboard the *Franklin* and the *Washington*.

† He was a nephew of Napoleon Bonaparte.

two regions voted to join the emerging kingdom of Italy, and the drive for unification was on once again. Garibaldi had fought a guerilla action against the Austrians in 1859 with an army of about three thousand men, operating in the area of Lakes Como and Garda. He had watched with extreme bitterness as his birthplace, Nizza, had been ceded to France in a rigged plebiscite, and he had even contemplated trying to occupy it militarily with his guerilla army. But now the Sicilians were preparing an uprising against the Bourbons and they asked the general to lead them. Start it, he said in effect, and my men and I will join you. It seemed a propitious time. King Bomb had just died, and the new Bourbon king, Francis II, was inexperienced, weak, and surrounded by blindly reactionary ministers who were even talking of a campaign against the stronger and more determined Piedmontese in the north. When Sicilian patriots staged a suicidal revolt in Palermo early in 1860, Garibaldi, after some hesitation, decided that the moment had come for him to invade the South.[19]

The *Lombardo* and the *Piemonte* steamed into Marsala, on the western tip of Sicily, six days after having left Genoa. They were just in time, as a squadron of Bourbon warships was closing in on them. Fortunately, there were also some British ships anchored at Marsala, and the Bourbon naval commander, seeing the red shirts of the Garibaldini through his telescope, held his fire for fear they might be British troops.[20] This gave the Thousand time to scramble ashore with their supplies before the *Lombardo* and *Piemonte* could be blown out of the water.

From that point on, nothing could stop Garibaldi's insurgent army. The British naval captain at Marsala had already observed that "the patriots stood fire splendidly and appeared to be altogether a fine body of men." [21] Their first battle in Sicily was decided by a bayonet charge up a steep hillside against a much larger Bourbon force supported by artillery. Before the charge, the fire coming down the hillside had been so heavy that one of Garibaldi's officers had suggested a retreat. *"Dove?"* cried Garibaldi. *"Qui si fa l'Italia o si muoie."* ("Where? Here we either make Italy or we die.")

He led the bayonet charge himself and when the Bourbon troops broke and ran, the way to Palermo was open. Now groups of peasants armed with scythes and ancient muskets rode on muleback to join Garibaldi, and the liberation of Sicily began to assume the characteristics of a popular rebellion. In certain areas estates were seized and land redistributed — though the Garibaldini themselves checked the most radical of these initiatives. When he occupied Palermo, Garibaldi casually proclaimed himself dictator of Sicily. It was a temporary title only. He had no time to deal with the complexities of the Sicilian situation, nor any clear-cut social program. He was fighting a war and his mission was the unification of Italy.

"I came here to fight for the cause of Italy, not of Sicily alone," he said in Palermo. "If we do not free and unite the whole of Italy, we shall never achieve liberty in any single part of her." [22]

On the eighteenth of August, 1860, Garibaldi's red-shirted army crossed the Strait of Messina to the Italian mainland. As Garibaldi began to push the Bourbon army up the boot toward its capital of Naples, Cavour, in Turin, took steps to make certain that Garibaldi would not achieve the liberation of Italy with popular forces. He had already written, at the time of Garibaldi's invasion of Sicily, "If the insurrection is put down, we shall say nothing; if it is victorious, we shall intervene in the name of law and authority." [23] Cavour was an aristocrat. He was a conservative, though a dedicated patriot. He was prime minister to a king. The last thing he wanted was for the collapse of authority in the kingdom of Naples, to trigger a social cataclysm — peasant rebellions that might lead to a civil war and destroy Italy's status in the eyes of the European powers at the very moment when Italy was becoming a nation.

Cautiously, Cavour used the Piedmontese army to block any further advance by Garibaldi's forces. Garibaldi, having taken Naples, was preparing to march on Rome, and there, in the ancient capital of the Italians and the lost battleground of 1849, to proclaim the unification of Italy. But by creating a series of incidents in central Italy, Cavour was able to rush the Piedmontese army southward on the pretext of saving the Papal States from "revolution." [24]

When Garibaldi's Red Shirts met the Royal Piedmontese army at Teano, still in Neapolitan territory, on October 26, 1860, it was Garibaldi who took the subordinate part. He had been standing for hours in front of a tavern watching the splendidly uniformed Piedmontese regiments march past when suddenly men began shouting "the King is coming." So now the old warrior mounted and rode towards Victor Emmanuel, waving his black biretta and shouting, *"Saluto il primo Re d'Italia."* ("I salute the first King of Italy.") As they clasped hands Italy became a nation and a kingdom.

But it was not a nation in the hearts of many of its citizens. Cavour had been perfectly right in fearing a release of bottled-up frustrations, particularly in the south of Italy — the cry for social justice that had been suppressed for centuries. A peasant rebellion broke out in the former kingdom of Naples as soon as the Piedmontese army moved in to restore order, and a crude form of guerilla warfare raged for months. Any peasant found carrying arms was summarily shot. "This was a ruthless declaration of war on people who had no other means of defense, and it reaped the whirlwind. Captured soldiers were sometimes tied to trees and burned alive; others were crucified and mutilated." [25] The army's countermeasures were even more brutal. Whole villages were razed, entire families imprisoned or shot because of one suspected offender.

By 1862, there were some eighty thousand armed rebels in the Neapolitan provinces.[26] Some were bandits, others guerilla soldiers. A parliamentary report of 1863 called on the new Italian government to "extend education and see to a fairer distribution of land. Roads must be built, marshes reclaimed, public works begun, and the forests looked after. . . ." The report also identified the causes of lawlessness in the South: "the existence of a bandit has many attractions there for the poor laborer . . . and brigandage becomes a savage protest against centuries of injustice by men reduced to the utmost poverty. With such people there is an absolute lack of confidence in the law and the exercise of justice. . . ." [27]

The solution was to carry out a long-term program of social reform. But it is doubtful whether Italy's ministers had really grasped the dimensions of the problem in the South, which had intensified because of unification. Agricultural prices fell, taxes rose; a tariff war with France closed traditional markets for Sicilian fruit and wines. The birth rate was now increasing, which meant more people on the land, more underemployment and poverty. In the meanwhile, military repression was deemed a necessary course. Soon, half the Italian army was concentrated in the south of Italy and in Sicily, suppressing "bandits." [28]

To many in the South, the new Italian government appeared to be just another form of rule by foreigners. The national parliament in faraway Rome (at first it met in Turin, then Florence), levied new taxes, heavier even than those imposed by the Bourbons. Some, like the grist tax on the grinding of wheat and corn, could not be evaded even by the very poor. A character in Verga's novel *The House by the Medlar*

Tree complained, "Now they're going to put a tax on salt. The druggist said he saw it printed in the paper. Then there'll be no more salting of anchovies, and we may as well break up our boats for firewood."

The dominant mood in the South was one of resignation. The peasants soon realized they were being cheated just as blatantly as before. In 1876, for example, the government expropriated Church lands and placed them on the market. The idea was that the peasant would gain ownership of these lands. But the moment the law was announced, land values were immediately depressed, and peasants found it hard to borrow money with which to purchase the newly available land. Instead of the peasants getting these properties, they went almost entirely to speculators and big landowners.

The deforestation of former church lands — totaling nearly a million acres — was another consequence of unification. Even the Bourbons had taken some pains to conserve remaining woodlands. But now widespread cutting of the forests brought many parts of southern Italy close to ecological ruin. When Norman Douglas visited Calabria at the end of the nineteenth century, he noted that "the friable rock, no longer sustained by plant-life, crashes down with each thunderstorm, blocks up the valleys, devastating large tracts of fertile land; it creates swamps in the lowlands and impedes the outflow of water to the sea." [29] The stagnant deposits of water created in these marshes served as a vast breeding ground for mosquitoes.

There are indications that malaria may have been present in southern Italy even in Greek times. The careful sanitary procedures indulged in by the Sybarites, including plumbing — which later Roman historians held up as indications of their degeneracy — may have actually represented an effort to check the disease. In many cases, man destroyed the environment and thus helped spread malaria. The city of Brindisi on the Adriatic, with a fine natural bay, first became malarial after the civil war between Caesar and Pompey. In trying to bottle up Pompey's fleet in the harbor, Caesar had his engineers dump thousands of tons of earth, uprooted trees and building materials into the channel at the mouth of the bay. The sea had almost cleared it again when the prince of Taranto, in the fifteenth century, sank ships in the channel to block an enemy fleet. By the middle of the eighteenth century, the marshy land created around the harbor had become so malarial that the population had declined from around fifty thousand in Roman times, to some eighteen thousand during the Middle Ages, when Brindisi served as a port of embarkation for the Norman crusaders, to no more than five thousand in 1766.[30]

The scourge of malaria lay over hundreds of southern towns and villages. At the Calabrian village of Foca, for example, parish records between 1850 and 1900 showed 319 births and 516 deaths,[31] and most of the survivors were ill with the disease. When not fatal, malaria was enervating. It made children dull-eyed and listless, and it made men impotent by their late twenties. The brisk northerners who visited the South in the years following unification would invariably return home with tales of southern indolence. The people of the South, they said, were constitutionally lazy; they were content to sit in the sun and spin dreams. But often what these northerners mistook for willful indolence was simply malaria.

The south of Italy had always been a land of hunger, and backbreaking toil. It took the people a while to realize after unification that their real standard of living had not only failed to improve after they had been "liberated" from the backward and inefficient Bourbons, it had deteriorated. The men from the North who ran industry and generally ran the Italian government could not believe this, being imbued with the kind of hearty middle-class optimism typical of the Victorians. But while the middle class in the North sat down to enormous meals, the hunger of the southern peasant increased — and his toil remained undiminished. A few slices of bread dipped in olive oil was a peasant's lunch, a plate of beans his supper. Even spaghetti, that most Italian of all dishes, was a rare treat in millions of homes. Meat was eaten twice a year, at Christmas and at Easter. Wine was reserved for the man when he returned exhausted from the fields.

And yet such peasants were considered, and considered themselves, fortunate. They had land, whether it was their own or someone else's. The dispossessed could be found at dawn every morning in any village square, squatting against a wall waiting to be hired for the day. These were *braccianti*, from the Italian *braccia*, meaning "arm," a pair of arms to be hired for the day. (There are roughly a million *braccianti* in the south of Italy even today.) A *bracciante* might be hired to help a wealthier peasant with some task, or to work on an estate at harvest time. He was lucky if he could find work a hundred days a year. And because the number of these day laborers continued to rise, it was impossible to maintain a minimum agricultural wage.

It was the pressure of these many forces, extending deep into history

— the ruin of the land, disease, hunger, poverty, but above all power-lessness and the continuation of intolerable social injustice in an age that was bright and promising elsewhere — that caused so many southern Italians to become emigrants. They did so at a time when Italy was a bustling European power, when its cities in the North and center of the peninsula hummed with activity, when factories in Milan and Turin were turning out heavy machinery, when hydroelectric dams were being built in the Alps and pre-Alps, when Italy was universally respected as a fountainhead of culture. What educated man had not been to Italy at least once? Italy was not backward in the sense that Egypt or India were. In the North, and in the large cities, Italy seemed a modern technological nation, with its navy, its empire, its stock market, its opera houses and elegant cafés.

But the common people, particularly in the South, were not part of that plastic and rapidly evolving society. Though their history went back thousands of years, they remained outside it. As Carlo Levi wrote, describing the villages in the remote fastness of the Calabrian mountains:

Christ never came this far, nor did time, nor the individual soul, nor hope, nor the relation of cause to effect, nor reason nor history. Christ never came, just as the Romans never came, content to garrison the highways without penetrating the mountains and forests, nor the Greeks, who flourished beside the Gulf of Taranto. None of the pioneers of Western civilization brought here his sense of the passage of time, his deification of the State or that ceaseless activity which feeds upon itself. No one has come to this land except as an enemy, a conqueror, or a visitor devoid of understanding. The seasons pass today over the toil of the peasants just as they did three thousand years before Christ; no message, human or divine, has reached this stubborn poverty.[32]

Among these villages where Christ had never come, the word began to spread in the second half of the nineteenth century that there was a better life to be had elsewhere. It spread from ear to ear, a kind of wind, an osmosis of promise. If the promise was often false, if it was rigged at the start by the steamship companies, the mills, the mines, the railroad gangs and plantations that awaited these people at the other end of their voyage, they did not know it. They became convinced in their slow, stubborn and fearful dialogue with themselves that there was a life *da Cristiani,* a life fit for Christians, across the sea.

Mulberry Bend

THE MEN LEFT FIRST.

Italian immigration to the United States at the turn of the century is easily characterized. The immigrants from Italy were eighty percent male. Eighty percent were from southern Italy. And eighty percent were between the ages of fourteen and forty-five — working age. As Oscar Handlin stated, "A definite economic cause drives the poor *meridionale* [southerner] from his home, and a definite economic cause and not a vague migratory instinct brings him to America. He comes because [this] country has the most urgent need of unskilled labor." [1]

These Italians were following a well-established pattern. Early in the nineteenth century, groups of laborers from depressed areas of northern and central Italy had begun crossing the Alps to do seasonal work. Many would work as field hands at harvest time, or as laborers. Others were skilled masons, and stonecutters, and quarrymen. At the end of the year they would return home with their savings. As travel became easier in the course of the nineteenth century, these migratory workers, or "swallows" as they termed themselves, became more adventurous. They went further afield. Italians built railroads in the Balkans, in Russia and in North Africa. They worked on the Suez Canal, and helped construct the first Aswan dam. Some of these men ultimately settled in the lands where they worked, often becoming shopkeepers or skilled craftsmen, so that by 1900 there were colonies of Italians throughout Europe and the Mediterranean basin.

By the middle of the nineteenth century, the focus of this seasonal immigration had begun shifting towards South America — and particularly towards Argentina, for a special reason. Argentina was below the equator. Its seasons were nearly the reverse of the Italian seasons, and this meant that the peasant laborer could till his fields and harvest his crops in Italy for one half of the year, and then work as a migratory farm laborer in Argentina the other half. Packing only a few clothes in a bag, these swallows, or *golondrinas* as the Argentines called them,[2] left Italy in October or November when the Italian harvest was finished. From November through April, they went from province to province in Argentina, harvesting wheat, corn, and other crops. In late April they sailed back to Italy for their own spring planting. Tens of thousands of Italian laborers made this crossing annually; some veteran *golondrinas* migrated twenty or more times.

As in Europe and North Africa, not all remained swallows. Some married local girls or they brought over their families, and so made their emigration permanent. As Nathan Glazer wrote,

Between 1860 and 1900 Italian immigration transformed the economy of Argentina, where many settlers of Spanish descent had disdained manual labor. A great stream of Italian laborers and farmers put the broad plains under plow, laid a railroad network, and built the city of Buenos Aires, largely along Italian lines. Almost half the immigrants to Argentina between 1857 and 1926 were Italians. The role of Italians in Brazil was also great, though in that enormous country they formed a much smaller proportion of the population. More than a third of all the immigrants to Brazil between 1884 and 1941 were Italians, and they were the single most numerous immigrant group.[3]

After 1880, Italian immigration began shifting towards its final, and greatest, goal — the United States. Italian immigrants to America in the 1880s and 1890s were chiefly seasonal laborers, swallows, humble commuters drawn to America by the labor needs of an expanding industrial system. As many as sixty percent returned to Italy at least once. Some went back and forth dozens of times. Meanwhile, the yearly number of Italian immigrants entering the United States swelled from 12,354 in 1880, to 100,135 in 1900.

It was relatively easy to come to America. The steamship companies were making so much money off the steerage traffic — clearing as much as $60,000 per one-way voyage — that they sent their own agents fanning out through the Italian countryside, offering jobs in America. If the peasant could raise the $30 fare — by mortgaging his house, or farm land if he had any — the shipping company would take care of the rest. No matter that these contracts were sometimes specious, and were illegal after 1885. They drew laborers. The peasant might hear about job prospects by word of mouth — someone from a neighboring village having just returned from *"laggiu,"* or "down there" as Italians invariably called the entire American continent, perhaps because they went first to South America in large numbers or perhaps simply because it was over the rim of the horizon. But the most powerful inducement of all was a letter from a member of the family who had gone over, and was now sending back for a brother, a cousin, or a friend.

Apart from the cost of the ticket, the immigrant needed very little money, just enough to survive his first few days in America in case his contract turned out to be fraudulent or he was unable to locate his relative, or friend. The average sum carried by Italian immigrants processed through Ellis Island — and this included families as well as single men, particularly in the years after 1900 — was a mere $17.

Once his ship had reached New York, the immigrant was ferried to Ellis Island and lined up with others in his same manifest group — there were thirty to a group and each person wore a name tag with a letter and number (e.g., Mario Rossi, C–5).[4] Going indoors, the immigrant shuffled nervously past a double row of medical examiners who would reach out every few minutes with a piece of chalk and mark a large X on someone's coat. This X was followed by another symbol or symbols: L meant lameness; CT, trachoma; G, goiter; H, heart; Pg, pregnancy; S, senility. Anyone with a chalk mark was shunted into a separate waiting room for a more thorough examination — by now sick with fear if nothing else. About fifteen percent of the immigrants were detained for medical reasons.

Then came the questioning, carried out as rapidly as possible by tired, harassed inspectors. The key question was number 21, regarding labor contracts. In an effort to protect the laborer from exploitation, a law was passed in 1885 making it illegal to recruit immigrants before they had entered the United States. An immigrant therefore had to reply to question 21 that no, he had not signed a contract, but yes, he had a job waiting for him. (Men nervously rehearsed this reply for days aboard ship.) The questioning done, the immigrant's money was counted and he was issued a card stamped *"admitted."* [5]

Now the immediate problem was to start working. The average $17 possessed by the Italian immigrant laborer might allow a single man to survive for two or even three weeks without work, but no longer than that. If he did not already have a job waiting for him, he quickly had to find one. This situation helped to create the class of middlemen called *padroni*.* An Italian lad from Naples who disembarked at the lower tip of Manhattan around the turn of the century described how he and another teen-age boy were recruited by a *padrone* named Bartolo, just minutes after they stepped off the ferry from Ellis Island:

We came to Brooklyn to a wooden house in Adams Street that was full of Italians from Naples. Bartolo [rented] a room on the third floor and there were fifteen men in the room, all boarding with him. He did the cooking on a stove in the middle of the room and there were beds all around the sides, one bed above another . . .

The next morning, early, Bartolo told us to go out and pick rags and get bottles. He gave us bags and hooks and showed us the ash barrels. On the streets where the fine houses are, the people are very careless and put out good things, like mattresses and umbrellas, clothes, hats, and boots. We brought all these to Bartolo, and he made them new again and sold them on the sidewalk. But mostly we brought rags and bones. The rags we had to wash in the back yard and then we hung them to dry on lines under the ceiling in our room. The bones we kept under the beds till Bartolo could find a man to buy them.

Most of the men in our room worked at digging the sewer. Bartolo got them the work and they paid him about one quarter of their wages. Then he charged them for board and he bought the clothes for them, too. So they got little money after all. Bartolo was always saying that the rent of the room was so high that he could not make anything, but he was really making plenty. He was what they call a *padrone* and is now a very rich man. The men that were living with him had just come to America and could not speak English — Bartolo told us all that we must work for him and that if we did not the police would come and put us in prison.

The worst of the *padroni*, men like Bartolo, were real flesh-peddlers. They recruited peasants either in southern Italy or at the Battery, stuck them into small, close-smelling rooms lined from floor to ceiling with bunks, and then took about sixty percent of their wages. If the men rebelled, they were threatened with the police. An Italian who wrote a bitter account of his experiences in America in the 1890s reported seeing *padroni* armed with rifles and pistols supervising ditch-digging gangs in the Five Points area of New York. The *padrone* system flourished for two reasons. Italian immigrants could not speak English. They could

* *Padrone* is "boss" in Italian.

not find work by themselves, nor discuss terms with an employer. Also, most of them had never been in a city before; they were bewildered and afraid. The *padrone* was usually able to exploit an immigrant for about two years. After that the man went back to his village in Italy, or learned enough English and acquired enough self-confidence in his American environment to threaten the *padrone* with the police — or simply to walk out on him.

Not all the *padroni* were evil. Some genuinely helped the arriving immigrant to find a job and helped him in moments of trouble with the law, or when he was in debt. But these "ethnic brokers" were in the minority. A fifteen-year-old boy recounted how he was hired in Ohio to work on a railroad gang:

> The boss said that if I wanted to work I would have to come to him, because Americans wouldn't hire any Italian except through him. I didn't want to sign up for four months' work. I was in a hurry to get back to New York, but my money was nearly gone. So I finally put my name down. The *padrone* wanted $6 *bossatura* [the fee for the boss], but as I had only $3 left, he took that and agreed to have the railroad company give him the other three out of my first pay envelope.

The boy told of what he found when he reached the railroad gang:

> There were nine dilapidated box cars, six for the half hundred men, one for the hand-cars, one for the tools, and the last for the *padrone* and time-keeper. I was allowed to live with them. Ours was the only car with windows. On both sides of the laborers' cars there were rusty tin boxes, propped up by stones. Heaps of rubbish covered the ground, and there was an awful stench. After the first day I often went among the men and talked with them in the evenings. You must remember there were no windows. The "dogs" did not need fresh air. As I entered one car for the first time, the odor choked me. I saw eight beds of boards placed across two boxes. On these lay bags of straw, and for a covering the men used old tan coats or horse blankets. The blankets were covered with vermin. Dirt of two years covered the mattresses.

The men got up at three every morning, washed themselves as best they could, and made themselves some coffee.

> Sharply at five o'clock the boss leaped from his car and began cursing at the men. The poor laborers trembled and hurried. In a moment five hand cars were on the rails. After riding six miles, we arrived at our destination. Amid more cursing the men took the cars off the track and began to tear up the old rails. In a few seconds the sweat was rolling in streams. The rails were

heavy and the men worked with might and main all morning. There was no
let-up, no mercy. From shortly after five until noon, about seven hours, the
men labored without rest. "The beasts," said the *padrone,* "must not be given
a rest, otherwise they will step over me." As the men silently appealed to him
for mercy, I was filled with pity, and often during the day tempted to beg the
padrone to let them rest. But how could I approach a raging maniac? He was
what the railroads wanted. After seven hours of the hardest labor the young
men had sausages and bread; the older men were satisfied with bread alone.
Yet, with nothing but coffee in the morning and bread at noon, these men
worked for ten hours every day under the blistering sun or in pouring rain.
Stopping work at four, the men returned to their ramshackle cars to cook, eat,
and sleep.

The boy added that many of these laborers were anarchists — not surprisingly.

In *I Trapiantati,* the Italian writer and journalist Giuseppe Prezzoloni
insisted that "the Italian immigrant who did not become a criminal, or
go mad, was a saint." But the immigrant from the south of Italy had
escaped conditions almost as pitiless as those just described. The Italian
immigrant endured. He persisted. He saved. If his pay was $1 a day,
which was a typical wage, he gave the *padrone* 60 cents, spent 15 cents
on tobacco, or whatever, and saved 25 cents. A man who works six days
a week and saves a quarter every day will have $150 after two or three
years. And usually, after two or three years in America, the Italian
laborer would go back to his native village to rest, to embrace his family,
sometimes to find a bride, and to boast a little after such a long fast of
humility.

One day he would reemerge among the olive trees, a small figure
walking up a well-remembered path — usually carrying the same suit-
case he had left with, now held together with string. He would stop
frequently to look at plots of land, his mind revolving backward to another existence. Then a shout of recognition would rise from some peasant working one of those plots, a cry, one of those rough, crooning yells
in dialect that every once in a while break the stillness of those hillsides.
Then a chain of cries surging up the hillside towards the village. And
the man was home.

The man's family, and all his relatives, would be spilling out of their
doorways now, making an impromptu procession to the foot of the village. Who can count the number of those reunions? That day, in the
returned immigrant's house, wine would be drunk and meat eaten.
Neighbors would call, trying to conceal their avid curiosity. How much

money had he brought back with him? Rumors were spread, to be analyzed minutely by all the village crones. The prodigal son might open his mouth in a belly laugh and reveal a *gold tooth*. Nothing stunned those poor villagers in the south of Italy more than the sight of a gold tooth, blinding in its substance. If a man could afford to put gold in his mouth, only the Devil knew how much he had secreted away in a bank.

The immigrant recounted his experiences. Old women who had never been farther than a mile from the village would sit nodding as they listened to descriptions of the hearty, hard-drinking Irish, the phlegmatic Poles and bearded Russians, and blacks, the old women turning to gaze at the horizon trying to imagine where these outlandish foreigners might live, beyond the ridge of what mountain. Many had never seen the ocean, and could not conceive it. The young males were the most eager listeners. A twelve-year-old boy in a village in southern Italy was already "grown up." His schooling was over. In economic terms, he was a man. In his dreams, when he listened to the tales of returned immigrants, he was already an immigrant.

The swallow might linger a while, pass the winter; even buy a plot of land or a house for his old age. But presently he would set forth again for America, and on the second or third trip he might take a wife with him. He knew the way now, the procedures. He could hold her hand and comfort her in the groaning, creaking, dark bowels of the ship during a night of storm, lead her through the maze of questions at Ellis Island to a home in the New World. In most cases, when the immigrant and his bride arrived at New York, they headed straight from the Battery about thirty blocks uptown to Mulberry Street.

Today, the Mulberry Street area is an unexceptional Lower Manhattan neighborhood. It is not very Italianate in its appearance, except for shop names; but it has character, and inside the aging brick façades of the tenements are comfortable, well-furnished apartments. Three-quarters of a century ago, when southern Italians were pouring in at the rate of hundreds per day, the "Mulberry Bend," as it was then called, was the worst slum in New York. A dozen immigrant populations had already passed through its fetid rooms by the time the Italians arrived.

The best descriptions of the Bend were written not by an Italian but by a Dane, Jacob Riis. He too had first come to America as a steerage passenger and an immigrant. After several years of semipoverty in New York, he had mastered English well enough to land a job as a police reporter for the New York *Tribune.* Riis had his office directly across the street from police headquarters, and the streets and back alleys of the Bend were his beat. "For years," he recorded, "I walked every morning between two o'clock and four o'clock the whole length of Mulberry Street, through the Bend and across the Five Points down to Fulton Ferry." [6] A compassionate observer, Riis deliberately set out to describe the horrors of slum life so that it would one day be eradicated. As he wrote in the preface to his best-known book, *How the Other Half Lives:*

Long ago it was said that one half of the world does not know how the other half lives. That was true then. It did not know because it did not care. The half that was on top cared little for the struggles, and less for the fate of those who were underneath, so long as it was able to hold them there and keep its own seat. There came a time when the discomfort and crowding below were so great, and the consequent upheavals so violent, that it was no longer an easy thing to do, and then the upper half fell to inquiring what was the matter.[7]

One of the New Yorkers who was most interested in finding out what was the matter, and what could be done about it, was Theodore Roosevelt, then serving as chairman of the New York Police Commission. The future President would often accompany Riis on his nocturnal walks through the Bend down to Fulton Ferry. "We were brothers in Mulberry Street," Riis wrote about those years, and he and Roosevelt remained lifelong friends.

"Where Mulberry Street crooks like an elbow," in Riis's phrase, was the Bend, "the foul core of New York's slums." [8] There, southern Italian immigrants lived in conditions as terrible as any depicted by Dickens in the slums of London earlier in the century. As Riis pointed out, the greatest crowding in Old London had been 175,816 persons per square mile. In the Lower East Side, there were 290,000 persons per square mile — and the Bend was the most crowded of all. In one tenement block containing 132 rooms lived 1,324 Italian immigrants — most of them male Sicilian laborers sleeping in tiers of bunks; over ten persons per room for an entire block. Riis reported "one room 12 × 12 with five families living in it, comprising twenty persons of both sexes and all ages, with only two beds, without partitions, screen, chair or table." [9]

These were the most dramatic examples. But the constant influx of new immigrants from Ellis Island meant that lodgings of any sort were always at a premium and rents were high. Out of his monthly wage of

$30, the Italian immigrant laborer paid $10 to $12 in rent for two or three miserable little rooms. During a survey of the Bend, city officials discovered that of 4,367 "flats," only nine were vacant.[10] The real meaning of those figures was that the owners of these tenements were under no economic pressure to improve them. Wallpaper hung in shreds. The hall sink and the squeaking water pump would be dry through the hot summer months. Many rear flats, whose windows gave out on narrow airshafts, had virtually no daylight at all — ever. The city finally stepped in and demolished the worst of these buildings.

From Mulberry Street itself, the Bend did not look that awful. It was colorful, animated. The "curious wanderer," having turned into Mulberry Street, entered "what might better be the market-place in some town in southern Italy than a street in New York," Riis wrote. Though the houses did not look Italian, being unmistakably New York tenements, the people were unmistakably Italian. "When the sun shines the entire population seeks the streets, carrying on its household work, its bargaining, its love-making on street or sidewalk, or idling there when it has nothing better to do. . . ." [11] Along the curb on either side of Mulberry Street was a double line of carts, dispensing none-too-fresh vegetables, secondhand pots and pans, chipped tableware, secondhand clothes — the commodities of the desperately poor. Women and girls wearing turbanlike bandannas, used for cushioning the weight of loads of firewood or produce that they carried on their heads, stood chatting in dialect as they might have in a southern Italian village. In the evenings the men, home from their jobs as laborers, stood in the doorways smoking clay pipes, or sat outdoors playing cards, while children ran screaming with excitement among the carts and tables.

But no amount of ebullience in the Italian spirit could entirely offset the grimness of life inside the tenements, where children struggled to survive and their mothers wept at night with their foreheads resting on the iron bars of the fire escape because they were homesick, because a child had just died and another was on the way. These women often made heroic efforts to keep their homes tidy and to give their children a sense of order, and of discipline. Riis described one flat where

five children slept with their elders. How many of those there were I never knew. There were three big family beds, and they nearly filled the room, leaving only patches of the mud floor visible. The walls were absolutely black with age and smoke. The plaster had fallen off in patches and there was green mold on the ceiling. And yet, with it all, with the swarm of squirming youngsters that were as black as the floor they rolled upon, there was evidence of a desperate, if hopeless, groping after order, even neatness. The beds were made up as nicely as they could be with the old quilts and pieces of carpet that served for covering. . . .[12]

Riis has left an indelible description of summer in the Bend:

With the first hot night in June, police dispatches that record the killing of men and women by rolling off roofs and window sills while asleep, announce that the time of greatest suffering among the poor is at hand. It is in hot weather, when life indoors is well-nigh unbearable, with cooking, sleeping, and working, all crowded into the small rooms together, that the tenement expands, reckless of all restraint. Then a strange and picturesque life moves upon the flat roofs. In the day and early evenings mothers air their babies there, the boys fly their kites from the house-tops, undismayed by police regulations, and the young men and girls court. . . . In the stifling July nights, when the big barracks are like fiery furnaces, their very walls giving out absorbed heat, men and women lic in restless, sweltering rows, panting for air and sleep. Then every truck in the street, every crowded fire-escape, becomes a bedroom, infinitely preferable to any the house affords. A cooling shower on such a night is hailed as a heaven-sent blessing in a hundred thousand homes.

Life in the tenements in July and August spells death to an army of little ones whom the doctor's skill is powerless to save. When the white badge of mourning flutters from every second door, sleepless mothers walk the streets in the grey of the early dawn, trying to stir a cooling breeze to fan the brow of the sick baby. There is no sadder sight than this patient devotion striving against fearfully hopeless odds.[13]

In one block in Mulberry Street, in 1888, the death rate for adults and older children was 15.78. For infants and children below the age of five it was 136.70.[14] In perpetually dark, airless rear tenements, as many as a third of all babies born died before their first birthday. In summer, Riis wrote, despite the efforts of special teams of doctors and nurses, "the grave-diggers in Calvary work over-time, and little coffins are stacked mountains high on the deck of the Charity Commissioners' boat when it makes its semi-weekly trips to the city cemetery." [15]

The majority of Italian immigrants to America spent their first years in this sort of purgatory — if not in the Bend then in similar slums in Boston, Philadelphia, or Chicago. What prevented their rapid exit was not merely the language barrier, but the fact that so many laborers from southern Italy had reached America illiterate or semiliterate. These men who crossed and recrossed oceans to find work could not even read a steamship ticket in their native Italian. Only those with exceptional energy were able to return home from a ten-hour day of ditchdigging or plastering and sit down with a grammar to learn English. This kept them tied to the Italian slum neighborhoods, where they could at least make themselves understood.

For all their hardships, however, as Riis conceded, these southern Italian laborers had powerful and fundamental virtues. They were the poorest immigrants in the city — and had one of the lowest rates of pauperism. Only a tiny fraction wound up on relief. If they could not find work digging (which, as peasants, they were accustomed to), they would go through ash barrels for usable rags, for bones, for objects that could be salvaged. Riis tells of gangs of southern Italians who actually paid Irish workmen to let them trim the garbage scows before they were towed down the river to the dump; in trimming the scows (which meant distributing the garbage evenly over the barge), they were able to find enough old clothes, rags, bones and other objects to enable them to maintain their families, and to survive.

Not only did most of these immigrants manage to put aside a little bit in savings every month, but the amounts that they sent back to their relatives in Italy in the form of postal remittances are staggering when one recalls that they were earning, many of them, $1 a day. The United States Immigration Commission reported in 1908 that during the preceding year Italian immigrants had sent $85 million in remittances to Italy. The figure is probably inflated, but there is no question that these remittances were in the area of tens of millions of dollars a year.* By World War I, Italian immigrants in America had sent nearly $750 million to their relatives in the mother country.[16]

This represented one of the benefits the Italian government derived from emigration. The toil of all those laboring backs and biceps became a vital source of income and of foreign currency for the fledgling kingdom of Italy. The other benefit was that immigration acted as a safety valve to forestall social turmoil during the years before World War I. Had this safety valve not existed, a class revolution might well have occurred first in Italy.

As the new century began, the rate of Italian immigration to the United States continued to rise. In 1903, it went over 200,000 for the first time. The peak year was 1907, when 285,731 Italians passed through New York and other American ports. In the first decade of the twentieth

---

* According to a New York *Times* story dated March 9, 1964, Italian-Americans were still sending $100 million per year to their relatives in Italy.

century, 2,045,877 Italians entered the United States. By 1921, when Congress passed the first Quota Act, the Italians had leapfrogged the Irish to become the second most numerous foreign stock in the American population after the German-Americans.

For many Italian immigrants, the Mulberry Bend and similar enclaves in other major ports — like Boston's North End — became their permanent destination in the United States. There they lived out their lives. But for other Italians the "Little Italies" of Boston and Providence, New York and Philadelphia were only temporary way stations to the larger, more open America that lay beyond the end of the trolley lines. Groups of Italians went up the Hudson to riverside towns like Piermont, or further north to Buffalo, Rochester, and Rome. Tens of thousands settled in the cities and towns of Connecticut and Rhode Island. Normally their migration was dictated by the availability of work. It was above all the railroad gang that first acquainted Italian immigrants with upstate New York. Stone quarrying created a community of Italians at Barre, Vermont. Others found jobs and established themselves in the mill towns of Massachusetts and New Hampshire, or in the coal towns of Pennsylvania, Ohio, and West Virginia.

In the cities and towns where they settled they clung together primarily because of their inability to speak fluent English and because they had only recently left those hilltop villages where all "strangers" were suspect. What reinforced this clannishness for years, however, was the amount of prejudice they encountered when they stepped outside their neighborhoods. Though many Italian immigrants made friends with other Americans, and a few became so wealthy and successful that they were able to shield themselves from prejudice, in the main the Italians were considered inferior, even contemptible, and — with four million of them pouring into the United States in the three decades between 1891 and 1920 — they were increasingly visible. No longer was the prevailing image of the Italian that of Garibaldi, or Avezzana, or "General" Luigi Palma di Cesnola. The nativist prejudice of the Know-Nothing 1840s and 1850s that had largely spared Italians because there were so few of them was now directed against them by all social classes and particularly by American workingmen, who saw in all these "dagoes" a threat to their livelihood and their values.

The extent of this prejudice has been partially forgotten by present Italian-Americans, which is natural. But it was all too real then. Between

1874 and 1915 thirty-nine Italians were lynched or shot by vigilantes in the United States. The worst of these attacks occurred in New Orleans, in 1891.

This was a city where Italians had done very well. It was where the Marquis Sant'Angelo had published the *Correo Atlantico,* where several Italians had become shipping or fruit-importing magnates, and also where a great many Sicilians had settled, working chiefly as fishermen, or as truck farmers on the outskirts of the city. They had brought the Mafia with them, but not in the form of organized crime. Their Mafia consisted chiefly of mayhem among themselves — feuds, vendettas, knifings, blackmail and extortion. When the New Orleans police chief was killed during an investigation into these Mafia activities, and evidence pointed to the Sicilians, a hysterical backlash against Italians occurred in the city. There were wholesale arrests. The mayor swore, "We must teach these people a lesson they will not forget for all time." [17] Ten Sicilians were arrested and brought to trial for having murdered the police chief and when a jury acquitted them, a mob that contained many of the city's most respectable men shot the Italian defendants to death in their cells. The eleventh Italian, whom the mob shot and then hanged while he was still alive, was in jail for some petty crime.

Many Americans approved. The New Orleans lynching marked the introduction of the Mafia as a symbol of fear and a threat to American values. The New York *Times,* while rebuking the mob for its "lawless and uncivilized" conduct, also concluded that "these sneaking and cowardly Sicilians, the descendants of bandits and assassins, who have transported to this country the lawless passions, the cut-throat practices, the oath-bound societies of their native country, are to us a pest without mitigation." [18] When the Italian government protested the lynchings, and requested an indemnity for the wives and children of the victims, Secretary of State James G. Blaine responded contemptuously. The Italian government then recalled its minister from Washington.

Internal hatred and external conflict now interacted directly, John Higham wrote in *Strangers in the Land,* producing an explosion of feeling against Italy and enormously magnifying the fear of Italian-Americans. A belief that the Italian fleet might suddenly descend on the United States gained fairly wide credence, and patriots flexed their muscles in preparation. Italians within the country now appeared as a potential fifth column; obviously these people could not be depended upon in times of national danger. There were reports of Italian immigrants riddling an American flag with bullets; a rumor circulated that several uniformed corps of Italians were drilling in New York.[19]

(This last would have been news to residents of the Bend.)

Three Italians were lynched in Hahnville, Louisiana, in 1896; five in Tallulah, Mississippi, in 1899. In 1895, six Italian laborers were lynched in Walsenburg, Colorado, following the murder of a saloonkeeper. Other acts of injustice, if not brutality, were inflicted on Italians in the 1880s and 1890s, like mass arrests following a knifing between hot-tempered Sicilian laborers. The victims of lynchings and punitive arrests were almost always southern Italians, who were not only feared as ignorant but also as swarthy, and dark. Even Ralph Waldo Emerson had rejoiced that early nineteenth-century immigration was bringing to America "the light complexion, the blue eyes of Europe," leaving behind, "the black eyes, the black drop, the Europe of Europe." [20]

But by 1900 the character of immigration had changed. Now a great many "black drops" were arriving from Europe, and a growing number of Americans sympathized with the emotions expressed by Thomas Bailey Aldrich in his poem "Unguarded Gates":

> *Wide open and unguarded stand our gates*
> *And through them presses a wild, motley throng*
> *Men from the Volga and the tartar steppes,*
> *Featureless figures of the Hoang-Ho,*
> *Malayan, Scythian, Teuton, Celt, and Slav,*
> *Flying the old world's poverty and scorn.* . . .[21]

Though southern Italians were not singled out among the wild, motley throng, clearly many Americans considered them both unpromising and dangerous. The Italians were not statistically more criminal than any other immigrant group. This is borne out by police records from Boston, Providence, and New York at the turn of the century. In Boston, where Italians constituted 7.0 percent of the foreign-born, their rate of arrest came to 6.1 percent of arrests of foreign-born residents. In Providence, where they constituted 11.2 percent of the foreign-born, their arrest rate was 10.8 percent. Only in New York, which contained the Bend, was Italian criminality slightly higher than average. Italians made up 11.5 percent of New York's foreign-born population, and their arrest rate was 12.3. But with the public already morbidly fascinated with the Mafia, and its Neapolitan counterpart, the Camorra, Italians

soon acquired a reputation as bloodthirsty criminals. . . . A penologist was wondering how the country could build prisons that Italians would not prefer to their own slum quarters. On the typical Italian, the prison expert commented: "The knife with which he cuts his bread he also uses to lop off another *Dago's* finger or ear. . . . He is quite as familiar with the sight of human blood as with the sight of the food he eats." [22]

Had Italian immigration to America been largely confined to middle-class exiles as it was in the first two-thirds of the nineteenth century, prejudice against the Italians might never have arisen. There might have been no use of "Dago," "Guinea," or "Wop." Racial prejudice is also class prejudice. The southern Italian was unwanted because he was ignorant or poor.

But now another kind of violence began to be associated with Italians in the public's mind. Because so many labor agitators were foreign-born, by the time the nineteenth century ended Americans had become intensely afraid of foreign ideologies. This fear first became widespread in 1877, when someone at a meeting in Chicago's Haymarket Square threw a bomb into police ranks, and police in reprisal shot down some forty or fifty strikers. The violence appalled America. As John Higham wrote, "For years the memory of Haymarket and the dread of imported anarchy haunted the American consciousness. No nativist image prevailed more widely than that of the immigrant as a lawless creature, given over to violence and disorder." [23]

The anarchist movement had deep roots in Italy, roots implanted by the Russian revolutionary Michael Bakunin during the period when he was contending with Karl Marx for control of the First International. Some Italian laborers, usually from the north of Italy, arrived in America already converted to the anarchist cause; others, usually southern immigrants, acquired anarchist ideas in America because of the conditions under which they worked and lived.

And so as the twentieth century began, with immigration from the south of Italy and Sicily assuming tidal proportions, the idea of the Italian as criminally inclined and the idea of the Italian as a dangerous political radical began to intersect.

9

Bread, and Roses

"STRIKE! STRIKE! STRIKE!" shouted the young Italian, waving his torn pay envelope in defiance. Down the long, dimly lit corridor he ran. Some workers remained at their looms; others swarmed around, taking up the cry.

"*Strike!*" A tall Syrian pulled a switch, turning off the speed belts that transmitted power to the machines.

Then the destruction began.

The Sicilians were carrying knives with them, and in a few minutes practically every belt had been slashed apart, the ends dangling from the pulleys. Gears were smashed as workers vented their frustration on the idle, silent looms. Windowpanes were kicked out.

It was Friday, January 12, 1912, and the great Lawrence textile strike, led by Italians, had begun.

The role of Italian immigrants in the labor struggles that convulsed American life in the last decades of the nineteenth century and up to the outbreak of World War I was initially slight. Though half a million of them had passed through Ellis Island by 1900, most were intent only on their personal survival and that of their families. To eat and sleep today and tomorrow was the limit of their ambition — as it had been in the arid lands of their birth. They possessed an atavistic sense of self-preservation developed amid injustices so permanent, so deep in their history that the idea of changing them through solidarity with other disadvantaged people took time to comprehend and accept. The irony is that, having entered a society that prided itself on competitiveness, they brought with them the psychological scars and deep-rooted diffidence of men who had been forced to compete against one another for the elemental right to live. Distrust of others, security only within the family and its network of blood relationships had been the first rule of survival in the villages of southern Italy, and Sicily. *Chi gioca solo non perde mai* was an ancient Sicilian maxim.[1] "The man who plays a lone hand never loses."

It was not surprising, therefore, to find that Italians often acted as scabs and strikebreakers. They helped the mineowners to ride out the Pennsylvania coal strike of 1887–1888. They helped to defeat a longshoreman's strike in 1887 and a Chicago meat packers' strike in 1904. They broke into the garment industry in New York and other cities because of their willingness to underbid other workers, and to step into jobs when other workers went on strike. An Irish employee in a textile plant complained: "These dagoes, who come to this country and takes the vittles right out of our mouths by workin' for nothing only wants more money to send home to Italy." [2]

The strike at Lawrence was a stunning reversal of this pattern. Not only were southern Italians, both men and women, the backbone of the strike, but they accepted the leadership of radical organizers from the controversial Industrial Workers of the World, or IWW. By 1912, many Italian immigrants had been in the country long enough to have been exposed to the idea of class solidarity. For people who had always believed that "the man who plays a lone hand never loses," the truly radical step was that of trusting strangers. At Lawrence, Massachusetts, Italian laborers not only linked arms with strangers but led them, passionate new converts to the idea of a brotherhood of workers.

At the time of the strike, Lawrence was the biggest textile manufacturing town in the world.[3] Located in northeastern Massachusetts, along the mill-bearing Merrimack River, it had 85,000 inhabitants, most of them immigrant millworkers whose pay for a fifty-six-hour week averaged $8.76.[4] The mills where they worked were owned chiefly by a huge trust, the American Woolen Company, which employed close to 40,000 people in Lawrence. Its 1911 output had been valued at $45 million. Though the mills paid their stockholders dividends every year of from seven to twenty percent, wages were at the subsistence level — and between 1890 and 1905, according to the U.S. Census, there had been an overall decrease of textile wages relative to production of twenty percent.[5]

Now, wages were to be cut directly. The Massachusetts legislature had humanely voted a reduction in the hours of work from fifty-six to fifty-four a week, and the millowners had humanely decided to pass on the reduction in their workers' pay envelopes.

Though immigrants from a dozen nationalities worked in the Lawrence mills, the majority were southern Italians. "Of all the mingled peoples of Lawrence," journalist Ray Stannard Baker wrote,

none are so humble as the Italians, none so eager for work at any price, and none so ill-paid. . . . When these people opened their envelopes, they found that there was a reduction of pay corresponding to two hours of work in a week — the price, perhaps, of three or four loaves of bread. A small matter, indeed, the comfortably fed outsider may observe, but in Lawrence, where many adult workers make only $6 to $7.50 a week, it is not an unimportant matter. A matter, indeed, of very great importance!

"It was like a spark of electricity," an overseer described it to me.

It changed instantly the discipline of years; it brought about a sudden wild confusion. One of the bosses, attempting to restore order with the threat formerly as potent as magic, shouted to one of the Italians:

"Tony, if you don't get back to your place, you'll lose your job."

"To hell with the job," responded Tony. "I'll pitch it."

And "pitch it" they did. They swept out of the mill, taking hundreds of others with them, they marched to the other mills and called out hundreds more. On the way, a few belts were cut, a few windows broken — losses not serious in themselves, but symbolic of the temper of the men, suggestive of future possibilities. And with marching and singing through the main streets of the town, the strike began.[6]

Before that morning, Lawrence had not been a fertile ground for labor organizers. The AFL United Textile Workers had organized some two thousand five hundred men into three locals, but at the time of the strike only about two hundred members were active. To the left of the AFL was the militantly anticapitalist IWW, whose members were known by the half-derogatory term of "Wobblies." Founded in Chicago in 1905, only seven years prior to the Lawrence strike, the IWW was growing in strength and influence. It preached the abolition of the wage-earning system, and sought ownership of the means of production by the workers themselves. Though some of its members were Marxists, and others anarchists, the IWW was a native American labor movement that had grown up in reaction to the often brutal working conditions, and miserable wages, of unskilled labor in the 1880s and 1890s. Its leader was William D. Haywood, a huge, unruly man whom his followers called "Big Bill."

The IWW chapter at Lawrence on the outbreak of the strike was barely larger than that of the AFL, with about three hundred dues-paying members. But, as Patrick Renshaw wrote, the Lawrence strike was made for the IWW. It involved a large number of poorly paid, unskilled immigrant laborers and it "came at a time when the socialist revolution seemed near, for it coincided with the climax of years of labor unrest in other countries." In Canada, Australia and New Zealand, as well as the United States, "1912 was a year of industrial turmoil. Even in the United States, Eugene Debs polled nearly one million votes as Socialist candidate for President. Encouraged by all these activities, the IWW went about its work at Lawrence with a will, and during the nine week strike it suddenly found its feet as a militant industrial union." [7]

That the foreign workers at Lawrence should have rallied so solidly behind the IWW was symbolic of their economic plight, and of their sense of being outcasts from the American promise. They had marched out of the mills in a spirit of revolt, and this remained the mood of the strike. "Better to starve fighting than to starve working!" was their initial slogan. [8] Baker wrote that some of the tenements in the drab slums of Lawrence were the worst he had ever seen. Rents and food prices were as high as those in New York. As Baker noted,

No man can support a family on $300 to $400 a year, even though he lives in the meanest way. The result was that the wife also had to go into the mills, followed by one child after another, as they arrived at the legal age. It took the combined earnings of many members of the family to feed and clothe the family. This meant the break-up of all decent family life and all effort towards real civilized development. It meant living in dark tenements; it meant taking in lodgers to the point of indecent crowding. [9]

When "Big Bill" Haywood arrived at the Lawrence station he was met by fifteen thousand cheering, surging workers. Haywood had had experience with foreign workers before. He knew they could understand little English, and so he made his points simply as he explained the difference between the AFL and the IWW. Holding up one of his huge hands with the fingers spread out, he would tell them, "The A.F.L. organizes like this," — naming his separate fingers — "weavers, loom fixers, dyers, spinners. . . ." Then he would bellow, "The I.W.W. organizes

like this" — clenching his fingers into a fist — shaking it at the bosses.[10]
It was the kind of crude, simple rhetoric even an illiterate immigrant
laborer had no trouble comprehending.

Because so many of the strikers were foreign-born — and the majority
of them Italians — the IWW dispatched a telegram to New York, summoning their twenty-seven-year-old Italian-American organizer, Joseph
Ettor. Brooklyn-born, stout and homely, with gentle, wide-set eyes and
a prominent nose, Ettor was a member of the IWW executive board.
He had been to Lawrence before and knew many of the Italian workers
personally.[11] He himself had been a worker on a railroad gang, in a saw-
mill, and in a San Francisco shipyard before joining the IWW in 1906.
He had helped lead strikes of West Coast miners and lumberjacks, had
led the foreign-born workers of the Pressed Steel Car Company in the
1909 McKees Rocks, Pennsylvania, strike, and the Brooklyn shoemakers
the year before Lawrence.[12] With him, Ettor brought along a friend —
Arturo Giovannitti, Italian-born poet and editor of the Italian Socialist
Federation's newspaper *Il Proletario*. A year older than Ettor at twenty-
eight, Giovannitti had never been to Lawrence and had never been in
the storm center of a major strike. His first reaction, when Ettor had
contacted him, had been to decline to go to Lawrence. He finally decided to accompany Ettor, but with a sense of foreboding.

Never before had mass picketing occurred in New England. Yet now
the radical, "un-American" IWW had moved in and taken command of
the strike. The reaction at the State House in Boston and in the courts
of the Commonwealth of Massachusetts was alarm. Stop the strikers at
once, magistrates warned, before the agitation spreads. Teach them a
lesson. Many of the native-born workers at Lawrence, including second-
generation Irish, were almost as hostile, and even the Italian middle-class
community in the town, consisting chiefly of small merchants and shopkeepers, refused to support the strikers. To show their disapproval of the
IWW, Lawrence citizens wore miniature American flags pinned to their
lapels or coats. The state militia was called out to reinforce state and
local police, patrolling the mills to guard them from further sabotage.
Each day, meanwhile, columns of strikers paraded down the main streets
of Lawrence behind American flags. Wearing long overcoats against the
bitterly cold weather, they shouted and sang. Now and then police
would move in, breaking up the lines, arresting strikers who resisted.
The militia was generally more hostile to the strikers than the Lawrence
police. One militia officer was quoted as saying in *Outlook* magazine:

"Most of our men had to leave Harvard [to go to Lawrence], but they rather enjoyed going down there to have a fling at those people." [13]

The first serious clash occurred on January 15. Some fifteen thousand strikers demonstrating outside the Prospect Mill were doused with ice-cold water by militiamen armed with fire hoses. Rather than breaking the strikers' will, the shock of that icy water infuriated the workers and made them even more determined to resist.[14] A near-battle ensued as workers from adjoining rooftops hurled chunks of ice down on the militiamen. In the pursuit, thirty-six strikers were arrested and most of them sentenced to a year in prison. Said one magistrate, when asked about the harshness of those rulings, "The only way we can teach them is to deal out the severest sentences." [15]

With public opinion solidly behind them, the millowners were confident of being able to suppress the strike eventually. But now some of them blundered hugely. In an attempt to frame the IWW, twenty sticks of dynamite were planted in three different locations — one of them next to a printer's shop where Ettor received his mail. But when IWW leaders pointed out that Boston newspapers had rushed into print with the story of the dynamite sticks even before they had been found in Lawrence, the police, after investigating, arrested a local businessman named John Breen. Breen was a prominent figure in Lawrence, the son of a former mayor and a member of the local school board, and his arrest became a lit fuse burning fitfully towards dynamite of another sort. What had started as an attempt to frame the IWW would turn into a scandal reaching deep into the Boston offices of the woolen trust.

On the day of Breen's arrest, however, an Italian woman striker, Anna LoPizzo, was shot to death in a melee as police broke up a picket line. The violence had followed a huge demonstration earlier in the day when Ettor had addressed the strikers at Lawrence Common. Though he was three miles from the picket line where Anna LoPizzo was shot, at a meeting of German strikers, Ettor was arrested as an accessory to the murder and charged, under the conspiracy law, with having created and provoked the violence. Arrested with him on the same charge was Arturo Giovannitti. The two young men, if convicted, faced long prison terms or even the electric chair.

Ettor's arrest did not cripple the strike. He had foreseen that eventuality, and had helped the strikers to organize their own executive committee, composed of two members from each of the nationalities represented among the workers. This committee met daily, and had become so effective that the arrest of Ettor and Giovannitti only strengthened the resolve of the strikers to hold out. Also, another Italian organizer, Carlo Tresca, now arrived to lead the IWW local. The strikers grimly continued picketing in the raw February and March weather. More militiamen had been called out to patrol the streets of Lawrence, and public meetings had been banned. Many of the strikers, though they lived in a textile center where surpluses of production were common, were thinly clad. To keep their spirits up, they marched behind American flags and they sang. Baker wrote: "It is the first strike I ever saw which sang. I shall not soon forget the curious lift, the strange sudden fire of the mingled nationalities at the strike meetings when they broke into the universal language of song. And not only at the meetings did they sing, but in the soup-houses and in the streets." [16] Women and girls marched beside their men. During the first weeks of the strike, Haywood had held "special meetings of women and children. He used simple, down to earth language and made sure the foreign-born workers understood him. He helped the women overcome their husbands' idea that women should stay at home and not go on the picketline or to the meetings. You are strikers as well as wives and mothers, he said, and you are just as brave fighters as your men." [17]

For all its cold, gray setting, the strike had a passion to it that moved every observer who went to Lawrence. It produced poetry as well as song. The women made banners for the picket line, and when the writer James Oppenheim saw young mill girls carrying a banner with the message, "We want bread and roses too," he wrote a poem for them. It was published under the title "Bread and Roses":

> *As we come marching, marching in the beauty of the day,*
> *A million darkened kitchens, a thousand mill lofts gray,*
> *Are touched with all the radiance that a sudden sun discloses,*
> *For the people hear us singing: "Bread and roses! Bread and*
> *roses!"*
>
> *As we come marching, marching, we battle too for men,*
> *For they are women's children, and we mother them again.*
> *Our lives shall not be sweated from birth until life closes;*
> *Hearts starve as well as bodies; give us bread, but give us roses!*
>
> *As we come marching, marching, unnumbered women dead*
> *Go crying through our singing their ancient cry for bread.*

Small art and love and beauty their drudging spirits knew.
Yes, it is bread we fight for — but we fight for roses too!

As we come marching, marching, we bring the greater days,
For the rising of the women means the rising of the race.
No more the drudge and idler — ten that toil where one reposes,
But a sharing of life's glories: Bread and roses! Bread and roses!

It was the immigrant women of Lawrence who finally broke open the strike. They sent their children away, to safety and sustenance. In part this was a tactic copied from Europe, where French and Italian strikers in similar circumstances had sent their children to board with sympathetic families in other cities. In part it was an imperative. The IWW strike fund was meager, and each family received only 33 cents a day with which to buy food and coal.[18] It was decided, as conditions deteriorated, to evacuate the children rather than go back to work on the millowners' terms.

On February 10, some 120 children were put aboard a train for New York, where they were met by three thousand members of the Italian Socialist Federation. When the train arrived at Grand Central Station, onlookers "wept as they saw the obvious signs of poverty and suffering these half-starved children had endured. Newspapers that had attacked the IWW suddenly turned the full blast of their criticism on the wool trust." [19] Many of the children had rickets, a bone disease caused by undernourishment. ("These children had been starving from birth," Haywood told a crowd at Cooper Union. "They had been starving in their mothers' wombs. And their mothers had been starving before the children were conceived." [20])

Aware that public opinion was beginning to shift in the strikers' favor, the Lawrence city fathers clumsily ordered that no more children could be evacuated. It was an unenforceable fiat, and on February 24 an incident so grotesque occurred at the Lawrence railroad station that it finally aroused the conscience of the nation. As 150 children prepared to board a train for Philadelphia, two companies of militia and some fifty policemen rushed into the station. According to sworn testimony by a member of the Philadelphia Womens' Committee:

When the time came to depart, the children, arranged in a long line, two by two in an orderly procession with the parents near at hand, were about to make their way to the train when the police . . . closed in on us with their clubs, beating right and left with no thought of the children who were in desperate danger of being trampled to death. The mothers and the children were thus hurled in a mass and bodily dragged to a military truck and even then clubbed, irrespective of [their] panic-stricken cries.[21]

Twenty-five women, including some who were pregnant, were arrested and booked on charges of neglect. Ten frightened children were packed off to the Lawrence Poor Farm. A cry of indignation rose from every part of America. New England's most distinguished literary figure, William Dean Howells, called it "an outrage; who could think it anything else?" The editor of the Kansas *Emporia Star*, William Allen White, concluded after a personal visit to Lawrence that "the strikers were justified, and there was no excuse for the violence by the police and the military." Samuel Gompers, the president of the AFL who had bitterly criticized the IWW for its radicalism at Lawrence, called the clubbings and arrests "a crime." The United States solicitor general, Frederick W. Lehmann, asked, as many Americans did, "What right did they have to do that? It is the right of any parent to send his children anywhere if he is guided by parental foresight and acting for their welfare." Even the Republican senator from Idaho who had prosecuted Big Bill Haywood in 1907, William Borah, termed the police and militia action, "an invasion of constitutional privilege." [22]

Spurred by thousands of letters and indignant editorials in the press, Congress opened an investigation. The wife of the President of the United States, Mrs. William Howard Taft, made it a point to attend. She was in the galleries when a pregnant woman striker testified how she had been beaten by police. Other strikers, male and female, showed their pay envelopes and described their working conditions. The committee also heard the testimony of fourteen-year-old Camella Teoli. One of the five children of an Italian textile worker, she was employed at the wool mill for $6.55 a week. But she had previously worked in another mill where she had been injured.

CHAIRMAN: Now, did you ever get hurt in the mill?
TEOLI: Yes.
CHAIRMAN: Tell us about it now, in your own way.
TEOLI: Well, I used to go to school, and then a man came up to my house and asked my father why I didn't go to work, so my father says I don't know whether she is 13 or 14 years old. So, the man say you give me $4 and I will make the papers come from the old country saying you are 14. So my father gave him the $4 and in one month came the papers that I

was 14. I went to work and [in] about two weeks got hurt in my head.
CHAIRMAN: How did you get hurt, and where were you hurt in the head; explain that to the committee.
TEOLI: I got hurt in Washington.
CHAIRMAN: In the Washington Mill?
TEOLI: Yes sir.
CHAIRMAN: What part of your head?
TEOLI: My head.
CHAIRMAN: Well, how were you hurt?
TEOLI: The machine pulled my scalp off
CHAIRMAN: The machine pulled your scalp off?
TEOLI: Yes sir.
CHAIRMAN: How long ago was that?
TEOLI: A year ago, or about a year ago.
CHAIRMAN: Were you in the hospital after that?
TEOLI: I was in the hospital seven months.[23]

Low salaries. Abuses (such as having a week's pay withheld every year). Hazardous working conditions. The Lawrence strike marked a turning point in the history of American labor. As a result of the congressional hearings, President Taft approved a nationwide investigation into working conditions. For the first time the trade union movement gained widespread sympathy.

The millowners, who had started in a dominant position, were now becoming aware of the force of public opinion in a democracy. Fearful that Congress would cut the high tariffs on imported textiles, the giant American Woolen Company capitulated on March 12, agreeing to all the strikers' demands. By the end of March the smaller textile firms had followed. Wages were raised from five to twenty percent not only in Lawrence but in mills throughout New England, though the millowners were able to partly offset these wage increases by speeding up their machines.[24]

The great Lawrence strike was over. There remained one piece of unfinished business. Ettor and Giovannitti were still in jail, awaiting trial for a crime they had obviously not committed.

It may be said for the prison system of Massachusetts, at least at that time, that no attempt was made to stifle the voices of these two "anarchists." Ettor and Giovannitti turned "their jail cells into studies. They read through the warden's library and then the books — Paine, Carlyle, Shelley, Byron, Kant — sent in by sympathizers. Ettor, interested in organizational methods, requested Burke. Giovannitti held what he called his 'afternoon matinees,' reading an annotated edition of Shakespeare that had been sent to him by a Harvard student." [25]

Though Ettor was an eloquent spokesman of the workers' movement and a man of courage, Giovannitti was the more fascinating of the two. He saw himself as a Byronic man, a poet, an individualist, an aristocrat of mind and tastes drawn by a powerful feeling of sympathy to the Socialist cause. As he had written in an introspective poem called "Atavism":

> *My mother's sires were men of solemn looks,*
> *Long-haired, bewigged, lace-collared and rapiered,*
> *Who served the King, obeyed the Pope and feared*
> *Nothing, save God and books.*
>
> *My father's folks were of the common sap,*
> *Poachers and court physicians, and such breed,*
> *Who had nothing but princely veins to bleed*
> *And royal game to trap.*
>
> *And thus, entangled in such strange discords,*
> *In strange contrasts my twofold nature raves,*
> *And now it loves to kick and flog the slaves,*
> *And now to hang their lords.*[26]

Born in the Abruzzi, in a tiny village near Campobasso, he was, as the poem indicated, the son of a druggist who also served as the village physician. The boy emigrated to Canada in 1900, at the age of seventeen — probably under some pressure from the police since, like other Italian students at the turn of the century, he had become attracted to anarchism.

After living in Canada for several years, where he worked briefly on a railroad gang and attended McGill University, Giovannitti came to New York. He took courses at Columbia and though he never graduated he was a brilliant linguist, able to speak and read Italian, French, Spanish, English and Latin. After working for a few months as a miner in Pennsylvania, he returned to New York and began editing *Il Proletario*. At the time of his arrest in Lawrence, he was deeply in love with, and engaged to, the daughter of Russian-Jewish immigrants. When her parents moved to St. Paul, Minnesota, she remained in New York to live with him.

Giovannitti was a dashing and flamboyant figure. Dark, with patrician good looks, just under six feet tall, he wore a velvet jacket, a Byronic collar and large, scarflike cravats. People who saw him and heard him for the first time took him for an English lord rather than an Italian immigrant. His language was rich, and fabulous. (Once in New York he had used the word "succor" in conversation with a striking truck driver, and had received a black eye in return.)

While in prison Giovannitti wrote a dozen poems that were reprinted in literary magazines throughout the United States. One of them, "The Walker," aroused great admiration when it was published. Writing in *Forum*, critic Kenneth McGowan said that in this poem, Giovannitti had "painted the prison as no man, not even Wilde, has done." Though its Whitmanesque style is somewhat dated, the poem is still believable and strong.

When Ettor and Giovannitti remained in jail throughout the spring, summer, and then fall of 1912, without a date for their trial being set, the case began to ignite protests in America and overseas. The Socialist candidate for President, Eugene Debs, had already sent the prisoners a fiery telegram: "CONGRATULATIONS. VICTORY IS IN SIGHT. THE WORKING CLASS WILL BACK YOU TO A FINISH IN YOUR FIGHT AGAINST PEONAGE AND STARVATION," it read in part. He continued to call for their release.

Though the IWW had insisted all along that Anna LoPizzo had been shot by a policeman, in April an Italian millworker, Joseph Caruso, was arrested and charged with the crime. While he had taken part in the strike, Caruso was a simple workingman. He was not a labor organizer like Ettor or a poet like Giovannitti and held no strong political views. As weeks passed without the three defendants being brought to trial, demonstrations were held in several American cities. In New York, Haywood and Elizabeth Gurley Flynn led some twenty-five thousand marchers from Union Square up Seventh Avenue, while in Boston demonstrators covered the Common. Sixty thousand dollars was raised as a legal defense fund.[27]

Meanwhile, in midsummer, the truth about the dynamite plot emerged. The contractor who had built the Wood Mill of the American Woolen Company, Ernest Pitman, confessed to the district attorney that plans for framing the IWW had been worked out in the Boston offices of the Lawrence textile companies. Ordered to testify before a grand jury, Pitman committed suicide. The president of the American Woolen Company, William N. Wood, was implicated in the plot.[28] Wood was ironically the son of an immigrant Portuguese fisherman from the Azores, who had worked his way up on sheer ability and had married the boss's daughter. He was a millionaire now. After Pitman's death, Wood was exonerated in court.[29] But the scandal again emphasized the injustice of keeping Ettor and Giovannitti, who were innocent of any physical crime, locked up in prison while the man who had planted sticks of dynamite around Lawrence, John Breen, had long since been released with a $500 fine.[30]

After fifteen thousand Lawrence workers had staged a twenty-four-hour sympathy strike, and with Haywood threatening a general strike throughout the country, the Commonwealth of Massachusetts at last brought the three defendants to trial at the end of September. The trial was held at Salem, and in a judicial procedure of the era that seemed in keeping with that city's worst traditions, the defendants were manacled together in a large green iron cage in the courtroom. This increased the sympathy that many Americans already felt towards the defendants — partly as a result of Giovannitti's poems. Crowds of people massed outside the courtroom every afternoon to cheer on the three Italians as they were led from the cage back to their prison cells. Dockers in France and Sweden threatened to boycott American ships unless the men were acquitted, and in Milan a mass rally was led by a young Socialist firebrand named Benito Mussolini.*

The lawyer who defended Ettor and Giovannitti was courtly James Sisk of Massachusetts. But the marshalling of witnesses and evidence was mostly handled by a flamboyant young lawyer from Spokane, Washington, Fred C. Moore. At the outset of his career Moore had been an ambitious West Coast company lawyer. But then he had dropped out to become a defender of radical causes and the legal Lochinvar of the

---

* After Mussolini had seized power in 1922 and become the Fascist Duce, Giovannitti, now his bitter enemy, would write prophetically:

> *A man may lose his soul for just one day*
> *Of splendor and be still accounted wise,*
> *Or he may waste his life in a disguise*
> *Like kings and priests and jesters, and still may*
>
> *Be saved and held a hero if the play*
> *Is all he knew. But what of him who tries*
> *With truth and fails, and then wins fame with lies?*
> *How shall he know what history will say?* [31]

IWW. Nine years later, at Dedham, Massachusetts, he would defend two other Italians also charged with murder by the same commonwealth — Bartolomeo Vanzetti and Nicola Sacco. His role in that case would be bitterly controversial.

At Salem he was less in evidence, though his investigative work all but destroyed the state's case. Company detectives who swore that they had heard Giovannitti urging strikers, during a rally, to "sleep in the daytime and prowl around like wild beasts at night," [32] were forced to admit they knew no Italian; Giovannitti's speech on that occasion had been delivered in Italian. Witnesses testified that Joseph Caruso was home eating supper at the time Anna LoPizzo was killed. Caruso said he was not an IWW member and had never even heard Ettor or Giovannitti speak during the early days of the strike. He added truculently, however, that the first thing he would do if he got out of jail would be to join the Wobblies.[33]

The issue was simply one of freedom of speech — whether belief in syndicalism was a capital crime in the Commonwealth of Massachusetts. Both Ettor and Giovannitti were allowed to make closing statements to the jury. Ettor said in part:

Does [the district attorney] believe for a moment that, beginning with Spartacus, whose men were crucified for miles along the Appian Way, and following with Christ, who was adjudged an enemy of the Roman social order and put on the cross — does he believe for a moment that the cross or the gallows or the guillotine, the hangman's noose, ever settled an idea? It never did.

If the idea can live it lives, because history adjudges it right. And what has been considered an idea constituting a social crime in one age, has in the next age become the very religion of humanity. The social criminals of one age have become the saints of the next.

The District Attorney talks to you about Massachusetts. Sixty years ago, gentlemen — seventy years ago — the respectable mob — not the mob in the mills but the respectable mob, the well dressed mob — dragged the propagandists and agents of a new social order and a new idea through the streets of Boston, and the members of that same respectable mob now — now that the ideas of Wendell Phillips have been materialized into something, now that the ideas of Garrison* and the rest have been proven of value, the off-spring of that social mob rises up and says, "The traditions of Massachusetts."

Gentlemen, the traditions of Massachusetts have been made by those who made them and not by those who speak of them. John Brown was hanged

---

* Wendell Phillips (1811–1884) and William Lloyd Garrison (1805–1879) were reformers and militant abolitionists.

and the cry went up, "a social criminal," — not even that dignity to him — just a criminal. Within two years the youngest, and the noblest, the strongest this nation could offer, were marching through the fields of this country singing:

> *John Brown's body lies mouldering in the grave*
> *But his soul goes marching on.*

My ideas are what they are, gentlemen. They might be indicted and you might believe, as the District Attorney has suggested, that you pass judgement and that you can choke them; but you can't. Ideas can't be choked.[34]

Then it was Giovannitti's turn. Dressed with his customary elegance in Byronic collar and Beau Brummel tie, he faced the jury members and told them solemnly that he was about to make his first speech in the English language. This was not strictly true; it was a piece of poetic license. But the remark had its effect and the speech itself was so spellbinding, delivered in Giovannitti's calm, beautiful voice, that a veteran newspaperman came out of the courtroom afterwards shaking his head and saying, "in twenty years of reporting I have never heard the equal of that speech." [35] Personal magnetism was an element that Giovannitti possessed in abundance; present in that Salem courtroom, it is now missing, on paper, sixty years later. But the courage of the speech is still intact, when one remembers that it was spoken by a young man on trial for his life. In closing he told the jury:

Weigh both sides and then judge. And if it be, gentlemen of the jury, that your judgement shall be that this gate will be opened and that we shall pass out of it and go back into the sunlit world, then let me assure you of what you are doing. Let me tell you that the first strike that breaks out again in this Commonwealth or any other place in America where the word and the help and the intelligence of Joseph Ettor and Arturo Giovannitti will be needed and necessary, there we shall go again regardless of any fear and of any threat.

We shall return again to our humble efforts, obscure, humble, unknown, misunderstood — soldiers of this mighty army of the working class of the world, which out of the shadows and the darkness of the past is striving towards the destined goal which is the emancipation of human kind, which is the establishment of love and brotherhood and justice for every man and woman in this earth.

On the other hand, if your verdict shall be the contrary . . . if it be that these hearts of ours must be stilled on the same death chair and by the same current of fire that has destroyed the life of the wife murderer and the parricide, then I say, gentlemen of the jury, that tomorrow we shall pass into a greater judgement, that tomorrow we shall go from your presence into a presence where history shall give its last word to us.[36]

On November 25, the jury began its deliberations. The next day it acquitted the three defendants of all charges.

Though Italian radicalism in the United States has become almost synonymous with the Sacco-Vanzetti trial in 1921, which resulted, after worldwide agitation and long appeals, in the execution of the two men for a dubiously proven crime, its high watermark actually came about ten years earlier, with the Lawrence strike and a similar mass strike the following winter at Paterson, New Jersey, again involving Italian mill-workers and the IWW.

The Paterson strike was Lawrence all over again, but in more savage form. A textile town of 123,000 people, fifteen miles from New York, Paterson "had a reputation as a 'hot bed' of anarchism." [37] There had been a flourishing and sometimes violent anarchist movement among Italian workers in Paterson for many years. A young Paterson anarchist, Gaetano Bresci, had returned to Italy in 1900 and had shot to death the Italian king, Umberto I, in a crime planned in New Jersey. Because of these antecedents, Paterson was already torn by seething hatreds, and when twenty-five thousand workers went out on strike in February 1913, closing down three hundred mills, a confrontation was almost inevitable. In an outburst of repression, two Italian workers were shot to death and no less than one thousand three hundred strikers arrested in picket line clashes with the police.[38] IWW leaders were arrested, including Patrick Quinlan who received a sentence of between two and seven years. Despite a lavish "red" pageant staged at Madison Square Garden by the IWW on behalf of the workers, which drew fifteen thousand people, the strike ultimately failed. By midsummer, the millworkers, hungry, depressed and frightened, abandoned the IWW and agreed to negotiate shop-by-shop settlements with the millowners.

Two factors now intervened to deprive the syndicalist movement of the 1900s and early 1910s of its strength. One was the First World War, which made industrial strikes look like deliberate acts of treason (a U.S. senator charged at the time that IWW stood for Imperial Wilhelm's Warriors). On September 5, 1917, the Department of Justice staged simultaneous raids on forty-eight IWW locals across the country, seizing files, pamphlets, and other documents.[39] On the twenty-eighth of September, 165 IWW leaders were indicted on various counts. By that time Ettor, Giovannitti and Carlo Tresca had resigned from the movement because of conflicts over policy; though Ettor and Giovannitti were both arrested, they were released, along with Tresca, on the grounds that they had left the IWW prior to the period covered by the indictment. But 101 defendants, including Haywood, were tried, found guilty, and sentenced to long penitentiary terms and a total of $2.5 million in fines. During the "anti-Red" hysteria that followed World War I, several IWW leaders including one veteran were lynched, and hundreds beaten.

The other factor was the Bolshevik revolution. Though most Italian and Italian-American anarchists were initially enthusiastic over the "worker's state," the 1920s and the 1930s were a time of growing disillusionment with the Communist system in Russia. This was particularly true in the 1930s. While in America the reforms carried out by the New Deal improved the life of the common man and abolished many of the injustices that had brought the anarchist and the syndicalist movements into being, the brutality of the Stalin era in Russia, with its Kafkaesque trials and millions shipped to Arctic concentration camps, caused most Italian socialists and radicals in the United States to draw closer in their thinking to the values of the western democracies. By the outbreak of World War II, their enemy was no longer primarily American capitalism but Italian fascism and, in many cases, Soviet communism.

10

"Il Grande Far West"

THE IMMIGRANTS who settled in New York, in Providence or in Boston still hugged the Atlantic. They were on the other side of the ocean from Europe but even so, only water and sky separated them from the Old World. That ocean was like a pane of blue-green glass in the minds of homesick women during their first few years in America. The same rolling beast that had carried them to New York harbor, their hearts like butterflies in its great iron gut, could bear them home again for the price of a steerage ticket.

It took much more strength, after having reached New York with only $17 and the memory of a long, frightening crossing, to uproot oneself again and move west, towards the Pacific — an ocean far removed from Europe, facing distant Asia. Though great handfuls of Italian laborers were constantly flung by their *padroni* into the American plains, working on railroad gangs and other construction jobs, most of them trickled back to the East Coast and into the Italian tenement slums, or drifted into the Italian neighborhoods of Chicago, or Indianapolis, or Kansas City.

Going to the Far West was usually a question of superior strength, ambition, and resources. The very size of the continent, not yet bridged by highways and air routes, inhibited Italians from leaving their neighborhoods in the Eastern cities. But the Italians who did manage to cross the Mississippi and settle in the West usually had a far better chance of rising economically and socially. They were newcomers in an opportunistic, if frequently dangerous, world of newcomers — the homesteaders, miners, and cowboys of the West in the late nineteenth century. As Andrew F. Rolle has written, "What proved to be more important than nationality were such more tangible matters as how well a man integrated himself into frontier life; how quickly he could put up a house or clear a field; how well he could break the sod. These qualities frequently determined acceptance. In this sense the frontier did not coerce, it emancipated." [1]

Though their number was limited to a few thousand everywhere except in California, Italians did play a role in the history of the American West. Among the earliest white men to follow Lewis and Clark into the Northwest were Italian Jesuits, like the Roman-born Gregorio Mengarini who built Montana's first church in the 1840s and studied the language and culture of the mountain tribes.[2] In 1877 he published his *Dictionary of the Kalispel or Flat-Head Indian Language*. A Sicilian-born Jesuit, Cataldo, taught himself nearly twenty Indian languages and dialects, and helped negotiate a truce in the Nez Percé war of 1877.[3] (Cataldo, Idaho, is named for him.) Father Anthony Ravalli of Ferrara, who had studied medicine in Italy, served as a physician and surgeon to the Montana tribes. "For decades Ravalli, in boots and long overcoat, with a breviary in his pocket, medicine and surgical instruments in his saddlebags, was a familiar figure as he rode an Indian pony through winter snows and summer heat to minister to the sick and injured." [4]

The lone survivor of General George Armstrong Custer's doomed column at the Battle of the Little Bighorn was an Italian immigrant lad, Custer's trumpeter John Martini. Before leading his two hundred men on their fatal charge, Custer gave Martini an oral message for Captain Frederick Benteen that his adjutant wrote out: BENTEEN: Come on. Big village. Be quick. Bring packs.[5] Martini galloped alone, over miles of grasslands until his horse was near collapse; he did deliver the message to Benteen, but by then Custer and his men were being massacred. Another Italian who fought in the same battle as a U.S. cavalryman was Lieutenant Charles Camilius DeRudio, a veteran of the defense of Rome in 1849. DeRudio, who was in Major Reno's command, also survived.

One of the most famous cowboys in the West during the climactic period of the cattle drives was the son of an Italian immigrant who had settled in Texas. "Charlie" Siringo (baptized Angelo Siringo) started herding longhorns for cattle baron "Shanghai" Pierce when he was in his teens. For ten years he drove herds of cattle up to the Kansas cow-towns. He went into Mexico after cattle thieves, and he led the posse that captured Billy the Kid at Stinking Springs. By 1883, however, Siringo had grown weary of the saddle, and he opened a store in Cald-well, Kansas. One of his advertisements in the local newspaper read: "Charlie Siringo wants every cowpuncher, nester, and Chinaman in the United States to know that he makes a specialty of fine cigars and to-bacco." A year later, he started writing the story of his adventures. This autobiography, entitled *A Texas Cowboy, Or Fifteen Years on the Hur-ricane Deck of a Spanish Pony,* was an anecdotal but accurate descrip-tion of the cowboys' life, and, as such, the first true "western." It sold nearly a million copies and became known throughout the West as the cowboy's Bible.[6] In fact, some cowboys never read anything in their lives but Siringo's book and probably some verses from the Bible itself.

Italian laborers worked on track-laying gangs in the western United States and in Canada during the building of the transcontinental rail-roads. They toiled as miners or stone-quarriers in the Rockies. The largest block of marble ever processed, used to make the Tomb of the Unknown Soldier in Washington, D.C., was worked and polished by Italians in Colorado.[7] There were even Italian families, recruited in Liguria and Piedmont, among the Mormon pioneers in Utah. But to most Italian immigrants, the American West meant one state — Cali-fornia. In the eyes of Italians it was superior to any other part of the New World. Up around the bay and beautiful city named for their most be-loved saint, St. Francis of Assisi, they found their best home of many immigrant homes in many countries.

Before the Union Pacific's transcontinental line was opened in 1869, a traveler from Italy bound for California had to round Cape Horn and come up the west coast of South America past Mexico. It was usually a journey of several months. This was the itinerary of Richard Henry Dana, son of the United States chargé d'affaires to the Court of Catherine the Great, Francis Dana; in 1840, Richard Henry Dana published his classic account of this journey, *Two Years Before the Mast.* While sailing off the Monterey coast in the 1830s, Dana had encountered Italian fisher-men "in blue jackets [and] scarlet caps . . . singing beautiful Italian boat songs all the way in fine full chorus." Ashore Dana saw "three or four Italian sailors mounted and riding up and down the beach on the hard sand at a furious rate." [8]

Of all migrants, fishermen are at once the most mobile and self-sufficient. The sea is their broad highway. They can pay for their journey by selling the fish they catch, and they themselves can subsist on fish. In the 1820s and 1830s, San Francisco Bay was already full of Genoese and Sicilian *feluccas,* and Chinese junks, along with Russian fishing boats. The state was still Mexican territory; not until 1848 was California ceded to the United States by the treaty of Guadalupe Hidalgo. What drew all these fishermen to San Francisco were some of the best fishing grounds in the world. The Chinese specialized in shrimp fishing, even shipping four-fifths of their catch back to China to be marketed there.[9] The Russians went after salmon and shad. The Italians, ranging as far north as Alaska, where they competed with the Russians for salmon, caught every kind of fish and shellfish.* North Beach, the Italian area of San Francisco, was contiguous to the fishing wharves and remains Italian today despite Bohemian inroads.

The gold rush of 1849, following hard on California's Americanization, attracted some Italian adventurers. But the predominant Italian tradition in California is agricultural, and it dates to the 1850s, 1860s, and 1870s. When immigrants from the north of Italy reached the state, many of them were prosperous enough to buy land in the fertile and beautiful valleys of northern California, what the Spaniards called *Alta California*. There had always been a kind of mystique about California in European eyes. The word itself was created by the Spanish dramatist Ordonez De Montalvo in 1510,[10] just after Columbus's discovery of the New World, to designate a fabulous island ruled by Amazons and situated near the center of the Earthly Paradise. By 1840, Genoese sailors serving aboard vessels of a dozen nationalities had spread word of the area's fecundity and charm throughout their native province of Liguria. A "chain" of immigration developed, consisting in part of fishermen and their families from Rapallo, Portofino, Camogli and other Ligurian fishing ports, and in part of affluent middle-class landowners determined to establish ranches in California. This is why the California wine industry was built largely by Genoese, though the province of Liguria, apart from a few excellent dry white wines grown on terraced slopes above the sea, is not a major Italian wine-producing area.

The most interesting of these Ligurians, and the first of two brilliant populist bankers among the Italians in San Francisco, was Andrea Sbar-

---

* San Francisco was only one of a series of major Italian fishing communities. Others were Boston, Tampa, New Orleans and Galveston, Monterey and Astoria, Oregon.

boro. Born in Genoa of well-to-do parents who moved to San Francisco in 1852, he established some of the first immigrant building and loan associations in California. By making small monthly deposits, his Italian clients could borrow money with which to buy land and build their own homes. Many *padroni* of course had run the same kind of money-lending operation, generally charging very high interest rates. But Sbarboro's ideas were of a different order entirely.

He was a reformer, in part inspired by Mazzini's social theories and in part by the ideas of the English utopian Robert Owen, who had established an experimental factory complex in New Lanark, Scotland, early in the nineteenth century, providing his workers with housing, schools, and nurseries.[11]

Sbarboro's dream was to found a cooperative vineyard in California along the lines of New Lanark where he could settle about a thousand unemployed Italian immigrants. He was already well known among San Francisco's Italians as a social activist. In his twenties, he had founded a night school for the Sicilian fishermen of North Beach and their children, even writing his own textbook. He had helped other Italian immigrants to buy farmland and equipment. Now, as a successful banker, he was able to raise the capital to establish the vineyard. With two partners, he bought a fifteen hundred-acre tract of rolling hill country in the Sonoma Valley, about a hundred miles north of San Francisco. Because a number of his prospective workers had emigrated from the Italian-speaking part of Switzerland, the Ticino (which had been part of the Duchy of Milan until the Italian wars in the late Renaissance), Sbarboro called his cooperative the Italian-Swiss Agricultural Colony.

The heart of Sbarboro's plan for the vineyard was to issue stock to the workers and therefore — as Mazzini had preached — to make them joint owners in the enterprise. In exchange for a small monthly deduction from his wages, the worker in the cooperative would receive shares that could either be held for their value or exchanged for acreage which the worker could then farm independently. The trouble was that while prospective workers were satisfied with the pay of $30 to $40 a month in addition to housing, food and wine, they flatly objected to the notion of having even a portion of their pay withheld — and finally Sbarboro, though disappointed, had to modify his plan.

The workers unwisely spurned Sbarboro's offer, since the Italian-Swiss vineyard was more successful than even its founder could have foreseen. Stock worth $135,000 when it was issued in 1880 was worth an estimated $3 million by 1910, thirty years later.[12]

For a while, it seemed the workers' skepticism might be justified. What Sbarboro and his partners had bought was a sheep range, forested with oak trees that had to be cut down and uprooted. More capital was raised for this clearing operation. When the vines were planted — imported cuttings from the leading vineyards of France, Italy, and Germany — they were almost immediately attacked by phylloxera, the plant disease that had already ravaged the vineyards of southern Italy during the nineteenth century. The Russian River overflowed several years in succession, swamping the lower slopes. Finally, Sbarboro's marketing plan had been to produce table grapes, which in the 1870s were selling at around $30 per ton; but by the time the Italian-Swiss colony's first grapes had been harvested, the price had fallen to $8 a ton because of overproduction. At that point, the colony's directors had no choice but to switch to making wine. Within a few years their wine chemist, the Piedmontese Pietro Rossi, had produced a good vintage and by 1890 the colony was a success. Sbarboro set up a merchandising network that made Italian-Swiss wines available nationally. Production grew so rapidly that by 1897 there was no longer "enough barrel cooperage in all California to hold it. Sbarboro, therefore, ordered a reservoir built in solid rock which became the largest wine tank in the world. It was eighty-four feet long, thirty-four feet wide, and twenty-five feet high; its highly glazed surfaces held five hundred gallons of wine." [13]

Other Italians did very well in agriculture, establishing million-dollar businesses in California. Joseph and Rosario di Giorgio developed such vast fruit orchards in the San Joaquin Valley that they ultimately became the world's largest shippers of fresh fruit, controlling more than forty thousand acres spread over California, and extending into Mexico and Central and South America. Their fruit was canned under the S & W label. Marco J. Fontana, who arrived from Italy in 1859, founded the California Fruit Packing Corporation, or Calpac, which became the largest fruit and vegetable canning organization in the world. By 1965, its annual sales had reached about $400 million. Fontana, too, was a Ligurian. With another Genoese, Antonio Cerruti, he started a canning company under the name Marca del Monte (in English, "brand of the mountain"), which was later shortened to Del Monte.[14] Julio and Ernest Gallo, the sons of an immigrant from Piedmont, today own one of the country's largest privately held firms and produce nearly half of all California wines. The Gallo winery had revenues of $250 million in 1971.

As Italian farmers and fishermen prospered in northern California, they began to bank their money in Italian savings and loan associations. There were quite a number of these by the turn of the century; Sbarboro alone had founded half a dozen. In 1899, he started the Italian-American Bank. But he was overshadowed as a banker by still another Genoese, Amadeo Giannini.

The third week in April 1906, was a time of special excitement for San Francisco's Italians. The great Caruso was in town for the first time. It was a significant event for other San Franciscans also, since no form of entertainment was more popular in the West at the turn of the century than grand opera, and no social commingling quite as glamorous as a gala performance in the opera house. Divas like Adelina Patti and Luisa Tetrazzini were more famous than actresses. Patti often traveled in a private railway car, and when she had sung in San Francisco in 1884, the opera house had suffered $3,000 worth of damage as rabid fans had "knocked out windows and even stood on tops of new pianos with hob-nail boots, demanding the last unsold tickets." [15]

No fans, understandably, were more enthusiastic than the Italians. Whenever a few more voices were needed to swell the chorus, the manager would send a messenger racing down to the wharves of North Beach, since all the Sicilian fishermen there knew the score of *La Traviata* or *Rigoletto* by heart.[16]

On that fateful evening of April 17, 1906, Caruso sang the part of Don José in *Carmen,* with the visiting Metropolitan Opera Company, before an adoring and chic public. Afterwards, hundreds of dinner parties went on until the early hours of the morning. At 5 A.M., actor John Barrymore was still up, examining a collection of Chinese glass at a friend's house. Caruso, restless for no apparent reason, had just fallen asleep in his suite at the Palace Hotel. Dawn broke, the sky lovely and clear.[17]

It was Wednesday, April 18, 1906, the morning of the great earthquake that struck at 5:12 A.M. and lasted exactly twenty-eight seconds.

Not the heaving earth but the subsequent fire devoured San Francisco. Though a few poorly built houses did collapse, in most neighborhoods damage was only moderate despite the violence of the shocks. But as people ran into the street in their nightgowns and bathrobes, black plumes of smoke were already beginning to rise from buildings that had caught fire, usually as a result of broken gas mains.

Had the city's firemen been able to douse the flames quickly the fire might have been checked in its first hours. But water mains had snapped as well as gas mains, and so the fires mingled together and began marching from block to block — this advancing wall of heat setting on fire shingles, draperies, rugs, and furniture hundreds of yards ahead of it. The city's magnificent new eighteen-story skyscraper, the Call Building, ignited from within; windows suddenly exploded in a shower of falling glass and flames and smoke poured out.[18] Troops from a nearby army base vainly dynamited houses and office buildings, trying to establish a fire break.

On that same morning, a broad-chested, strikingly handsome man six feet two inches tall walked through the gate of his ranch, "Seven Oaks," about an hour after the quake, starting on foot for the city. It was a seventeen-mile walk from San Mateo on the south side of the bay to San Francisco, and it was noon before Amadeo Giannini reached the three-story building in North Beach where his Bank of Italy had its modest offices. He conferred with subordinates. North Beach, the city's Italian district, located close to the waterfront, seemed safe from the flames. But by early afternoon the district was burning as the fire swept on inexorably — it would finally devour 2,593 acres. Inside the doomed little bank, Giannini and a half dozen employees loaded their cash reserves, about $80,000 in gold, into orange crates and then casually lifted the crates onto the back of a ramshackle horse-drawn wagon identical in appearance to the wagons used to haul produce. The orange crates containing the gold were cautiously overspread with a layer of fruit, and the wagon began to roll through the streets with Giannini and two hefty subordinates dressed as Italian fruit vendors. As an extra precaution they stopped at a friend's house on the outskirts of the city and replaced the fruit with furniture and bedding, to look like refugees.

By midnight, the wagon rolled slowly into Seven Oaks, and as thirty-six-year-old Clorinda Giannini ran out of the doorway to embrace her husband, his assistants cleared away the covering and brought the orange crates into the house, where they were hidden in the rear of a spacious fireplace. The men ate, drank some wine from the nearby Santa Clara Valley vineyards, and caught a few hours of sleep. Amadeo would be returning to the city at dawn, without the gold this time. He would be seen that day walking along the piers, hiring captains to sail their vessels to the Oregon coast to load up with lumber so that North Beach, still emitting a skein of greasy black smoke, could be rebuilt at once. No one asked Amadeo Giannini to do this; but because of it, North Beach would be the first neighborhood in San Francisco to recover from the fire.

He was the son of immigrants. In 1869, when the transcontinental railroad was complete, one of the Union Pacific's first westbound trains had carried a young Italian couple to San Francisco. Luigi Giannini, twenty-two years old, and his fifteen-year-old bride, Virginia, were both Ligurians. Luigi Giannini possessed the drive and business acumen characteristic of the Genoese. Though he was struggling to learn English — practicing it with his fellow passengers during the long rail trip across the United States — he had enough capital with him to lease a small, twenty-room hotel in San Jose, in the rich fruit-growing area of the Santa Clara Valley just southeast of San Francisco Bay. There Amadeo Giannini was born. Since he was American-born his parents gave him an English middle name, Peter. So he was Amadeo Peter, a name that would prove too disturbingly Italian for a businessman; the lyrical Amadeo would be crushed into A. P.

After a few years of managing the hotel, Luigi Giannini was able to save enough money to buy a forty-acre spread at Alviso near the south end of the bay. This was the immigrant's dream, and the dream fructified. Luigi's farm prospered. Two more boys were born to Virginia Giannini, so that Amadeo had playmates all day long. But when he was seven years old, Amadeo saw a nightmare enacted before his eyes. The boy whose bank vaults would one day contain millions saw his father stabbed to death in front of their house by a neighbor in a quarrel over a one-dollar debt.

The young, attractive widow, with three small boys, married a second time a year later. Amadeo's stepfather was a farmer and small business-man from Lucca, Lorenzo Scatena, who had worked his way to San Francisco as a sailor. He was twenty-six when he married Virginia Giannini, and "his capital was a team and wagon in which he hauled ranchers' produce to the dock at Alviso on the Bay." [19] Though all three of the Giannini boys seem to have developed a strong affection for their stepfather, Amadeo and Lorenzo Scatena became particularly close. When Amadeo was twelve, the family moved to San Francisco where

Lorenzo took a job in the North Beach market area working as a commission merchant for an Italian fruit wholesaling company. Within a year and a half he had started his own firm, L. Scatena & Co.

The wholesale market was Amadeo's first, deeply exciting taste of the world outside the schoolroom and the home. On Friday night, he would be allowed to accompany his stepfather after supper.

In the dark, Lorenzo and Amadeo would climb into the firm's wagon and rattle over the cobblestones of Green Street on the way to the wharves to meet the fruit and vegetable boats from the Sacramento and San Joaquin rivers, from Alviso, and from the other little ports dotting the far shores of the bay.

At the waterfront Lorenzo would encounter his competitors from Washington Street. Many were Italians, like himself; also, there were Chinese, Portuguese, Irish, Jews, Syrians, as well as what we like to call representatives of the old American stock. Amid a babel of tongues, bidding and buying were keen. Several times Lorenzo Scatena would fill his wagon — with beans, potatoes, celery, corn, peas, turnips, cantaloupes, grapes, pears, cherries, plums. . . .[20]

The wharf and the Washington Street market were Amadeo Giannini's business college. By the age of fifteen he had joined the firm of Scatena & Co. full time — a strapping, six-foot teen-ager able to take care of himself on the North Beach waterfront. "At seventeen Amadeo was making buying trips for the firm. He toured the Santa Clara, the Napa and the Sacramento valleys lining up commodities. The youth was a mixer and popular. He was liked by the ranchers, by the townspeople, by the rival buyers he met at nights in the country hotels. He worked longer hours than his colleagues. Soon the big San Francisco houses which for years had had standing arrangements with certain growers found L. Scatena & Company getting a share of the business." [21]

When Amadeo was twenty-one, Lorenzo made him a full partner. He was described as "the handsomest man in North Beach," tall, square-shouldered with a rugged face, dark, full eyebrows and black hair. The North Beach girls would watch him pass from behind the lace curtains of their parlor windows, aware that Amadeo, splendidly attired in "top hat, gloves, and a Prince Albert," was courting the daughter of North Beach real estate magnate Joseph Cuneo. In 1892, when they were both twenty-two, Amadeo and Clorinda Cuneo were married. Within a few years Amadeo would buy Seven Oaks, in San Mateo, their lifelong home after the first years of marriage in San Francisco.

It was marriage that turned Amadeo Giannini into a banker. By 1901, he had retired from the fruit and vegetables commission business, having invested enough of his earnings in real estate to have a monthly income of $250. Beyond this, he had an income from the ranch. He was at a crossroads. There was no business that particularly interested him. He was thinking about a possible political career, when his father-in-law's death in 1902 channeled his energies in another direction. Joseph Cuneo left an estate of half a million dollars, mostly in North Beach property, and by the common desire of his eleven children Amadeo was appointed custodian of the estate for ten years, with the stipulation that he would receive twenty-five percent of whatever profit he could make. (Amadeo managed to increase the value of the estate by $160,000 in those ten years.) But along with the job of managing this inheritance, Amadeo also received Joseph Cuneo's seat on the board of directors of a small immigrant bank, the Columbus Savings and Loan Society.

The Columbus was the pioneer Italian savings and loan association in the San Francisco area. It had been started by an immigrant, John F. Fugazi, who had reached the West Coast in the waning months of the gold rush, hoping to make a fortune as a miner. When this effort failed, Fugazi became the San Francisco agent for the White Star Line, a shipping company with regular service to Italian ports. Because Italian immigrant laborers and fishermen often brought him their gold to ship back to relatives in Italy, Fugazi bought a safe. This was his entry into banking. In 1893, he enlisted the aid of an established San Francisco banker, Isaias W. Hellman, and opened the Columbus Savings and Loan Association. "As the first bank in North Beach the Columbus performed an unquestioned service to the community. It provided residents with a secure place to keep their money — hard money still being the rule on the West Coast — where it would earn interest. This was a big improvement over hiding coin about the house." [22]

But while the Columbus did loan money for home building and the purchase of farmland, it was a conservative institution. Its directors concentrated on negotiating big loans at the highest possible interest. In 1899, Andrea Sbarboro — the founder of the Italian-Swiss Agricultural Colony — established a rival bank specifically aimed at helping the small Italian merchant and farmer. It offered checking services, as well as savings, and with its more liberal loan policies it began to overtake the Columbus.

Amadeo not only believed that Andrea Sbarboro was correct in his banking policies, he wanted to go much further. Newly arrived Italian immigrants usually needed to borrow money; land prices were high, and by the time the settler had bought equipment, and seeds, and harvested his first crop, he might easily have invested $20,000. Often, the immigrant had nowhere to turn but to loan sharks. Though San Francisco was the financial capital of the West, providing funds for the development of Los Angeles County, and of Oregon and Washington to the north, the banking establishment was interested chiefly in big accounts.

It was true that Andrew Sbarboro's bank had been established to satisfy the needs of small immigrant entrepreneurs. But its clientele was generally limited to the North Beach Italians of San Francisco. Amadeo had a different vision of banking. He knew from his past business trips that Italian farmers and fruit growers were spread all over northern California, and beyond its borders into the northwest. And Italians were only a small minority of millions of immigrants or native-born Americans who had migrated to the West. Most of these people needed capital.

He opened his bank on October 17, 1904, on the premises of a former saloon. Amadeo had wanted to call it the *Italian Bank of California,* but Sbarboro had objected that this sounded too much like his own Italian-American Bank. So the fledgling institution was called Bank of Italy, and in Italian, *Banca d'Italia.* Its initial capital of $300,000 had been raised by selling three thousand shares at $100 each. Amadeo had hoped that many working-class people would buy two, three, or four shares — and in fact, after he had gone around to all the Italian fishermen, grocers, produce handlers, bakers and cobblers in North Beach, over half the shares were purchased by these small stockholders.[23] The bank's personnel was entirely Italian, and so were most of the initial depositors. They were people whom the popular Amadeo had met professionally or personally, so that he was able to greet almost everyone by name when they came into the bank.

To San Francisco's banking establishment the opening of the Bank of Italy was a source of some amusement; good naturedly, they took note of "that little Dago bank in North Beach."

This was the situation two years later in April 1906, when the earthquake struck San Francisco. A little Dago bank, prospering but still much smaller than its intended rivals, the Columbus and the Italian-American banks. It had a staff of seven, including a tall, handsome director serving as a vice president at a salary of $200 a month.

When the last flames burned themselves out in the half-gutted streets, and the task of reconstruction began to take form in the minds of San Francisco's city fathers, one of their first acts was to call a short bank holiday. Nearly all of San Francisco's banks had either burned to the ground or had suffered extensive damage. Though their deposits were safe in vaults, these underground vaults were still hot and it took several days before they cooled down enough to be opened. A far greater problem was the destruction of records. A bank no longer knew who its depositors were, or how much they had possessed in their accounts. The bank holiday was extended, therefore, for over a month.

Amadeo Giannini had no such problems. He had taken his gold reserves home in orange crates, along with the bank's records. Besides, he knew almost every one of his customers personally. Four days after the earthquake, as the city still smouldered, Amadeo sent a circular to the bank's depositors, announcing that the Bank of Italy had absolute confidence in San Francisco's future and was ready to lend money for rebuilding. It was opening temporary quarters at two locations: the house of Giannini's younger brother, Attilio, who was a doctor, and on the Washington Street wharf. From the first, the wharf became the Bank of Italy's chief place of business — and part of San Francisco history. Operating from a plank propped up by two barrels, Amadeo approved loans on the spot. He had the $80,000 in cash, backed by deposits of $846,000. To spread the money as widely as possible, he asked loan applicants to take half of what they requested.[24] If an applicant was unknown to him, Amadeo would often ask the man to show the palms of his hands. Anyone with calluses on his hands received a loan — with calluses as the only collateral.

It was a splendid scene: the big, hale man, confident and inspiring confidence. North Beachers never forgot it, and when the Bank of Italy reopened formally on May 22 in a real estate broker's office, thousands of new depositors placed their savings in Amadeo's hands. Money which had been hoarded under bricks or loose boards, or simply kept in glass jars, came out from those domestic hiding places and went into the Bank of Italy's vault. By the end of 1906 — the earthquake year — deposits had risen to $1,355,000 and the number of depositors had doubled.

Early in 1907, Amadeo took his first trip to New York and to other eastern cities. It was partly business, partly a vacation. His wife Clorinda accompanied him. He had been working hard for over three years, and now that the bank was firmly established, and San Francisco's rebuilding was moving along, he could afford to take a holiday.

In the East, he found a disturbing situation. A number of bank failures had already occurred in Europe. The phenomenon had started in Egypt with the failure of a large bank in Alexandria, then had spread throughout Europe, Japan, and South America. Everywhere, credit seemed overextended with deposits often tied up in speculative ventures, and when the panic struck and depositors clamored for their money, banks closed. Amadeo talked to bankers on Wall Street and then left for the coast, determined to save the Bank of Italy. When the panic reached New York a few months later, only the personal intervention of J. P. Morgan, who raised $25 million, averted a catastrophe. As it was, six banks and four trust companies failed. (Out of this debacle came the Federal Reserve System, and modern banking legislation from Congress.) By the end of the year the panic spread westward to San Francisco. Amadeo had prepared for the crisis. For months, he had cut back on loans and had convinced depositors to make withdrawals in paper money rather than in gold. While other banks were failing he kept the Bank of Italy's gold in full view, behind a metal grill, to reassure customers. The Bank of Italy not only survived; its deposits increased.

When the American Bankers Association met in Denver in 1908, the principal speaker was the president of Princeton University, Woodrow Wilson. He was sharply critical of the banking profession, and most of the delegates listened to his remarks with a certain hostility. But Amadeo Giannini felt that Wilson, the future President, had said exactly the right things, things he himself believed.

Wilson chastised bankers for concentrating on speculative investments, and suggested, instead, that money should be radiated out to the communities through a system of branch banks, to "quicken and fertilize the country." He said, "If a system of branch banks . . . could be established, which would put the resources of the rich banks of the country at the disposal of the whole countryside . . . the attitude of plain men everywhere towards banks and banking would be changed utterly within less than a generation." [25]

The majority of the bankers at Denver were skeptical. Branch banking had been tried successfully in Canada, and in various European countries, but not in the United States. Also, most bankers were not interested in concentrating on the small depositor. But Giannini listened carefully to Wilson's suggestions. And though few of his fellow delegates knew who he was, or paid any attention to him, he would come to personify American banking in the years of the New Deal just as J. P. Morgan had personified banking in an earlier age.

In March 1909, the California legislature passed a bank act that provided for "the most rigid supervision and regulation of state banks that had been imposed by any state government" [26] — this in the wake of the panic of 1907, which made a reform of banking practices mandatory. The issue of branch banking, however, was virtually ignored by the act since branch banking hardly existed. The only rule laid down was that a bank had to add $25,000 to its capital for every new branch, a simple enough requirement to fulfill.

By the end of 1909, Amadeo was ready to test his ideas of expanding in the direction of the small rural customer. The Bank of Italy's deposits had passed $2 million and its assets were over $3 million. Now, in a step unprecedented in American banking, the Bank of Italy, based in San Francisco, opened a branch in a farming community fifty miles away where business needs were wholly different from those of the city.

The bank Amadeo and his fellow directors had bought out was the Commercial and Savings Bank of San Jose in the heart of the Santa Clara Valley. "The banks of the valley," wrote Marquis and Bessie James,

had been founded by the landowning gentry and were run for their benefit. In boom times these people were rich and the banks paid whopping dividends. In hard times the people borrowed more from the banks and increased the mortgages on their land. By and large those who made the land productive were hard-working immigrants who cultivated every corner of their small ranches. The banks made the task harder than it should have been.[27]

The Commercial and Savings Bank occupied a handsome Spanish-Moorish-style corner building in San Jose. When the doors reopened on January 2, 1910, Amadeo was on hand to greet new and old depositors. San Jose was his birthplace, and he had a special feeling for the community. As a shrewd businessman, and good citizen, he had taken pains to retain local stockholders and to keep many of the bank's former employees. He had advertised that there would be tellers at the bank who spoke French, Italian, Spanish, and Portuguese, a service for immigrant depositors whose English was halting. If a depositor came in with a child, Amadeo would take a gold dollar from his pocket, give it to the parent and suggest that a savings account be opened in the child's name.

He had that great quality of never appearing pressed for time, or impatient, stopping to chat with people who came into the bank, looking over their accounts personally.

In 1911 and 1912, Amadeo and his fellow directors at the Bank of Italy seriously considered opening a branch in New York. Though it was a continent away, in an age when communications were much slower than they are today, still New York had eight hundred thousand Italians and not a single adequate bank for them. But there were so many problems involved in operating in two different states, and at different ends of the country, that the directors decided ultimately to limit their expansion to California. There, they moved very rapidly, taking over three banks in the Los Angeles area by 1913 amid a good deal of resistance. As at San Mateo, Amadeo went after new business aggressively. Since there were only 3,802 Italian-born residents in Los Angeles, he clearly had to attract other customers. THE BANK FOR JUST PLAIN FOLKS, he advertised; and WOULD MONEY HELP YOU? [28]

If such slogans are common enough today, they were unorthodox at the time and caused raised eyebrows among bankers in Los Angeles and San Francisco. No one took Giannini very seriously yet, though his bank's growth was striking. By the end of 1913, the new Los Angeles branches had deposits of over $2.5 million, while the bank's headquarters and branches in northern California now had deposits of $11,682,000. This was quite a performance for a "little Dago bank" that had started only nine years before with assets of $300,000. Even more unusual was the fact that almost all of the Bank of Italy's depositors were "just plain folks." In a newspaper interview in Los Angeles, Amadeo reiterated his business philosophy: "We have no money for speculators," he said. "We consider the wage-earner or small businessman who deposits his savings regularly, no matter how small the amount may be, to be the most valuable client our bank can have." [29] In this he was reflecting the attitude of millions of Italian immigrants who religiously saved a portion of their income, however meager, from every paycheck.

Until 1915, Amadeo continued to serve as vice president of the Bank of Italy, with an annual income of $9,000. Though he was distinctly the boss, his stepfather had been the bank's president during its first decade. On September 22, 1915, Lorenzo Scatena was elevated to the position of chairman of the board and Amadeo Giannini officially became president of his bank, with a salary of $25,000 a year.[30] He was forty-four years old, a superb executive, shrewd, demanding, driving, but also public-spirited and generous in his ideas. His largely Italian staff was expected to work harder than most bank personnel. In return, they were well paid and received liberal benefits.

The war years between 1916 and 1918 were boom times for California's farmers. With Europe's fields cratered and the sea lanes disrupted, there was a worldwide demand for food and prices soared. In those years the Bank of Italy, riding that crest of high prices and fat harvests, opened eighteen new branches, most of them in the agriculturally blessed San Joaquin Valley that stretches three hundred miles from northern to southern California behind a protective reef of coastal mountains. The bank's growth was phenomenal. By the end of 1918 its deposits were $85,937,839 and it had become the fourth largest bank in California. In 1919 it added another $41,320,000 in deposits, the greatest increase of any American bank that year. The most significant statistic, however, was that this obscure Bank of Italy now had 189,511 depositors, more than any other bank in the United States including the gigantic financial castles of New York.

What Amadeo Giannini had done in a mere fifteen years with his immigrant bank was to comprehend that the real energy behind America's growth lay with the common people. All his life, he would derive as much strength from his contact with the people as any politician. Despite his bank's enormous growth, Giannini resisted the isolation and self-importance that often accompanies great power. He could be curt, demanding, and unjust. One of his executives recalled a few years after his death, "I had a wonderful, simply terrific time working for A. P. and all because I started out on the proper footing and didn't knuckle under to him when I was in the right." [31] But he was basically an earthy, unaffected man who was not embarrassed to shout a greeting to a friend across a cavernous bank lobby and who made a point of taking his own telephone calls in the office without having them screened by a secretary. Thousands of Californians called the Bank of Italy every year, asked for "A. P. Giannini, please," and a moment later heard the gruff, booming voice saying, "This is A. P. Giannini." The same obsession with keeping the banker close to the people caused Giannini to restructure the interior of every bank he absorbed. Bank executives who had once been comfortably closeted in the privacy of rear offices found themselves out on the floor, separated from the public by only a low wooden rail. They either adapted or left. Giannini, who lived for his work, kept his own life simple. In the morning he arrived in his office around 9:30. At

12:45 he would go to lunch, invariably eating at the Chas. Fashion restaurant either with bank associates or occasionally with a politician. At about 6:30 he would leave for San Mateo, have dinner with his family, and take a walk after dinner if the weather was seasonable. His business fascinated him and was never far from his thoughts. "My brain never stops," he once said. "I think while I sleep." [32] Yet he spent much time with his family at Seven Oaks and was particularly close to his son Mario, who bore the cross of hemophilia. Mario grew to manhood and even outlived Amadeo by a few years, but he was never free from physical suffering. Shorter than his father, pale, reserved except among close friends, Mario would himself become a brilliant banker. Yet even during the years when he was president of the Bank of America, he would frequently be forced to transact business from a hospital bed. After Mario joined the bank in 1919 at the age of twenty-five, father and son worked as a team.

The year 1919 in many ways marked a turning point in Amadeo Giannini's business career. He had built a superbly functional bank in California whose branches were able to shift capital from one agricultural zone to another as seasonal crops came in and farmers looked for new short-term loans. If surpluses drove down the market price of a crop, Giannini's local branches were able to call on the resources of their kindred banks throughout the state and advance huge sums of money to the beleaguered farmers to see them through the crisis. This was Giannini's particular innovation, and the cornerstone of his banking empire; but, then, few bankers had grown up handling heads of cabbage and shaking hands with men whose hands were veined with soil and manure.

As industry began to move into California in the 1920s, the Bank of Italy was ready to negotiate long-term loans, often taking chances that more conservative institutions would not take. At a time when the nascent film industry in Hollywood was viewed by most bankers as a congregation of wild-hunch players, temperamental geniuses, and dizzy blondes, Giannini loaned vast sums to movie producers. Many of the classic films of Chaplin, Mack Sennett, and the young Darryl Zanuck were made with Bank of Italy money. [33]

The problems that still confronted Giannini in California were, for a man of his creativity, secondary ones. A master at cutting the Gordian knot, he quickly resolved crises that would have blighted the business careers of less daring men. When a bank run began at a branch in Sacramento, for example, Amadeo hired a plane, jammed it full of sacks containing a million dollars in cash and, without worrying unduly whether this flying armored truck might crash, accompanied the money up to Sacramento. Panicky depositors standing in line outside the branch were startled to see Giannini himself, bellowing out friendly "hellos" and "how are yous," shouldering his way through the door. Behind him came men carrying sacks stuffed with money. The run stopped at once, and Amadeo coined what is probably the greatest three-syllable epigram in the English language. "Money talks," he told a reporter.

All he could really do in California was to expand, and if federal laws and a succession of state banking superintendents had not combined to check his acquisitive drive, Giannini would have started or absorbed new branches even more rapidly. As it was, by 1927, when he had swallowed up the state's Liberty banks, he possessed the third largest bank in the United States, with over a million depositors. "The multiple consolidations that had resulted in the Bank of Italy National Trust and Savings Association," wrote the Jameses, "represented the most gigantic undertaking of that kind America had ever seen. . . ." [34] In the following year, 1928, Giannini joined a very select group of tycoons whose enterprises had resources of more than one billion dollars. Already some reporters were talking of Giannini's Bank of Italy as "the octopus" — a charge that would gather strength during the *Grapes of Wrath* depression years when hundreds of struggling farmers went bankrupt in California and the Bank of Italy, through a subsidiary called California Lands, Inc., found itself in possession of 2,642 farms comprising over half a million acres. But the bank was never a blood-sucking enterprise, and before the Depression its foreclosures had averaged only slightly more than one farm per year per branch. [35]

By the start of the decade of the Roaring Twenties, Giannini had largely accomplished his work in California. His eyes were turned eastward, towards the Rockies and the plains beyond, and the industrial centers of the Midwest; towards New York, and Europe.

Not since 1836, when President Andrew Jackson had succeeded in blocking the recharter of Nicholas Biddle's Bank of the United States in a landmark struggle over the future structure of the American economy, had anyone seriously set out to build a national bank. But Giannini's point of departure was different enough, at least in his own eyes, for him to believe that he would be able to convince the government to modify its banking and antitrust laws. What he proposed to establish was an international bank with thousands of branches oriented to the needs of the common man. After 1919, his moves were predominantly in pursuit of this vision.

Italian immigrants in New York had been urging Giannini to create a bank for them since 1911. In 1919, he bought the East River National Bank of New York. It was his first acquisition outside California. He also began buying up small banks in Italy, which he merged in 1922 with the *Banca Italia Meridionale* to form his enduring Italian bank, the *Banca d'Italia e d'America*. It would survive fascism and the war and grow into the second largest private bank in Italy. In 1925, Giannini strengthened his base in New York by purchasing the Bowery National Bank and merging it with the East River National to form a $70 million bank with twelve branches. By 1928, its resources had grown to $106 million.[36] In February of 1928, Giannini made an even more significant acquisition: He bought the Bank of America, a small but venerable New York institution with offices at 44 Wall Street and financial kinship with the house of Morgan.[37] Though this purchase would give Giannini the ultimate name for his huge California bank — still called the Bank of Italy — it also brought him into conflict with powerful Wall Street bankers who had little sympathy for this immigrant's son from California, this former fruit peddler whose manner was often abrasive and whose appetite for banks was apparently insatiable (he also tried to buy the Manufacturers Trust in New York).[38] The press was enchanted with Giannini, seeing in him a new kind of Western hero and a self-made financial colossus in the very spirit of the twenties. But now the 1928 market, probably with a little help from various Wall Street bankers, gave the new colossus a lesson in the old economics.

In the spring of 1928, with investment fever high all across the land, the publicly traded stock of Bank of Italy and its parent company, Bancitaly, became the target of speculative buying on the San Francisco exchange. For months, Giannini had been warning San Francisco's Italians, "Our shares are too high. Don't gamble on them." [39] By May, the bank's shares were ripe for a bear raid. Giannini, who saw it coming, vainly wired messages of alarm from Rome where he had gone on vacation and fallen ill. When the Federal Reserve Board raised the discount rate — just as rumors circulated in San Francisco that A. P. had suffered a paralytic stroke — thousands of Bank of Italy and Bancitaly shares were suddenly unloaded at the San Francisco exchange, driving the price down steeply and setting off a wave of selling. It is likely that Wall Street assisted in organizing the panic. Tens of thousands of Italian-Americans in California who had invested their savings in Bank of Italy shares saw values decline by nearly half in only a few days. Some sold out; others hung on, trusting Giannini. Amadeo and Mario Giannini took the only course open to them. They backed their shares with some $60 million, buying them to stabilize the price. They stopped the panic — though it cost them an estimated $20 million to do it.

This setback did not separate Giannini from his dream of establishing a nationwide network of branch banks. But the 1928 break, followed by an involved battle with J. P. Morgan & Co., did modify Amadeo's approach to Wall Street. As the Jameses wrote, "The breach with Morgan left Giannini looking for talent that knew the ways of Wall Street, had the proper entrée there and a sympathetic understanding of nationwide banking." [40] Early in 1929, Giannini believed he had found the right man. This was forty-nine-year-old Elisha Walker, a New Yorker, a graduate of Yale and MIT, and president of the blue-chip New York investment house of Blair & Co., whose staff of bright young executives included the French industrial expert Jean Monnet. A deal was struck whereby Blair & Co. was merged with the Bank of America in New York. "Walker became president of the securities affiliate of the bank, Bancamerica-Blair Corporation, and chairman of the executive committee of the bank." [41]

Giannini was now sixty. It seemed an appropriate time to draw back and let younger men carry forward his ideas. He had already retired from the presidency of the Bank of Italy in California five years earlier, in 1924, being succeeded by the forty-two-year-old Italian-American James A. Bacigalupi, one of Giannini's closest collaborators for years. To bring his California and New York operations together under one corporate roof, before relinquishing the active stewardship of his banks as he then believed he would do, Giannini created a vast holding company to which he and Mario gave the name of Transamerica — a name significant of its intentions. Under the law, only by creating such a holding company could an enterprise own banks in different states. Its assets were valued by Giannini at nearly one and a half billion dollars. The name Bancitaly now disappeared, and in the following year, 1930, the old name Bank of Italy was finally dropped to be replaced by Bank of America National Trust and Savings Association. Though Transamerica was to be the parent company for the Bank of America, what Giannini had created in effect was an elephant with a head at either end. One head was the mammoth California bank with its headquarters in San Francisco and staffed by long-time Giannini associates, many of them Italian-Americans. The other head, Transamerica, was the holding company with its headquarters in New York with Elisha Walker as chairman of the board. It was run initially by a mixture of Giannini men and members of Walker's team from Blair & Co. as well as other Wall Street bankers, though the organization rapidly developed a seismic crack that turned old and new friends into bitter enemies.

The effects of the stock market crash in October 1929 probably made the conflict between Elisha Walker and Amadeo Giannini inevitable. As the value of Transamerica's shares began to precipitate, Walker's reaction was to reduce operations while Giannini's was to call for continued expansion. By 1931, the breach had become complete. The 1930 annual report, reflecting Giannini's views, had suggested optimistically, "It is now generally conceded that the trend of public opinion is increasingly favorable to the [nationwide] extension of branchbanking." But in the fall of 1931 Walker issued a statement stating bluntly, "There is no apparent likelihood that nation-wide branchbanking will be authorized by law in the near future." [42] This was the least of the bitter surprises awaiting Transamerica's founder, who was again in Europe and again ailing. Walker announced that Transamerica's books were padded, that the Gianninis had overvalued its worth by some $800 million, and that Transamerica would sell off Giannini's banks, including the Bank of America in California. Giannini, his brother, his son Mario, and nineteen other directors were dropped from Transamerica's board. A hard-nosed Texas banker who in the words of the press "did not allow sentiment to get in the way of collateral," was appointed president of the Bank of America until a purchaser could be found.

On September 22, 1931, the New York *Times* carried the headline: GIANNINIS LOSE CONTROL OF HUGE BANK CHAIN.[43] Throughout that winter of 1930–1931, Giannini had been desperately ill with polyneuritis. It appeared that he might be permanently crippled. But the news of Walker's brusque dismantling of his life's work spurred him to regain his health. From Lucerne, where he was recuperating, Giannini cabled Mario on August 17: LET'S CALL THEIR BLUFF.[44] Indulging in a bluff of his own, he booked passage to Quebec under the name S. A. Williams, arrived undetected, met Mario secretly in Vancouver, and was practically back in his office at 1 Powell Street before anyone spotted him. By then, his associates at the Bank of America had formed a stockholders' protective association and Giannini was ready to launch his counterattack for control of Transamerica.

Even so, he was given virtually no chance of succeeding. Walker controlled more than 375,000 shares and could count on the support of Wall Street institutions that owned large blocs of shares. Most of Giannini's partisans were small private shareholders and he himself had only 56,000 shares.[45] But for Amadeo Giannini it was the battle of his life. He barnstormed California where he was still a magical figure among the thousands of Italians whom he had helped to prosper in better times. Though the value of Transamerica's shares had dropped from a high of 67 in 1929 all the way to 2 at the time of the proxy battle, these small investors still believed in Giannini as he had believed in them. When the ballots were counted, most of the New York financial press could not believe its own stories. Giannini had won back Transamerica by a lopsided margin of 63 percent of the stockholders' proxies.[46]

In full control of his business again, Giannini continued to scheme and negotiate for the establishment of a nationwide branch bank. He was an early backer of Franklin Roosevelt and one of the few bankers in sympathy with the aims of the New Deal. As he told the press in 1933, "The system has to be changed. There is something wrong with a system that lets 14,000,000 men get out of work." [47] Two years later he was one of the few important bankers in America to support a bill concentrating authority over credit with the Federal Reserve Board. "The control of money is a real power for good or evil," he told reporters. "Personally, I would rather that this power be exercised by a public body in the public interest than by the New York banking fraternity." [48] Giannini was undoubtedly a sincere admirer of FDR, and of the New Deal in its early stages. But he may have also have believed cannily that the new Democratic administration, with its hostility towards Wall Street, and towards the big New York bankers in particular, might look favorably on his undiminished ambition to be a people's banker all through the land. Despite dinners at the White House and polite notes from the President each time Giannini defended the New Deal, however, this ambition was never satisfied. Not only were the banking laws not changed in his favor, but by 1938 Giannini himself had become a target for some of the more ambitious New Deal trustbusters. His periodic grumblings about "those goddamned New York bankers" were now increasingly interspersed with tongue-lashings directed at the Treasury Department and its "goddamned bureaucrats." He was "fed up with some of the people down in Washington," [49] he informed the press.

On the twelfth of December, 1938, the Securities and Exchange Commission threatened to delist Transamerica stock, citing eighteen specific charges. Giannini roared that he was the victim of a "diabolical conspiracy" to steal his banks from him as Walker had tried to do, and demanded a congressional investigation. For several years thereafter, he and Treasury Secretary Henry Morgenthau, Jr., engaged in an acid, if long-distance, feud, but Giannini was shrewd enough to parry any really effective action against him by separating the Bank of America from its holding company, Transamerica, and diversifying Transamerica's portfolio by purchasing other businesses — among them the Occidental Life Insurance Co. of Los Angeles, which under Transamerica's wing became one of the largest in the country.

The friction between Giannini and Morgenthau did not destroy the banker's friendship with FDR, however, and a few days after Pearl Harbor Giannini spoke to the President to assure him that there would be no security problem on the West Coast in regard to the Italian-Americans and that the government should count on their loyalty rather than humiliating them by regarding them suspiciously — as was done with the Japanese-Americans over the protests of J. Edgar Hoover, among others. On Columbus Day 1942, the President acknowledged the loyalty of Italian-Americans by declaring that America was at war with the Fascist government and not with the Italian people, and by announcing that Italian citizens would no longer be classified as enemy aliens. After the liberation of Italy, Giannini is widely believed to have played a role in the selection of a new Italian government. It was not really his business, but in his position as the head of the *Banca d'America e d'Italia,* as well as the foremost American banker of Italian origin, he had influence over the granting of desperately needed loans to Italy for relief and industrial reconstruction. Giannini was then at the zenith of his power as a banker. Though he had retired a half-dozen times already, nothing could keep him from his office in the bank's new building at 300 Montgomery Street. He resigned as chairman of the board of the Bank of America in May 1945, at the age of seventy-five, and assumed the honorary title of founder-chairman. But no major decision was taken at 300 Montgomery, as the bank's headquarters was known, without Giannini's approval. Moreover, the war years had brought people, jobs and money to California, and the Bank of America had continued its protean growth. In April 1946, as its employees celebrated with California champagne, the Bank of America National Trust and Savings Association surged ahead of the Chase Manhattan in total deposits to become the largest private bank in the world. It had over five and a half billion dollars in deposits and 3,300,000 depositors.[50]

For another three years, the big, white-haired, white-moustached banker continued to plan the Bank of America's future expansion, including its overseas operations.* He tried to convince his son Mario to work a little less hard, and kept an eye on promising young executives like the Swedish-born Rudolph A. Peterson, who would become president of the Bank of America in 1961. He once growled to his staff, "If I ever hear that any of you are trying to play the big man's game and forgetting the small man, I'll be back in here fighting." [51] But the time for fighting was past and Giannini knew it. At a party celebrating his seventy-ninth birthday in 1949, he told reporters with brusque premonition that it would be his last. A week later, at Seven Oaks, he died of a heart attack.

Mario succeeded him for a few years only, dying in 1952. Amadeo's strong-minded daughter, Mrs. Claire Giannini Hoffman, took her father's seat on the board of directors. (In 1963, she would be appointed the first woman on the board of Sears, Roebuck & Co.) Another extremely powerful Italian-American banker of Genoese extraction and a Giannini protégé, Frank N. Belgrano, Jr., became the president and chairman of Transamerica. For a time Belgrano attempted to revive Amadeo's dream of a vast interstate bank. By 1957, Transamerica had become the world's biggest bank holding company with assets of over three billion dollars. But a congressional law (aimed particularly at Transamerica) forced the company to get out of banking or divest itself of its other holdings. Transamerica dropped out of banking and became a financial conglomerate.

In writing Amadeo Giannini's obituary, *Fortune* reported, "The quality of greatness is not easily defined. Yet few would deny that last month marked the death, at seventy-nine, of the greatest U.S. banker since the elder Morgan." [52] For a man whose bank vaults had contained billions, Giannini left a characteristically temperate estate of $489,278, nearly all of it willed to the Bank of America–Giannini foundation that he had established in 1945 to provide educational scholarships for Bank of America employees and to finance medical research, particularly into the

* The Bank of America is still the world's largest private bank, with total resources of more than $30 billion.

disease that had tormented Mario Giannini all throughout life, hemophilia.

The quality of Amadeo Giannini's mind was reflected in the wording of the document creating this foundation. He wrote these final paragraphs:

The Trustor at his desk in his office, in the City and County of San Francisco, is executing this Declaration. The thoughts in his mind at this time are intimate and personal. He does not behold his Trustee as a cold, corporate entity, breathing only the life derived by it from the law. He sees through and beyond the corporate form, beholding the men and women who have worked by his side for the last forty years. To these devoted co-workers he cannot speak in the stern formalism of the law. His mind and his heart speak:

Administer this trust generously and nobly, remembering always human suffering. Let no legal technicality, ancient precedent, or outmoded legal philosophy defeat the purposes of this Trust. Like St. Francis of Assisi, do good — do not merely theorize about goodness. This is my wish and I confidently commit this Trust to your hands for its fulfillment.[53]

11

"... in which man was wolf to the man"

SET IN A WALL in a square in Palermo is a bronze tablet with a brief inscription. It reads: "Killed in the discharge of his duty, March 12, 1909. Lt. Joseph Petrosino, New York City." [1]

A muscular, square-faced man, Petrosino was a New York police detective and head of the Italian Squad — twenty-seven agents, two of them Italian-speaking Irishmen, who worked exclusively in the Italian tenement areas, sometimes peddling vegetables from a cart or swinging a pick in ditch-digging gangs to ferret out *Mafiosi,* and *padroni* who were exploiting the immigrants. Himself an immigrant born near Naples, Petrosino had come to America at the age of eight. In 1909, in order to investigate the Sicilian Mafia on its home ground, he boarded a ship and crossed the Atlantic to Palermo. But word of his mission preceded him, and at 9 o'clock on the morning of March 14 as he walked into Marina Square in Palermo, Petrosino was gunned down in a Mafia ambush. He pulled out his own revolver and fired one wild shot before falling dead.

The American people had been familiar with the term Mafia since the New Orleans lynchings of 1891, and the penny journals fed their readers a stream of gory, romanticized tales about banditry in the south of Italy. But the Petrosino murder was shockingly real. It proved the existence of something that bridged the ocean, an international crime conspiracy of Sicilian origin. A good deal of resistance to further immigration from Italy would henceforth be based on fear that the weed of the Mafia could run rampant in the American garden.

So much has been written about the Mafia recently that anything more may seem superfluous. One point that has not been stressed, however, is that the same Sicilians from the very same villages emigrated to the countries of South America as came to the United States. Yet there is no Mafia as we know it in Brazil or Argentina.

It is a truism that the Mafia expresses the decay and frustration present in Sicilian history. But its explosive metamorphosis only occurred when those historical forces reacted with forces of wide-open opportunity, materialism, and daring in America — creating an unforeseen fusion, a fireball.

The Mafia's political origins are said to go back to the Sicilian Vespers in the thirteenth century, a popular insurrection against French officials in the waning years of Norman power. But those origins probably extend even farther back into Sicilian history, perhaps to the slave revolts of Roman times, when Sicily was Rome's chief source of grain, and its fertile lowlands were farmed as great plantations. At the time Christ was being tempted by Satan in the mountains of Judea across the Mediterranean, in Sicily escaped slaves of a dozen nationalities were already climbing into the fastness of the island's arid, volcanic peaks, seeking security in their eagles' nests and building their first crude villages out of stones — insurgents against government and law. For every Spartacus remembered in history because he was a gladiator who nearly overthrew the Roman Empire, there must have been a hundred Sicilian Spartacuses forgotten by history.

Though it probably did begin as a resistance movement, the Mafia became something else during the centuries of stagnation and poverty endured by Sicily after the Norman era. In those Sicilian villages human energies were compressed into a slow, often subtle competition for power among people who were basically powerless. From birth, the overriding challenge was to defend one's position in the social hierarchy. The Mafia, this former rebel force, in time became a kind of unofficial secret police that enforced order and maintained the status quo. It could be hired by landowners to break peasant rebellions. It could, however, also avenge a poor peasant whose daughter had been abducted or whose sheep had been stolen. A *Mafioso* could also kidnap the sheep (or daughter), or kidnap and hold for ransom the landowner, the baron whom he had protected against his rebellious peasants. Like a Hindu deity the

Mafia grew many arms, many eyes, noses, ears, lips and expressions. It became a Sicilian god, and monster.

When the Sicilian immigrants reached America in great numbers at the turn of the century, they brought with them their sense of hierarchy — and the Mafia. The early *Mafioso* in America was both a benevolent and evil presence. The *Mafioso* might be a *padrone*. He might exploit immigrant laborers. He might shake down Italian grocers, fish peddlers, anyone who dealt in a commodity. But he might also protect the laborer, the grocer, the fish peddler. He might act as a strong, paternalistic presence in the neighborhood, a judge, a lawgiver, a defender of tradition, a moralist. He did not live ostentatiously as did American gangsters later on, but in the tenements, an immigrant among immigrants.

As Riis and other observers emphasized, there was a conspicuous absence of what could be called organized crime among southern Italians when they first reached America. The earliest crimes were economic ones, perpetrated by the *padroni* against their weaker countrymen — and the *padroni* were not necessarily members of the Mafia. Rather, they were middlemen useful to the American industrial system, since they supplied the raw labor that was needed for expansion. Italian crimes involving blood were chiefly stabbings over women, over a bottle of wine, a deck of cards or an insult. Again, these pathetic misadventures did not usually involve the Mafia except that the victim, if he recovered, might go to a *Mafioso* to obtain revenge.

The first distinctive Italian criminals to emerge from the big-city slums were the practitioners of the *Mano Nera*, or Black Hand — or as the tabloids called it, the Dirty Mitt. These extortionists were sometimes *Mafiosi* but not always. They were chiefly southern Italians practicing a form of banditry that had existed for centuries in poverty-ridden societies throughout the world. Just as the *padroni* preyed off poor and ignorant Italian immigrants, so the practitioners of the *Mano Nera* preyed off Italians who had managed to gain some measure of affluence. A letter would arrive in the mailbox suggesting that the recipient deposit a considerable sum of money in a specified place, or else risk a violent death.

One such note, demanding $2,000 within a week or "not even the dust of your family will exist," ended in a typically rococo salutation: "With regards, believe me to be your friend." [2]

Tired of being victimized and slandered by the activities of the Black Handers, Chicago's Italians founded the White Hand Society in 1907, a law and order group organized by the city's Italian consul, Guido

Sabetta.[3] Despite a great deal of publicity (which further embarrassed respectable Italians) the White Hand was ineffectual and was finally disbanded in 1913. In the 1920s, laws were passed making the use of the mails for extortion a federal crime. The FBI went after the Black Handers and virtually eliminated that activity within a few years.

There had been gangs and gangsters in the slums of American cities decades before the arrival of the southern Italians. There had been Anglo-Saxon, Irish, and German gangs just as today there are black and Puerto Rican gangs. These gangs were the product of poverty and of the protean competitiveness of American life. A late nineteenth-century Irish gang in New York, the Whyos, even advertised its brutal services with a printed brochure. For both eyes blacked, the charge was $4. Breaking an arm or a leg, $19. For stabbing, $25. For murder, $100.

By the early years of the twentieth century, Italians were forming their own gangs or were joining Irish gangs (and sometimes taking them over). Italian racketeers began to muscle into Italian fraternal organizations that had been formed originally for the protection of immigrants. Using these benevolent societies as a cover, the racketeers then engaged in loan-sharking, gambling, prostitution, strikebreaking, and murder. They also shook down Italian merchants and grocers. One Italian gangster was known as the "artichoke king" because he forced grocers to buy high-priced artichokes from his wholesaling firm. Another packaged cheap black cigars in a fancy box with his portrait on the cover and then forced merchants to stock his brand.[4] There were dozens of similar rackets. But Italian-American crime was localized, and it was practiced chiefly among Italian-Americans in the Italian ethnic neighborhoods.

Then came January 16, 1920.

The Volstead Act not only turned bootlegging into a billion-dollar business, but it turned millions of otherwise law-abiding Americans into lawbreakers. They were committing a crime for which they felt no particular guilt or revulsion. Judges drank on the sly and so did most jurymen. And since all these white-collar criminals needed the bootlegger — the serious criminal — in order to go on drinking, the distinction between what was permissible and intolerable in the society was blurred. By then, swarms of Italian gangsters armed with black touring cars and Thompson submachine guns were fighting other gangsters, including Irishmen, Jews, Germans and Anglo-Saxons, for the millions of dollars to be had in big-time crime. The new Mafia, the American Mafia, was born in the 1920s.

An event at the end of the decade confirmed this. In a violent uprising known as the Night of the Sicilian Vespers, some forty old-time Mafia chieftains were eliminated in a single coast-to-coast bloodbath by younger, American-born or at least American-educated *Mafiosi*. The old-timers, "Mustache Petes" as they were called, had wanted to keep the Mafia in America similar to what it had been in Sicily, small, suspicious of "foreigners," and limited to Sicilians related to one another by family ties. The young *Mafiosi* were hungrier, and they yearned to dominate American crime through alliances with non-Sicilians, and with non-Italians as well.

It is doubtful whether even a majority of the gangsters who flourished during Prohibition were Italians. They came from many backgrounds. The man who established the first major whiskey smuggling business was the gambler Arnold Rothstein. What he did was to buy liquor in England and ship it to New York, bribing customs agents. "As the competition grew, Rothstein stopped bringing in his own whiskey and started hijacking his rivals' liquor shipments on their way to distribution points. For this purpose he used such gunmen as Legs Diamond (real name John T. Noland) and Dutch Schultz (Arthur Flegenheimer.)" [5] It was this violent struggle for markets that produced the headline-grabbing murders of the Prohibition era. When Lucky Luciano and other younger mobsters came to the conclusion that these gang wars were bad for business, attempts were made to form a nationwide "syndicate." Nicholas Gage told how an alliance was formed in the late 1920s called the Eastern Syndicate. "It included members of many ethnic groups; Anglo-Saxons such as Owney 'The Killer' Madden, Irishmen such as William 'Big Bill' Dwyer, Jews such as Meyer Lansky, and younger *Mafiosi* such as Luciano." [6]

By the late 1920s, successful gangsters had become the equivalent of the Robber Barons fifty years earlier. Meyer Lansky, who had reached America as an immigrant from Russia named Maier Suchowjansky in 1911, amassed a personal fortune estimated at between $100 million and $300 million. Al Capone, one of the nine children of an immigrant from Naples named Gabriele Caponi who earned $11 a week as a barber in Brooklyn, ran his Chicago crime operations out of a six-room suite in the plush Hotel Lexington. A pitiless killer when crossed, the deceptively sleepy-looking, cherubic Capone possessed an army of seven hundred to a thousand gangsters, "some under his direct command, others available to him through allied gang chieftans." [7] Sacks of money often lay propped against the walls of his suite, waiting for transfer to a bank, and on his middle finger the former slum urchin wore a $50,000 blue-white dia-mond.[8]

"I call myself a businessman," he said blandly. "I make my money by supplying a popular demand. If I break the law, my customers are as guilty as I am." [9]

Capone, and men like him, flourished during a time of unrestrained materialism in America. The idea of a consumer society was shiningly new, unclouded by car graveyards or other pollution. Many consumer products had just been invented, or were just coming into reach of the average pocketbook through mass production. Much of the nation was infatuated with Wall Street and it seemed that prosperity might soar effortlessly from one plateau to the next. The President himself had said that the business of the American people was business. Sinclair Lewis had created Babbitt, the national archetype. It was no wonder that with materialistic values prevailing so strongly, gangsters bred in the ten-to-a-room tenements of the slums should have fought their way upward with the weapons at hand. Many of their methods were borrowed from legitimate business — the fleet of armor-plated speedboats used by Frank Costello to run whiskey down the East Coast from Canada, the fleets of trucks, the company lawyers — above all the concept of volume, of mass sales. Banditry in southern Italy had consisted of crouching behind a tree trunk in readiness to draw a flour sack over the passing wayfarer's head, or to fire a *lupara* into the breast of an enemy in a hundred-year-old vendetta. It had been a personal, even parochial matter.

There is, however, a moral limit to this analogy between crime and legitimate business. The Mafia's power in southern Italy had always rested on brutality, and its methods had included blackmail, rape, tor-ture, and murder. These same methods were later employed by Italian-American gangsters on a larger scale. One of the first successful Italian racketeers in America, the Calabrian-born James "Big Jim" Colosimo, earned some $600,000 a year from his string of whorehouses in the Chicago area,[10] and in order to keep the houses stocked he had working-class or immigrant girls lured to false job interviews, drugged, and then broken in by professional rapists. The Mann Act was a response to this proliferating "white slavery." Some gangsters were naturally sadistic, and suspected informers or rivals were sometimes hung from meathooks and slowly tortured to death until their remains no longer resembled those of a human being.

The less sadistic and more intelligent Italian-American *Mafiosi,* on the other hand, developed political connections and often made an attempt at respectability. To the extent that they understood it, they admired American society and tried to launch at least some of their children into the law-abiding mainstream by giving them a good education. In their personal lives, such *Mafiosi* have often been faithfully devoted husbands and fathers. Some have donated large sums to charity. They retained the Janus-like double image of the old Sicilian Mafia, a face that was benevolent and a face that was evil.

By the mid-1930s, many of the gangsters who had reigned like feudal lords during Prohibition were dead or in prison. Capone was number 40822 in the Atlanta Penitentiary — he would be freed only to be re-incarcerated on Alcatraz, dying of neurosyphilis in 1947. Colosimo was murdered. Rothstein was murdered. Schultz was murdered. Luciano was deported. The man who had brought Capone to Chicago, "Terrible John" Torrio, had withdrawn to Sicily after several attempts on his life.

But because of its cohesive, family-centered structure, Italian-American crime survived the 1930s and became increasingly powerful and subtle. It is an academic question whether or not these Italian-American families went by the name of *Cosa Nostra* as Joseph Valachi testified in 1964. Undoubtedly, Italian criminals in America did have dealings among one another, but they did not exclusively control crime in the United States nor did they deal exclusively with criminals of their own nationality. Even Valachi, after having testified for weeks about what he called the *Cosa Nostra,* "was bewildered when he was told that his testimony had raised a clamor of protest from Italian-Americans who felt he was smearing them and their ancestors. 'I'm not talking about Italians,' Valachi explained, 'I'm talking about criminals.' " [11]

The Mafia does not appear to be very large in terms of its key people. Gage put the number of families at twenty-six and the number of full-time members of the American Mafia at around five thousand. In a report covering the FBI's activities in the crime-fighting sector during fiscal 1969, the late J. Edgar Hoover spoke of "some 3,000 members of *La Cosa Nostra* 'families' operating in the United States today." Shortly thereafter, the Justice Department was instructed to stop using the terms Mafia or *Cosa Nostra* in its press releases because of protests from Italian-Americans who felt that the constant use of these terms was demeaning. Ironically, Mr. Hoover's report was entirely to their advantage. It shows that out of some 15 million Italian immigrants and their descendants in this country, about three thousand are members of the *Cosa Nostra* — a statistically insignificant .0002 percent.

Yet the American *Mafiosi* are of course not insignificant in terms of their power. The President's Crime Commission has estimated the Mafia's income from illegal activities at around $7 billion a year. Presumably much of this money is deposited in banks and can be reinvested selectively. The most striking thing about the American Mafia remains its success. It represents a great and mysterious paradox, how a tiny immigrant group, a clan steeped in feudal fantasies created a thousand or even two thousand years ago in a backward rural society, has been able to impose its will for close to half a century on the strongest, most open and swiftly changing society in the world.

For a brief period, between the end of World War I in 1918 and the onset of Prohibition in 1920, it seemed that the Italian anarchist might eclipse the *Mafioso* as a figure of popular fear and approbation in America. It was the time of the "great Red scare," to which Italian immigrants contributed appreciably.

On June 2, 1919, a bomb exploded in front of the residence of A. Mitchell Palmer, attorney general of the United States. It exploded prematurely, and its carrier — later identified as Carlo Valdinoce, an Italian anarchist from Paterson, New Jersey — was blown into fragments of bone and flesh. The front of the attorney general's home was damaged, and his lawn, like that of his neighbor, Assistant Secretary of the Navy Franklin D. Roosevelt, was showered with pink leaflets proclaiming "class war." The leaflets bore the title *Plain Words* and were signed, "The Anarchist Fighters." [12] The FBI traced these leaflets to an Italian printing shop in Brooklyn, where in February 1920, agents arrested Roberto Elia, a printer, and Andrea Salsedo, a typesetter.

After the two men had been detained at FBI headquarters in New York for over a month, a group of Italian anarchists in Massachusetts who had begun raising a defense fund sent a personal emissary to find out what more they could do in behalf of Elia and Salsedo. The emissary was a Plymouth fish peddler, Bartolomeo Vanzetti. On the evening of April 25, 1920, the tall, stoop-shouldered Vanzetti, his long face traversed by a wide drooping moustache, boarded a train for New York. Though he must have known he was fishing in troubled waters, he could not suspect as the train pulled out of the Boston station that he had just taken his first step towards the electric chair.

The number of Italian anarchists active in America just before and after World War I was probably no greater than the number of *Mafiosi* cited by Hoover — perhaps some three thousand or so. Their numerical strength in Italy was around ten times that figure, still small in a country of nearly 40 million people.

In Italy particularly, anarchists tended to come from the extreme ends of society. Many of the movement's leaders were young noblemen in revolt against the class system. In this they followed the pattern established by Michael Bakunin, the Russian aristocrat who is generally regarded as the most influential nineteenth-century European anarchist. As important to the history of the Italian movement, however, was the duke of San Giovanni, Carlo Pisacane.

Pisacane was an exceptionally interesting man. He had taken part in the revolutions of 1848 and had been chief of staff of Avezzana's Army of the Roman Republic — Garibaldi's superior in Rome. After the defeat of the Republic, Pisacane retired to his country home for nine years during which he read deeply into French revolutionary philosophers, particularly Proudhon, who had argued that because the upper classes had exploited peasants for centuries, all accumulated property was the product of theft. As Pisacane became more radicalized, he was moved to work out his own anarchist philosophy. He came to believe that the Italian people could only be truly liberated if the peasants were freed from landowners at the same time that Italy's Austrian and Bourbon masters were overthrown. Pisacane "demanded, like Proudhon, that every man have 'the fruit of his own labor guaranteed,' and that 'all other property be not only abolished but denounced as theft.' Pisacane, in fact, went beyond Proudhon in the direction of collectivism, since he wanted industrial plants to become collective property and the land to be cultivated by . . . communes in such a way that the people should share equally in the produce of agriculture." [13] But Pisacane, like many other anarchists, was not a Marxist. He did not want to see the establishment of a powerful proletarian state, but the abolition of the state entirely. People would voluntarily enter into a collective form of life after an anarchist revolution had opened their minds to new concepts of life.

"Ideas result from deeds," Pisacane wrote, "not the latter from the former, and the people will not be free when they are educated but will be educated when they are free." [14]

In 1857 he again served the cause of Italian independence and in a preview of Garibaldi's invasion of Sicily three years later, sailed from Genoa in the steamship *Cagliari* at the head of a small army of patriots and invaded Calabria. The Bourbon forces surrounded him, defeated his small army and shot him to death. Pisacane, the duke of San Giovanni, thus passed into Italian history as a hero of the Risorgimento, though he would have violently rejected the Italy that emerged from the Risorgimento with its class structure largely intact, a neocapitalistic society dominated by a few thousand rich industrialists and landowners, most of them in Milan and Turin.

Errico Malatesta, the most important Italian anarchist leader after the Risorgimento, was the son of a landowner in the south of Italy. He had grown up surrounded by scenes of desperate peasant poverty. Though Malatesta was opposed to random acts of violence, he believed firmly in an anarchist revolution. "Don't you know," he cried to workers in denouncing the prosperous Italian elite, "that every bit of bread they eat is taken from your children, every fine present they give to their wives means poverty, hunger, cold, even prostitution for yours?" [15] The same cries would be echoed by the agitators of the IWW before crowds of immigrant workers in America.

The laborers who followed leaders like Malatesta were often men who had been uprooted. They had started life as the children of peasants. Then they had emigrated north to the factories of Milan, or across the Alps to France and Belgium, or across the Atlantic, working as laborers or as fodder for giant industries that treated them impersonally and harshly.

It was men such as these who at the end of the nineteenth century put into action at the grossest level Pisacane's dictum that ideas should follow deeds, launching a spectacular wave of assassinations that made them hated and feared throughout Europe. In 1894 they murdered the French president, Sidi Carnot. Three years later they shot to death the prime minister of Spain, Antonio Canovas. The following year Luigi Luccheni in a particularly revolting crime, stabbed to death the Empress Elizabeth of Austria in Geneva.[16] In 1900, a young Italian immigrant returned to Italy and, at Monza, shot to death King Umberto in revenge for the suppression of strikers. When President McKinley was assassinated in Buffalo, New York, in 1901, Italian anarchists were at once suspected.

In many ways, though he was almost certainly a nonviolent man, Bartolomeo Vanzetti was a typical Italian convert to the anarchist cause. In prison, he wrote a brief autobiography, *The Story of a Proletariat Life,* in which he recounted his sufferings and his alienation from middle-class society both in his native Italy and in America.

Born in a relatively prosperous farming community in Piedmont in 1888, the lanky, ugly boy adored school and was a bright pupil, but his peasant father forced him to drop out at the age of thirteen and apprenticed him to a baker. A dreary succession of jobs in restaurant kitchens and pastry shops followed until Vanzetti decided to emigrate to America in 1908. His mother had just died, the one person to whom he had been truly close.

"It was I who laid her in her coffin," he wrote of her death. "I who accompanied her to the final resting place, I who threw the first handful of earth over her bier. And it was right that I should do so, for I was burying a part of myself . . . the void left has never been filled." [17]

From Le Havre, the twenty-year-old Vanzetti traveled to New York in the steerage compartment of an ocean liner and his first contact with America chilled and disoriented him.

How well I remember standing at the Battery, in lower New York, upon my arrival, alone, with a few poor belongings in the way of clothes, and very little money. Until yesterday I was among [people] who understood me. This morning I seemed to have awakened in a land where my language meant little more to the native than the pitiful noises of a dumb animal. Where was I to go? What was I to do? [18]

He found a job as a dishwasher in an elegant restaurant, working alternate twelve- and fourteen-hour days with five hours off on Sunday, for a salary of $5 to $6 a week. "The vapor of boiling water where the plates, pans, and silver were washed formed great drops of water on the ceiling, took up all the dust and grime there, and fell slowly one by one upon my head, as I worked below." [19]

He quit, tramping around New York for three months alone and destitute while the terrifying contrasts between the Mulberry Bend and the affluence of Fifth Avenue burned into his mind. He was an incipient anarchist already, dreaming of a new and ideal society where men would be equal. With another young unemployed Italian he wandered through the Connecticut countryside asking for jobs and handouts. At Meriden he worked for a time in the stone quarries. He drifted back to New York and worked as a pastry cook in a restaurant and then at a hotel. Unemployed again, he slept in doorways with newspapers stuffed under his clothing to keep from freezing.[20] Finally, he was hired to work in a railroad construction gang near Springfield, Massachusetts. When that job was done he went over to Plymouth, where he worked in a loading gang at the Plymouth Cordage Company. But his participation in a strike cost him his job there and at last, tired of working for others, he bought a pushcart and began to peddle fish. To make ends meet he did odd jobs as well, but finally he was his own master.

A lonely, introspective man, Vanzetti found a certain contentment at Plymouth, lavishing his affections on his Italian friends and their children. Many nights, he would lie awake until almost dawn reading the social philosophers — Pisacane, Mazzini, Marx, Bakunin, Malatesta. At Plymouth he boarded with the Brini family. Vincenzo Brini was an Italian immigrant, a steady wage-earner but also a free-thinker sympathetic to the anarchist movement. "The Brini house," wrote Francis Russell, "was a way station for every passing anarchist. Luigi Galleani had stopped there, and big, genial, bearded Carlo Tresca, and the poet Arturo Giovannitti, and Malatesta himself, the aristocrat turned radical, with his beautiful voice. Night after night they used to sit in the Brini kitchen, talking, talking, talking of the brave new world to come." [21]

Arriving in New York on the evening of April 25, 1920, stepping off the train from Boston at Grand Central Station, Vanzetti was met by Tresca, who had succeeded to the leadership of the Italian anarchists in America due to Luigi Galleani's deportation. Vanzetti also saw Luigi Quintiliano, secretary of the Italian Workers' Defense Committee charged with aiding Elia and Salsedo. What Tresca and Quintiliano had to say to Vanzetti was hardly cheerful. Dozens of Italian anarchists had already been rounded up and deported on Attorney General Palmer's orders. Now the Defense Committee's lawyer, an American, was predicting an even more thorough crackdown by the Justice Department.[22] Italian anarchists in New York had begun destroying their flyers and pamphlets to avoid incrimination. Unable to discover anything specific about Elia and Salsedo, Vanzetti returned to Boston.

It was a particularly tense moment in American history. President

Wilson lay in the White House still convalescing from a stroke he had suffered on October 2, 1919; he had been President since 1913 and he was old, tired, querulous, and discredited because of the peace that had failed. Americans who had believed with wartime fervor that the defeat of the Central Powers would usher in a period of worldwide democracy were now being forced to adjust to the reality of a world in turmoil. The First World War, far from being simply a struggle between the democracies and the spike-helmeted Germans and Austrians as it appeared to be, would mark in violence the end of Europe's long domination of the globe and the beginning of the end of colonialism. The genie of revolution loomed suddenly above the charred battlefields, and the creation of a proletariat state in Russia was hailed by sympathetic workers throughout the exhausted countries of Europe. In Germany, the Spartacists had tried to proclaim a Soviet republic. In northern Italy workers occupied over five hundred factories, and the country, along with several Balkan nations, seemed on the verge of revolution. Red flags appeared on the streets in England and France. The old order was passing, and with its passing the democracies of the West entered into a time of unrelenting pressure and adaptation.

In America, too, "Reds" posed a grave threat in the minds of many people. The nation's first general strike, in Seattle, followed by a wave of vicious bombings, appeared to herald an era of leftist violence. The reaction was a sharp crackdown on Wobblies, Bolshevik sympathizers, and anarchists — many of whom were foreign-born laborers rebelling against their conditions of work and their sense of powerlessness. Attorney General Palmer, shocked by the attempted bombing of his own home, warned Congress that the Reds were planning "to rise up and destroy the government at one fell swoop." [23] All over the country dangerous aliens were rounded up for deportation. At one California banquet, a speaker had suggested indignantly that "these murderous wild beasts of our otherwise blessed Republic should be given a pint of meal and a bottle of water and shoved out into the ocean on a raft, when the wind is blowing seaward." [24] This policy was adopted, almost literally. Several hundred "Bolshies" were arrested at a meeting commemorating the second anniversary of the Russian Revolution. After a swift screening, they were put aboard the transport *Buford* — popularly known as the Soviet Ark — and shipped to Russia.

On January 2, 1920, Palmer launched the more extensive raids that would come to bear his name. Alien anarchists and Bolsheviks were rounded up for deportation in thirty-three cities. In all, some six thousand people were arrested.[25] "The victims were loaded into trucks, or sometimes marched through the streets handcuffed and chained to one another, and massed by the hundreds at concentration points. . . ."[26] Though ultimately only some five hundred of these alien radicals were deported, the Palmer raids were cheered by millions of Americans. They provided a focus for emotions and a national catharsis. The crescendo of labor violence and bombings after World War I, and the residue of unspent, unsatisfied emotions raised by the war, came together in that winter of 1919–1920. There was a power vacuum in Washington and for a few months Palmer filled it, eyeing the White House ambitiously. But he pressed his anti-Red drive so far that by the spring of 1920 even the conservative Republican National Committee had swung against him. When Palmer rashly predicted a mass uprising of radicals on May 1, 1920 — May Day — and the day instead passed peacefully, the attorney general was finished as a national figure. The "Red Scare" would subside as quickly as it had arisen. But not before it had netted Vanzetti and the man whose destiny would become linked to his, Nicola Sacco.

On May 2, 1920, in Boston, Vanzetti, Sacco, and a group of their anarchist colleagues met to decide how to best gather up and destroy anarchist literature they had already distributed. It was pointed out that Mario Buda, a young Italian anarchist living in Bridgewater who called himself "Mike" Boda, owned an Overland car which he had stored in a shed belonging to Ferruccio Coacci, another anarchist.[27] Though dilapidated, the Overland might be used to collect the incriminating propaganda.

And here the two versions of the Sacco-Vanzetti case diverge. The Bridgewater police chief, Michael E. Stewart — who baited a trap with the Overland — was certain that Sacco and Vanzetti tried to obtain the car in order to use it in a robbery attempt. There had been a sharp rise in crimes of violence in the industrial towns of Massachusetts in 1919, and it was Chief Stewart's belief that this phenomenon was due to the presence of anarchists trying to raise money for their cause, rather than ordinary criminals. On the day before Christmas 1919, four "foreigners" driving a touring car had attempted to hold up a payroll truck in broad daylight in downtown Bridgewater. The truck was carrying $30,000 in a strongbox locked and bolted to the floor, so that the bandits would have had to kill all the guards and then steal the truck itself to get at the money. They approached it head-on and began firing at random from a distance. As the guards returned this fire, a streetcar rumbled between the two vehicles, allowing the truck to pull away. Its driver lost control and crashed against a telegraph pole, but by then the bandits had sped off.

It did not look like the work of professional criminals. Anarchists, was Chief Stewart's suspicion. He began checking the area and soon enough turned up "Mike" Boda and the Overland. When Stewart returned a second time to the shack where Boda was living to question him, the Italian slipped out, reached East Boston and hid out there with friends.[28]

If the day-before-Christmas robbery at Bridgewater had been a farce, a payroll robbery four months later at nearby South Braintree was a different matter. Five "foreigners" shot two payroll guards dead and stole $16,000 outside the Rice & Hutchins shoe factory. It became Chief Stewart's conviction, and that of District Attorney Frederick G. Katzmann who soon entered the case, that the South Braintree crime, involving a brutal double murder and robbery, had been committed by Sacco, Vanzetti, "Mike" Boda, Ferruccio Coacci, and another Italian anarchist, Ricardo Oriciani. They also believed that some of these men, including Vanzetti, had staged the earlier attempt at Bridgewater. However, they were able to indict only Sacco and Vanzetti for the South Braintree crime, which all eyewitnesses agreed had been the work of five bandits. Of the other three Italians, Coacci had been deported just after the crime. Boda, after lying low in East Boston, Portsmouth, and then Providence, received a passport from the Italian consul under his original name of Buda and sailed to Italy. He thereafter steadfastly refused to return to Boston to testify in behalf of Sacco and Vanzetti because he said his life would be in danger. The third man, Oriciani, had a watertight alibi. His factory time card showed he had been at work during both the Bridgewater and South Braintree crimes.[29]

In the eyes of their defenders, Sacco and Vanzetti were guilty only of being anarchists. On the evening of May 5 they blundered into Chief Stewart's trap out of anxiety to collect possibly incriminating anarchist literature. This anxiety had been heightened by the news that Salsedo's crushed body had been found lying on the pavement in front of FBI headquarters in New York, fourteen stories below the window of the room where he had been held. According to Elia's subsequent affidavit, he and Salsedo had remained voluntarily at FBI headquarters, having been warned that the alternatives might be jail or deportation.[30] Their lawyer and their families knew that they were there and could visit them. Though Elia said he was well treated throughout this detention, Salsedo was apparently beaten at the start by agents trying to discover the identity of the man who had blown himself up while attempting to bomb Attorney General Palmer's house.[31] After Salsedo admitted to having printed *Plain Words,* there were no more beatings and he and Elia were taken out for walks and even to a movie. But as their detention continued Salsedo became more and more despondent and, according to Elia's deposition, mentally unbalanced. He finally took his own life. The Italian anarchists in Boston, however, knew none of this background. They assumed that Salsedo had been tortured and then pushed out the window, and they now feared the same kind of treatment themselves. They may also have known what FBI agents presumably learned from Elia and Salsedo — namely that the *Plain Words* leaflets which Salsedo had printed had been ordered by members of Luigi Galleani's group,[32] and that Galleani's followers had probably been responsible for numerous bombings.

On the evening of May 5, therefore, Sacco, Vanzetti, "Mike" Boda, and Ricardo Oriciani set out for the Overland, which had been towed to the garage of Simon Johnson of Bridgewater since it lacked a 1920 registration. While Johnson stalled the men, his wife called the police. Their suspicions aroused, the Italians left abruptly. Boda and Oriciani drove off in a motorcycle with a sidecar, while Sacco and Vanzetti, who had known each other for three years and had become steadfast friends, took the Brockton streetcar bound for Sacco's house. While still aboard the streetcar they were arrested by officer Michael Connolly at Chief Stewart's request.

At the Campello station, the Italians were searched and then questioned by Stewart. Vanzetti was carrying a loaded .38 calibre revolver, four shotgun shells and a pocket knife. Sacco was armed with a .32 calibre Colt automatic, with eight cartridges in the clip, one in the chamber, and another twenty-three loose cartridges in his pockets.[33] Both men, questioned separately, lied about the reason they had visited the Johnson garage and denied knowing Boda or Coacci. Both men were draft dodgers, having fled to Mexico together in 1917 to escape induction (from which they would have been exempt anyway, though they did not know it). Both were aliens. Both were anarchists. Sacco was carrying an announcement in Italian that Vanzetti had scribbled that same evening.

It began: "Proletarians, you have fought all the wars. You have worked for all the owners . . ." and ended with an invitation to hear Vanzetti speak on the subject of exploitation. "Freedom of discussion for all. Bring the ladies with you." [34]

Though District Attorney Katzmann was able to indict Sacco because a bullet taken from the body of one of the dead payroll guards at South Braintree appeared to match test bullets fired from Sacco's Colt .32, he did not have enough evidence to prosecute Vanzetti. This dilemma was resolved when eyewitnesses to the earlier bungled robbery attempt at Bridgewater identified Vanzetti as one of the four "foreign" bandits — despite the fact that Vanzetti did not altogether resemble any of the men originally described.

Thus, it was decided to first try Vanzetti separately on the charge of attempted robbery at Bridgewater. This trial was held in Plymouth, Massachusetts, in June 1920. Shackled by an inept defense and by his own decision not to testify, Vanzetti was found guilty and sentenced to twelve to fifteen years at hard labor.

The following year, in 1921, Sacco and Vanzetti were tried together at Dedham for the murders and armed robbery at South Braintree. By that time, of course, Vanzetti was already a convicted criminal.

Of all the factors that damaged Vanzetti at his first — and crucial — trial at Plymouth, none stands out so clearly as the prejudice against Italians shared by Judge Webster Thayer (who would also preside a year later at the Dedham trial) and the jurymen. This prejudice may in part have been provoked by Vanzetti's anarchist beliefs, but it still denied him a fair trial. One of the reasons Vanzetti chose not to testify at Plymouth was that his alibi seemed so strong. Over a dozen Italian residents of Plymouth came forward to swear under oath that on December 24, 1919, Vanzetti could not have been involved in the robbery at Bridgewater because he had been delivering eels to their own homes in Plymouth. These eels, however, had a significance that was entirely alien to the non-Italian judge, district attorney, and jurymen. For Catholics, the day before Christmas is a day of fasting; and southern Italians traditionally break this fast at the evening meal on Christmas Eve by eating eels that have been boiled and then marinated in vinegar. This was an important observance, and it was natural for the Plymouth Italians to be able to recall that on December 24, on precisely that morning, Vanzetti had delivered their eels. He was accompanied on his rounds by thirteen-year-old Beltrando Brini, who also testified. The fact that the Brini household was a way station for Italian anarchists allowed District Attorney Katzmann to suggest that the boy's testimony had been prepared for him, that he was lying. The surprising thing is that Katzmann was able to destroy, in the same manner, the testimony of the other Italian witnesses, all of whom were adults and most of whom had no sympathy for Vanzetti's political ideas. One of these witnesses, Vincent Longhi, was a native son of Plymouth and a World War I veteran. Though he testified that on the morning of December 24 Vanzetti had entered his kitchen to deliver eels, he was not believed.

The Italian witnesses were hectored by Katzmann. When housewife Margaret Fiocchi was testifying, the district attorney suddenly asked her to tell him what kind of a moustache the court stenographer had "without looking at him." Not unnaturally, Mrs. Fiocchi glanced at the stenographer, and Katzmann cried triumphantly, "And this the way you tell the truth about the eels — because you talked with somebody before you took the stand, is it not? Some of those Italians up there told you what to say?" [35]

Herbert B. Ehrmann, junior defense counsel in the final weeks of the Sacco-Vanzetti trial, wrote of Vanzetti's alibi witnesses that "these men and women were stable, longtime residents of the town. The prosecution was apparently unable to find a single blemish on their reputation as law-abiding people. Most of them had lived in the same homes and held the same jobs for years. . . ." [36] They were not believed, he wrote, because Katzmann successfully insinuated that they had been coached in their testimony, and perhaps also because of the basic substance of Vanzetti's alibi. Eels. Had Vanzetti been delivering turkeys to the homes of Plymouth's native American citizens on the day before Thanksgiving, one wonders if there would have been a Plymouth trial at all, let alone if the state could have convicted Vanzetti on the kind of evidence it produced. The Plymouth trial, Ehrmann concluded, furnished "an excellent casebook for a study in prejudice." [37]

Unlike Ettor and Giovannitti, who had been tried in Massachusetts a decade earlier under similar but decidedly more ennobled charges, Sacco and Vanzetti were able to speak only mangled English. This too was against them. "I am suffering because I am a radical," Vanzetti said to the jury in his final statement, "and indeed I am a radical. I have suffered because I was an Italian, and indeed I am an Italian." Three phrases more and he was finished. But as Judge Webster Thayer began to pass sentence, proscribing that Nicola Sacco would "suffer the punishment of death by a passage of a current of electricity through your body," Vanzetti spoke up again. He had wanted to say something more about Sacco. Judge Thayer interrupted him to finish passing sentence on him. Vanzetti was not allowed to say what he had wanted to say, so he wrote down those remarks and passed them afterwards to Italian friends.

"I have talked a great deal of myself," he wrote,

but I even forgot to name Sacco. Sacco too is a worker from his boyhood, a skilled worker lover of work, with a good job and pay, a bank account, a good and lovely wife, two beautiful children and a neat little home at the verge of a wood, near a brook. Sacco is a heart, a faith, a character, a man; a man lover of nature and of mankind. A man who gave all, who sacrifice all to the cause of liberty and to his love for mankind; money, rest, mundain ambitions, his own wife, himself, and his own life. Sacco has never dreamt to steal, never to assassinate. He and I never brought a morsel of bread to our mouths, from our childhood to today, which has not been gained by the sweat of our brows. Never.

Oh yes, I may be more witful, as some have put it, I am a better babbler than he is, but many, many times in hearing his heartful voice ringing a faith sublime, in considering his supreme sacrifice, remembering his heroism, I felt small at the presence of his greatness and found myself compelled to fight back from my eyes the tears . . . to not weep before him — this man called thief and assassin and doomed. But Sacco's name will live in the hearts of the people and in their gratitude when Katzmann's and [your] bones will be dispersed by time, when your name, his name, your laws, institutions, and your false gods are but a [dim remembrance] of a cursed past in which man was wolf to the man. . . .[38]

It will seem unjust to some readers that the Mafia, and Italian anarchists such as Pisacane, Malatesta, Tresca, Sacco and Vanzetti, should have been linked together in this fashion in the same chapter under what could be called a general heading of "Italian violence." Italians (in Italy) would object immediately that anarchists are men of the left, and idealists, while the Mafia is a phenomenon of the right and its members are criminals.

But there is another point to be made. The conditions under which Italian immigrants lived when they came to the United States was bound to call forth a reaction. That reaction took two extreme forms, both representing a basic emotional alienation from the democratic system. Italians were not "biologically" disposed to violence, as many Anglo-Saxons in America believed. If anything, their personal lives were characterized by a basically conservative and stable Catholic morality. The Italians who committed acts of criminal violence in America were already full of hatred when they crossed the Atlantic because of the history of exploitation and injustice that lay behind them. They did not see the Statue of Liberty. They did not see the rolling farmlands of Pennsylvania, nor the wide Mississippi, nor the vineyards planted by Italian hands on the hillsides of California. They saw one thing only. They saw the contrast between the Mulberry Bend and the mansions of Fifth Avenue.

12

Little Italies

THE GREAT MAJORITY, the ninety-nine percent of Italian-Americans, had nothing to do with either the Mafia or the anarchist movement. They were aspiring American citizens, sober, law-abiding people, possibly even more fervent in their loyalty to the United States than older residents who tended to take their loyalty as a matter of course.

"I have never heard such moving expressions of love for this country as I have heard [among Italian-Americans]," wrote William Foote Whyte in his study of Italian street gangs in the 1930s. "But," he added, "if a man wants to forget that he is an Italian, the society around him does not let him forget it. He is marked as an inferior person — like all other Italians. To bolster his own self-respect he must tell himself and tell others that the Italians are a great people, that their culture is second to none, and that their great men are unsurpassed." [1]

Truly, the Italian-Americans of the first and second generations were people between two worlds.

Though the older immigrants surrounded themselves nostalgically with Italian foods, Italian songs and photographs of Italian opera singers, actually they had barely participated in the rich culture of Italy. Even though they now began to speak with aggressive pride of Michelangelo and of Marconi, *those* men had been part of that other Italy, the Italy across the tracks, north of Naples, the Italy of Botticelli painting Simonetta Vespucci as Venus and of Galileo staring at the universe through his telescope. And that other, highly civilized Italy, which had not wanted

the immigrants, did not now care to acknowledge them as "sons of Italy."
It was a source of continuing embarrassment to upper- and middle-class
Italians that their country should be represented in the eyes of the
Anglo-Saxon world by all these southern immigrants, unschooled, and
censured in the press for their violence.

"Oh, but they're not really *Italian*," the more fastidious Italians said.

Not Italian. Not yet American. "Still eating spaghetti," an American
social worker reported after a visit to an Italian neighborhood, "not yet
assimilated." These people, who had come mostly from villages with
powerful local traditions and loyalties, now turned their tenement blocks
in the heart of the American city into substitute villages, hung crucifixes
on the bedroom walls and cloves of garlic on the kitchen walls, spoke
Italian dialects among themselves — re-creating in their lives a semblance of emotional order, because the transition they faced was enormous. It was not simply a case of forgetting Italian and laboriously
filling their mouths with thick English words, or abandoning spaghetti
for stew and potatoes.

A slow, measured cycle of seasons, of simple repetitive tasks had been
the experience of these people in their villages, the pace of their lives
slow, consistent — men returning home at sunset, walking uphill slowly
beside their mules, women pounding their wash on warm, flat stones
beside a stream, pausing to gossip; bells ringing for vespers in the
twilight, smoke rising from chimneys. No telephones. No cars. No
speeds, really, greater than the speed of the human footstep. Their
landscapes were full of permanences. The look of a village changed
very slowly. A house might be abandoned, another built, only once in
ten years. The terraced land of the hillsides for miles around remained
wrought in the same configurations for a man's lifetime, his son's and
grandson's lifetimes.

The New World into which these immigrants were plunged was truly
a new world for them, of motion, of change and psychological stress beyond anything they had previously experienced. Their reaction was to
strengthen even more firmly the bonds of family life and of the neighborhood.

In ancient Rome, the great three- or four-story tenement houses where
the poor lived jammed together were called *insulae*, or islands, because
they occupied an entire block with streets on all four sides. Now, in the
New World, these poor relations of the Roman World re-created their
own kind of *insulae*, ethnic islands that consisted of a cluster of build-

ings occupied by Italians, often families from the same village or the same province. In Chicago, there was a Tuscan enclave at 24th and Oakley, a community of Genoese in the Near North Side, and one of Sicilians along Chicago Avenue.[2] Often, these "Little Italies" were contingent to one another, and as the years went on and children were born in America, the separate islands tended to form archipelagoes. People who had been supremely conscious of having come from the area around Naples, or from some village in Calabria or the Puglie, assumed a broader identity as Italian-Americans.

These Italian enclaves were sometimes tiny. When in the late 1960s the city of New York decided to build a new high school and athletic field in the Corona section of Queens, the Planning Commission informed sixty-nine homeowners along four blocks that their property would have to be razed — with compensation, of course.

The affected residents organized and fought back, and soon the New York press began taking an interest in these embattled homeowners of Corona. The press discovered that in crime-ridden New York this *insulae* of Corona represented, as the New York *Times* reported, "one of the few crime-free oases" remaining in the city. All its residents worshiped, were confirmed, married, and mourned at St. Leo's Roman Catholic Church, and their children went to Public School 14. They were nearly all Italian-Americans who formed a tightly knit villagelike community in the midst of the sprawling borough of Queens. They had shared memories, some of them sorrowful. No less than eighty of their sons had served in World War II, and many had not returned. The GI insurance of those dead soldiers had helped pay off the mortgages on homes that the city now wanted to destroy. "It's not just 69 houses or even 138 families," said one resident who had lived there for forty-five years, "it's like one family."[3] She might have been speaking for many other Italian-American communities.

In other ways too, Corona typified the Italian ethnic neighborhoods spread throughout the eastern seaboard of the United States, in parts of the Middle West and along the West Coast. The men were good with their hands, their wives diligent housekeepers. There were usually masons, stonecutters, wood-carvers, plumbers, house painters and gardeners living in an Italian-American community — and the appearance of those neighborhoods showed it. As at Corona, the houses were neatly kept and inside a visitor would find a sense of order and comfort.

"My father built one of these houses with his own hands," said Mrs.

Lillian Manasseri of Corona to a reporter. "People here never went on relief. We worked hard. Even these sidewalks here we put down ourselves and we repair." [4]

At the turn of the century, when Jacob Riis and Theodore Roosevelt had gone on dawn patrol along its dreadful streets, the Mulberry Bend had symbolized a disastrous and hopeless slum. Yet even there the Italian-Americans wrought a steady, patient transformation. The district began to improve in the 1920s as people moved to other parts of Manhattan, or to the Bronx or Queens. On tenement floors where four or five families had lived in nearly intolerable conditions of overcrowding, one family now remained. The peeling wallpaper was replaced, the floors were resurfaced with linoleum, and soon brand-new sofas, stuffed chairs, double beds with coil spring mattresses were being maneuvered up those narrow but no longer malodorous stairs.

Wherever soil could be gathered, in window boxes or little backyard plots, or even out in vacant lots where no one else would bother to hoe and plant, the Italians put down their herbs and strung their vines of tomatoes, their beans and zucchini.

No other ethnic group remained so loyal to its own foods, or had so great an influence on what other Americans ate. Even the lowly pizza, which had nearly become extinct in its place of origin, Naples, before being resurrected in 1905 on New York's Spring Street, now rivals the hot dog and hamburger in popularity.* At least a dozen Italian dishes have become American favorites, including spaghetti and other forms of pasta, lasagne, ravioli, minestrone, chicken cacciatore, and veal scaloppine. But beyond that, the Italians introduced color and flavor to the American table. The vintages bottled in the largely Italian-owned vineyards of California helped make wine part of American meals. After World War II, housewives all over the United States began discovering cheeses like parmesan, mozzarella and ricotta, the use of peeled tomatoes, of tomato and meat sauce, of tomato paste, of herbs traditional to Italian cooking, of olive oil and vinegar dressings on salads.

The popularity of Italian foods, and Italian restaurants, seems so obvious today that it takes an effort to recall how queer they seemed to the

---

* Nearly two billion pizzas are consumed annually in America, along with 600 million pounds of mozzarella cheese and 80 million pounds of tomatoes. Moreover, the American pizzas are as good as those in Naples.

American people at the turn of the century. The average American housewife would no more have thought of buying a box of rigatoni than of wrapping her potatoes in coconut leaves. "Not yet assimilated, still eating spaghetti," sounds quaintly funny now, like saying about German-Americans, "Not yet assimilated, still driving Volkswagens." But the social worker's earnest judgment reflected a powerful American bias against foreign things. It was the immigrant who was expected to adapt to American styles of self-expression, of dress and of cuisine. But however hard they tried otherwise to conform, Italian immigrants were not willing to give up their traditional foods.

One reason for this stubbornness goes far back into Italian history. The diet of Italian peasants, and of southern Italians in particular, had for centuries been almost exclusively vegetarian. Though there were herds of goats and sheep being tended on the mountainsides by shepherds, the goats were kept primarily for milk and the sheep for their wool. The more prosperous peasants regularly ate ham — in the form of salami and *prosciutto* — and also chicken, but the daily meal of humbler Italians consisted mainly of corn or wheat flour products, of bread or sometimes of pasta, supplemented by vegetables and fruit. The typical Italian immigrant to America had been accustomed to eating meat perhaps a dozen times a year — and most of that poultry, a little bacon, an infrequent leg of mutton. These people could not easily adjust to an American diet, based as it was on the cooking of northern Europe, on chunks of meat and overboiled vegetables and the sturdy but bland flavors of foods like porridge. Thus the very first shops that flowered in the Little Italies, shops whose windows lent a characteristic color to the neighborhood, were those that retailed foodstuffs — cans of imported olive oil stacked in pyramids, sausages and cheeses hanging in profusion, baskets of onions and cloves of garlic, pungent herbs, big, firm sacks of rice from the Po Valley. Peddlers sold vegetables, fruit, or fish from their carts, and each morning the laborers trudging to work with their shovels would stop at the baker's shop with its pervasive, unmistakable aroma of fresh bread still warm from the oven.

Social life revolved around the preparation and offering of food, as it had in southern Italy. Very little hard liquor was drunk, but wine was important not only to restore a man's strength when he came home exhausted in the evenings but as a mark of hospitality. In a proud household there was always a glass of wine to be offered to whoever might cross the threshold, not excepting a doctor, a health department inspector, a policeman. The glass of wine might be refused but the gesture of offering it was important. Italians were not hard drinkers and deeply resented Prohibition, which puzzled and disgusted them. Above all, why should it be applied to wine — a product of grapes, of a fruit, a thing healthful and joyous since the earliest times in the Mediterranean? This was an aspect of Puritan, Nordic America that the Italian-Americans could not accept, and politicians in their wards regularly produced shouts of approval and thunderous ovations when they denounced the ban on drinking wine.

Care in preparing and serving food also underscored the basic sensuousness of the Italian-Americans. This sensuousness had nothing to do with the nerve-caressing sensuality of the Italian upper classes — it was physical, earthy, the inheritance of people who for generations had lived close to imperishable things, to sunlight, to the smell of newly turned earth or freshly baked bread, to the colors of the land, of olive leaves, of clouds massed over the sea. This was a heritage shared by all Mediterranean peoples, the Greeks, the Spaniards, the Turks, the Arabs, and the Jews, as well as the Italians, and it could not be quenched in the gray tenement squalor of the big city. It rang out in people's voices, in their mobile and expressive hands, in the intensity with which men looked at women, in the way life moved outdoors into the street where the cobbler stood outside his shop doorway pounding nails into a shoe, where men bought and sold merchandise out on the pavement, and the funeral of a child was a pageant involving a thousand, two thousand people between those in the procession and those at windowsills.

The street was not only an escape from the dark, overcrowded tenements, but an arena in which to debate, to gossip, to examine the gills of fish for freshness or the color of a bolt of cloth, to stand listening to a neighbor's radio or watching his daughter — above all to observe other people.

No one has caught the exact timbre of this kind of earthly sensuousness better than Mario Puzo in *The Fortunate Pilgrim:*

"Che bella insalata" — what beautiful salad — the words rose up to the sleeping children at their moment of awakening. They all sprang out of bed, and Gino looked out the window. Below was the hawker, standing on the seat of his wagon as he held up to the sky and the watching windows a pearly green lettuce in each outstretched hand. *"Che bella insalata"* he said again, not asking anyone to buy, only asking the world to look at beauty. Pride, not cajolement, in his voice, he repeated his cry each time his horse

took a mincing step along the Avenue. In his wagon were boxes of onions dazzling white, great brown potatoes, bushels of apples, bouquets of scallions, leeks, and parsley sprigs. His voice rose rich with helpless admiration, disinterested, a call to lovers. "What beautiful salad." [5]

This Italian sensuousness was reflected in the community's religious festivals — occasions that scandalized the more puritanical Irish hierarchy in the Catholic church in America. "The Italians are not a sensitive people like our own," confided an Irish prelate to the archbishop of New York in 1917. "When . . . told that they are about the worst Catholics that ever came to this country, they don't resent it or deny it." [6] But much of this Irish finger-wagging was misapplied. St. Peter's itself is a sensuous basilica, though the priesthood is an ascetic confraternity. Rome is a sensuous city, and Italy's three thousand-year-old traditions of magic, of ritual and superstitious belief in deities flowed tranquilly into Christianity when it became the religion of Rome. The frankly pagan enjoyment of religious feasts has been a part of Italian life for centuries. Much of Leonardo da Vinci's time in Milan was consumed in designing costumes and mechanical devices for pageants. Year after year Roman aristocratic families vied for the honor of building the most spectacular float for the week-long carnival preceding Ash Wednesday; the Orsinis once raised an artificial mountain with caves from which pretty maidens emerged.

The further south one went on the peninsula, the more fantastic and extravagant religious processions became. For the feast of Santa Rosalia, patron saint of Palermo, the city's normally dark, austere cathedral glowed like an immense diamond, illuminated by fifteen thousand candles reflected in gold- and silver-colored mirrors.[7] Patrick Brydone, writing in 1770, described a float built in Palermo for this same feast that was seventy feet long, thirty feet wide, and drawn by fifty-six mules in double file. "The traditional shape of this float was that of a conch (or a Roman galley) with raised prow, while the stern expanded into an oval amphitheater to hold a large orchestra. . . ." [8] Above the orchestra was a dome supported by six Corinthian pillars, and above the dome rose a huge silver statue of Santa Rosalia.

Even remote villages vibrated to the cycle of these annual festivals. Often, villagers would walk for miles over hill trails to sanctuaries where a saint's day would be celebrated. As women pressed into the chapel, praying, asking the saint's image for miracles, outside the chapel hawkers sold goods while hunters with shotguns sprawled on the grass, drinking wine and eating their bread and tomatoes, and onions, perhaps roasting game. Boys and girls wandered off into the bushes — all of it a scene from some southern Breughel.

This same atmosphere, half sacred, half roisterous, characterized the religious feasts of the Italian immigrants in America. During the annual procession in East Harlem honoring Our Lady of Mount Carmel, thousands of men and women, some of them barefoot, many carrying candles, would wind in parade under the hot, humid July night through streets decorated with lanterns, as bands in the line of march played a half-dozen different hymns all at the same time. As the statue of Our Lady of Mount Carmel was borne past them, women rushed up to pin dollar bills onto her vestments, hoping for a miracle. The route was lined with booths where vendors sold sausages grilled on skewers with tomatoes and peppers, or rich Sicilian cakes. Overhead, fireworks suddenly lit the sultry New York skies.

During the early years of Italian mass immigration, Protestant denominations in the United States made a sustained effort to wean Italians away from Catholicism. Some nativists viewed such conversions as a crucial part of the process of Americanization. An article in a Presbyterian journal in 1907 lamented that with emigration from Italy and eastern Europe, America was being penetrated by "the continental idea of the Sabbath, the socialist's idea of government, the communist's idea of property, and the pagan's idea of religion." [9] It concluded that there was an urgent need "that the gospel be preached to this new immigration." But despite the activity of nearly three hundred Protestant missionaries in the Italian slum areas, few Italian immigrants were converted. Though some of the men might be anticlerical because of papal opposition to Italian unification, the Catholic church was too large a part of their tradition to be easily shed. In one case it was a Protestant missionary who became, in a sense, the apostate. As a young man Norman Thomas labored among Italian immigrants as a pastor in East Harlem. The poverty he saw there turned him into a Socialist, and ultimately into a six-time presidential candidate for the Socialist party in America.

The Catholic church itself was not, of course, inactive among the immigrants. In 1887, Bishop Giovanni Battista Scalabrini of Piacenza had founded the Congregation of the Missionaries of St. Charles to aid Italian immigrants overseas. But the sudden rise and then the tidal overflow of Italian immigration to the United States swamped these efforts.

Well-established Irish parishes resented the sudden influx of Italians, who for their part often found the Irish priests cold and indifferent, if not overbearing. For years, Italians worshiped in the basement of Catholic churches like members of some persecuted sect, gathering to hear mass said by an Italian priest and to confess in their own language. In time, they were able to worship at their own parishes. Where there had been only thirteen Italian parishes in greater New York in 1900, there were forty-four a quarter of a century later. But ironically, Italian-American priests remained subordinate to the Irish hierarchy for decades in their own Roman church. There has never been a single Italian-American cardinal, and the first Italian-American auxiliary bishop, the Most Reverend Joseph M. Pernicone, was only appointed in 1954.

There was another basic difference between earlier Irish immigrants and the southern Italians who swept into their neighborhoods around the turn of the century. However bitter the Irish might feel about the centuries of British oppression they had endured, they could speak English. The Italians initially could not, and were lampooned for decades by stereotyped figures like the swarthy, moustachioed fruit vendor who spread his hands out and confessed, "I-a no speak-a da Eng." Actually, the sprinkling of vowels into English phrases was an effort to bridge the tonal gap between musical Italian, rich in vowel sounds, and English. This problem of language not only kept the Italian neighborhoods insular, but produced a distinctive Italian-American culture that flourished for several decades. Radios and newspapers talked to the immigrants in their own hybrid language, composed mainly of English words and Italian sounds.

A small body of literature even exists, or existed, written in Italo-American. Plays were performed on the stage in the Mulberry Bend or in East Harlem. The protagonist was often Farfariello, a Punch-like character from the Neapolitan folk theater. Only in this case Farfariello represented the *cafone*, the trusting, helpless immigrant from southern Italy just off the boat, being swindled by the padrone, picked on by the Irish cop, and snubbed by the girl eager for social advancement. Men who had lived these same experiences would sit in a small, dimly lit theater roaring with laughter, the tears running down their faces as they saw themselves parodied by the heavily made up, rhetorical, mimicking figure on stage.

There were also hundreds of poems written in Italo-American. One of the most ambitious had Dante arriving as an immigrant. After being processed through Ellis Island, Dante was disembarked at the Battery where he was met by Virgil who escorted him through the Lower East Side to Mulberry Bend — a tour of Purgatory. But the majority of these Italian-American poems were short, bitter commentaries on the indignities and injustices of immigrant poverty. This is a free-verse translation in English of a sonnet written in Italian but employing such Italian-American terms as *bricchelieri* (bricklayers) and *ruffo* (roof).

> *The bricklayers came over by the thousands,*
> *A whole Italian gang with calloused hands,*
> *To raise a building forty stories high*
> *Not counting in the basement or the roof.*
> *The skyscraper's now done; it towers up,*
> *A symbol of American achievement.*
> *But who recalls the greenhorns, the paesani,*
> *The ones who died without the sacraments?*
> *What did they gain when error or misfortune*
> *Came crashing down upon them on those floors?*
> *Poor Guinea, helpless, God-forsaken Dago . . .*
> *Seated before his thick half-pound of steak*
> *The boss just laughs and shows his golden tooth.*
> *"Who's dead is dead. I'm breathing. I don't care."* [10]

This Italian-American culture was destined to have a life of about half a century. It clung to the older generation of immigrants along with their dialects, their folk songs and the women's superstitious beliefs in the magic of lucky numbers in dreams, and of *corni* — red, horn-shaped amulets. The younger Italian-Americans, born on American soil and educated in American schools, regarded it all with a certain contempt.

The conflict of generations was an inevitable part of the immigrant experience. The children of the immigrants responded naturally to other influences and another pace that rushed at them whenever they stepped outside the house. They had no direct personal experience with the old country. As Jo Pagano wrote,

Myself, for example, born in America, brought up in the schools and the streets of the New World, creating a life and being created by it — what knew I of Italy? A country built like a deformed shoe descending from maps of Europe pored over in musty schoolrooms; a name, a flavor, a language, which my people spoke; what reality was there in all this, what remembrance? [11]

Yet the children of Italian immigrants were expected to obey codes of behavior that were strictly Italian, some of which went back to the remote past. The Roman poet Horace, a quarter century before Christ, recounted how a peasant lad in Italy, after working in the fields all day, would not dream of recrossing the threshold of his family's cottage without bringing home a bundle of firewood which he ceremoniously placed inside the door before entering the house himself — wood he had cut down and collected on common land.* When Swindburne visited Calabria in the eighteenth century he found this same custom still being observed by peasant boys. It was a practical custom, since the wood was used for cooking and heating. But it was also a tribute, a sign of filial respect and of a son's willingness to serve and obey his parents. In many Italian-American households, so long as a son lived under his parents' roof, though he might be thirty years old, he was expected to turn over his pay envelope to them unopened. He received an allowance in return.

The American-born son was usually not averse to helping out his family, and thousands of Italian-American boys still in their teens supported parents, grandparents, and a brood of smaller brothers and sisters. But he might chafe at old-world forms of obedience, at a pattern of family hierarchy that seemed unrealistic in America and at variance with its spirit of personal independence.

With every passing year, moreover, the psychological bond of filial obedience grew weaker. Fathers and mothers lost their absolute powers, and logically so. In all agrarian societies, the elders had commanded respect not only because they represented the accumulated wisdom of the community, but because they were the exact living image of what every young person would become after having passed through the same experiences — on and on for generations. This was as true in southern Italy as in China or Japan. Now, in America, the conflict was not only between old Italian influences and new American influences, but a more subtle and profound challenging of the elders by young people who intended, in their hearts, to become as different from them as a man is from a minotaur — to surpass them, to have more personal freedom, to be smarter, to make more money, to live better.

---

* This may be the origin of the symbol of a bundle of rods, or sticks, that appears also on American coins.

This conflict of generations was often sharpest, and most painful, for daughters, who in many Italian-American families had little freedom. Though upper-class women in Italy had always possessed a more complete equality with men, intellectual, physical, and emotional, than perhaps anywhere else in Europe, in the economically hard-pressed laboring classes women were expected to serve both as the anchoring strength of the family and to submit to the often capricious will of their husbands and fathers. They were expected to be eternal mothers — eternally loved and tyrannized. And many Italian-American girls, born and educated in cities, seeing the same movies and reading the same magazines and books as their native American counterparts, found themselves summoned to behave like incipient grandmothers when they were still impatient virgins — to listen respectfully to the advice of all the village-born crones in the neighborhood, to have their dates and even their husbands picked for them. Their own ambivalence in this situation was reinforced by that of Italian-American boys, torn souls who could not decide whether it was more desirable for a girl to be briskly independent in the American manner or Italian and submissive. "Irish girls are more fun than Italian girls," said an Italian boy interviewed by psychologist Irving L. Child in the late 1930s. "The Italian girls have more old-fashioned ideas." But another boy from the same neighborhood said, "A girl has no business staying up late and fooling around. She's got to respect the older people." [12]

As the years passed, it was the older generation's ideas that changed more radically to conform to the new reality of America. What had helped hold the Italian-American families and neighborhoods together through the buffeting forces of change was not only the strong bond of love among relatives and friends, but the bond of a shared experience. They were all moving together through a difficult period of testing and adaptation, towards goals of security, of social acceptance and the advancement of their children. The Italian ethnic neighborhoods, in this sense, were a transitional phenomenon. They served as decompression chambers. By the late 1930s, as the economy recovered under the New Deal, Italian-Americans began abandoning the Little Italies. East Harlem, which had swelled with Italians moving uptown from the congestion and dirt of the Mulberry Bend, now began losing these Italian families to Queens, to the suburbs of Yonkers and Long Island. Puerto Ricans moved in, to the extent that East Harlem is today known as Spanish Harlem.

The move to the suburbs represented almost as great a break with the past, psychologically, as the crossing over from Italy. In the Italian ethnic neighborhoods, the immigrants had re-created a semblance of Italian village life, a rough, rather gaudy but at all times warm, familiar and self-protective environment. Men sitting outdoors in the sunlight on chairs or benches, reading *Il Progresso Italo-Americano;* from open windows came the blaring tones of a tarantella, the baying of a tenor, interspersed with breathless commercials for some Italian-American's furni-. ture store in Brooklyn. The suburbs would not look, sound, or feel like that.

13

Fiorello

THE ONLY PEOPLE who seem to mention La Guardia today are New Yorkers of the older generation nostalgic about their city in its better years. He is publicly remembered as a somewhat comic, volcanic little man (OUR OWN LITTLE STROMBOLI, a Republican paper once headlined acidly),[1] an irrepressible jack-in-the-box jumping out of old Graphlex photos with his plump index finger raised indignantly, high falsetto voice mugging as he kept children up to date on the adventures of Dick Tracy during the newspaper strike. Fiorello, the little flower. Even his name seems to diminish his stature. What schoolchild today can identify a single accomplishment of his apart from the fact that he was mayor of New York?

Yet he was more than just a good mayor of a troubled metropolis. During the 1920s he was an important political thinker, an aggressive champion of the rights and aspirations of the American people. La Guardia was a reformer who sought to improve the system from within. He succeeded in many ways, and people forget today that he was considered by his enemies a radical, or as he himself liked to say — taking the phrase from Nietzsche — a fighter against his time.

The gods could not have put together a more heterogeneous man. His father, Achille, was a southerner from the beautiful high plains of the Puglie beloved by Frederick II. (Near Foggia, Achille La Guardia's birthplace, is the town of Manfredonia named for Frederick's son Man-fred, the last Hohenstaufen king of Sicily.) By profession Achille was a musician who in his early years played in orchestras throughout Europe and even shipped out to the Dutch East Indies, where he was a bandmaster. On his return to Italy he married Irene Coen, a plump, dark, intelligent young woman from Trieste whose mother's family, the Luzzatis, had been distinguished citizens of the republic of Venice for centuries.[2] Irene was Austrian in citizenship, Italian in culture. In 1880 the newlyweds emigrated to America, settling in the Italian section of Greenwich Village and it was there that Fiorello was born. He was named after his maternal grandmother, Fiorella Coen.

A few months after the boy's birth, his father enrolled in the U.S. Army as a bandmaster and the whole family moved to Prescott, Arizona. The West was still being settled, and it was there that Fiorello grew up. "All my boyhood memories are of those Arizona days," he wrote in his autobiography, "To me that is truly God's country. I love everything about it. . . . Our playground was not measured in acres, or city blocks, but in miles and miles. We could do just about everything a small boy dreams of." [3]

There were only two thousand inhabitants in Prescott then. No cars, no telephones, no movies; the first electric lights were just being installed. Life was simple and rugged, and all through his political career La Guardia would trace his self-reliance and toughness to that Arizona frontier upbringing.

He was a tiny, aggressive, charming boy — a hummingbird. When his sister Gemma invited her girlfriends over to play, he would jump on the table and harangue this captive female audience on the proper raising of children.[4] He was terribly sensitive about his height, and would not be ridiculed.

No one, Gemma remembers, could taunt her brother about his size without his flying into a rage. This would always be true. And when he got into a fight, particularly against bigger boys, he preferred to be walloped rather than budge an inch. "I licked him every day," boasted Joe Bauer, one of his classmates — every day because Fiorello came back for more. Once, to give an extreme example, he was fighting a lad in the schoolyard who was so much taller than he that his fists couldn't reach [the boy's] face. Sobbing, Fiorello broke off, ran into the building, returned with a chair, got up on it, and began swinging away.[5]

There were other taunts, too — about being a dago. These puzzled and hurt the boy. "I must have been about ten when a street organ-grinder with a monkey blew into town. He, and particularly the monkey, attracted a great deal of attention. I can still hear the cries of the kids: 'A dago with a monkey! Hey Fiorello, you're a dago too. Where's your monkey?' " [6] The boy was mortified when his father, chatting with the organ-grinder in Italian, expansively invited him over for dinner. "The kids taunted me for a long time after that. I couldn't understand it. What difference was there between us? Some of their families hadn't been in the country any longer than mine." [7]

Irene Coen seems to have tried to minimize her son's feeling of being different. Though Jewish, she did not keep a kosher home. People in Prescott, regarding her as an Italian, assumed she was Catholic. Wanting her children to be as much like other American children as possible, she sent them to an Episcopal Sunday school and brought them up as Protestants. "Fiorello was indifferent to religion as a boy and he would suffer no qualms of conscience in marrying a Catholic in the rectory of St. Patrick's Cathedral, and, after her death, a Lutheran in a ceremony performed by a Lutheran minister." [8] The original human melting pot, Fiorello thought of himself as an Italian-American. Though his ability to address crowds in Yiddish would win him votes in the Lower East Side, Fiorello was not apparently deeply conscious of his Jewish heritage until World War II, when with rage and heartbreak he learned that his sister Gemma was in a Nazi concentration camp. She — a Protestant — had married a Hungarian Jew and had beeen arrested with her husband. He died, but she survived and returned to America after the Allied victory.

At fifteen, Fiorello became a high-school dropout, though involuntarily. In February 1898, the *Maine* was blown up in Havana harbor and on April 25 President McKinley declared war on Spain. Achille's unit, the Eleventh Infantry, was sent to Mobile, Alabama, on the Gulf of Mexico while dependents were transferred to a barracks in St. Louis.[9] Fiorello had tried to enlist but he was underage and puny. Nevertheless, he managed to join the troops through a feat of bravado and La Guardia fluency, persuading a skeptical editor of the St. Louis *Post-Dispatch* to send him down to Mobile as a war correspondent.

On May 18, the paper carried his first by-line piece under the headline EVERYBODY IN FINE SPIRITS. The men, reported the fifteen-year-old correspondent, "are ready and anxious for the order to go to Cuba." [10] But war is suffering, and this Spanish-American War that had offered Fiorello such high adventure would sear him more terribly than he could foresee. In Tampa, Florida, where the Eleventh Infantry was sent before embarkation for Cuba, Achille came down with malaria and his health was permanently damaged when he ate diseased beef that had been sold to the army by war profiteers. "My father became so ill as a result of eating some of this diseased beef that he had to be discharged from the service on account of disability. Though we did not know it then, he had only a few years to live because of the work of crooked Army contractors." [11]

Reduced to living on a pension of eight dollars a month, the La Guardias returned to Trieste in 1898. They boarded with grandmother Fiorella. But three years later the former bandmaster was dead and, at eighteen, Fiorello became the head of the family.

He had not even finished high school. Though not unattractive, he was under five feet tall, glandular, with a falsetto voice. Yet over the next twenty years Fiorello La Guardia would live a life that most young men only dream about: he would represent his country abroad, become fluent in three languages, be challenged to a duel, have love affairs with talented, sophisticated and beautiful European women, protect the weak, the poor and defenseless, be admitted to the bar in New York State, learn to fly an airplane not much different from the one designed by the Wright brothers, be elected to Congress, and become a war hero.

At the ripe age of eighteen, Fiorello went to work at the American consulate in Budapest. The city, as La Guardia recalled nostalgically towards the end of his life "was at the height of its glory in the ten years before the First World War smashed the Austro-Hungarian Empire forever. One could hear more good music in Budapest in 1902 and 1903 than in Vienna. The town was considered the gayest in Europe, and many American dancers and other entertainers turned up there." [12]

Though La Guardia had been hired as a clerk, his duties were more challenging and varied than that modest title would imply. His superior in Budapest was Frank Dyer Chester of Boston, a brilliant linguist with a Ph.D. from Harvard in Semitic languages. "Chester was reserved, correct, well-dressed and delicate to the point of effeminacy." [13] They were a study in contrast, the cool, fastidious Bostonian and his brash, eager, hot-blooded assistant.

There were inevitable clashes when Chester, with his headmaster mentality, sought to impose his standards on La Guardia's private life. "Among the vaudeville performers, musicians, actors and actresses who passed through the Budapest consulate," La Guardia recalled," was a bleached blonde. Mr. Chester warned me and [another] clerk at the Consulate that if he caught us going out with her, he would fire us at once. That was enough for us, so that evening we called at the actress' hotel and took her to the Folies Bergeres. Mr. Chester must have suspected us, for he appeared at the theater, too, and promptly fired us." [14] The following day, however, Chester relented and the two smirking clerks were back at their desks. Another time, after listening to one of Chester's frequent tirades against women, La Guardia handed him a revolver, inquiring brusquely, "What do you have to live for?" [15] But there was also respect on both sides. Under Chester's direction, the young La Guardia received the equivalent of a college education. Not only did he handle much of the consulate's routine business, but at the consul's urging, studied languages and history. One summer, Chester even sent him to Croatia for four months to study that little-known language, and La Guardia, in this and other trips through the Balkans, was able to observe firsthand an area where many races lived together amid constant stress and conflict.

After three years as a clerk in Budapest, La Guardia was appointed by Chester as director of a branch office of the consulate in the Adriatic port of Fiume — then the main point of embarkation for Balkan immigrants bound for the United States. Despite its Italian name, Fiume was in Austro-Hungarian territory. The consular branch, located on Fiume's most elegant avenue, consisted of two sparsely furnished rooms, one the office, the other La Guardia's bedroom. But the appointment was a vital step forward in La Guardia's career. Three years earlier he had been hired at a salary of $100 a year. At Fiume he earned eight times that. He was his own boss, with the title of consular agent. "Since I was not yet twenty-one, I could serve only as Acting Consular Agent until February 1904 when my commission, signed by Secretary of State John Hay, was sent to me." [16]

About thirty thousand immigrants a year sailed from Fiume aboard the ships of the Cunard and Adria Lines. They were "Slavs and Magyars, Germans, Jews, Italians — nearly every variety of people who inhabited pre–World War I polyglot Hungary." [17] Though the regulations governing immigration specified that immigrants should be in sound health at the time when they boarded ship, neither at Fiume nor at any other port of embarkation were the immigrants actually checked by a doctor. This often led to heartbreak at Ellis Island, and terrible subsequent hardship for a family.

Several hundred immigrants daily were found to be suffering from trachoma and their exclusion was mandatory. It was harrowing to see families separated because the precaution had not been taken, of giving them prior examinations on the other side. Sometimes, if it was a young child who suffered from trachoma, one of the parents had to return to the native country with the rejected member of the family. When they learned their fate, they were stunned.[18]

Many immigrants had sold their homes and furniture in their native land; they had nowhere to return to, unless a relative could be found who was willing to shelter the outcast.

While still in Budapest, La Guardia had read through the consulate's files on immigration; at Fiume he talked with immigrants and saw for himself the needless misery they were sometimes forced to suffer. For years, hundreds of officials had turned their backs on the problem of health checks for immigrants at the port of embarkation. La Guardia was not even twenty-one. He was inexperienced. But he did what he thought was right and necessary.

On his first day as acting consular agent, La Guardia took a local doctor aboard the Cunard Line's *Aurania*. No, he said, he would not sign a required bill of health — previously regarded as a formality — until the doctor was permitted to inspect the immigrants on board. "The Cunard officials insisted vigorously that I had no authority to inspect immigrants, told me that they had been carrying passengers to America since before I was born, and stated flatly that they would not permit either my doctor or myself to 'look at an immigrant.' " [19] La Guardia went back to his office, refusing to sign the bill of health. After a day of tension and bickering, the Cunard Line gave in. Back marched La Guardia to the *Aurania*. "The immigrants were all on deck. . . . I examined each one of them with my doctor and stamped their cards, while the Cunard representative and the British Consul filed a formal protest against my action." [20] Though the protest was forwarded to Washington by a somewhat apprehensive Chester, La Guardia won the battle. "The State Department ruled that only the consular agent of Fiume could execute the immigration laws of the United States." [21] From then on, the shipping lines not only allowed La Guardia's doctor to check each immigrant but also paid the doctor's fees.

"The sight of immigrants embarking got to be not only popular but fashionable," La Guardia wrote. "Big shots would obtain permits from the Hungarian officials to watch the scene, and there would often be as many as thirty or forty visitors. They would stand on the first-class deck where they could get a gallery view of the entire procedure." [22] Most vessels took aboard between a thousand and fifteen hundred immigrants who lined up on the dock with their baggage and children, stepping onto a platform where they were inspected for medical defects and trachoma, and where their temperature was taken. This was the spectacle the "big shots" came to watch.

One day La Guardia received notification that immigrants were to be embarked on the S.S. *Panonia* three days prior to sailing because Her Imperial Highness, the Archduchess Maria Josepha, had asked to watch an embarkation. "I was visited by the senior Hungarian official in charge of the port. He explained that the situation would permit no alteration, told me how important it was, and assured me that I would be given the great honor of having tea with her Imperial Highness on board ship . . . it would only be necessary to inspect two hundred immigrants, as it would be too tiring for Her Highness to watch any more." [23] Too tiring for Her Highness! When at least two hundred men, women and children, already facing a miserably long journey, were going to be kept cooped up in steerage an extra three days just to put on a show for an archduchess. La Guardia exploded. He refused to sign the bill of health and refused to take tea with Her Imperial Highness. Hungarian officials cajoled and threatened, but to no avail. La Guardia vanished, and the archduchess was forced to take tea on the *Panonia* with the British consul and the governor general while heel-clicking officials reported with embarrassing frequency that the immigrants could not be boarded because the American consular agent was nowhere to be found. "They roasted me alive," La Guardia wrote. "I had affronted a member of the Imperial family; I was rude and discourteous." [24] It was just the kind of fight La Guardia really loved, showing up some "spoiled big shot," some big name, in order to protect the anonymous little people. An official protest was lodged with Chester, who duly forwarded it to Washington and tried to forget he was paying La Guardia's salary out of his own pocket.

His young appointee was becoming very self-assured and aggressive. While the Hungarian officer in charge of the port was bowing to Maria Josepha and admitting that no, Herr La Guardia had not yet been located, "if he had only known, I was having tea at his own home with his wife," La Guardia boasted afterwards.[25] Despite his bantam size, the young diplomat was cutting quite a figure with the ladies at Fiume. "He still parted his hair in the middle, but wore it stylishly longer. He had taken to wearing a bow tie, Prince Albert coat, and derby rakishly angled on the back of his head." [26]

When he was promenading with a good-looking young woman one evening during the interval of a masked ball, the girl's fiancé, enraged, intercepted them and attempted to pull off her mask. Fiorello decked him with a right cross. The fiancé turned out to be an officer in the Hungarian army who would be disgraced if he did not challenge the American to a duel. So a few days later two young men, wearing top hats and Prince Albert coats, called on La Guardia and asked him to name his seconds.

Well, I named my seconds. One was a Mr. Radmonovic, who was head of the Royal Hungarian tobacco monopoly in Fiume. He was a fine, most serious gentleman and had been a good friend of my predecessor and was a good friend of mine. He helped us both in our German, which he spoke perfectly. The other second I named was the Turkish consul, who was a rogue. I selected him for the fun of it. He was a notorious roué, had married an old and ugly widow with plenty of money, and his chief mission in life was spending her money on other women. This is how we became friends — aside from our formal official contacts — for he swiped a girl from me, a singer in light opera. My $800 a year could not compete with his wife's millions. The old effendi was a card, and he was much amused when I told him the story and, of course, consented to act in this "affair of honor." [27]

Next, La Guardia looked up a Lieutenant Karl Selak of the Hungarian army, another friend.

Off Karl and I went to to the garrison gym. All afternoon he coached me in lunges and thrusts with a sword. It seemed reasonably certain that our duel would be with swords. Our bellies and throats would be bandaged for protection. At least, that was the way Karl Selak doped it out. By the time he was through describing the procedure to me I was really worried. We considered our plan of attack. At the word go I was to spring an *ausschlag*, "down full left swing and thrust for the head." [28]

He would probably have tried it, but there was no need. When the principals met at five o'clock the next morning at the best café in Fiume, considerable paperwork was prepared and signed and it was agreed that everyone's honor had been satisfied. Fiorello was startled but relieved. The two principals toasted one another with cognac and went home, kissing the dawn.

When he had served in Fiume three years, La Guardia resigned.

Chester had told him frankly from the very first that without a Harvard degree, and perhaps without a different social background, he would never be able to have a career in the Foreign Service. After having instituted health checks for departing immigrants, there was not a great deal more that La Guardia could do in Fiume. He was twenty-three, ambitious, and bored. "I felt that the life I was leading was too easy. Too much of the time I had nothing to do. I wanted more action, and I did not see any future for myself in diplomacy. . . . After [my resignation] was accepted, I had to pay for my passage home by working on a British ship. I acted as interpreter and assisted the ship's doctor in vaccinating 1,800 emigrants on board." [29]

La Guardia was a native New Yorker, born in Greenwich Village. But he hardly knew the city, having grown up in Prescott and having matured into a man in Budapest and Fiume. The life he returned to in America was hard and humble. In Fiume he had been someone — both professionally and socially. In New York he was simply another poor young man taking evening courses in law at New York University, sometimes having to blink to stay awake because the day had been so long. After finding a $10-a-week job as a translator for the Society for the Prevention of Cruelty to Children, then a $15-a-week job as a clerk at a shipping company, then a $20-a-week job as a stenographer at Abercrombie & Fitch, he finally secured a civil service appointment as an interpreter at Ellis Island, which paid $1,200 a year.[30]

It was a strange destiny that led him back to working with immigrants again, some of whom would one day vote for him, address requests to him, and cheer him when he passed in a city motorcade. At Fiume La Guardia had possessed sufficient power to stop ocean liners from sailing, and to insult an Imperial Highness. But no archduchesses stepped ashore at Ellis Island, and the ferries brought their human cargo whether he desired it or not. He was just another uniformed official, asking the same questions over and over in Italian, German, Croatian.

His civil service appointment had been granted in November 1907 — the peak year for Italian immigration and one of the busiest moments in the history of Ellis Island. With more than a million immigrants arriving each year, the overburdened staff was on a seven-day week. Barely had one agonizing human problem been clarified, and a decision reached, when another came along. In the morning, La Guardia got up in time to catch the 8:40 ferry. Then, after working on the island all day, he would take the 5:30 ferry back to the Battery, have a quick evening meal, and rush to his classes. Whatever studying he managed to do, he did after 11 P.M. Still, he found the energy and will to write to senators and representatives in Washington, urging a reform of immigration laws. Most immigrants were still arriving at Ellis Island without having had a prior medical examination, and thousands were rejected for medical reasons. Each day La Guardia saw appalling scenes. Immigrants were pouring in at a rate of more than five thousand a day, and while most inspectors were basically well intentioned, and dedicated, they were tired, irritable, prone to making snap judgments that could literally kill people.

"I always suffered greatly when I was assigned to interpret for mental cases in the Ellis Island hospital," La Guardia wrote.

I felt then, and I feel the same today, that over fifty per cent of the deportations for alleged mental disease were unjustified. . . . One case haunted me for years. A young girl in her teens from the mountains of northern Italy turned up at Ellis Island. No one understood her particular dialect very well, and because of her hesitancy in replying to questions she did not understand, she was sent to the hospital for observation. I could imagine the effect on this girl who had always been carefully sheltered and had never been permitted to be in the company of a man alone, when a doctor suddenly rapped her on the knees, looked into her eyes, turned her on her back and tickled her spine to ascertain her reflexes. The child rebelled — and how! It was the cruelest case I ever witnessed on the Island. In two weeks' time that child was a raving maniac, although she had been sound and normal when she arrived at Ellis Island.[31]

One of his duties as an interpreter was to escort immigrant couples to City Hall to be married. Often the bridegroom was a "swallow" who had come to the United States first, found a job and sent for his bride. It was Fiorello's first experience with the underside of New York politics. The marriages were performed by aldermen who overcharged for the service and were often drunk. "Some of the aldermen would insert into their reading of the marriage ceremony remarks they considered funny and sometimes used lewd language, much to the amusement of the red-faced cheap 'tinhorn' politicians who hung around them to watch the so-called fun." [32] And this was a young woman's introduction to America, the country of her dreams! Day by day the young La Guardia was accumulating within himself the rage, the compassion, the realism that would bring him to power.

The first step was his law degree. He was, through physical tiredness, a poor student. In eighteen courses, he earned six Ds and eight Cs.[33] But the main thing was graduating. In June 1910, he received his degree. That summer he took his last ferry ride to Ellis Island, put on his uniform for the final time. In the fall, he was admitted to the New York State Bar, renting a tiny room at 15 William Street in the firm of McIllheny & Bennet. He was twenty-eight years old, and his own boss again. "On his desk he placed a six-inch romantic looking bust of Napoleon Bonaparte, General of the French Armies at twenty-eight." [34]

He developed a practice, logically enough, in immigration law. This is a somewhat unusual specialization within the field of law, and not a remunerative one, since deportation orders generally fall only on poor people. The fee charged by F. H. La Guardia was $10 per case, if the defendant could pay. His former associates on Ellis Island sent him all the business he could handle.

Though he had always regarded himself as an Italian-American by birth, La Guardia had returned to New York in 1906 with an entirely different background from the Italian-Americans on Mulberry Street and in East Harlem. His boyhood out West and his consular experience in the Austro-Hungarian Empire set him off as something of an oddity, and he was unusual, too, for the intensity of his social conscience and the complexity of his ambitions. Yet La Guardia could hardly interpret for Italian immigrants on Ellis Island, help them, advise them, defend them in court, without becoming recognized as one of the natural leaders of the Italian-American community in New York.

He had peers. There was a group of talented young men among the first- and second-generation Italian-Americans in New York who were known informally as the "green geniuses." [35] Most are now forgotten. An early friend of Fiorello's was Raimondo Canudo, born in Bari and a graduate in law from the University of Messina in Sicily. Canudo, a lawyer, also edited a weekly newspaper called *Sicilia,* which tried to advise Sicilian immigrants about job opportunities, about their legal rights and responsibilities as Americans. With Canudo, La Guardia established a second practice devoted to helping Italian immigrants with their legal problems. The two young men kept office hours in the Village in the evenings and on Sunday.[36]

Arturo Giovannitti was a close friend of La Guardia's, as was another poet, Antonio Calitri, and a sculptor, Attilio Piccirilli. The Renaissance man among these "geniuses" was Onorio Ruotolo, who painted, sculpted, wrote verse and edited a little magazine in Italian, *Il Fuoco.* But the real genius among them was the airplane designer Giuseppe Bellanca, a Sicilian by birth. When Bellanca established his aircraft company, La Guardia served as his attorney. The capital for the fledgling company had come mostly from Italian-American cooks and waiters in various New York hotels, each of whom had put up $100.[37] In return for his legal services, La Guardia received flying lessons from Bellanca at a tiny field at Mineola, Long Island. It was only a few years after the Wright Brothers, and the airplane in which La Guardia learned to fly was a Blériot-type monoplane with a motor that developed fifteen horsepower. "We flew irregularly," La Guardia recalled, "whenever we had the time and whenever the wind was right." [38] The other students included a New York City detective named "Mile-a-Minute" Murphy who had raced a Long Island train on a bicycle before taking up airplanes, a Chinese, a young Vermont farmer, and a very pretty girl "who had a perfect wardrobe of flying clothes but who showed up very seldom for her lessons." [39]

Fiorello became a very close friend of the other Bellanca brother, August, a physically frail but courageous labor organizer. It was August who really introduced Fiorello to New York politics, asking the young lawyer to handle picket cases in court when the men's clothing workers went on strike in New York in December 1912. August Bellanca was the head of the Italian section of the Amalgamated Clothing Workers of America, a crucial post for the union because of the tension that had existed between Jewish and Italian tailors and seamstresses at the turn of the century. Every time the politically conscious Jewish workers had tried to launch a strike against low pay, long hours and sweatshop conditions, management had been able to hire Italians fresh off the boat for wages even lower than the ones the Jews were rebelling against. It took a great deal of patience and perseverance on the part of Jewish garment workers before they could educate the Italian workers to understand that if they thought only of short-term advantages, and let employers use them as a weapon to beat down other workers, their suffering in the long run would be much greater.

Before the strike, male garment workers had been on a sixty-hour week, earning between $5 and $14.50 per week. Four years earlier, in 1909, women garment workers had gone on strike, twenty thousand of them, in what became known in American labor history as "the uprising of the twenty thousand." [40] Over seven hundred women pickets had been arrested during the three-month strike. Thugs and even prostitutes had been hired by manufacturers to beat up the workers and discredit them.[41]

"I was studying law and working at Ellis Island . . . when this big strike was going on," La Guardia wrote, "and did not take any direct part in it. But I followed its progress and was particularly interested in the picketing problem in New York.

"During that period, the right to picket depended on who was doing the picketing and who was being picketed. Politicians turned picketing into a racket. Unless Tammany lawyers were retained, pickets were jailed." [42] Already disgusted with the corruption that flourished under the Irish-led Democratic machine in New York — known as Tammany because it was first organized as a patriotic society in 1786 and named after an Indian chief — and sympathetic to the cause of the workers, La Guardia agreed enthusiastically to represent the union when approached by Bellanca.

They were a formidable team. Bellanca, who spoke English only imperfectly, was nevertheless a subtle, skilled negotiator adept at keeping various factions within the union in harmony, while La Guardia, with his Italian-Jewish background, was the ideal figure to heal the distrust between Italian and Jewish workers in the Amalgamated. Most of the sixty-five thousand striking garment workers were Jews of various nationalities or Italians, and La Guardia, racing from picket line to picket line, taunting the Tammany-controlled police to arrest *him*, flamboyantly dressed in a black ten-gallon hat and a string bow tie,[43] was instantly recognized by those struggling Lower East Side immigrant workers as a new leader.[44]

When officials of the United Garment Workers announced on February 28, 1913, that they had reached a settlement without having consulted the workers, La Guardia was one of the rebel leaders who convinced the rank and file not to accept it, and to keep on picketing despite the now-hardening opposition of Mayor Gaynor, the courts and even some of the left-wing Yiddish papers. Though the mayor ordered police to break up picket lines on the grounds that the strike was over, the garment workers stayed off the job and a month later won better terms from the employers, including a $1-a-week raise for fewer hours of work.

As La Guardia's biographer Arthur Mann has noted, the strike was an important experience for the young lawyer and incipient politician. "It was not N.Y.U. but the East Side that grounded La Guardia in the slashing, hot-gospel style of oratory for which he was known." [45] The strike also introduced Fiorello to New York labor leaders who would one day support him for political office. Among these men were Sidney Hillman, the first president of the Amalgamated Clothing Workers of America, and the Socialist lawyer Jacob Panken, who had led the 1913 strike crying in Yiddish to fifty thousand workers in Union Square, "let your hands, which you have just raised, become paralyzed if you touch a needle or a machine under non-union conditions!" [46] Among the Italians were Luigi Antonini, president of the biggest local in the International Ladies Garment Workers Union, and Salvatore Ninfo, one of the chief organizers for the ILGWU. Some of these labor leaders were Marxists, others were simply to the left of La Guardia. But political differences did not prevent him from liking these men and understanding their sympathies and their causes. They would regard him as an odd Republican and a lovable man.

He had begun reading the *Congressional Record* on his return to New York from Fiume. "Somehow, I did not know how, I had a feeling that some day I would get into Congress. I kept my eyes open, but I felt that my chances in New York City were very slight." [47] He had also joined the Republican party because there was nowhere else for him to go. He was not a Socialist, and his experiences with the corrupt Democratic politicians, the Tammany Hall mob, had left him disgusted and eager for a change to provide an alternative. "I joined the Republican Party because I could not stomach Tammany Hall." [48]

His congressional district, the Fourteenth, which covered both Greenwich Village and the Lower East Side, had a particularly progressive Republican Club, and in 1914, only a year after the successful end of the garment strike, Fiorello was able to get the congressional nomination almost by default.

Actually he had been eyeing it for some months and had tried to line up support among active Republicans of his own generation. Even so, he nearly lost his chance when the man who was compiling the petition said " 'Hey, La Guardia, what's your first name?' I said 'Fiorello.' 'Oh hell,' he said, 'let's get someone whose name we can spell.' " [49] A violent argument followed, until Fay, seeing how passionately the little Italian-American lawyer wanted the honor of running for office, even in a hopeless cause, finally upheld La Guardia. (His name appeared on the official New York State manual as Fluollo.)

Because the Fourteenth was predominantly a district of poor immigrants living in tenements who voted the straight Democratic ticket, many of whom were beholden to Tammany Hall for patronage or a favor of some kind, the district was Tammany's firmest stronghold — it automatically went Democratic. Never since the Civil War had a Republican been elected to Congress from the Fourteenth, a period of nearly half a century.

When the eager, youthful La Guardia announced that he intended to make a serious try at winning, Republican veterans laughed. Just help elect the ticket, they told him.

He tried anyway, giving a dozen speeches a day from the rooftop of his secondhand Ford. If his base was in the Italian section of the Village, where he could count on the aid of the Bellancas, Ruotolo, the sculptor Piccirilli and other volunteers from among the green geniuses, he found support in other bits and pieces of his polyglot district. It included the heavily Irish western part of the Village, a good part of the predominantly Jewish Lower East Side, and finally the fashionable Wasp area of Washington Square and Lower Fifth Avenue that would vote for him simply because he was a Republican. He ran as a reformer, a radical Republican, the friend of labor and of minority groups. When he was not holding forth shrilly from the rooftop of the Ford, he was climbing tenement stairs to talk to immigrant families (some of whom he had processed on Ellis Island), and attending every wedding, funeral, confirmation, and bar mitzvah he and his staff could locate.

Though the Socialists had also entered a candidate, syphoning voters away from La Guardia, his only real competition was the Tammany front runner, Michael Farley, a saloonkeeper who was innocent of any political views. La Guardia roasted him as an illiterate barkeep, calling him everything but a drunken sot. He hit so hard that the Republican bosses warned him against overdoing it;[50] but Farley, assured of victory, loftily ignored the attacks of his gnatlike challenger. And on election day, in fact, Farley won comfortably.

But not crushingly. Farley's predecessor, Jefferson M. Levy, had swept the district with a plurality of nearly 6,000 votes. Farley's margin was 1,700. And while the Democrats had swamped Fiorello in the Irish wards, and even carried the Italian section, La Guardia had done remarkably well in other parts of the district. It was assumed that he would receive the Republican nomination again two years later, in 1916, and that his chances then of pulling off an unprecedented Republican victory would be nearly even. In the meanwhile Fiorello needed a post that would keep him in the public eye, and in January 1915, he was appointed deputy attorney general for the state of New York, in New York City.

It was a patronage job. Like his candidature in the Fourteenth District, he was not really supposed to take it seriously. But coasting was not La Guardia's style, and as deputy attorney general he launched a Nader-like crusade to defend the public interest against big business. Sixty years ago, ecology was not an issue in America, but La Guardia's first major case was an attempt to prosecute air polluters. Factories on the New Jersey shore of the Hudson River were emitting noxious fumes that were blowing into Manhattan — as, of course, they still do today — and La Guardia, after weeks of intensive preparation, working far into the night studying precedents of law, filed seven complaints with the Supreme Court.

The fact that the State of New York was filing seven cases at one time against seven large corporations attracted attention, and there was some publicity. I was quite proud of having finally started the actions which had been kicked around the office for at least five or six years. Imagine my surprise when I got a good calling down for proceeding so precipitately. . . . I soon learned the reason for it. The kick came from Governor Whitman. The party big shots were closely connected with the matter. These corporations had used their tremendous influence and I was given orders to take no action from now on unless I got direct approval from the chief of the bureau, who, in turn, had to get direct approval from the Attorney General.[51]

Nothing was done.

Another case La Guardia prosecuted involved the protection of sea life. Big fishing companies were taking scallops under a year old in the Long Island Sound, which was against the law. Five times La Guardia went to court, and five times the judge granted an adjournment. On the sixth occasion, La Guardia had barely sat down at the counsel table when he was informed that the New York State legislature had just amended the fishing law to cover only public waters where small fishermen operated. Since the big companies leased their fishing grounds, they were now exempt from prosecution.

The last major case La Guardia handled was against large packinghouses, for selling underweight hams and bacon and misstating the weights on their labels. It was the same hanky-panky all over again. The defense lawyer was State Senator James J. Walker, later the flamboyant mayor of New York in the 1920s, who himself had written the law he was trying to circumvent. As Walker explained to the judge, the hams and bacons were exempt since they were in wrappers, not in a container. "And of course," La Guardia wrote,

he knew, for he had written the bill.

He also knew the judge, who was an affable Tammany judge. He went out of his way to be nice to Jimmy, and my case was dismissed then and there. I started to protest — for all the good it did me! I had known Jimmy for some time, and after the case was dismissed . . . Jimmy and the judge invited me to have a drink. . . .

"Jimmy," I said, "how can you possibly appear in a case to defeat your own law?"

And Jimmy, in his urbane way, said, "Fiorello, when are you going to get wise. . . . Why are you in the Attorney General's office? You're not going to stay there all your life. You make your connections now, and later you can pick up a lot of dough defending cases you are now prosecuting." And of course, the judge acquiesced in all that.

"But," I said, "a lot of little storekeepers have been fined for selling the same kinds of hams in wrappers."

"Fiorello," said Jimmy, "you stop worrying about those things. What are you in politics for, for love?" [52]

It was a relief for La Guardia to return to the politics of love — running for the congressional seat in the Fourteenth District. Not that he had ever really stopped running. Even as deputy attorney general he had driven himself to participate in every public function he could uncover. It seemed that no christening could take place, no dance start, no one could be married or buried unless the ubiquitous Fiorello was on hand. As his principal lieutenant recalled, "There was not a meeting of five or ten people in that congressional district that Fiorello and I didn't attend for two solid years." [53]

Feeling he had a chance to win, La Guardia was horrified when he discovered that his former backer, Clarence Fay, had all but promised the candidature to Hamilton Fish, Jr., who was not even a resident of New York City. The distraught La Guardia went to state chairman Fred Tanner, who overruled Fay and promised La Guardia full support, including funds for his campaign. La Guardia also obtained the Progressive party's nomination, increasing his chances for victory. "In September 1916, the little man with the big hat and stringy bow tie and squeaky voice was seen again in a battered flivver speaking energetically and multi-lingually at hundreds of street corners." [54]

His opponent was Farley again, an incumbent congressman running for a second term with an undistinguished record. There was, moreover, a new and potent issue to be used against him. The First World War had broken out, and that conflict dredged up deep emotions in the hearts of the Fourteenth's foreign-born immigrants. The Irish, reacting to the Easter Uprising, were passionately anti-British, as were the Germans. Italian-Americans, instead, were fervently pro-Allied because of Italy's intervention the previous year on the side of Britain, France and Russia. The Habsburg subjects were divided, some favoring Italy's enemy, Austria, some yearning for Czech and Hungarian independence. The Russians dreamed of revolution against the Czar.

While Farley stayed clear of these turbulent waters, La Guardia plunged in, exploiting the issue with all the skill of a former diplomat in the Balkans. He was all things to all ethnicities, berating the British before Irish crowds, then tearing across the East Side in his Ford to roast the Czar or to dismember the Habsburg Empire. As for Farley, La Guardia "accused him of selling 'rotgut' to his customers and, after they passed out, of throwing them into the snow to freeze to death." [55] It was a savage campaign. To garner every possible vote, La Guardia got up before dawn on election day and went down to the Bowery, picking bums up off the sidewalk and treating them to a bacon and egg breakfast.

He won, by a margin of 350 ballots (or bums) out of 18,670. La Guardia's heaviest pluralities were ironically among silk-stocking Republicans in the Lower Fifth Avenue area, voting a straight ticket — and often not realizing that they were sending a champion of the lower classes to Congress. The Italian-Americans, who should have been his staunchest backers, either didn't bother to vote or voted for Farley. The Socialist candidate picked up twice as many votes as in 1914. Yet Fiorello won. Many professionals couldn't believe it. Not only was he the first Republican from the Fourteenth District in half a century, but the first Italian-American congressman who had put together a victorious coalition of many ethnic groups. He was an urban populist two decades before the New Deal, and this, rather than his Italian name, was what sent him to Congress.

He did not remain there long. The most urgent business before the Sixty-fifth Congress was war. On April 2, 1917, the young Italian-American representative sat in a hushed joint session of Congress as President Wilson quietly and eloquently spelled out the reasons why America was forced to declare war on the Central Powers and make the world safe for democracy. On April 6, Good Friday, the vote was taken, and La Guardia voted yes. Politically, it was not an easy decision for him. His district included Socialist strongholds fiercely opposed to the war, viewing it as a clash of capitalistic interests; some of his personal friends would stand trial in wartime America for those beliefs. He had been elected in part by the votes of German-Americans who would suffer insults, and persecution, after the American entry into the war.

Yet there were other considerations. As an Italian-American congressman, could he vote against the overriding sentiment for war? He fought small, obscure, rear-guard battles for civil liberties, opposing the conscription of alien immigrants who had not taken out citizenship papers but who were liable to the draft under the Selective Service Act of May 1917. He vainly tried to attack the Espionage Bill, which he called "this un-American and vicious legislation." [56] But at heart Fiorello was a happy warrior. He had been raised among soldiers, and the sound of the drum, of the bugle, of marching feet and the sight of the flag being lowered at sunset quickened his blood.

During the debate on the draft bill, a congressman opposing it had asked caustically how many members of the House "who were going to vote to send boys to war, would go themselves." [57] Fiorello was one of five members who stood up. He was probably the only man in Congress who could fly a plane, and so, on a hot July day in 1917, he presented himself at the Southern Railway Building in Washington to enlist in the Air Corps at the age of thirty-four. He was commissioned a first lieutenant the following month and was sent to his old field at Mineola, Long Island, where Major Leslie McDill was assembling a unit for the Italian front. Most of the 150 cadets at Mineola did not know how to fly. They were college boys eager for adventure. Among them were Albert Spalding, the violinist, and Elliot Springs, who would become one of the ace fighter pilots of the war.[58]

From the very start Fiorello commanded tremendous respect — both as a congressman and as a man of the world about ten years older than most of his "boys." For all his minute size and slightly comical look, Fiorello had that classic male combination of virtues: he was a strict moralist and a carefree lover. (Once, when a German-born politician on the East Side had asked him politely where he had learned German, La Guardia replied boastfully, "In a whore-house in Trieste." [59])

There was a kind of breeziness about the Air Corps that matched Fiorello's style. One day McDill told La Guardia to go and book passage on a ship to Europe for the unit. La Guardia drove to New York, and after shopping around a bit, bought 156 first-class tickets on the Cunard Line's S.S. *Carmania.* He knew all about ships from his Trieste days, and this was a good deal. "Major McDill's eyes almost popped out when I showed him the big bunch of first class passages. He remarked that if we got away with that, we were good, but warned me that the responsibility was mine." [60] Happily for Captain La Guardia, the army assented — otherwise he would have had to pay $23,400 out of his own pocket, the difference between first class and steerage. By one of those coincidences which lead people to believe in a fateful cycle, the field in Italy where La Guardia's unit was stationed was Foggia, his father's birthplace. Fiorello would be flying on missions over the Adriatic, his destined sea — both his mother's birthplace of Trieste, and Fiume, where he had spent three years as consular agent, were Adriatic ports. His future wife's birthplace was also Trieste.

The base at Foggia was a joint command. The flying instructors, planes, and ground crews were Italian, the cadets Americans. And since personnel of both nationalities jointly ran the operation, La Guardia, perfectly bilingual and at home with Italian customs, was an invaluable liaison officer, hurrying to Rome between missions to serve as the army's representative on the high-level Army and Navy Aircraft Committee in Italy.

The nearly seven hundred cadets at Foggia, who now included Walter Wanger, the future Hollywood producer, and Yale's All-American halfback, Steve Philbin,[61] were in training with their Italian instructors when the Battle of Caporetto took place.

Russia was on the point of collapse and revolution, releasing dozens of German divisions from the eastern front. Aware that the arrival of American forces on the Western front in France would tip the balance of power against them within less than a year, the German generals decided to concentrate all their available forces against Italy, knock Italy out of the war with one massive offensive, and then concentrate all German and Austrian forces against the Allies on the Western front in a final, overwhelming drive on Paris early in 1918. It almost worked, like most German military plans. At two o'clock in the morning on October 24, 1917, the Italian lines around the mountain village of Caporetto were overrun. The rumor that a million Germans had been added to the Austrian forces and were spearheading the attack turned the Italian retreat into a rout.* On the fourth of November the Italian army, bled and shaken, began its withdrawal to the Piave River just above Venice. But there, under the command of a peppery little general, Armando Diaz, the recovery began. "By November twenty-second, the Italians had held their lines firm and were counter-attacking. British and French divisions which had been rushed to the front but held in reserve aided the Italians in December. The last Austro-German attack was repulsed on Christmas Day, turning a tide that threatened disaster for the whole Allied cause." [62]

That was the situation on the ground when La Guardia and his "boys" took to the air. Just after Caporetto, about a hundred of them were posted to a front-line airfield near Padua; from there they flew regular bombing missions throughout that grim winter against snow-covered freight yards, railroad depots, munitions dumps and Austrian-held air-fields. Their planes were three-motored Caproni bombers, with two spacious wings and a little well in front, just ahead of the pilot and copilot, for a machine gunner; the rear machine gunner stood up within a tubular frame so that he could fire over the upper wing. All four crew members flew with at least their heads and shoulders exposed to the open air, which of course was bitingly cold in the winter season, and in an area just below the Tyrolean Alps. An efficient airplane, the Caproni cruised at about 110 mph loaded with bombs en route to the target and about 10 mph faster on the way home.

Fiorello was not a born pilot. On a training flight he had become lost, run out of gas, crashed and narrowly missed being pinned under one of the motors. But he was an aggressive crew member. He normally flew as copilot and bombardier with the gigantic Italian flier, Major Piero Negrotto. They were an unusual crew — Negrotto a deputy in the Italian Parliament and La Guardia a United States congressman; Negrotto huge and fierce, La Guardia tiny and choleric. "Negrotto . . . used to show his scorn for Habsburg lackeys by taking off his goggles in the midst of an enemy barrage and adjusting his monocle." [63] He and La Guardia sat next to one another in the cockpit, and their dialogue was probably better than any movie version could make it. Their Caproni was hit many times by antiaircraft fire. Once, they had swooped low over Austrian positions to see the effect of their bombing when they were suddenly jumped by two Austrian fighter planes. After the cumbersome Caproni had been riddled with holes, and the Austrian fighters were maneuvering for their final pass, a squadron of friendly fighters suddenly

* Among the Germans at Caporetto was a youthful officer, Erwin Rommel.

appeared, turning the tables and saving the two legislators from extinction.

In August, La Guardia was promoted to major. King Victor Emmanuel personally decorated him with the Italian War Cross after which General Diaz sent him on a private mission to General Pershing in Paris. He was becoming famous on both sides of the Atlantic. The New York *Times*, which had previously ignored him, did a profile of him in its Magazine. To bolster Italian morale in those final weary months of the war, the American ambassador in Rome, Thomas Nelson Page, had La Guardia tour major Italian cities where he addressed huge and enthusiastic rallies. Then he would hurry back to his unit and go off to bomb the Austrians again.

La Guardia left the front a month before the armistice; General Pershing had received a War Department cable summoning the congressman home, ostensibly to train Caproni crews but actually to campaign. Fiorello disembarked in New York on October 28, 1919, one short week before election day. He had returned to fight for his House seat. Despite his dashing appearance now, as he campaigned in his crisp major's uniform replete with cavalry boots and riding crop, La Guardia had not exactly represented his constituents in Washington over the past two years, and a good many of them resented it. Also, the Fourteenth was a Socialist stronghold and the carnage that had taken place in the trenches for four years — one million French and German youths killed at Verdun alone in 1916 for an advance of a few miles — only confirmed them in their pacifist opinions. They detested La Guardia, and in January 1918, had petitioned to House Speaker Champ Clark for a special election to unseat the absent congressman. (Shown a copy of the petition in Rome, La Guardia had replied histrionically, "If any signers of the petition will take my seat in a Caproni biplane, I shall be glad to resume my upholstered seat in the House." [64])

So polarized had feeling on the war become in New York's immigrant districts that Republicans and Democrats had decided to run fusion tickets against the anti-war Socialists. La Guardia coolly accepted Tammany support in his race for reelection against Scott Nearing, a former economics professor whom the Socialists had selected as their candidate in the Fourteenth. It was no contest. The tough Irish wards were solidly for La Guardia, and when he walked through Little Italy, "trim, tan, and decorated with the Merit of War, the Italian War Cross, and the Knight Commander of the Crown of Italy" [65] nearly two thousand wildly excited, cheering Italian-Americans followed him around. This was the one time he would really attract the Italian-American vote. Normally, the *prominenti* rejected him as a leftist and fought him with their newspapers. They wanted to be respectable. He was a noisy reformer, a troublemaker, a rebel. But in 1918, with his wings and medals, La Guardia was respectable and they supported him. La Guardia won, with 14,523 votes to Nearing's 6,214.

On November 11, a week after the election, Germany signed the armistice. And a month later, having resigned from active duty, Congressman Fiorello La Guardia walked down the aisle in the House to take his seat once more, as fellow members reached out admiringly to shake his hand. When he had first entered the House in 1916, crafty old Joe Cannon had sometimes pretended to mistake him for a page, sending the tiny, boyish congressman on errands; and Fiorello, seeing the old man's eyes twinkling, had played along. No one would dream of doing that now. At thirty-six La Guardia had achieved a degree of personal fulfillment that most people never attain, and on the eighth of March, 1919, he completed his life by marrying the girl he had left behind, Thea Almerigotti. She was twenty-four, pretty and frivolous, and fun, and close friends who saw them frequently reported that the newlyweds were as happy as newlyweds should ideally be. Theirs would be a beautiful marriage. And a tragically short one.

A changed La Guardia returned to the House. War had changed him. He had drawn away from the ideals of internationalism espoused by his Socialist and radical friends among the green geniuses. The victory of Lenin in Russia had also disillusioned him, and when Attorney General Mitchell Palmer began raiding the headquarters of "foreign radicals" and jailing them, La Guardia, who in the past had been a fiery civil libertarian, went along with the majority. He was, however, still a populist muckraker, and he continued to flog big business at every opportunity. He went after the meat packers, the hated trust of his boyhood, for advising the Bureau of Surplus Supplies that millions of cans of beef and bacon intended for the war front were not fit for the American domestic market. And when the hapless Bureau director ventured the opinion, in committee hearings, that those millions of surplus cans might be shipped to Rumania, Fiorello nailed him with the caustic reminder that there was probably not a single can opener in the entire Balkans.[66] "When I got back to the House," La Guardia wrote in his autobiography, "I certainly found the profiteers buzzing around the capital." [67] Always a good hater, he was still in the cockpit of his Caproni dropping bombs on his favorite targets. But Fiorello was an ineffective congressman during his second term. Every bill he introduced died in committee. He took potshots at every domestic and foreign problem, consistently underestimating, as Mann has pointed out, the intelligence and motives of others. Once, at a Washington dinner party, he began violently berating a man who was talking about the situation in the Adriatic. "What do you know about Croatia and Dalmatia?" La Guardia insisted. "I've lived in that part of the world for three years and I know what I am talking about." The man replied, "I am the Serbian Ambassador here."

Later, at the same party, someone asked him if he was enjoying himself. "Why, I never saw such a bunch of nuts before," La Guardia said truculently. "I'm going. Want to came along?"

"I can't," the other replied. "I'm your host." [68]

It was La Guardia who was considered the nut in Washington. He seemed unable to assimilate the forces arising out of his own background — the radical streak born of his compassion for the immigrant poor, now overlaid by an angry patriotism. He was groping for a mental attitude as linear and effective as his prewar conviction that the biggest issue in American society was the cause of the people against vested interests. He would return to this conviction in time, but now he entered a period of eclipse, frustration, and personal tragedy.

In 1919, the Republican bosses in New York decided to run La Guardia as their candidate for president of the City Board of Aldermen in that year's municipal elections. Though Fiorello would have preferred staying in the House, he had no real choice and the quid pro quo was that if he ran successfully, he would receive the Republican nomination for mayor of New York in 1921. The reason why La Guardia was asked to leave Congress and run for a dreary political office in New York was that so many normally Democratic voters in the city were upset over President Wilson's peace policies. German-Americans and Austrian-Americans were resentful over the crushing reparations imposed on the Central Powers — Irish-Americans because Wilson had failed to press the cause of Irish independence; Italian-Americans because Italy had not been given the Adriatic port of Fiume in the peace settlement. The state's Republican leaders now saw a chance to lure these ethnic voters into the GOP, and Fiorello — himself a hyphenate, a war hero, and a critic of Wilson — was to be the bait. Running against a vague, tongue-tied florist, La Guardia threw himself into the campaign with typical zeal, popping up everywhere to berate the President and Tammany Hall, speaking in as many as sixteen places in a single evening. Though he won by a margin of less than two thousand votes, "the smartest of the Tammany politicians perceived that the Little Flower was a prevision of a radical shift in New York politics." [69] The city had been run for years by increasingly conservative Irish politicians. But as one of them said to La Guardia after the 1919 election, "Some day an Italian and a Jew will be Mayors of New York, and the Italian will come first." [70] Being of Italian-Jewish parentage, La Guardia could only smile.

During the Tammany heyday in the 1880s, when Boss Tweed had run New York, the president and the Board of Aldermen were known informally as Ali Baba and the Forty Thieves. But the thieves' hands had been cut off legislatively, and the board now concerned itself only with picayune routine matters. Fiorello soon longed for Washington. He had been forced to resign his congressional seat in order to take up his new duties — the second straight time he had left the House during his term. And compared with serving in Congress, presiding over the New York Board of Aldermen was a pathetic joke. During La Guardia's tenure, the aldermen passed resolutions honoring St. Patrick's Day, condemned dog-stealing and debated whether one-piece bathing suits should be allowed on the beach at Coney Island.[71] (One of La Guardia's reforms when he later became mayor was to abolish the Board of Aldermen.)

But if nothing else the post was a chance for him to examine how New York was run. Though La Guardia was attuned to the city's ethnic pressures and balances, there was more to running New York than simply appointing an Irishman, an Italian, and a Jew to public office, with an occasional Wasp for seasoning. Each city department had its traditions, and needs; with five boroughs comprising everything from the density of the Lower East Side with its bulging tenements, to the almost pastoral eastern end of Staten Island where windmills looked out over the Atlantic and cows walked home with tinkling bells, the government of New York City was as complex and delicate a mechanism as any in the world. La Guardia studied it from the inside. To the amazement of the press, he worked so hard at his undemanding job that he twice collapsed from exhaustion. Many evenings, after an eight- or ten-hour day at his desk, he was out addressing a banquet. Reporters, who would interview him as he chomped on a sandwich for lunch and gulped down a glass of milk, could not stop writing about him.

Though La Guardia was an effective voice for the Republican party among Italian-Americans, dutifully stumping Italian neighborhoods for Harding in the 1920 presidential election, he was making enemies among the conservative upstate Republicans in the Albany legislature. He criticized them when they unseated five Socialist assemblymen for belonging to a "subversive and unpatriotic organization." The Albany Republicans, Fiorello complained, were putting peaceful Socialists who believed in the ballot box in the same category with bomb-planting anarchists, and he was disturbed that his upstate party colleagues were regarding foreign-born and subversive as practically synonymous. (Italian-Americans felt particularly vulnerable because of the Sacco-Vanzetti trial in Massachusetts). "All you hear upstate now is: 'We were born here, they were not,'" La Guardia said dejectedly.[72] Nathan Miller, the Republican governor who took office in 1921, hated Socialists, was suspicious of liberals, distrusted immigrants, disliked New York City, and was anathema to La Guardia who clashed with him publicly. La Guardia began saying at this time that rather than be ruled by Albany, New York City should secede and become the forty-ninth state. He took his battle to the clubhouses, where his volent polemics incited brawls; in Brooklyn, he arrived to make a speech only to find the doors locked and the clubhouse dark. The Hearst press meanwhile egged him on, touting him as the champion of the people against Wall Street interests. (Miller was a former corporate lawyer.)

By the spring of 1921, Miller and conservative Republicans in New York City had decided to dump La Guardia — he would not be the GOP candidate for mayor that year. He had given up his congressional seat for nothing. The only course open to him was to enter the Republican primary, win it, and receive his nomination from the voters. "Don't do it, Fiorello," his old political mentor Sam Koenig advised him. "This town isn't ready for an Italian Mayor. You'll lose and you won't be able to make a living." [73] But La Guardia insisted, obstinately running in what came to be called by his partisans the "penniless primary" because he was so low on campaign funds. His strategy was to appeal to the votes of Italian-Americans and of women, promising that he would appoint women in his administration. "Women in politics are the hope of American politics," he preached. "They are either going to break the control of the bosses, or put the political parties out of business."

But it was the party machine that broke La Guardia. In the primaries he failed to carry a single one of New York's boroughs and the total vote was almost three to one against him. With bitter satisfaction, he watched the conservative Republicans lose the election later that year in what amounted to a Democratic sweep. He had been right in his conviction that the Republican party could win in New York City only if it represented the little people. But his own political career seemed finished amid a residue of bitterness and derision.

The year had been a terrible one for him. He and Thea, whom he adored, had lived in the Village between March 1919 and December 1920 surrounded by their Italian friends — the Bellancas, the sculptor Ruotolo, Giovannitti — entertaining Caruso and other Italian celebrities. A daughter had been born to them in June 1920, while Fiorello was president of the Board of Aldermen. They had named her Fiorella, after his maternal grandmother. She was truly the little flower, and "La Guardia, who was enormously fond of children, lavished on his own child the love of a man who comes late to fatherhood." [74]

That winter he learned that both his wife and daughter had tuberculosis. He moved them to a quiet tree-lined area of the Bronx, hoping the cleaner air might make a difference. But the disease consumed them. In May 1921, Fiorella died. Then, on November 29, 1921, his beautiful Thea died, despite the efforts of the best New York doctors. They had been married less than three years.

A lesser man might have been broken. And in his final months as president of the Board of Aldermen, La Guardia was wildly irascible in his grief, lashing out at a growing list of enemies while the newspapers ridiculed him. There were rumors that he was drinking heavily. But he survived, returning to private law practice, teaching immigrant children at the Columbia Grammar School.[75] And when he returned to politics the following year in 1922, he was again an insurgent, a spokesman of the people.

In 1923, he was back in Washington as a congressman.

His political recovery had begun early in 1922, while he was still mourning Thea. Though whipped in his battle with the Republican machine for the mayoral nomination in 1921, his campaign had helped awaken Italian-Americans to the idea of political power. Now he returned to those same Italian-American clubhouses, pounding home the simple message that Italians would never obtain their share of the American dream until they organized and put their own representatives into office. In various parts of the state, as well as in New York City, he lined up support from small but aroused Italian-American Republican clubs. In his heyday as a war hero, just after the armistice, Fiorello had flirted with the dream of a wide constituency, and his political views had edged towards the mainstream of the Republican party. But Miller had been too much for La Guardia to stomach, and now he was building a solid, if narrow, base, among the poor immigrants whose cause he had always felt most deeply, and championed most effectively. By shrewdly allowing New York's Republican bosses to believe he was gearing up to challenge Miller for the governor's seat in Albany,[70] he wrung from them an all-important concession. They agreed to run him as the Republican candidate from the Twentieth Congressional District of East Harlem.

By 1920, this area of closely packed tenements had become the largest Little Italy in America. It was a natural base for La Guardia. Because there were poor Jews living in East Harlem, as well as Italians and some Puerto Ricans, the Tammany machine selected an unknown Jewish lawyer, Henry Frank, as their candidate in 1922, while the Socialists, well organized in this area of struggling proletarians, put up a labor lawyer, William Karlin. The three candidates came out with almost identical campaign promises to fight the government's restrictive immigration laws, increase welfare, and oppose prohibition of beer and light wines. These were the issues that appealed to the immigrant poor. For several months, as he drove through the neighborhood on a truck, addressing small crowds at nearly every street corner, La Guardia struggled in his speeches to disassociate himself from the image of the Republican party as the ally of big business. He was a progressive, he explained over and over, running on his own platform. "I stand for the Republicanism of Abraham Lincoln." [77]

It was an extremely close race up to the last week when Frank, possibly unaware of La Guardia's Jewish ancestry, tried to smear him with anti-Semitism. It was a clumsy mistake to say the least. Boiling mad, Fiorello switched from Italian to Yiddish and even offered to debate Frank publicly in Yiddish. During one speech before a Jewish crowd, the indignant La Guardia ridiculed Frank with the crack "is he looking for a job as *schamas* [custodian of a synagogue] or does he want to be elected Congressman?" [78] His audience roared with laughter, and some of the Yiddish papers, censuring Frank, backed Fiorello. He beat Frank by the tiny margin of 168 votes, with the Socialist Karlin running a poor third, and though Frank sued for a recount, the House of Representatives upheld La Guardia's victory.

Though he is remembered as probably the best mayor New York has ever had, La Guardia's most important political achievements occurred during the ten years he served as congressman from East Harlem. The Roaring Twenties were a period of restless, uneasy change for the American people. Perhaps because of this unease, politically the twenties were a time of Republican "normalcy." The term was first used by President Harding, whose administration was one of the most corrupt and inept in American history. (Harding died suddenly in San Francisco in August 1923, and was so spared the exposure of the Teapot Dome scandal.) His vice president and successor from 1923 to 1929 was Calvin Coolidge, austere, personally honest, and an exponent of laissez-faire capitalism. "The chief business of the American people is business" was his famous dictum. Big business was again in the saddle, and La Guardia, radical Republican in a decade of Republican normalcy, fought a long, lonely battle of dissent.

He returned to the House in 1923 wiser, shrewder, more purposeful and effective than he had been in his first two terms. But he was still Fiorello, the iconoclast, the little Stromboli of American politics. His office was a madhouse, La Guardia jabbering away excitedly in Italian or Yiddish while respectful midwestern tourists, awed by those otherwise hushed congressional corridors, scurried past his door round-eyed with amazement. Those daring enough to take a peek were scandalized by the portrait that hung on the congressman's wall — not of the President but of Rudolph Valentino. Yet Fiorello, for all his antics, was one of the hardest working representatives in the House. His private life was spartan; he roomed with Ole J. Kvale of Minnesota, an ordained Lutheran minister. He worked even on Sunday, eschewing Washington parties. In the morning he would be "waiting impatiently for the convening gong which would send him tearing from his office down the House corridors on his short legs. Ordinarily the first in the Chamber, where he might munch from a bag of peanuts, he was also the last to leave." [79]

To many of his colleagues, he was no longer the heroic flier of 1918, Major La Guardia, but a confirmed eccentric. Denied a seat on every important congressional committee, he concentrated on issues, accumulating a staggering body of knowledge on the workings of the U.S. government.

The twenties were a period of resurgent racism. After having absorbed 45 million immigrants, middle America was sated, and unhappy.

The breaking down of European colonialism following World War I and the Russian Revolution both contributed to this vague but powerful sense that the civilization of white people, practicing free enterprise, was no longer as masterfully dominant as it had been in the past. Hitler's theories of Aryan supremacy were in fact partly borrowed from the writings of an Englishman, Chamberlain, and two Americans: Madison Grant, a New York lawyer, who assured his readers in the best seller *The Passing of the Great Race* that Jesus was a Nordic; and a Harvard scholar, Lothrop Stoddard, who claimed among other things that Dante and Michelangelo were the offspring of husky blonde ancestors. (Curiously, Dante and Michelangelo were both small and dark.)

La Guardia fought a bitter rearguard action against the notion that America, in Mann's felicitous phrase, had once been "a paradise of Protestant Nordics living on farms and in small towns" [80] before being overrun by an immigrant horde. The Johnson-Reed Bill, which President Coolidge signed in 1927, limited the quota of immigrants to two percent of their ethnic ratio as calculated under an extremely complex formula. The result of this discriminatory bill was to restrict immigration of Italians, Greeks, and people from eastern Europe. The Italian quota was established at about six thousand immigrants a year, in contrast to a quota of almost sixty-five thousand a year for British subjects. And while there were tens of thousands of Italians eager to enter the United States, the "Nordic" quotas were regularly unfilled.

Though the national quota portion of the bill only went into effect in 1929, other provisions became law immediately and La Guardia, with his background in immigration law, had many requests from Italian laborers who found that as aliens they could not bring their wives and children to join them in the United States. All La Guardia could do was to sympathize and counsel patience. From his House seat he waged a guerilla war on the Nordic supremacists, knowing he was all but helpless against the national mood.

Denounced one day by a southern congressman for having criticized the Johnson Bill before a meeting of immigrants in Philadelphia, La Guardia retorted, "everybody could come to that meeting, and at that meeting everybody's face was visible." [81] That was his style, counterpunching with ridicule, exposing attitudes where he could not determine issues. He was still the scrapper in Arizona who had run back for a chair to stand on so he could reach the enemy's jaw. [82]

Many of his colleagues, particularly among southern conservatives, disliked La Guardia. In their eyes he was a false Republican, a radical, a Dago, a Jew. He was boisterous and insulting, and too isolated to be effective — even if he did work hard. "I am doomed to live in a hopeless minority," Fiorello lamented.[83]

Yet if he failed to put his name on a single important piece of legislation in the 1920s, his record in opposition is one of courage and intelligence. His record in many ways foreshadowed the New Deal, and he foresaw that America would have to deal with its basic problems more maturely than the nation was apparently willing to do in the 1920s, which was a kind of grace period for provincialism. One could believe in Fundamentalism and damn Darwin. One could believe in Prohibition. One could believe that "niggers" and "Chinks" were inherently inferior and that the British colonial system was the best thing that had ever happened to India. Amid all the racy newness of the twenties, there was also a great nostalgia for the certitudes and the ruddy morality of the Victorians, and in politics the Republican party expressed that nostalgia.

La Guardia dissented. He asked the hard questions. He clashed with Treasury Secretary Andrew W. Mellon, a multimillionaire, whose indulgent, self-serving credo was, "Any man of energy and initiative in this country can get what he wants out of life."[84] In reply to the complacent optimism of Mellon, and the whole Republican leadership, Fiorello asked: if it was so easy to get ahead, then why were there so many millions of poor Americans living in tenements? Why were there so many second-class Americans?

La Guardia ripped into big business again and again. He went after the beef industry, the bread trust, landlords, coal mineowners, and the big utility companies. "The supreme issue is the encroachment of the powerful few upon the rights of the many," La Guardia said when he bolted the Republican party in 1924 to endorse the Progressive candidate Senator Robert M. La Follette of Wisconsin against Coolidge. "I would rather be right than regular."[85]

His election that year was a personal triumph. At Madison Square Garden La Follette told a huge crowd, "Do all you can to send La Guardia back to Congress. Not only the people of New York, but the people of the country need him there."[86]

La Guardia's foes denounced him as a left-wing radical, but his poor constituents in East Harlem did not mind that. They were perfectly willing to listen to a radical. The stock market boom was not making them rich and now the government would not even let them drink wine.

La Guardia understood and sympathized with these people. Mann describes how Fiorello, in his East Harlem office, talking to constituents in English, Italian, Yiddish, occasionally German, "might register disgust, surprise, outrage, sorrow, weariness, or sympathy. 'Funny country, isn't it, Pop?' he said, understanding the baffled chagrin of a proud old Italian immigrant who had been summoned to court for beating an eighteen-year-old daughter who went to the movies and came home late with a boy of whom he disapproved." [87] He organized about a thousand young Italian-Americans of the Twentieth District into an enthusiastic group called the *Gibboni* that got out the Italian vote, traded punches with Tammany roughnecks, and monitored polls on election day. Tammany again nominated Frank but this time Fiorello crushed him, 10,756 votes to 7,141.

It would be La Guardia's greatest electoral margin in East Harlem. In 1926, back in Republican ranks, he won by only 55 votes.

His intensity, the underlying seriousness with which he took his responsibilities as a congressman, were impossible to ignore. He had always tended to talk on every subject before the House, even when he was out of his depth, but now, matured by experience and armed by the enormous amount of reading he did, he was becoming one of the most knowledgeable legislators on the Hill. In the Seventy-first and Seventy-second congresses, he would speak out more often, on more subjects than any other representative. By the middle 1920s, he had put together a record that showed he was not only a fighter against his time, but a political thinker ahead of his time. He had fought for civil liberties, minimum-wage laws, old-age pensions, workmen's compensation and taxes on luxury items. He was in favor of public utilities and of government aid to farmers, who were going bankrupt while the business sector prospered. He was against monopolies, against child labor, against racial discrimination, and against arbitrary injunctions to bar strikes. His was a uniquely realistic understanding of what the American electorate would need, and want, in the future. Virtually every one of these positions discussed and defended by La Guardia in the 1920s would be enacted under the New Deal, and would come to be accepted by the Republican party in the 1950s and the 1960s.

And finally, there was a heroic element in the little man that commanded respect. When the Navy submarine S–4 collided with a Coast Guard vessel in Provincetown Harbor on December 28, 1927, its crew trapped in the sub at a depth of a hundred feet, La Guardia arrived on New Year's Day for a firsthand inspection. At first inclined to blame the Navy, he spent thirty-six hours at the bottom of the harbor aboard another submarine, the S–8, during the week-long (and unsuccessful) rescue attempt. His report to Congress was factual, objective, and convinced his colleagues, rather than making a drastic cut in the submarine program, to raise the pay of submarine crews. "You've got to give him credit," was how most of his colleagues felt.[88]

In 1929, La Guardia again tried for the mayoral election in New York; his first try in 1921 had been a disaster, but this time he at least won the Republican primary. He also remarried on the eve of the campaign. The new Mrs. La Guardia had been his secretary for years, Marie Fischer. They were close and the marriage was a happy one. Unable to have children of their own, they raised an adopted son and daughter.

La Guardia was not an unpopular candidate for mayor in 1929. He was the first representative of the new immigrants to have a serious chance at what many people considered the second or third most important elective post in the nation. But he was running against Socialist Norman Thomas, himself an eloquent reformer, and against a popular incumbent, the Democrat Jimmy Walker. A magic figure of the 1920s, Beau James had risen from a poor Irish background to become a songwriter on Broadway (*Will You Love Me in December as You Do in May?*) and a stylish man about town.[89] Though he devoted very little time to City Hall, people loved his charm, his wit, the elegance of his clothes, and they seemed to share vicariously in his carefree enjoyment of life. He belonged wholly to the Roaring Twenties, whose collapse began one week before the election; October 24, 1929, came to be known as Black Thursday, the day the panic started on Wall Street. But the crash did not come in time to save La Guardia. Walker, busy attending the rehearsals of a Broadway play in which his mistress was appearing, barely campaigned. He won in a landslide, with a margin of nearly 500,000 votes. La Guardia did not carry a single district.

But he still had his seat in Congress, and now, with the Depression spreading across the land and the optimists falling silent, La Guardia at last began to achieve recognition as one of the leading intellects in Washington. His had been a voice crying in the wilderness, denouncing the trusts, disputing the convenient Republican premise that by letting business have its way the entire country would benefit. Now the country was a shambles, and Fiorello would neither forget nor forgive. "The bastards broke the People's back with their usury," he raged to an aide.

"Let them die; the People will survive." [90] He urged the impeachment of Secretary of the Treasury Andrew Mellon, whom he had always despised. As a member of the Judiciary Committee of the House, La Guardia grilled bankers and Wall Street operators. He called for federal relief for farmers and federal slum clearance projects, and when Hoover warned that government projects such as those would destroy the ruggedness of the American character, La Guardia contemptuously dismissed the President — and the leader of his party — as a mediocrity. He spelled out his own convictions in a letter to Senator George Norris of Nebraska, dated March 1931:

There is a tendency on the part of leaders in both of the major parties to continue to legislate on fundamentals laid down in the age of the stage coach, the spinning wheel and tallow candles. This tendency has resulted in the concentration of great wealth under the control of a few families in this country with the large masses of workers entirely at their mercy for their very existence. Legislation has not kept abreast with the progress in mechanics, electricity, chemistry, transportation and the sciences. The result is that we find ourselves with an unprecedented wealth, with warehouses full and millions of willing workers out of employment and large numbers dependent upon private charities. When millions of workers through no fault of their own are thrown out of employment it is the duty of government to give them relief and not force them to apply for private charity.[91]

This was a lucid analysis of the legislative task the New Deal would be facing. But Hoover's term had still two years to run. When the President sought to revive the economy by applying a $600 million dollar sales tax, an indignant Fiorello bucked his party leadership and in a fierce two-week battle engineered the biggest upset of the Seventy-second Congress. La Guardia simply did not feel that in depression times, as Mann has written, the poor should carry the rich on their backs. "The House, surly and contentious, confused and disorganized since the opening day of the session, and preparing for the coming election, suddenly stampeded to a leader who embodied the resentments that would sweep Herbert Hoover out of the White House in 1932." [92]

Though the defeat of the sales tax was something of a negative triumph, other congressmen were impressed, at last, by La Guardia's long record of insurgency. His hour had come. For the first time he was able to introduce legislation and have it acted upon. He had always been a rebel; now he was a rebel leader. He introduced a bill establishing federal insurance for savings deposits, which would serve as the model for a bill enacted under the New Deal. He wrote an amendment to the Federal Home Loan Bank Bill making it easier for the common man to buy a home by making low-interest loans available. He championed the Omnibus Relief Bill, introduced by Democratic Speaker John Nance Garner, and he swung enough Republican votes to have the measure passed; it authorized nearly $3 million for unemployment, relief and public works and was vetoed by President Hoover in July 1932.[93] But Fiorello's major legislative achievement, which capped his ten years of struggle in Congress, was the Norris–La Guardia Anti-Injunction Act.

This key piece of legislation — considered by many to be labor's Magna Charta — established the right of all American workingmen to bargain collectively, and made it the government's duty to maintain that right. The act restrained courts from issuing strike injunctions unless management could show that it had already bargained responsibly, or been intimidated by violence, or would be financially ruined by the continuation of a strike. It invalidated so-called "yellow dog" contracts, which enticed workers to sign on favorable terms with the stipulation that they would not join a labor union while employed. For years La Guardia had represented the interests of workers — in the great garment strike of 1913, as a labor lawyer and as a congressman. Many of his closest Italian-American friends had been labor crusaders like August Bellanca, Arthur Giovannitti, Joseph Ettor, Silvio Ninfo and Luigi Antonini. Though Fiorello might disagree with them politically, he had remained faithful to their common vision of aiding and liberating the workingman.

The Norris–La Guardia Act would stand as his major achievement. It was passed by the House and Senate with huge majorities, and signed into law by President Hoover in March 1932 — in the knowledge, Norris claimed, that Congress would override his veto.

In July, when Fiorello returned to East Harlem to open his campaign for reelection, he was probably the most respected and best-known congressman in the nation. Five months later he was on the street, unemployed. Despite a typical all-out La Guardia campaign, speeches before large, cheering crowds, the support of the Liberal party and effective block-by-block canvassing by the *Gibboni*, he lost the election to a young, affable, politically unknown Italian-American, James J. Lanzetta, the Tammany candidate, whose margin was a solid 16,447 votes to La Guardia's 15,227. "Oh, man," asked a dazed Fiorello the day after, "how did we lose?" [94]

He had lost in a half a dozen ways. Nineteen thirty-two was the year of Roosevelt's landslide victory, and FDR's margin of over twenty thousand in East Harlem had helped Lanzetta, a fellow Democrat. Jews had been moving out of the district and Puerto Ricans moving in, and Tammany had been actively recruiting many of East Harlem's new Puerto Ricans. Finally, the Italian-Americans had let Fiorello go under. Older Italians often did not vote. The younger Italian-Americans switched to Lanzetta because he was popular among them and they liked his style.

In a democracy, of course, there is no law that says public office is a sinecure. And while Fiorello had lost his seat in the House, he would still play an important role in the waning months of the Seventy-second Congress, helping to usher in the politics and the legislation of the New Deal. Later that year, 1933, he would be elected mayor of New York in a crushing victory over Jimmy Walker's successor, John O'Brien.

Yet his defeat in the congressional election, on the eve of the New Deal and in light of his triumphs in the House over the previous two years, does indicate that the East Harlem Italians who should have been his staunchest supporters did not yet see political choice as a vital ingredient in their lives. They were fond of Fiorello, and proud of him, and would be even prouder when he was mayor. But he was never the magnified image of his Italian-American constituents. There were too many elements in his background that they did not possess. He was ahead of them in the depth and scope of his political vision, and in 1932, when he might have expected recognition at the polls, they instead brought him home to New York.

14

The Turbulent Thirties

IN THE GRIMMEST MONTHS of the Depression, some Italian-Americans began having second thoughts about the decision they or their parents had made in leaving Italy. Despite the new President's air of resolve, and his forceful confidence, industrial output by the spring of 1933 had fallen to half its 1929 level; there were 14 million unemployed, or twenty-five percent of the labor force; and the banking system was on the verge of collapse. Everywhere there was hunger and the threat of civil disorder. In Italy, on the other hand, there was no disorder, no hunger; officially there was no unemployment; and the figure of the Duce, warmed and illuminated by the sycophantic praise of the Fascist press, appeared to radiate a virile strength for himself and for Italy. As he assembled his plasticine Third Roman Empire, Il Duce had words of praise and of solidarity for the millions of Italians settled in other lands, who seemed to represent so many outposts of Italian civilization, and, potentially, of fascism. He saw them as people enriched by the industrial skills they had learned, saw them also as possible collaborators, and their sons as soldiers. "An Italian," he assured them, "remains an Italian no matter in what land he lives, even to the seventh generation."

A few thousand Italian-Americans were lured back to Italy during the Depression years, and about a thousand young men went to fight in Ethiopia.[1] Nearly all would rue that decision as they were caught by

World War II, mistrusted first by suspicious Fascist police and later by officials of the Allied occupation.

It was hardly surprising that Italian-Americans should be dazzled by Mussolini. For years, on the pavements of America, they had been insulted as "Wops" and "Dagoes." Ten years before his successful presidential race in 1912, Woodrow Wilson had published a five-volume *History of the United States*. In the fifth volume, he took up the question of aliens, and his verdict on the Italian immigrants then arriving by the hundreds of thousands was that they came from the "lowest class from the south of Italy." He found them a people with "neither skill nor energy nor any initiative of quick intelligence," adding, in a double-edged slur, that "the Chinese are more to be desired, as workmen if not as citizens, than most of the coarse crew that comes crowding in every year at the eastern ports." [2] A navitist newspaper had put it even more crudely, characterizing most Italian immigrants as "steerage slime." While these attitudes of Anglo-Saxon superiority towards southern Italians were not universal, they were not unusual. To Italian-Americans, therefore, the Duce's great initial appeal was that he seemed to be making Italy respected by the Anglo-Saxons.

Hardly a day passed without their hearing Italy, or Mussolini, mentioned on the radio. When Italian laborers came home in the evening and opened their newspapers, they saw articles on Italy that made them proud. In one photograph, distinguished foreign ministers might be shown arriving in Rome for an important conference arranged by the Duce; in another, a smiling Italian aviator leaned from the cockpit of a seaplane after having broken a world's record. Much of Mussolini's own press was favorable. Thomas Edison went so far as to call the Duce "the greatest genius of the age" [3] — an extravagant compliment from a man who was a genius. After meeting the dictator for the first time in 1927, Winston Churchill, then chancellor of the exchequer, turned to Mussolini in front of a group of foreign correspondents and said, "If I were an Italian, I am sure I would have been with you from beginning to end in your struggle against the bestial appetites of Leninism." [4] Senator Hiram Johnson of California, returning from a trip to Rome, said, "I have seen the marvel of modern Italy, Signor Mussolini." [5]

U.S. Secretary of the Treasury Andrew Mellon was also an admirer. As part of the settlement of Italy's war debt with the United States, negotiated by Mellon, a consortium of Wall Street banks led by J. P. Morgan & Co. loaned the Fascist government $100 million to help stabilize the Italian lira. The loan provoked a furious debate in Congress. Senator Kenneth McKellar of Tennessee termed the Duce "perhaps the greatest evil that has befallen the Italian people in 100 years." [6] By then, Hiram Johnson had lost his earlier enthusiasm for Mussolini, and he too attacked the loan. But in vain. The debt settlement package was approved by both the House and the Senate in 1926.

The high point of *Il Duce*'s popularity among Italian-Americans occurred in 1929, with the signing of the Concordat, or Lateran Treaty. Ever since the unification of Italy in 1860–1870, relations between the Italian government and the Vatican had been strained. Rome had been conquered in 1870 by an Italian army of sixty thousand soldiers; other Italian units had occupied the remaining cities of the Papal State that still comprised some seventeen thousand square miles of the peninsula. The unhappy Pius IX, Pio Nono, barricaded himself inside the Vatican, an area one-seventh the size of New York's Central Park. "This brooding confinement within the Vatican by Pope Pius IX, and his successors Leo XIII, Pius X, Benedict XV, and (for part of his reign) Pius XI, became symbolic of the papacy's refusal to accept the loss of sovereignty over Rome and the territories of the Papal State." [7]

On February 11, 1929, the Fascist government announced that an agreement had been reached with the Vatican to end this nettlesome "Roman Question." On that same day, the Duce's representatives and those of Pius XI signed the treaty in Rome's Lateran Palace, from which it took its name. The pact not only normalized relations between the Vatican and the Italian government, but created Vatican City as an independent state, made religious instruction compulsory in Italian schools, and made the Italian government responsible for paying the salaries of parish priests. It also compensated the Vatican for the loss of its former territories and established canon law as the civil code regulating marriage (thus voiding divorce except in cases of special dispensation).

If the treaty was a relief for the Vatican, it marked a triumph for Mussolini. In his youth, the future Duce had been a militant atheist and radical. During a period of exile in Switzerland in 1902, going hungry and being jailed as a vagrant because he could not find work, the one possession he had clung to had been a cheap metal medallion of Karl Marx.[8] But after he had abjured socialism and employed his truncheon-wielding Fascist squads in raids to break the revolutionary spirit of Socialists, Mussolini had become respectable in the eyes of Catholic conservatives. The Lateran Treaty solidified his position at home, and its effect reached every country where the Catholic church was well established. The Duce now stood forth not only as a powerful bulwark against Marxism, but also as a defender of the Catholic faith.

In America, however, the signing of the Lateran Treaty coincided with a scandal over the Fascist League of North America, which had been founded in 1925 and counted some fifteen thousand members. An article by Marcus Duffield in *Harper's Magazine* detailing the activities of the league so embarrassed Rome and the Italian embassy that the league was prudently dissolved before Congress could investigate it.[9] But funds and support for Fascist sympathizers among the Italian-Americans continued to arrive from Rome through an official Association of Italians Abroad headed by a general in the Fascist militia. The most strident champion of fascism in the New York area, where the largest concentration of Italian immigrants lived, was a rabid anti-Semite, Domenico Trombetta. He published an Italian-language newspaper, *Il Grido Della Stirpe* (*The Cry of the Tribe*), which he characterized as "the faithful voice of Fascism in North America." [10] An Italian-American, Paul Castorina, led an organization of U.S. blackshirts called The American Union of Fascists. In all, the Fascists could count on the support of about one hundred thousand sympathizers in America. In New York alone there were some fifty Fascist clubs where members sat around wearing black shirts, playing cards, and reading propaganda. The Cine Roma, a New York movie house, showed films shipped from Rome with titles such as "Dynamic Fascism" and "Decaying Democracy." [11]

Though this Fascist proselytizing was destined to have little effect on the loyalty of Italian-Americans toward their adopted country,* the 1930s marked a time of turbulent conflict within many Italian neighborhoods. In 1933, for example, Italian-American blackshirts and anti-Fascists clashed at the Garibaldi memorial on Staten Island, leaving one dead and several wounded. The verbal battle in the Italian-American press was continuous and fierce. Though the anti-Fascists were probably in the minority throughout the 1920s and 1930s — a fact that never failed to amaze those Italians fresh from Fascist prisons in Italy who were seeking asylum in the land of the free — the anti-Fascist movement brought an even more distinguished group of exiles to

* After Pearl Harbor, the F.B.I. took only some 400 Italian-Americans or Italian aliens into custody; most of them were released within a few months.

America than had arrived a century earlier from the Austrian dungeons of Lombardy and Venetia.

They included Arturo Toscanini, who had refused to play the Fascist hymn, "Giovinezza," at his concerts; Carlo Sforza, the former Italian foréign minister; the novelist Giuseppe Antonio Borgese, who taught Romance languages at the University of Chicago; Gaetano Salvemini, who taught history at Harvard; and Max Ascoli, for many years editor of *The Reporter*.

The most important of these exiles in terms of America's destiny in the twentieth century was Enrico Fermi, who, instead of returning to his laboratory at the University of Rome from Stockholm, where he received the 1938 Nobel Prize for physics, escaped with his family to the United States. The famous letter written by Albert Einstein to President Roosevelt and mailed in Peconic, Long Island, on August 2, 1939, first suggesting the possibility of building an atomic bomb, began with the sentence: "Some recent work by E. Fermi and L. Szilard which has been communicated to me in manuscript, leads me to expect that the element uranium may be turned into a new and important source of energy in the immediate future." [12] Though Fermi was only one of the European physicists working in the United States during World War II, it was the group led by Fermi that produced the world's first self sustaining nuclear chain reaction at 2:20 on the afternoon of December 2, 1942, under the west stands of Stagg Field, the University of Chicago football stadium. (It was also Fermi who, with his somewhat crude English, baptized the nuclear reactor as a "pile," selecting the English word for heap.)[13] When American physicist Karl T. Compton called James B. Conant at Harvard to break the news, he said in a guarded wartime metaphor, "Jim, you will be interested to know that the Italian navigator has just landed in the New World." [14]

While the names of Toscanini and Fermi became world-famous, possibly the two most interesting anti-Fascists of the period were a priest who arrived in America only in 1940, aboard an English ship that had been dive-bombed and strafed by Nazi planes, and an anarchist who by 1940 had been imprisoned by the United States government thirty-six times.

During the three years of turmoil that preceded the march on Rome in October 1922, the Italian who appeared to have the best chance of emerging as the alternative to Mussolini, or to the Marxists, was a tall, jut-jawed Sicilian priest named Luigi Sturzo.

He had been born in the Sicilian town of Caltagirone in 1871, the year after Rome and the Papal States had been wrenched from the pope's hands. By the time he was twenty, Don Luigi Sturzo was already regarded as an unusual man. Spare and phlegmatic where most Italians were given to forensic arabesques, towering over his fellow Sicilians, he was also a political activist at a time when the Catholic church was still recoiling from any direct involvement in the critical political struggles of the industrial age. By the turn of the century, Sturzo had been elected the mayor of Caltagirone and — in a Sicily ruled by conservative landowners who often used the Mafia to bludgeon social protest — had led protest strikes of up to eighty thousand peasants. He was mayor of Caltagirone for fifteen years.

By the eve of World War I, this brave, far-sighted priest had done more than any other individual to turn the Vatican away from social isolationism. *Non Expedit* (it is not the case) had been the reply given by the Sacred Penitentiary Congregation to Italian bishops who had asked whether Catholics could run for political office, or even vote. Sturzo, like other young prelates, believed that the Church could not continue to offer charity as a solution to the world's social problems. But his was a minority opinion. A fellow priest was even unfrocked in 1909 for having defied the *Non Expedit* and run for a parliamentary seat (successfully). "People today," Don Sturzo wrote in 1945, "have no idea of what it cost in patience and humility, obedience and sacrifice to overcome opposition all the more serious and bitter in that it was often inspired by zeal, by a sense of discipline, or by fear of errors falsely attributed to 'modernism.' " [15] Sturzo, however, had brilliant allies within the Church, including Angelo Roncalli — the future Pope John XXIII — and the present pope's father, Giorgio Montini, who was a respected and influential Catholic journalist.

By 1918, Don Sturzo had won his case in the high councils of the Vatican and was among the founders of the Christian Democratic party the following year — it was, however, decided to call it the *Partito Popolare,* or Popular party. Pope Benedict XV abolished the *Non Expedit* in time for the November elections, and the "Populars" won ninety-nine seats, making them the fifth largest group in Parliament. The Catholic party in fact appeared to have the best chance of challenging the Socialists for the support of organized labor in Italy. By

1920, unions affiliated with the Popular party had enrolled a million people and had a particularly strong following among agricultural workers.[16] The Populars might also have checked the Fascist onslaught but for the tragic fact that the death of Benedict XV in the crucial year of 1922 led to the elevation of Achille Ratti, who took the name Pius XI. Ratti sided with those Vatican conservatives who favored fascism as the most secure barrier against a Marxist revolution in Italy. By then, it had become clear that fascism, though it had presented itself at times as the "spearhead of a proletarian world revolution against conservatism," would instead strengthen the class system and protect industrialists and large landowners against the normal, democratic pressures of social change. This made it welcome to conservatives both outside and inside the Vatican. And while the Popular party included a conservative wing, its leaders, and in particular Don Sturzo, were pledged to a program of social reform.

In a move that may have laid the cornerstone for the Lateran Treaty seven years later, Pius XI withdrew his support from the Populars. When Fascist *squadristi* beat to death an activist priest, Don Giovanni Minzoni, in August 1923, in what would later appear as almost a dress rehearsal for the celebrated murder of Socialist leader Giacomo Matteotti the following year, the Vatican barely protested. Don Sturzo, having encouraged the Popular party to condemn the Fascists at its congress in Turin in the spring of 1923, had become an embarrassment to Pius XI. He was forced to resign his post as party secretary and to go into exile. (His protégé within the Christian-Democratic movement in Italy was a young, mild-looking but iron-willed journalist from the Tyrol, Alcide De Gasperi. Arrested by the Fascist secret police and sentenced to four years in prison, De Gasperi, after his release, eked out a living as a humble $80-a-month librarian in the Vatican archives.)

From France, meanwhile, Don Sturzo had gone to England where, like the anticlerical Mazzini of a century earlier, he produced a stream of publications and letters in the cause of freedom. But in 1940, suffering from a heart ailment, his London home damaged by Luftwaffe bombs, he was persuaded to seek sanctuary in America. After a year in a Florida hospital, he went to live in a modest home in the Bensonhurst section of Brooklyn, where he continued to write, to receive visitors, to encourage the anti-Fascists among Italian-Americans, and to prepare for the resurgence of the Christian Democratic movement throughout the Catholic world.

Though he was nearly seventy when he reached America, and ill with heart disease, it was while he was living in Brooklyn that Don Sturzo produced his most important book, *Italy and the Coming World*. In it, he wrote:

Men are so preoccupied with the search for personal well-being that they forget its sources, confusing material reality with moral values. But at the bottom of our two-thousand-year-old civilization the religious, moral spirit of the Classical and Judeo-Christian tradition is never missing, even in theoretical and practical deviations. Men who have denied or fought the Christian religion (or have ignored it) when they speak of liberty, justice, and moral values, of public and private honesty, of the rights of the human personality, mean more or less the same things that we mean, even without actually referring them to God.

. . . Liberty and Democracy must today be reviewed in the light of Christianity even by those who are without religious faith; they cannot but recognize the incoherence of modern society as founded on scientific materialism, or pragmatic positivism, or state, national, or racial pantheism. . . .[17]

In 1946, the seventy-seven-year-old Don Sturzo returned to Rome, a frail, ailing, and increasingly querulous elder statesman. But he had lived to see the rebirth of the political movement he had founded. In Germany, it brought to power Konrad Adenauer; in Italy the former Fascist prisoner and Vatican archivist De Gasperi, who more than any other man restored Italy's sense of direction after the shame, and confusion, and the crimes of Mussolini's last years.

The most stormy and persistent foe of fascism in America during the 1920s and 1930s was the anarchist Carlo Tresca. A tall, jovial southern Italian with the sparkling blue eyes of a Scandinavian, Tresca was a political ascetic possessed by sensual appetites. Perhaps because he wore his contradictions so openly, he was, as his friend Max Eastman wrote, "the only man left whom all the one hundred and seventeen varieties, divisions, denominations, sects, sections, and subsections of the revolutionary movement respect and esteem." [18]

It is one of the minor ironies of Italian history that this fiery anti-Fascist had roomed briefly with the future Duce in Switzerland, when both were youthful fugitives from Italian justice — Mussolini because he had refused induction into the army, and Tresca because he had jumped bail after having been convicted of slandering a government official. Tresca was en route to New York where his older brother Ettore had established himself as a general practitioner on Mulberry Street. Mussolini appears to have seriously considered going to America at this time, but in the end decided against it. And so one day, at the Geneva railroad station, Comrade Mussolini and Comrade Tresca embraced and parted, to go their separate ideological ways.

Carlo Tresca was born in 1879 at Sulmona, a backwater in central Italy noted chiefly as the site of a great fortress in Roman times barring Julius Caesar's path after he had crossed the Rubicon. (Caesar bought off the garrison and went on to occupy Rome.) The Trescas were a landowning family, so respectable socially that when the young radical went preaching revolution to the local peasants they sometimes replied, "as you wish, Don Carlo." But the family's fortunes were something else. The once-profitable vineyards had been all but destroyed by phylloxera and year by year the land was being sold off to pay bills. Though Carlo's older brother had managed to earn a degree in medicine before emigrating to America, there was no money left for Carlo's education, and he faced the dreary prospect of becoming a clerk. This undoubtedly made him sharply aware of social and economic distinctions at an early age, and it may have made him reject the comfortable middle-class optimism of his more fortunate schoolmates. There was a tradition of political activism in the Tresca family, too, since a favorite uncle, Paolo Tresca, was a veteran of Garibaldi's campaigns.

Just when "Don Carlo" was finishing high school, and struggling with the problem of his future, Sulmona received a sudden and unexpected influx of militant Socialists. These were leaders of the railway workers' union who had caused trouble elsewhere in the peninsula and so had been banished to this Adriatic Siberia. They at once organized a political club; fascinated, Carlo began attending their meetings. Within a few years, he had become the club's secretary and had founded *Il Germe* (*The Seed*), the first of his many struggling newspapers. Convicted of libeling a captain of the *carabinieri,* Tresca was soon spending two months in jail in the company of a Socialist agitator whose prison reminiscences were subsequently published in *Il Germe.* The story was picked up by Italy's major Socialist newspaper, *L'Avanti,* and Tresca was invited to a rally in the Colosseum. It was in 1901 — the first and last time that he would see the Italian capital. At the rally, he wept from emotion when the Socialist deputy Enrico Ferri mentioned his name as a promising young editor from the provinces. "I looked around to see if the people of Rome were taking notice of me," he wrote in his auto-biography. "I wanted to shout, 'Here I am! I am Tresca!' " [19]

He returned to Sulmona, and to a second conviction for libel. Sentenced to a year and a half of solitary confinement, he jumped bail, made his way to Switzerland and to his brief domicile with Mussolini, and then joined his brother in New York. He was twenty-three years old, and the squalor and coarseness of immigrant life in the Mulberry Bend made the same indelible impression on him as it had on Vanzetti and dozens of other Italian radicals of the period. He joined an anarchist cell that met in a cramped basement on Bleeker Street. The setting consisted of "a big barrel with two lighted candles on it and four men seated around it, urging the necessity of marshalling the power of the Italian workers for the coming general battle against capitalism. Conspirators? Why, yes! We felt as such. There was at that time in each and every one of us the conviction of an approaching apocalypse." [20]

Moving to Philadelphia in 1904, he edited *Il Proletario*, the weekly newspaper of the Italian Socialist Federation, for about a year. Barely able to speak English, living in slums among poor Italian laborers whom he tried to awaken and organize politically, he was seeing in this New World the reflection of the class structure of Europe. He admitted frankly, "I was still living in Italy, both with my heart and mind. My thinking, my conversation, my habits of life, my friends and my enemies, were all Italian. We called the sections of American cities inhabited by Italian immigrants *'colonie Italiane,'* Italian colonies." [21] Within those neighborhoods, and wherever Italian laborers were employed, Tresca continued his angry muckraking journalism. He worked in a Pennsylvania mine and on a New Jersey track-laying gang, slept (or did not sleep) in a Lower East Side hotel where homebound immigrants were said to be suffocated in their sleep and their savings robbed, and visited whorehouses where Italian peasant girls had been lured or forced into prostitution by white slavers posing as prospective American husbands. (The girls, Tresca complained, were always in a hurry, suspicious of his questions, and usually unwilling to talk.)

Soon, he drew his first American jail sentence in Philadelphia for having slandered the Italian government in an issue of *Il Proletario*. Of prison he wrote,

it destroys you unless you have an iron will. Alone in a small, poorly ventilated cell, with the darkness always overpowering the light; alone with your thoughts, the torturing thoughts of what you have lost, of what you need and long for; alone, with your silent and burning tears in a cell where a dog would be maddened after a single day's stay. To be there day after day, doing nothing creative, losing the sensation of time, indifferent to the sunrise and the sunset, always waiting desperately for something new, for someone to see, to speak to, for some noise to signify that you are not forgotten. All this is hell.[22]

Just before entering prison, Tresca, now twenty-six, had resigned from the Italian Socialist Federation. He was too intractable a spirit to accept the ideological dogma of the Socialist movement, still predominantly Marxist. He would henceforth call himself an anarchist, that most ambiguous of all political designations. But he was, unlike many of the Italian anarchists in America, a believer in organizing industrial strikes rather than plotting deeds of violence. In the language of the revolutionary movement of that time, this made him an anarcho-syndicalist, and it would lead him inevitably into the IWW. Like most Wobblies, Tresca believed that there must first be a revolution that would abolish the private ownership of industry. Once men were free of the wage system, they would work voluntarily. In this utopian view human beings, being free, would have no need of government and life would be organized around a loose association of trade unions and agricultural cooperatives.

These were the views he espoused in his new Italian language weekly, *La Plebe*. He had moved from Philadelphia to Pittsburgh in order to be closer to the large number of Italian laborers working in the mines and steel mills. For a few years, he wrote, debated, organized and led strikes in the drab mining towns of Pennsylvania, Ohio, and West Virginia. Because he was a hearty, fun-loving man, devoted to red wine and talk and the Italian card game of *briscola,* he was a welcome guest in the miners' homes. Often, an apologetic miner would offer to share his bed with "Don Carlo," and the visiting dignitary would accept only to discover that it also contained the miner's entire family.

Had Tresca limited himself to preaching revolution in Italian, to Italian workers, the authorities would probably have taken little notice of him. But he was also a confirmed priest-baiter, like so many Italian radicals of the nineteenth and early twentieth centuries, and he published some scurrilous attacks on local priests in *La Plebe* and in the newspaper that soon replaced it, *L'Avvenire* (*The Future*). Local Catholics protested, and Tresca was sentenced to nine months in prison. His attacks on the clergy, moreover, had stirred deep passions within the Italian community. As he finished addressing a rally on the eve of his imprisonment, a man slipped up behind him and tried to cut his throat.

The job would have been done perfectly but for the fact that I was able to realize what was coming as soon as I felt a strange hand over my cheek. As a defensive move I pressed my chin against my breast. The razor, instead of operating against my neck, as intended, started to work on my upper lips and, coming down it, found resistance on the jaw, so much so that the blade was broken when it reached the jugular vein, which was left untouched.[23]

It required twenty-six stitches to close the wound, and the scar was so disfiguring that Tresca thereafter grew a beard to cover it. The man who had slashed him was caught, tried, and acquitted. Two months later, however, the would-be assassin was killed by Italian miners.

From the hospital, Tresca went to prison to serve his nine-month term for libel. It was while he was in the county jail that news reached him of the uprising of Italian millworkers in Lawrence, Massachusetts. His friend Arturo Giovannitti was there, and it was all Tresca could think of. He headed for Lawrence the day he was released. "I went to Lawrence like Mohammed to Mecca; with burning faith in my heart. When the conductor called out 'Lawrence' at the station, my heart began to palpitate like the engine of a great electric generator." [24]

Arriving shortly after Ettor and Giovannitti had been arrested for complicity in the murder of Anna LoPizzo, he took charge of the Italian local of the IWW, personally visiting the homes of every man or woman whose dues were in arrears. He led the strikers to the Lawrence Common in defiance of a ban, and led them to the Boston Common for the huge rally in behalf of Ettor and Giovannitti. Lawrence rescued Tresca from the obscurity of Pennsylvania mining camps, and his obstinate priest-baiting, and brought him into what was then the most dynamic wing of the American labor movement. It also set his heart going like a generator in another sense, for it was at Lawrence that Tresca met Elizabeth Gurley Flynn, with whom he had the most durable of his numerous love affairs with ladies of the revolution. He already had an Italian wife, but he was something of an anarchist in personal matters also, and his passion for Gurley, as she was called, was deeper than convention. She herself was in her early twenties, a pretty, dark-haired and blue-eyed colleen, "in the slender fire-breathing charm of her indignant youth," as Francis Russell described her.[25]

From Lawrence, the lovers moved to New York where Tresca took part in the Hotel and Restaurant Workers' strike. He was now something of a celebrity, a debonair man of thirty with a Van Dyke beard, whose photographs show him wearing a pin-striped suit and vest along with the floppy tie and black ten-gallon hat that had become the anarchist symbols. So distinguished did he appear that during a street brawl along Broadway involving his waiters and dishwashers, a police officer politely cautioned him, "Please step aside, Doctor. We're arresting these men." By contrast, a few days later a detective who had been struck to the ground in another fracas shoved a gun into Tresca's face and threatened to blow his head off unless the strikers immediately dispersed. As he was being dragged to the paddy wagon, a copy of Elizabeth Barrett Browning's *Sonnets from the Portuguese* tumbled from his pocket, its tender passages underlined and the flyleaf adorned with an inscription from Gurley. The press went into titters, and the romance between the dashing Italian anarchist and the "East Side Joan of Arc" became public knowledge.

Booked and released, Tresca crossed the Hudson to Paterson, New Jersey, where he was at once recognized and arrested. The predominantly Italian millworkers were out on strike, and the mayor and chief of police were determined to crack down on agitators. John Reed, who would write the classic account of the Bolshevik revolution, *Ten Days That Shook the World,* was also arrested and thrown into the same cell with Tresca, who thought he was a police spy.[26]

Once they had been released from jail, Reed hurried back to New York where, with help from his friends in the theatrical world and the Village, he staged an elaborate Silk Strike Pageant at Madison Square Garden to raise funds for the strikers across the Hudson River. The pageant had a cast of one thousand two hundred, mostly Italian immigrants from Paterson. As the letters IWW blazed forth in red lights from the roof of Madison Square Garden, a sympathetic New York audience saw five mammoth scenes depicting the evolution of the strike and the fatal shooting by police of Valentino Modestino, an Italian striker. Even Modestino's funeral was reenacted, the coffin wreathed in red carnations. Tresca, Haywood and Gurley took their places beside the coffin and repeated the same orations they had spoken at the real funeral. In the final scene, depicting a strike meeting, all the people on stage turned their backs to the audience so that the public could feel itself part of the huge group of strikers as Haywood spoke to them. At the end, everyone stood and sang the "Internationale."

The gargantuan pageant, however, was so expensive to stage that instead of raising funds for the Paterson workers, it lost money. This as much as anything else doomed the strike, and by midsummer it was over.

Tresca took part in one more major strike for the IWW, at the Mesabi Range in Minnesota, where many Italians worked as miners. In 1916, they and thousands of other immigrant laborers walked out, demanding an eight-hour day. Tresca was arrested the moment he stepped off the train and was taken to the Duluth County jail. Shortly afterwards, police raided a Montenegrin miner's house and in the scuffle a deputy was shot. Tresca was charged with being an accessory to the murder, though he had never even been close to the miner's house. An elaborate bargain was worked out with the district attorney whereby the charges against Tresca were dropped and two miners received relatively light sentences after pleading guilty to manslaughter. But Haywood was furious when he learned of this arrangement, which had not been approved by him, and the result was that Tresca, along with Ettor and Giovannitti, who had also been at Mesabi, resigned from the IWW.

For Tresca, the World War I period was the loneliest and most dangerous of his life. Though he had severed connections with the IWW, he believed, like the Wobblies, that the war was simply a struggle over colonial possessions and markets. And like all anarchists, he identified authority itself as the principal evil. Men fought one another and exploited one another, he believed, because the ruling class used authority to its own advantage, manipulating the mass of human beings. Remove authority, do away with government altogether, and men would voluntarily work together in harmony. This profoundly optimistic vision of the future was shattered, of course, by what followed the Bolshevik revolution and above all by the figure of Joseph Stalin. But Tresca believed passionately in the ideal of total freedom in that final grace period of the utopian left, and believed, like Marx, that the working class, because it had not become corrupted by wielding authority over others, would bring about the regeneration of mankind.

"I had faith," he wrote, "faith in the invincible power of my creed, in the soundness of my principles and in the working class as a class that would, some day, find in itself the force to give to mankind a better world. . . ." [27]

Had Tresca been a theorist, a writer rather than a doer, he could have probably produced volumes of anarchist literature in some East Harlem walk-up without the government taking any particular notice. But he was supremely a man of action whose newspapers were merely polemical weapons. Not only did he continue to travel throughout the Midwest fomenting strikes among Italian laborers after his split with the IWW, operating alone, but he also opposed American participation in World War I. Already, he had been living dangerously — he had entered one mining town early in 1917 leading a procession of five cars filled with armed deputies, while along both sides of the town's main street were two columns of armed vigilantes shouting, "Damned agitator! Damned foreigner! Get the hell out of here!" After the American declaration of war on the Central Powers on April 6, 1917, he was under more or less constant police surveillance and he would frequently step off a train to find a sheriff's posse waiting to take him directly to jail.

But he never deviated from his solitary course, and after World War I he emerged as the leader of the Italian anarchists in the United States* (although, being anarchists, they never conferred the honor on him formally). Rather, they knew that Carlo was a man who could be trusted, who rarely refused to help anyone, and who risked his skin as a matter of course. When Bartolomeo Vanzetti took the train to New York to find out what had happened to Elia and Salsedo, it was Tresca he met with. And after Vanzetti had been convicted in the first trial at Plymouth on August 16, 1920, it was Tresca — angry at the Boston group of anarchists for what he felt was Vanzetti's inept defense — who sent Fred C. Moore, the IWW's former general counsel and the key to the acquittal of Ettor and Giovannitti, up to Boston to take charge of defending Sacco and Vanzetti at the second trial at Dedham. "If Massachusetts lawyers had been left to defend Sacco and Vanzetti," Russell wrote,

* They were concentrated mostly in Paterson, New Jersey, in the industrial towns around Boston, and in Barre, Vermont, where Italian stone quarriers had brought the anarchist creed with them. Their more or less acknowledged leader until April 1919, when he was deported by the United States government, was Luigi Galleani, the editor of *Cronaca Sovversiva*. One of the Italian anarchists of the period who had also been a member of the IWW, returned to Italy and ironically became one of the most powerful ministers in Mussolini's cabinet. This was Edmundo Rossoni. Conversely, Domenico Trombetta, the editor of the Italian-language Fascist newspaper, *Il Grido Della Stirpe (The Cry of the Tribe)*, had been an anarchist in Italy before World War I. Tresca contemptuously referred to Trombetta's paper as *Il Grido Della Trippa — The Cry of The Tripe*.

the obscure Italians, whether convicted or acquitted, would have never shed their obscurity. It was Moore, with his flair for propaganda and his contacts with many radical labor groups all over the country and abroad, who made the fate of the two immigrants into an international issue that blazed round the world. Tresca, by sending Moore to Boston, originated the Sacco-Vanzetti case.[28]

But now, Tresca himself went to prison.

In New York, Tresca had bought yet another struggling weekly newspaper from a fellow anarchist who had decided to operate on his customers' heads in a more practical way by becoming a barber. This newspaper Tresca called *Il Martello* (*The Hammer*). Borrowing art and cartoons from *The Masses*, which was edited by Max Eastman, Tresca wrote most of *Il Martello* himself, signing articles with various pseudonyms including *Ego Sum* and *L'Homme Qui Rit*.

On the thirtieth of October, 1922, Mussolini became premier following the march on Rome. Tresca, hailing the news as "a return to the happy days of the Inquisition," at once began attacking the Fascists. Since his paper was written in Italian, Tresca smuggled copies of it into Italy. Its effect was negligible — even in the New York area where most of its readership lived — but it irritated officials in Rome to the extent that in a speech at the Waldorf-Astoria in 1923, the Italian ambassador, Prince Don Gelasio Caetani, suggested that a certain newspaper that was slandering the Italian government should be suppressed.

The July 21 issue of *Il Martello* was held up in the mails without warning, and on August 10 Tresca was arrested. The attorney general's office reportedly offered not to prosecute if Tresca would leave the country.[29] He refused, and on October 30 he was indicted for having published a two-line birth control advertisement for a book entitled *The Art of Not Making Children*. On December 8, 1923, Tresca was convicted and sentenced to a year in the federal penitentiary in Atlanta.

He served only four months. The conviction had become an embarrassing scandal almost at once. The Baltimore *Sun* wrote scathingly in an editorial that "the time has come for an inquiry as to whence our Federal bureaucracies derive their power, from Mussolini or from the American people."[30] H. L. Mencken even reprinted the same advertisement in the *American Mercury* and challenged the government to arrest him. La Guardia raised the matter in Congress, and in May 1925 President Coolidge pardoned Tresca and ordered his release.

Tresca returned to New York and to his anti-Fascist fulminations in

Il Martello. He was now probably the best-known anarchist in the United States. Each time a bomb exploded anywhere in the vicinity of New York the detectives of the bomb squad paid him a routine call to see if he knew anything. "They are good fellows," Tresca once said. "They would ask me what I knew. I never knew anything, so we would have a glass of wine together." [31] And as he would try to explain to the New York *World,* "I don't carry bombs, despite the stories of the Mussolini government." But because he was an anarchist, others made the association for him. When he was living on Staten Island, he stepped out of his house one morning in his bathrobe to find it entirely surrounded by curious spectators. Opening the newspaper he discovered why. The Secret Service had identified him as the man who had planted a bomb outside the Morgan bank the day before. Italian friends came by to see if they could help organize his defense fund, and one even offered him a boat. That afternoon, Tresca took the ferry to lower Manhattan for a speaking engagement. On the ferry people pointed at him, whispering, "There he is, that's Tresca." He gave his speech and returned home but was unable to sleep. The next day he received an apology from the head of the Secret Service, William Flynn, for having inadvertently mentioned his name to the press. Tresca later told friends that he went to bed and slept for three days, waking up only to eat.[32]

He continued to be the object of violence. Having failed to quench *Il Martello,* the Fascist government apparently hired someone to have Tresca murdered. Tresca's contacts within the Italian community in New York were extensive, however, and he found out about it. For several months a sparring game ensued while Tresca took the precaution of sleeping in a different room every night. Finally, the would-be murderer came to Tresca, and asked him for $4,000 so that he could leave the country. He was a bootlegger, he said, and he had once heard Tresca speak at Paterson and did not want to kill him. A meeting was finally arranged in an Italian restaurant in Greenwich Village. The bootlegger kissed Tresca's hand in the presence of several *Mafiosi,* and there the matter rested. No matter how unorthodox his political views, "Carluccio" was a popular man in the Italian neighborhoods of New York and this afforded him some protection.

It did not keep the *Fascisti* from trying again. While Tresca was speaking at an anti-Fascist rally in East Harlem one evening, he was suddenly interrupted by a thunderous roar just down the block. A powerful bomb had exploded in a car containing three Italian-American Fascists, killing them instantly. Nothing could dissuade Tresca that had the bomb not exploded prematurely he would have seen it growing rapidly larger as it flew towards him.

By the late 1930s, however, he felt himself in danger of assault from the left as well as from the right. Like most revolutionaries, Tresca had responded enthusiastically to the founding of the Bolshevik state. Though this enthusiasm waned when the Soviet government began persecuting Social Democrats, anarchists, and other heretical leftists, for many years Tresca continued to regard the Communists as valid allies in the battle against fascism. While the U.S.S.R. under Stalin was clearly a totalitarian state, Tresca knew perfectly well that there were dozens of brave, self-sacrificing Communists as well as Socialists in Italy who were risking their lives every day or who were suffering in prisons for the same anti-Fascist cause in which he believed.

The Spanish Civil War wrought a decisive change in his attitude. Spain was the one country where anarchism had become a major political force. At the outbreak of the Civil War there were more than a million anarchist workers in the Barcelona area. After some hesitation, the anarchists made common cause with the liberals, Socialists, Communists and other groups in opposing Franco. This coalition, however, suffered from many weaknesses. The anarchists were frequently undisciplined. The Republic's armies lost ground steadily to the Fascists, which heightened tensions and bred suspicions among the various political factions. And finally, the Soviet Union was the only country to systematically supply the Republic with arms and money, and this fact reinforced the aggressiveness of the Spanish Communists at the expense of their allies. In May 1937, street fighting broke out in Barcelona between anarchists and Communists. Though a truce was quickly established, the Barcelona uprising was a signal for the Communists to crack down. As early as December 1936, *Pravda* had announced that "the cleaning up of Trotskyists and anarchists has begun [in Spain] and will be carried out with the same energy as in the U.S.S.R." [33] Now hundreds of anarchists and other non-Communist leftists disappeared, rounded up by the Communist-controlled police. Terrible rumors began to seep out of Spain, of ruthless interrogations by N.K.V.D. agents in secret prisons, forced confessions, and midnight executions. The details of these reports resembled the fearful tales emanating from the Soviet Union, where Stalin's manic trials were in full swing.

Repelled by these events, Tresca became as outspoken and uncompromising a foe of communism as he was of fascism. He was one of a handful of liberals, labor figures, progressives and radicals willing to serve on a committee headed by the philosopher John Dewey to investigate the purge trials in the U.S.S.R. After Tresca signed the Dewey report, the Communist press in New York denounced him—ironically—as a Fascist and as an enemy of the people.[34]

Tresca's increasingly bitter anticommunism also brought him into conflict with a man who in certain ways resembled him. Like Carlo Tresca, Vito Marcantonio was a fighter. He was brave, colorful, and *simpatico*. Born and reared amid the tenements of East Harlem, Marcantonio emerged in the 1920s as La Guardia's political heir. In 1934, he defeated James J. Lanzetta and recaptured La Guardia's former congressional seat for the Republican party. The party label, however, was purely a formality; while other Republicans were attacking the New Deal as socialistic, Marcantonio complained that most New Deal legislation did not aid the workingman nearly enough. Swarthy and pugnacious, a spellbinding orator, Marcantonio made himself an effective spokesman for his poor East Harlem constituents, and they sent him back to Washington for a total of fourteen years. An early champion of civil rights legislation, in foreign policy Marcantonio steered a course contiguous at least to that of the Communist party. When Stalin signed the nonaggression pact with Hitler in August 1939, Marcantonio became a strident isolationist, appearing at "The-Yanks-Are-Not-Coming" rallies and casting the only House votes against the Naval Ship Construction Bill and the Aviation Expansion Bill. Following Hitler's invasion of Russia on June 22, 1941, Marcantonio did an about-face and came out for immediate American entry into the war, arguing in a speech on October 16, 1941, that "the invasion of the Soviet Union by Hitler transformed that war which was predominantly imperialist into a war which is now essentially one of national defense." *

The Japanese attack on Pearl Harbor three weeks later brought America into the war as Russia's ally and, for the Italian anti-Fascist exiles in the U.S., brought them face to face with the problem of whether or not to collaborate with the Communists. This was an issue that had troubled

---

* It would be an injustice to Marcantonio, however, merely to dismiss him as a fellow traveler. For years he pursued his lonely, unpopular course with courage. In order to truly explore Marcantonio's tie with the Communists, one would have to undertake a meticulously detailed study of his voting record, speeches, and correspondence, something which is beyond the scope of this chapter.

the democratic left since the days of the Popular Front and the Spanish Civil War. To his friends in the Italian-American Labor Council and the Mazzini Society, the most influential anti-Fascist organizations in the United States, Carlo Tresca argued passionately that the totalitarianism being practiced in Stalin's Russia was not essentially different from the totalitarianism of Hitler's Germany, of Mussolini's Italy or Franco's Spain. All were police states. He warned that a postwar Italy dominated by the Communists, with Stalin determining policy from Moscow, would result in a regime even more repressive than the Fascist one. In the end, the Communists were generally excluded from these exile groups and from the important Pan-American conference of anti-Fascist organizations held at Montevideo, Uruguay, in August 1942. This was in contrast to the situation in Europe, where the Socialists, Communists, and representatives of the center-left movement *Giustizia e Libertà* had signed a tripartite agreement in Toulouse, France, in October 1941, that helped lay the groundwork for the Italian resistance. Men and women of many political shades, from conservative to Communist, eventually joined the resistance; after Mussolini's downfall in July 1943, when the German army occupied northern and central Italy, they were hunted by the Gestapo and many died in Nazi concentration camps, but many more survived to battle the Germans in the mountains and, during the climactic spring of 1945, in cities like Genoa, Milan and Bologna, which they liberated before the arrival of Allied troops.

On the night of January 11, 1943, with the streets of New York darkened by wartime blackout, Carlo Tresca left his office at the corner of Fifth Avenue and 15th Street. An elderly associate, Giuseppe Calabi, was with him. As Tresca and Calabi reached the corner and stood waiting for the light to change, a man stepped behind Tresca and fired four shots. The leader of the Italian anarchists in America fell to the curb with a fatal bullet imbedded in his brain, another in his back. He was sixty years old. Though two suspects were arrested, neither would talk and both were ultimately released. The murder became simply another of the thousands of unsolved homicides in New York. It was rumored that Tresca had been killed by Italian-American Fascists in a final gesture of revenge, or by agents of the N.K.V.D. because of his anti-Communist activities, or by the Mafia because of some obscure personal feud. It is unlikely that the truth will ever be known.

He is a difficult man to sum up. Though anarchism is at once the most beguiling of political philosophies, it is also, in its fanatic manifestations, the most repulsive. Carlo Tresca, as he once defined himself, was an "irreconcilable." Seeing only evil in the totalitarian state, he nevertheless continued to oppose even the capitalism of the New Deal because it perpetuated the wage system and measured human beings in terms of money. At the time of his death he was holding out the hope that the destruction of political parties and labor unions in Europe by the Nazis would "free" the workers for a great anarchist resurgence after the war. There was something stubbornly unrealistic about such a vision.

And yet, his was a formidable spirit. Perhaps his true place is within the history of nonviolent protest in America. Certainly, few other men can match his record of intransigence. In the United States alone he was arrested thirty-six times and tried by jury seven times for his political beliefs. His throat was cut. He was shot at four times and finally murdered. Usually alone, he had dared challenge the industrial system of America in the early 1900s with its company detectives and deputies, then the Fascists and Communists, with their respective secret police organizations. He was a great individualist, and in an age when the power of government has expanded and its abuses have grown, he was strong enough to stand against that power without an organization, or funds, or public opinion to sustain him.

There is a small monument to the memory of Carlo Tresca in his native Sulmona. Though a few older Italian-Americans still remember him, he is otherwise forgotten.

15

Columbus's Children

WEARING A POLO SHIRT because it was a humid New York summer day, Joseph Colombo, Sr., walked about restlessly beneath his namesake's statue on its tall granite column. The place was Columbus Circle, the date June 28, 1971.

Colombo was in high spirits. At least fifty thousand people, and perhaps more, were expected to attend this second Italian-American Unity Day rally, scheduled to begin at noon. It was now 10:45, and the dapper, forty-eight-year-old Colombo kept busy giving instructions to his aides, arguing with sidewalk peddlers who hoped to sell shirts decorated with the Italian boot, unloading police barriers himself from a truck. When he spotted a middle-aged woman sitting just in front of the speaker's stand, he barked out, "Not even the queen of Italy can sit here." The woman gave him a weary look. "Okay, okay," he relented, "but you'd better wear this," handing her an official badge of the Italian American Civil Rights League, the organization he had founded.[1]

Around the periphery of the rally site, vendors in stands gaily festooned with red, white, and green bunting hawked buttons affirming "Italian Power" and "Italian Is Beautiful." But these expressions of ethnic pride were also signs of protest, and in that old, inchoate surge of rebellion lay Joseph Colombo, Sr.'s own Italian power.

The Italian-Americans who boarded the league's chartered buses from the boroughs and suburbs of New York to attend the Unity Day rally were not necessarily minions of the Mafia. Most were ordinary citizens who spoke for a good many of New York's 1.6 million Italians. They were generally children of the original immigrants who had lived in the slums described by Jacob Riis; and they were just realizing that by the standards of America in 1970, they themselves were trapped in incipient slums, for all their patient years of striving. Most of them owned their homes, but those homes were likely to be still mortgaged to a bank even after a quarter century. The men worked hard, even hazardously, to earn somewhere between $7,000 and $12,000 a year, and now inflation was squeezing them mercilessly. Their sons were being shipped to Southeast Asia, and now even these Italian-Americans, infinitely loyal but possessed of a fundamental piety (their relatives in the villages of Italy had been bombed, too), were strained with doubt. Despite the strong Catholic morality of traditionally close-knit, warm Italian families, Italian youths had a high dropout rate and a disturbing number of them were becoming drug addicts. Many older Italian-Americans whose fathers had scorned relief during the Depression — so proud had these people been — found themselves forced to go on welfare. Their neighborhoods were deteriorating along with the rest of the inner city. Elderly immigrants who had loved the street, missing their village *piazzas,* were afraid to go out of their homes after sundown. They felt ignored, their problems forgotten. The only time they heard Italians mentioned in the media was in connection with organized crime. Organized, hell! They were the ones being mugged; the grocers and storekeepers being shot, whose names appeared in the *Daily News* and the *Post,* were their neighbors.

This was Joseph Colombo, Sr.'s constituency. This was why the hot summer zephyrs at Columbus Circle whistled through guy wires decorated with thousands of crackling red, white, and green plastic pennants. When Colombo had first appeared on Third Avenue the previous spring, emerging out of the obscurity of a Brooklyn real estate office to picket the FBI's New York headquarters, it had seemed a final extravaganza of pop culture. Here was the reputed boss of one of New York's five Mafia families, elegantly dressed, bullhorn in hand, protesting discrimination against Italian-Americans because of their Mafia image. The press snickered; serious Italian-American politicians were outraged. But it soon became apparent that Colombo was a genuine spokesman, a kind of Masaniello from the Brooklyn *bassi,* who had managed to give voice to a great many simmering frustrations among Italian-Americans.

In the year since that first Unity Day rally, moreover, Colombo had built up the Civil Rights League into an organization with offices on

Madison Avenue and enough support to persuade Attorney General John Mitchell that it would be politically wise for the Justice Department to stop using the terms Mafia and Cosa Nostra. A League benefit at the Felt Forum, to which Frank Sinatra, Vic Damone, Connie Francis and other entertainers donated their time and talents, had reportedly brought in $500,000. Colombo had appeared on the Dick Cavett show. He had been photographed shaking hands with Meir Kahane of the Jewish Defense League and Gordon Lynch of NEGRO, fellow ethnic leaders.[2] It seemed that this alleged *Mafioso* might be on the point of pulling together the first truly effective Italian-American organization since the *Gibboni* of East Harlem in the days of La Guardia and Marcantonio.

At 11:20, as Colombo was moving through the now-thickening crowd at Columbus Circle, greeting supporters and attending to last-minute details, a slender black youth carrying a movie camera asked him to pose. Colombo stopped and turned, obliging him; then, moving away, he began speaking to his son, Joseph Colombo, Jr. A volley of shots rang out, surprisingly mild in the overlay of New York traffic and crowd sounds.[3] Colombo slumped to the ground, blood streaking down the right side of his face. A few feet away the movie photographer lay face down on the pavement, dead. He was later identified as Jerome Johnson, twenty-four, of New Brunswick, New Jersey, a drifter with a record of seven arrests.

"This is a false alarm," a voice pleaded over the loudspeaker, while people screamed and ran back from the scene of the shooting. "This is a false alarm. No one has been hurt." [4]

As the unconscious Colombo, strapped to a litter, was lifted into an ambulance for the brief but critical dash to Roosevelt Hospital, police on the edge of the crowd were involved in protecting some black musicians from the wrath of Italian fists. High on his cylindrical pedestal, Cristoforo Colombo, the discoverer of America, continued to stare downtown towards the Atlantic — a memory, a legend, centuries removed from the violence below.

And yet his Italian children in America had been above all a physical people, familiar with violence. It was in their history, in their *animus*. When Norman Douglas visited Calabria at the turn of the century, he reported that one of the saints venerated by the peasants was a certain Saint Giangiuseppe della Croce, who had been able to foretell the deaths of children. Entering a cottage, the saint, with a jocular smile, had been wont to remark, "O, what an odor of Paradise," after which one or more of the children would die. "To a little girl who was crying in the street he said, 'I don't want to hear you any more. Go and sing in Paradise.' And meeting her a short time after he said, 'What, are you still here?' In a few days she was dead." [5] The saint's macabre gift of prophecy, Douglas concluded, was sometimes secretly welcome in desperately poor households, since a child's death meant one less mouth to feed. Poverty was always a far greater form of violence in the Italian South than the violence of rapes, knifings, and shootings. But the two were closely entwined. In times of disorder or famine, bandit chiefs like Caruso, Carmine Donatelli di Rionero, called Crocco, and Ninco Nanco became the Robin Hoods of southern Italy whose merry men were indigenous guerilla bands. They would kidnap and sometimes murder landowners, burn crops, plunder government supply trains and distribute wheat and salt free to the poor. Pitched battles were fought in wooded mountain passes between soldiers and bandits. These events always ended bitterly. Rebellious peasants stoically accepted the law's handcuffs and years of imprisonment with dull resignation. At the root of southern life was a desperation beyond measure. "If the world had only one enormous heart," the bandit Caruso is supposed to have said, "I'd tear it out." [6]

What most tormented the South's peasants and made their poverty inevitable was their inability to own the land they worked. This was a terrible form of emasculation. The folk songs of southern peasants at the time of mass immigration were full of a spirit of anarchic vengeance:

> *Now, landowner, you'll work your own fields*
> *Because we're going to America . . .*

It was as a physical people that the great majority of Italian immigrants reached America. They had been peasants in Italy; in America, they worked as unskilled laborers. To the New World they gave their sweat, and often their blood. Rock rumbled down on pick and shovel laborers digging subways, breaking legs and crushing lungs. Lead pipes filled with dynamite blew off the hands of miners. When Tresca went to work on a track-laying gang, the freight car in which he and a half dozen other Italian laborers slept was so filthy, the air so fetid, that he needed weeks to completely regain his health. In one of the most terrifying scenes in any work of fiction, the protagonist of Pietro Di Donato's *Christ in Concrete*, a bricklayer, pinned under a beam in the collapse of a half-completed building, sinks his teeth into the beam and grinds them so violently in his agony that the teeth snap off, leaving only stumps. Many hundreds of Italian laborers, maimed in industrial accidents in America as in other countries, picked their way back up the steep paths to their villages on crutches. Italian immigrants also sacrificed themselves physically in another sense, sometimes holding down two jobs to feed their big families, eating supper half stupefied with weariness, never taking a day's vacation except to rest at home. The women were constantly busy. If they took in piecework they sat over their sewing until late at night, helped by their daughters. Boys went to work in their teens.

Yet to the majority of Italian immigrants America's terms were bearable because here in this country, for the first time, they could free themselves from the grip of a rigid class system that had kept them in perpetual servitude. Here they could vote. They could challenge injustices in a court of law. Above all, they could own property — their own portion of the earth. In Italy, their plows had often turned up ancient Greek, Roman, Byzantine coins; they believed that a man brave enough to go out alone in the dead of night without a lantern might spy the faint radiance shining from Saracen gold secreted in caverns or buried underground. In America the land was bare of such treasures and of such symbols of antiquity, but it was theirs to be fertilized by the sacrifices of their labor and by the blood of their sons fighting in America's wars for those tangible freedoms, for that right to exist as individuals. America further toughened these immigrants from the villages and towns of the South. They had always been a stoic, persevering people. The New World made them aggressive, acquisitive. It also unlocked in them a vitality that had been half suppressed, or stunted, for generations.

In America, sons became taller, more self-assertive, more daring than their Italian-born fathers. The three youngest DiMaggio brothers, Vince, Joe, and Dom, whose father was an immigrant fisherman from an islet near Palermo called *Isola delle Femmine* — the Island of Women — grew up playing baseball under the shadows of gulls in San Francisco's North Beach, in a vacant lot with squashed oil cans for bases and a concrete block for home plate.[7] At first the elder DiMaggio raged at this baseball. A game! He rose and dressed at four o'clock every morning to thread his way through the dreams of sleeping children out into the predawn darkness, walking down to the wharves with other Sicilian fishermen. This was a man's life. Only gradually did he realize that America was different, that a strong, ambitious youth had options outside the linear pattern of a son gradually replacing his father and inheriting the fishing boat. It was Joe's older brother, Vince, who first broke into professional baseball when he played center field for the San Francisco Seals. He also had a voice so beautiful and strong that various San Francisco Italians, including Amadeo Giannini, talked of sending him back to Italy to study music. "Vince could have been a great opera singer," Dom DiMaggio wistfully told a reporter years later. "He wanted to go to Italy to study, but it couldn't be done." [8]

Along with the vitality they inherited from strong, hard-working parents, these young Italian-Americans often possessed talents that flowered in them spontaneously because they were the first generation to be liberated from that age-old bondage of humility. They emerged in the 1930s and 1940s as singers, entertainers, sports heroes. "I heard Sinatra sing at the Copa," wrote Frank Capra, "heard him grab that night club audience; heard him grab me. He knew the meaning of his lyrics and he sang them to you, powerfully, dramatically. Vocal cords swelling out from his thin neck, face contorted with passion, blue eyes moist with meaning — that thin vibrant man sang like nobody of the time. . . ." [9]

It was as a physical people, too, that many sons of the Italian immigrants emerged to positions of power and responsibility. Many of them worked their way up in trades like construction where a man had to be able to crack heads together to maintain discipline and to get things done. Even the patrician-looking Amadeo Giannini had proved his manhood on the San Francisco waterfront in his teens, when he had helped his stepfather in the produce business. One of the most representative Italian-Americans in public life today is New York Congressman Mario Biaggi, who received twenty-eight commendations for bravery and was wounded eleven times as a police officer before running for a House seat.

Nothing is more striking, in fact, than the contrast between the often exceptional combat performance of Italian-Americans in World War II and the lingering image of woebegone Italian soldiers surrendering by the tens of thousand in North Africa. Yet the genetic differences at the level of the first and second generation were virtually nonexistent. It should be apparent that Italian enlisted men, rather than lacking courage, were denied power in their society in peacetime to the extent that they continued to be alienated from it in wartime. The sheepishly grinning Italian prisoners in the 1942 newsreels looked exactly like what they were: laborers, fishermen and shepherds, glad, most of them, to be released from an obligation towards which they felt indifferent or hostile.

Italian-Americans, on the other hand, had a splendid record in World War II. Marine hero John Basilone, who was awarded the Congressional Medal of Honor for exceptional heroism on Guadalcanal, and who was killed in the Iwo Jima landings, was one of a dozen Italian-Americans who received the Medal of Honor. Ten won the Navy Cross, including the late A. Vernon Jannotta, a rear admiral in the Naval Reserve, who during a Kamikaze attack in the Philippines went aboard a flaming tanker loaded with 50,000 gallons of high octane gasoline and 160 torpedoes, rescued the crew, and then remained on the ship to extinguish the flames. Jannotta had also fought in World War I, having enrolled in the Navy along with his entire class from Cornell.* The leading ace among American fighter pilots in Europe was Donald Gentile, whose immigrant father had worked as a stone quarrier and coal miner in Ohio, and who had used his savings to buy his son a $1,400 biplane in 1939. Eager to become a fighter pilot, Donald Gentile enlisted in the Royal Canadian Air Force — transferring to the United States Air Corps after Pearl Harbor. He flew a total of 182 missions, and shot down 42 German planes.[10]

After the war, hundreds of thousands of Italian-American veterans returned to a country where there was no longer any untoward discrimination against them. Gone was the disdain their fathers and grandfathers had experienced. After 1945, in an increasingly liberal American atmosphere, and in a postcolonial age where it was no longer realistic to believe in a world dominated by the discipline and creativity of a few Nordic races, smart, ambitious Italian-Americans found themselves advantaged for the first time in the pursuit of personal goals. Many used the GI Bill to earn degrees and enter the professions. Others started businesses of their own, or joined large corporations — where they had not been significantly present before except in clerical jobs. And they shared in the flat-out expansion of the American economy in the postwar period, when business output nearly tripled, from $445.2 billion in 1946 to $1,059 billion in 1971. In the space of two generations, Italian-

---

* Admiral Jannotta was aboard the cruiser *San Diego* as a lieutenant j.g. in 1918 when it was torpedoed while on patrol duty in the Atlantic. He survived eight hours in the water. In civilian life Jannotta, whose father was born in Capua, near Naples, was an executive with the Jewel Tea Company. He died on May 31, 1972, and was buried at Arlington National Cemetery with full military honors.

American families that had once faced the strictures of poverty began to experience the more insidious problems of affluence.

At the same time, however, the public image of the Italian-Americans began to be seriously at variance with the reality of their lives, and their accomplishments. In every community where there was any number of Italian-Americans, they could be found as mayors, as city councilmen, as teachers, as fire captains and police chiefs. They were frequently among the most public-spirited citizens, solid family men and women who attended the local Catholic church regularly, who raised funds for charities and willingly gave of their time for the good of the community. But the public image of the Italian-Americans steadily deteriorated. No ethnic group had a more injurious press, or a more tarnished reputation. Italian-Americans came across to the public in the rasping Brooklynese of chain-smoking, square-faced Joseph Valachi. A small-time hoodlum serving a sentence at the Atlanta penitentiary, Valachi had become convinced that the Mafia wanted him dead after fellow prisoner Vito Genovese had supposedly given him the "kiss of death" in June 1962. In a frenzy of fear, Valachi beat to death an innocent inmate whom he wrongly suspected had been chosen to be his executioner. Sentenced to a life term for this murder, feeling alone and betrayed, Valachi agreed to break the ancient Mafia law of *omerta*, or silence, and to testify in Washington before the McClellan subcommittee on organized crime in the fall of 1963. He told an engrossing story of how the Mafia was organized into a group of families, all of them Italian and most of them Sicilian, identifying themselves as belonging to "la Cosa Nostra" — Our Thing. Valachi related some very hackneyed tidbits such as the story of his initiation into the Mafia, when a gangster pricked his trigger finger with a pin to draw blood while Mafia chieftain Salvatore Maranzano intoned, "This blood means that we are now one family." [11]

But as Valachi continued his revelations, to the amusement, unease, and scorn of a nationwide television audience, many Italian-Americans who had never been even remotely involved with Mafia activities, who considered themselves Americans with an Italian name, began to feel an understandable sense of shame, and of guilt by association. "I hand you my business card," Kansas City businessman Marion Trozzolo told a *Time* reporter, "and without even looking at me you see an image because of the name." And he added, "For some reason it works that way particularly with Italian names. Bugs Moran was a gangster, but he certainly didn't put such a long-lived blot on the Irish image."

Trozzolo was himself a representative Italian-American. Born in southern Italy and raised in Chicago, Trozzolo served in the army in World War II and was decorated with the Bronze Star for valor at the Battle of the Bulge. Graduating from the University of Chicago with a degree in philosophy in 1947, he received a master's degree in economics three years later and, moving to Kansas City, started his own plastics firm. When floods ravaged Florence in 1966, Trozzolo and other Kansas City businessmen and professional men of Italian background mounted a drive to collect relief funds that attracted ninety prominent sponsors. In 1971, Trozzolo organized the River Quay Association to restore Kansas City's historic riverfront section — a venture that has developed into one of the outstanding private urban renewal projects in the nation. But the prevailing image of Italian-Americans remains that of Joseph Valachi, not of men like Marion Trozzolo — even in Italy. When the Rome newspaper *Il Tempo* ran a photograph in the summer of 1970 showing a young Boston policeman of Italian descent dramatically risking his life to save a would-be woman suicide on a Charles River bridge, the caption was headlined: *They're Not All Bandits.*

This paradox — the private rectitude of the great majority of Italian-Americans and their destructive public image — has deep roots. Nothing is clear about the Italian-Americans that does not take into account their past in Italy. Most of the Italian immigrants who came ashore in lower Manhattan, with their admissions slips from Ellis Island and their patched-up suitcases, were surrounded by that past, by a Blake-like cloud of ancestors, of angels, saints, witches and goblins whispering to their emotions, a history of instincts — in the form of proverbs and superstitions. "Be on your guard," these ghostly voices counseled. "Trust no one but your own flesh and blood. Laws are made by the rich and powerful."

Not only were Italian immigrants mostly poor laborers. They were also people who lacked any experience in being part of a social dimension greater than that of their families, and their villages. The class system in Italy, strong and well entrenched, had operated for hundreds of years to estrange the poor from even a desire for power. And though personal relationships between a landowner and his sharecroppers were often warm, and even informal, when the Italian peasant found himself in trouble and looked around for help, when he needed assistance as a citizen, he saw nothing but a wary hostility in the faces of the mayor, of municipal officials, of the *carabinieri* and the police, and even, all too often, of the clergy. They were there to keep him in his place — just as fascism in the twentieth century would keep him in his place, masquerading as a popular revolution. So the Italian peasant, already bred to regard strangers, all strangers, as enemies, viewed even the hierarchy of his own village or town with diffidence.

A few years ago the popular reformer Danilo Dolci interviewed a Sicilian laborer named Vito, in Sicily. Some of their conversation went as follows:

"Have you ever been part of an organization?"
"What does that mean?"
"Have you ever participated in any organization, of any sort?"
"I've always been part of myself."
"Didn't you ever feel like belonging to a political party?"
"I put my name down for unemployment compensation. Wasn't that a political party?"
"What do you think a political party is?"
"A party is like the head of a family who can carry out certain tasks."
"Haven't you ever felt like joining a religious group?"
"No, never."
"Why?"
"Because I've always been on my own. I've never been led by anyone."
"How old are you?"
"49."
"Did you attend school?"
"A few days. I'm illiterate."
"Would it be wrong to say that your family is your political party?"
"No, that's exactly right."
"Your wife, your children, and who else?"
"My brother. I'm close to all of them."
"And other people?"
"No, not close. Almost distant. It's habit. The proverbs say, 'Whoever walks alone is well off,' 'The man who plays a lone hand never loses.' " [12]

When they came to America, the immigrants from southern Italy in particular brought with them this deep-rooted diffidence towards authority. They had recently witnessed the savage guerilla warfare that raged through portions of the South between troops of the Piedmontese-controlled Italian army and rebellious peasants. They had seen former Church lands fraudulently sold to landowners instead of to those who most needed land. They had been backed against a precipice of desperation by rising prices, by poverty and by their childrens' hunger. In America, they worked their way out of the depths of dark, airless rear flats in slum tenements, slowly creating their own middle class in the process. It was as if they had made a revolution and swept their landscape bare of kings, dukes, barons, big and little landowners, mayors and tax assessors; only instead of seizing power they had followed Columbus across the Atlantic. In a sense he was their Robespierre, their George Washington, the revolutionary hero whom they revered. For years in America they continued to live out this greatest of all peasant rebellions, wary of strangers, trusting in their own families, their own neighbors, even the *padroni* who swindled them, rather than in American authorities and American law.

This is why so many of the most significant Italian-Americans of the early twentieth century were outcasts in battle against a social system they perhaps understood only in terms of their particular historical bias — strike leaders like Ettor and Giovannitti, or anarchist laborers like Sacco, Vanzetti, or Carlo Tresca, the "irreconciliable" who was the personal friend of nearly everyone he met and the enemy of every social hierarchy that in his view limited human freedom. There is no question that the two most important Italian-American politicians of that period, La Guardia and Marcantonio, were both critics of the society, though Marcantonio's radicalism was more extreme than that of La Guardia. The representative Italian-American politicians today, instead, are fundamentally conservative, though not necessarily rightists. They are men like Philadelphia's former police commissioner and its Democratic mayor, Frank Rizzo; or Congressman Mario Biaggi; or the Republican State Senator from Staten Island, John Marchi.

It has often been pointed out that the Italian-Americans still occupy few positions of leadership in the United States. While some ten percent of the American people are of Italian descent, for years the only Italian-American Senator was John O. Pastore of Rhode Island. New Mexico Republican Peter Domenici was elected in November 1972. Out of a total of 435 House seats, no more than a dozen are filled by Italian-Americans. There has never been an Italian-American Kennedy, or Eisenhower, a man representative of the American people as a whole, even though Italian-Americans are just as numerous in the population as the American Irish, or the Americans of German descent.

The explanation most often heard for this phenomenon is that Italian-Americans have been unwilling to make the personal sacrifices necessary for a successful career in politics. Instead, they have preferred to spend more time with their families. There is probably some truth to this widely

held view, but it is only a partial truth — ignoring the fundamental historical reality of the Italian-Americans, which is that they passed through
a process of rebirth in coming to America, acquiring their civic traditions
from American culture rather than from Italian culture. During this
period of transition, when their rapidly changing ideas about themselves
and the society around them were new and fragile, they could hardly be
expected to lead others.

Today, the Italian-Americans are almost independent of the forms and
conflicts of their difficult past, and these survive as dramatic but illusory
echoes. The turbulent rebel tradition that accompanied their enormous
change from being rural Italians to becoming urban Americans has all
but ceased to exist. The radicals and anarchists are but a dim memory,
and it seems doubtful, too, whether another Joseph Colombo, Sr., will
ever arise within his particular milieu to lead an Italian-American protest
movement — with its echoes in the history of southern Italy. Today, in
fact, all the former leaders of the Italian-American communities a quarter century ago are passing from center stage, including the old-line
prominenti, whose function as "ethnic brokers" is almost superfluous.
While there were once over 150 Italian-language newspapers in the
United States, led by the late Generoso Pope's powerful *Il Progresso
Italo-Americano,* many have vanished. The biggest single fact about the
Italian-Americans now is that their middle class is indistinguishable
from the American middle class — is part of it.

When the Italian journalist Giuseppe Prezzolini interviewed newly
elected Governor John A. Volpe in Boston in 1961, the first question he
asked Volpe was what the Italian-Americans had contributed to the
United States. Volpe replied,

During the years of mass immigration, their contribution was mainly one of
hard, sweaty labor. They were people from the poorer classes and they
had little education. In those years their ambition was mainly to feed their
families and to give their children a better education than they themselves had
received. Their family life was exemplary, dominated by an ideal of devotion
to their faith, and full of examples of goodness. In those first years, their contribution to America was not really proportionate to their number. But that
is changing. We have seen these Italians mature as citizens, enter political life,
make a contribution to American culture, to music and the arts. Many sons
of Italians are scientists, or teachers. A great many, women as well as men,
have gone into the medical profession, others have studied law and provided
America with capable lawyers and judges, worthy of the traditions of the
University of Bologna. . . .[13]

(This realistic reply, Prezzolini wrote, pleased him a great deal.)

Volpe, the son of an immigrant plasterer, was himself an example of this will to succeed and to contribute to American society. Frustrated in his desire to study at MIT and forced to go to work as a plasterer just after high school to help his hard-pressed father, Volpe managed a few years later to save enough money to study architectural construction at the Wentworth Institute in Boston. In 1933, at the height of the Depression, he cashed in a life insurance policy for $300, borrowed another $200, and started the John A. Volpe Construction Company. During the war, he closed the firm and served as a lieutenant commander in the Seabees. By 1950, Volpe had made his first million dollars, and he was becoming known in Massachusetts as a public-spirited and personally charming, gregarious man active in many causes — among them raising funds for the Republican party. A reformer when he actively entered politics, he attacked the corruption within the Irish-dominated Democratic castles in Boston, just as La Guardia had attacked Tammany Hall in New York. Volpe was elected governor three times, twice in the face of overwhelming Democratic landslides for native son John F. Kennedy in 1960 and for Lyndon Johnson in 1964; during that last campaign tens of thousands of Boston Irish crossed party and ethnic lines to vote for Volpe, whom they considered an honest, forceful governor. After Richard Nixon appointed him secretary of transportation in his first cabinet, Volpe earned a reputation as one of the most able men in the cabinet. A relentless worker, he would regularly come home around 7 P.M. with as many as five briefcases of reading, finish it by midnight, and then be up at 6 A.M. for early morning exercises and early mass.

Volpe, in his sixties now, is a classic example of the immigrant laborer's son who worked his way up in a tough environment. But the Italian-American businessmen of the generation following Volpe's have tended to have careers more nearly resembling those of other middle-class Americans. Lee Iacocca, appointed president of Ford in December 1970, at the age of forty-six, graduated from Lehigh University, and then took a master's degree in engineering at Princeton. The president of Chrysler, John J. Riccardo, is the son of an Italian immigrant who worked in a bicycle factory in Little Falls, New York. Riccardo graduated from the University of Michigan. He was promoted to president at the age of forty-five. The number three man in the Chrysler hierarchy (after Chairman of the Board Lynn Townsend and Riccardo) is Brooklyn-born Eugene A. Cafiero, an Italian-American who is two years younger than Riccardo and who graduated from Dartmouth, where he majored in mathematics and psychology. Ralph D. DeNunzio, elected chairman of the New York Stock Exchange at the age of thirty-nine, graduated from Princeton, where he majored in classics and wrote his thesis, "Changing Manners and Morals in the Roman Republic." *

The majority of Italian-Americans who are now teen-agers or who are in college should be able to take their place in the society on equal terms with other Americans of their age. Inevitably, some of them will become political leaders — in effect the final step of assimilation. Already, an Italian name is no longer necessarily a political disadvantage in non-Italian neighborhoods. When twenty-nine-year-old Antonio G. Olivieri announced his candidacy for state assemblyman from the silk stocking Sixty-sixth Electoral District on Manhattan's East Side in 1970, several professional politicians advised him to at least change his first name to Anthony to make it sound less foreign. But Olivieri's Italian name was probably a neutral factor in the election race, which he won in an upset — becoming the first Democratic assemblyman elected from the Sixty-sixth District in fifty-seven years. He was reelected by a huge margin in 1972. An Exeter, Harvard, and Columbia Law School graduate (he majored in government at Harvard and received a magna cum laude from Henry Kissinger for his thesis), Olivieri, who looks somewhat like Teddy Kennedy, will find his Italian name an advantage in Italian neighborhoods if he continues to be elected, and runs for either a citywide office or a congressional seat.

These men — Volpe, Iacocca, Riccardo, Cafiero, DeNunzio, Olivieri — are not meant to be representative of all Italian-Americans; apart from the fact that they are exceptional as individuals, there is simply too great a diversity among the 15 million or so Americans of Italian descent to fit them into any one mold. Only two generalizations can really be made about the Italian-Americans today. One is that they are still in the process of changing. The generation that first came over from

* Other Italian-Americans prominent in American corporate life include Francis J. Palamara, executive vice president of the New York Stock Exchange and executive vice president of the Pittston Company; Benjamin F. Biaggini, president of the Southern Pacific; Martin J. Caserio, a vice president of GM and general manager of the Pontiac Motor Division; Joseph F. Alibrandi, president of one of the larger conglomerates, the Whittaker Corporation of Los Angeles. Alibrandi graduated from MIT in 1952 with a B.S. in mechanical engineering. A number of Italian-Americans founded large companies, such as Ross D. Siragusa who started the Admiral Corporation during the Depression and began manufacturing television sets in 1946. Thousands of other Italian-Americans are chief executives in smaller or medium-sized companies.

Italy was forced to be conscious of the exterior of their lives, the "foreignness" that set them off from the majority of Americans. In Italy, their way of talking, the clothes they wore, their customs had all fitted them as naturally as their skin — whatever their economic station. In America, they were often painfully concerned with adapting the surface of their lives to resemble other Americans. Their American-born children were frequently at midstream in this process of adaptation. They might still feel Italian deep within themselves because of the influence of the home, but they were more American in their outward appearance and more at ease outside the Italian ethnic neighborhoods. The third and fourth generations are not only much less anxious about having an Italian surface, but they are also increasingly American in their way of looking at themselves, of constructing their lives, and of approaching moral problems. This transition has been a change of perspective and of language. The illiterate Sicilian shepherd who lay down at night under the stars near his flock and thought about the meaning of God, and of the limits of human action and responsibility, was in no way a more superficial human being than his great grandson who is a senior at the high school in Tenafly, New Jersey, and plans to go to medical school. But the great-grandson's interior dialogue is far more subtle linguistically, richer in images; he is American in his introspection — and any nationality consists above all in its particular weave of introspection, which is also its literature and culture.

The second generalization that can be made about the Italian-Americans is that this process of transformation is well along. The melting pot is not cold, at least regarding the Italian-Americans. But while the melting pot once consisted of being ashamed of one's ethnic background and of wishing to shed as rapidly as possible those surface differences that gave one away as a non-Nordic, it now consists of affirming a sense of ethnic pride and of searching for a particular ethnic tradition.

This change was caused to a considerable extent by the dilemma of America's blacks. Not being able to modify their surface appearance to conform to the Nordic model, they had to go beyond, or beneath, that level in order to achieve a parity of respect for themselves, and to look for a process of cultural transformation different from that of the whites.

This black demand that their culture be respected is what provided the opening for Joseph Colombo, Sr., to launch the idea that the Italian-Americans, too, had a special ethnic tradition, an Italian soul, that should be treated with greater respect by the rest of America. There was just enough of a residue of resentment among Italian-Americans over the prejudice they had encountered before the 1950s to fill Columbus Circle on June 29, 1970. But the crowd at the second Unity Day rally — when Colombo was shot — already appeared to be much smaller, and the Italian-American Civil Rights League itself, deprived of Colombo's leadership, has rapidly faded from prominence.

Though some Italian-American spokesmen continue to complain of discrimination, particularly in the New York area, they are using the term as an umbrella for many kinds of discontent. In the big cities, blue-collar Italian-Americans see themselves trapped in a grim battle to maintain their deteriorating and increasingly dangerous neighborhoods. All their lives they grew up watching the sacrifice of their parents, who sometimes held two jobs and never went off on vacation together — what was the point of it all? Their parents and grandparents struggled so hard to set down roots in America, and now these roots, which took the form of houses, stores, schools, churches and even sidewalks, are being wrenched out if not by an avalanche of blacks and Puerto Ricans, then by the government which wants the land for a high school or an expressway. In the 1960s, after the black ghettoes had erupted, these poorer Italian-Americans saw the blacks receiving a great deal of attention from the press and from government agencies, while they who had been steadfastly loyal and obedient citizens, and were now sharing many of the same urban problems as the blacks, received no attention. This awakened them to the reality that they would only obtain assistance — and above all understanding — if they organized, put some pressure on the media, and began to elect Italian-Americans to office who would fight for the survival of their communities, and their values.

Though this resurgence of ethnic feeling among Italian-Americans has taken an initial form of protest, it seems essentially affirmative rather than defensive. For the first time, young Italian-Americans have gone to talk to the dean of admissions at Harvard to ask why there are not more Italian-Americans in the student body, and in New York they have called for more Italian principals in the city's high schools. They are more assertive than earlier generations would have dared to be.

On the whole, Italian-Americans seem satisfied with their accomplishments in America — and wish with a certain bitterness that these accomplishments were not obscured by the shadow of the Mafia which has involved so few of them and yet diminished them all a little. Many have done very well for themselves economically, without losing their virtues of warmth and concern for others. An example of this is Jeno Paulucci of Duluth, Minnesota, the son of an immigrant miner, who began selling home-canned pasta a quarter century ago, then borrowed $2,500 and pioneered the field of canned Chinese food, founding the Chun King brand. It was so successful that he was able to sell it in 1963 for $63 million. He then started Jeno's Inc., which makes frozen pizzas and other Italian specialties, and which had sales of $50 million in 1971. The majority of his employees are people that other businessmen might not hire: they are retarded, or deaf-mutes, or former convicts, or they wear leg or neck braces. In 1972, in recognition of his concern for the disadvantaged, Paulucci received the National Association of Manufacturers' Employer of the Year Citation.

Paulucci explained in a *Time* interview that his concern for the disadvantaged dates to "when I was a kid and a member of a real minority called a 'dago' and a 'wop.' I felt disadvantaged in my own way." But he adds, reflecting on his success and on the opportunity he found in this country, "I can't think of a better way to pay America back." Many Italian-Americans would second this sentiment.

One finds among them now a certain nostalgia for the past, as difficult as it was. Their immigrant parents and grandparents were heroic people — strong, self-sacrificing, and proud. The Italian values they had brought with them to America were direct and profound, emphasizing the dignity of the individual in the context of his or her responsibilities to the family and the neighborhood. Now, the society has become more tolerant of the individual's desire to make the outer world conform to his or her needs, and this change disturbs many Italian-Americans who grew up in households where a strict morality was taught and observed. Marguerite Novelli of Detroit, a comely young woman who in early 1972 became the highest ranking woman executive in the history of General Motors, and who was one of the twelve children of an immigrant laborer, feels that the most important influence on her life was that of her Italian parents, and their values. "If you've learned to take care of the family," she says, "you're going to act in the same manner towards other people. If you've grown up believing that the sun rises and sets on you, you don't realize that other people need your help and consequently your life has very little meaning." She can remember her father walking to work to save a nickel carfare. "My father always said to me, 'If you respect yourself, you'll respect other people.'" In the neighborhood where she grew up people were poor, but she can recall no vandalism or delinquency on the order that exists today in those same neighborhoods, and she wonders if children today, Italian or otherwise, are not being deprived of character-building values that she received from her family and from her Italian background.

The same questions are in the minds of many Italian-Americans. Rather than being concerned predominantly with prejudice, they are asking what lies beyond the material well-being and self-confidence they have achieved in America. Groups of young professional men of Italian background are meeting in cities like Buffalo and Syracuse to ponder whether their ethnic heritage, with its roots in Italian civilization and in Catholic morality, may not contain some new answers to the questions of American life today — and particularly urban life, with its increasing destruction of neighborhoods and depersonalization. In Italy, despite grave social problems, people lived happily together for centuries. The Italians, Stendhal once wrote, had mastered "the great art of being happy, which is here practiced with this added charm, that the good people do not know that it is an art, the most difficult of all." [14]

One man who believes, and hopes, that such a movement of ethnic awareness will spread among 15 million or so Italian-Americans is a wiry, youthful Scalabrini priest, Silvano Tomasi, who runs the Center for Migration Studies on Staten Island, a place of recurrent significance for Italian-Americans. There, he has been assembling thousands of books, letters, and other documents on Italian-American history. He believes that the Italian-Americans are now beginning to rediscover their tradition in terms of its values — even so simple a thing as the fact that those peasant villages from which the immigrants came were usually built around a piazza, an open space where people would constantly come together, see one another and talk to one another. The immigrants were on the whole happy to leave those villages behind them. But now their grandsons and great-grandsons, Father Tomasi believes, may see the values symbolized by the piazza as something desirable in their own lives and in their own communities. He defines the instinctive Italian values as "a sense of the importance of the family, a sense of religious life in terms of piety and acts rather than abstract theology, and a communitarian, community-centered view of life." Up to now, he feels, American society has tended to view these values as superseded and old-fashioned. The Italian-Americans, he says, were taught to "suppress and reject" these values, but they are now beginning to experience an ethnic reawakening based on their Latin, Catholic traditions.

It seems premature to try to guess what the future of such an ethnic movement will be. Clearly, many Italian-Americans are today responding to the complicated forces loosed by their assimilation into the American mainstream. The children of the Italian immigrants no longer feel Italian. They are American. In shedding a sense of apartness from American life, they have also relinquished their once-powerful emotional associations with a remote Italian world that they knew secondhand, from family recollections and legends. A void has been created, and they are now beginning to reevaluate their ethnic past — which is Italian-American rather than Italian — because it is an inescapable part of what they think about themselves, and what they tell their children. This backward look has been obscured by the issue of the Mafia, which is a great emotional obstruction. When viewed against the background of Italian history, however, the Mafia falls into perspective. It has been overemphasized and overdramatized in the last ten years, and it is, above all, only one aspect of a profound social drama. Far more important than the Mafia to Italian-Americans, as they evaluate their past, is that they can discover a tradition of idealism, and moral and intellectual courage. Yes, the major figures of Italian-American history were great men, but they were great men precisely because they were fighters against their time. They were remarkable individualists, even when their character was flawed, as in the case of Mazzei and Cesnola. The Italian radicals, personified by Ettor and Giovannitti and Carlo Tresca, had uncommon integrity and political courage, and even humble laborers like Sacco and Vanzetti were eloquent in their fidelity to convictions deeply held. The Italians who reached the New World, starting with Columbus, were usually outsiders struggling against great odds, and the best of them were brave, beautiful human beings full of warmth and a large-hearted concern for humanity.

This is the real tradition of the Italian-Americans. And precisely because the Italian-Americans, in being transformed into Americans, have acquired a more complex self-awareness and a different and richer introspection, their past should not appear to them as something crudely mythological and a source of confusion and even shame. It should give them strength.

ACKNOWLEDGMENTS

THIS IS Lou Howland's book. He is the editor at Little, Brown who conceived it and who guided me in writing it. Though its faults are mine, he shares in whatever virtues it may have. Luise Erdmann, the copyeditor, not only worked very hard on the manuscript but was always gracious and thoughtful, and I am glad to be able to thank her here. Joseph Consolino, Sr., of Little, Brown's New York office, contributed wise and valuable counsel.

I am deeply grateful to Jerry Korn for having supported my request for a leave of absence from Time, Inc., to write this book, and to Cal Whipple for having arranged an extension of my leave. *The Children of Columbus* would not have been written without their help.

Other colleagues at Time, Inc., contributed ideas or research, and kindly support, and I would particularly like to thank Ezra Bowen, Joyce Pelto, Doris Coffin, Washington correspondent Jerry Hannifin, and Rome correspondent Ann Natanson.

Though these distinguished men are in no way responsible for the opinions expressed in the book, I am indebted to His Excellency Egidio Ortona, the Italian Ambassador to the United States, and to Vieri Traxler, the Italian Consul General in New York, for their interest and suggestions. I would also like to acknowledge the many valuable suggestions made by Professor Giuseppe Cardillo, director of the Italian Cultural Institute in New York; Ruggero Orlando; Danilo Dolci; Professor John A. B. Faggi of Columbia University and the former director of the Casa Italiana; the Reverend Silvano M. Tomasi of the Center for Ethnic Studies; Frank C. Arricale; and Vanni Montana.

The late Professor Howard R. Marraro of Columbia generously helped me by making his many scholarly publications available and by contributing his ideas. Len Giovannitti was kind enough to lend me some of his father's publications and to read the chapter on the Lawrence strike. I am indebted also to Joanne Pellegrino for contributing her research on the nineteenth-century Italian exiles and for her kind assistance in reading a portion of the manuscript.

Robert Connolly of the Casa Italiana was exceptionally helpful. I am most grateful also to the entire staff of the Palisades Free Library who through the Ramapo-Catskill library system magically produced every book I requested, including the rare 1770 Swindburne. And I wish to thank Signora Maria Anita Gargotta of the Italian Cultural Institute, Mrs. Mae Bowler of the New York *Herald-Tribune* library, and the staff of the Manuscript Room of the New York Public Library. To everyone at Edit Ref, *un'abbraccio,* and to Miss Florence Conboy who typed the manuscript in record time, *un bacio.*

Finally I would like to thank my wife lovingly for all her support and many ideas; my mother and father, May and Daniele Amfitheatrof, for their constant help and advice; and my friends Ann Hancock and Jack Macrae for their many contributions to the book.

Sneden's Landing   — E. A.
Palisades, New York

July 1972

SOURCES AND REFERENCES

IN WRITING THIS BOOK, I have relied to a large extent on material already published. My task, as I saw it, was to explore the relationship between Italian history and the Italians who became part of American history. Precisely because I have drawn from the works of other writers, I wish to make this debt perfectly clear by listing sources and reference notes chapter by chapter.

Introduction

1. *Time,* 15 October 1965.
2. Ibid.
3. Ibid.
4. Yale University News Bureau press release, 11 October 1965.
5. Albin Krebs and Mylas Martin, New York *Herald-Tribune,* 13 October 1965.
6. Natalie Jaffe, New York *Times,* 13 October 1965.
7. William Foote Whyte, *Street Corner Society* (Chicago: University of Chicago Press, 1943), p. 274.
8. Richard Severo, New York *Times,* 9 November 1970.
9. Richard Gambino, "Twenty Million Italian-Americans Can't Be Wrong," New York *Times Magazine,* 30 April 1972.
10. Severo, New York *Times,* 9 November 1970.
11. Ibid.

Chapter 1

The basis for my portrait of Columbus and his nautical world has been Samuel Eliot Morison's classic biography, *Admiral of the Ocean Sea: A Life of Christopher Columbus.* For general background on the period,

John R. Hale's *Age of Exploration* in the Great Ages of Man series by Time-Life Books was most useful. A fascinating work is Edmundo O'Gorman's *The Invention of America: An Inquiry into the Historical Nature of the New World and the Meaning of Its History*, which was particularly valuable for its interpretation of Vespucci's role in uncovering the American continent. A fine biography of Vespucci was written by a distinguished Colombian diplomat, Germán Arciniegas. It was originally published in Spanish in Buenos Aires as *Amerigo y el Nuevo Mundo,* and was translated into Italian and published by Rizzoli in 1960 as *Amerigo Vespucci*. The brief portraits of John Cabot and Giovanni da Verrazzano in this chapter were draw chiefly from Morison's recently published *The European Discovery of America: The Northern Voyages*. Another source of information on the Italian explorers, as well as a basic reference work on Italian-American history, was Giovanni Schiavo's *Four Generations of Italian-American History* and, to a lesser extent, his *The Italians in America before the Civil War*. The recent publication of *The Voyages of Giovanni da Verrazzano, 1524–1528* by Lawrence C. Wroth for the Pierpont Morgan Library, with a translation of the Cellère "Codex" by Susan Tarrow, made available Verrazzano's fascinating account of his voyage along the coast of North America.

1. Samuel Eliot Morison, *Admiral of the Ocean Sea: A Life of Christopher Columbus,* 2 vols. (Boston: Little, Brown, 1942).
2. Ibid., p. 24.
3. Ibid., p. 30.
4. Quoted in ibid., p. 31.
5. Quoted in ibid., p. 30.
6. Morison, *Admiral of the Ocean Sea,* pp. 62–63.
7. Ibid., p. 69.
8. Ibid., p. 90.
9. Quoted in ibid., p. 81.
10. Quoted in ibid., pp. 86–87.
11. Quoted in ibid., p. 95.
12. Quoted in John R. Hale and the editors of Time-Life Books, *Age of Exploration,* Great Ages of Man (New York: Time, Inc., 1966), p. 59.
13. Quoted in Edmundo O'Gorman, *The Invention of America: An Inquiry into the Historical Nature of the New World and the Meaning of Its History* (Bloomington: Indiana University Press, 1971), p. 79.
14. Morison, *The European Discovery of America: The Northern Voyages* (New York: Oxford University Press, 1971), p. 158.
15. Ibid.
16. Ibid., p. 159.
17. Ibid.
18. Francis Parkman, *La Salle and the Discovery of the Great West* (Boston: Little, Brown, 1885), p. xxiv.
19. Letter from Lorenzo Pasqualino, quoted in Giovanni Schiavo, *Four Centuries of Italian-American History* (New York: Vigo Press, 1952), p. 54.

20. Quoted in Morison, *European Discovery of America,* pp. 190–191.
21. Ibid., p. 192.
22. Schiavo, *Four Centuries,* p. 47.
23. Germán Arciniegas, *Amerigo Vespucci* (Milan: Rizzoli Editore, 1960), p. 8.
24. Ibid., p. 41.
25. Ibid.
26. Ibid., p. 43.
27. Ibid., p. 189.
28. Quoted in O'Gorman, *Invention of America,* p. 113.
29. This copperplate engraving, which is in the Pierpont Morgan Library, is repro-
    duced in Lawrence C. Wroth, *The Voyages of Giovanni da Verrazzano, 1524–
    1528* (New Haven: Yale University Press, 1970).
30. Morison, *European Discovery of America,* p. 283.
31. Ibid., p. 285.
32. Wroth, *Voyages,* p. 142.
33. Ibid., p. 135.
34. Ibid., p. 136.
35. Ibid., pp. 136–137.
36. Ibid., p. 137.
37. Ibid.
38. Ibid., p. 138.
39. Ibid., p. 139.
40. Morison, *European Discovery of America,* p. 312.

Chapter 2

Will Durant's *The Renaissance: A History of Civilization in Italy from
1304–1576* A.D., Part V of his monumental Story of Civilization, is a rich
source of material on the Italian Renaissance. My portrait of Clement VII
is based largely on Durant's. *The Civilization of the Renaissance* by
Jacob Burckhardt is excellent for background, as is John R. Hale's *Renaissance* in the Great Ages of Man series. A particularly well-paced and
coherent history of Italy is Geoffrey Trease's *The Italian Story: From the
Etruscans to Modern Times,* and I have quoted from it several times in
the course of this book. The description of the battle of Fornovo in this
chapter was based in part on Luigi Barzini, Jr.'s much fuller analysis
of it in his splendid book *The Italians.*

1. Francesco Guicciardini, *The History of Italy,* trans., ed. Sidney Alexander (New
   York: Macmillan Co., 1969), p. 4.
2. Will Durant, *The Renaissance: A History of Civilization in Italy from 1304–1576*
   A.D. (New York: Simon & Schuster, 1953), p. 611.
3. Geoffrey Trease, *The Italian Story: From the Etruscans to Modern Times* (New
   York: Vanguard Press, 1963), p. 220.
4. Ibid., p. 221.
5. Durant, *Renaissance,* p. 630.
6. Ibid., p. 632.
7. Ibid., p. 636.
8. Ibid., p. 615.

Chapter 3

A source of much of the detail in my descriptions of Tonti's expeditions has been Francis Parkman's *La Salle and the Discovery of the Great West,* first published in 1885. I have quoted quite extensively from Parkman, in part because of the majestic roll of his prose, and have sought to make that clear in the text. Edmund Robert Murphy's *Henry de Tonty: Fur Trader of the Mississippi* is a valuable piece of research particularly in respect to the latter part of Tonti's life. The portrait of Tonti contained in Barbara Marinacci's *They Came from Italy: The Stories of Famous Italian-Americans* is particularly fine. An engrossing book to read for background on the exploration of the North American continent is John Bakeless's *The Eyes of Discovery.*

Nearly all the material on Filippo Mazzei, including the extensive quotations found in this chapter, was taken from his *Memoirs* as translated by the late Professor Howard R. Marraro of Columbia University, whose introduction includes an assessment of Mazzei's role in American history. Again useful for the record of early Italian settlers in America was Schiavo's *Four Centuries of Italian-American History,* as well as the late Michael A. Musmanno's *The Story of the Italians in America.*

1. Francis Parkman, *La Salle and the Discovery of the Great West* (Boston: Little, Brown, 1885), p. 441.
2. Quoted in Barbara Marinacci, *They Came from Italy: The Stories of Famous Italian-Americans* (New York: Dodd, Mead, 1967), p. 19.
3. Edmund Robert Murphy, *Henry de Tonty: Fur Trader of the Mississippi* (Baltimore: Johns Hopkins Press, 1941), p. 60.
4. Marinacci, *They Came from Italy,* p. 21.
5. Parkman, *La Salle,* pp. 153–154; and John Bakeless, *The Eyes of Discovery* (Philadelphia: J. B. Lippincott, 1950), p. 290.
6. Bakeless, *Eyes of Discovery,* pp. 292–293.
7. Parkman, *La Salle,* p. 201.
8. Ibid., pp. 201–202.
9. Ibid., p. 209.
10. Ibid., p. 212.
11. Enrico Tonti, "Memoir," in *Early Narratives of the Northwest,* ed. Louise P. Kellogg (New York: Barnes & Noble, 1959), p. 291.
12. Parkman, *La Salle,* p. 197.
13. Quoted in ibid., p. 220.
14. Parkman, *La Salle,* p. 277.
15. Membre, quoted in ibid., p. 279.
16. Parkman, *La Salle,* p. 279.
17. Ibid., p. 283.
18. Ibid., p. 285.
19. Louis XIV, quoted in ibid., p. 303.
20. Quoted in Marinacci, *They Came from Italy,* p. 31.

21. Murphy, *Henry de Tonty,* p. 84.
22. Ibid., p. 115.
23. *Memoirs of the Life and Perigrinations of the Florentine Filippo Mazzei, 1730–1816,* trans. Howard R. Marraro (New York: Columbia Press, 1942), p. 12.
24. Ibid.
25. Ibid., p. 13.
26. Ibid., p. 27.
27. Ibid., p. 16.
28. Ibid., p. 31.
29. Ibid., p. 52.
30. Ibid., p. 88.
31. Ibid., p. 98.
32. Ibid., p. 121.
33. Ibid., p. 125.
34. Ibid., p. 139.
35. Ibid., p. 165.
36. Ibid.
37. Ibid., p. 172.
38. Ibid., pp. 175–176.
39. Ibid., p. 187.
40. Ibid., p. 188.
41. Ibid., p. 192.
42. Ibid., p. 203.
43. Ibid., intro.
44. Ibid., p. 195.
45. Marinacci, *They Came from Italy,* p. 51.
46. *Mazzei,* p. 207.
47. Ibid., p. 228.
48. Ibid., p. 231.
49. Ibid., p. 302.
50. Ibid., p. 328.
51. Ibid.
52. Ibid., p. 331.
53. Ibid., p. 333.
54. Howard A. Marraro, "The Four Versions of Jefferson's Letter to Mazzei," *William and Mary College Quarterly* 22, no. 1 (January 1942): 9.
55. Quoted in Marinacci, *They Came from Italy,* p. 54.

Chapter 4

In writing this chapter on Italy during the Napoleonic years, during the revolutions of 1848 and during the Risorgimento, I have relied in particular on Christopher Hibbert's biography *Garibaldi and His Enemies: The Clash of Arms and Personalities in the Making of Italy.* Another key source of information on this period is Priscilla Robertson's *Revolutions of 1848: A Social History.* An invaluable source for American reaction to the events taking place in Italy is the late Professor Marraro's *American Opinion on the Unification of Italy, 1846–1861.* A most useful and thoughtful study of the intellectual-political history of Italy is Professor Giuliano Procacci's prize-winning *History of the Italian People,* translated into English by Anthony Paul. An extremely valuable source was *Italy: A Modern History* by Denis Mack Smith, as well as his *Garibaldi*. To gauge Napoleon's effect on Italy, I relied above all on Procacci, also on Trease, and, for certain details including Napoleon's Italian lineage, on the Horizon book of *The Age of Napoleon* by J. Christopher Herold.

1. Giuliano Procacci, *History of the Italian People* (New York: Harper & Row, 1970), p. 185.
2. Ibid., p. 206.
3. J. Christopher Herold and the editors of *Horizon Magazine, The Age of Napoleon* (New York: American Heritage Publishing Co., 1963), p. 48.
4. Quoted in ibid., p. 49.
5. Geoffrey Trease, *The Italian Story: From the Etruscans to Modern Times* (New York: Vanguard Press, 1963), p. 254.
6. Ibid., pp. 255–256.
7. Ibid., p. 256.
8. Christopher Hibbert, *Garibaldi and His Enemies: The Clash of Arms and Personalities in the Making of Italy* (New York: New American Library, Plume edition, 1970), p. 26.
9. Quoted in ibid., p. 24.
10. Howard R. Marraro, *American Opinion on the Unification of Italy, 1846–1861* (New York: AMS Press, 1969), p. 7.
11. Hibbert, *Garibaldi*, p. 27.
12. Ibid.
13. Priscilla Robertson, *Revolutions of 1848: A Social History* (New York: Harper & Row, Harper Torchbooks, 1960), p. 11.
14. Ibid., p. 35.
15. Ibid., p. 39.
16. Ibid., p. 216.
17. Marraro, *American Opinion*, p. 42.
18. Ibid., p. 12.
19. Ibid., p. 17.
20. Manin, as quoted in Robertson, *Revolutions of 1848*, p. 390.
21. Marraro, *American Opinion*, p. 37.
22. Robertson, *Revolutions of 1848*, p. 353.
23. Ibid., p. 365.
24. Ibid., p. 315.
25. Ibid.
26. Ibid.
27. Ibid., p. 318.
28. Garibaldi memoirs, quoted in Hibbert, *Garibaldi*, p. 6.
29. Hibbert, *Garibaldi*, p. 8.
30. Ibid., p. 18.
31. Ibid., p. 21.
32. Ibid., p. 41.
33. Joanne Pellegrino, "In Search of Freedom: Italian Political Refugees in America, 1831–1860" (M.A. thesis, CUNY, 1971), p. 47.
34. Quoted in Hibbert, *Garibaldi*, p. 45.
35. Hibbert, *Garibaldi*, p. 50.
36. Marraro, *American Opinion*, p. 69.
37. Ibid., p. 70.
38. Ibid.
39. Reported in Hibbert, *Garibaldi*, p. 55.
40. Marraro, *American Opinion*, p. 74.

41. Hibbert, *Garibaldi*, p. 56.
42. Ibid., p. 57.
43. Ibid., p. 59.
44. Marraro, *American Opinion*, p. 85.
45. Hibbert, *Garibaldi*, pp. 77–78.
46. Quoted in Marraro, *American Opinion*, p. 78.
47. Ibid., p. 77.
48. Reported in Marraro, *American Opinion*, p. 90.
49. Quoted in Hibbert, *Garibaldi*, p. 95.
50. Garibaldi's memoirs, in Hibbert, *Garibaldi*, p. 102.
51. Quoted in Hibbert, *Garibaldi*, p. 108.
52. Hibbert, *Garibaldi*, p. 113.
53. Ibid., pp. 116–117.
54. Quoted in Hibbert, *Garibaldi*, p. 118.
55. Ibid., p. 119.

Chapter 5

I was fortunate in being able to consult and quote from an unpublished M.A. thesis by Joanne Pellegrino, *In Search of Freedom: Italian Political Refugees in America, 1831–1860*, which contains much valuable information on the little-known Italian political refugees before the Civil War. A prime source on the courage and suffering of Italian patriots during the period of Austrian domination was Felice Foresti, whose monograph "The Fate of the Carbonari" was published by the Italian Historical Society in 1932 in a translation by Professor Marraro. Again, I am indebted to Christopher Hibbert and to Denis Mack Smith for information on Garibaldi's American year. Schiavo's *Four Centuries of Italian-American History* contains a long and detailed examination of Meucci's claim to be the inventor of the telephone; and a monograph by G. Favoino di Giura published in 1923 also presents Meucci's case in some detail.

1. Felice Foresti, "The Fate of the Carbonari," trans. Howard R. Marraro (New York: Italian Historical Society, 1932), p. 34.
2. New York *Times*, October 1836, quoted in Joanne Pellegrino, "In Search of Freedom: Italian Political Refugees in America, 1831–1860" (M.A. thesis, CUNY, 1971), p. 15.
3. Pellegrino, "In Search of Freedom," p. 54.
4. Ibid., p. 24.
5. Ibid., pp. 57–58.
6. Giovanni Schiavo, *Four Centuries of Italian-American History* (New York: Vigo Press, 1952), p. 271.
7. Pellegrino, "In Search of Freedom," p. 49.
8. Howard R. Marraro, *American Opinion on the Unification of Italy, 1846–1861* (New York: AMS Press, 1969), p. 95.
9. Garibaldi memoirs, quoted in Christopher Hibbert, *Garibaldi and His Enemies: The Clash of Arms and Personalities in the Making of Italy* (New York: New American Library, Plume edition, 1970), p. 121.

10. Quoted in Hibbert, *Garibaldi,* p. 121.
11. Hibbert, *Garibaldi,* p. 121.
12. Pellegrino, "In Search of Freedom," p. 42.
13. Garibaldi memoirs, quoted in Hibbert, *Garibaldi and His Enemies,* p. 122.
14. Hibbert, *Garibaldi and His Enemies,* p. 122.
15. Pellegrino, "In Search of Freedom," p. 46.
16. G. Favoino di Giura, "Antonio Meucci" (New York: Carroccio, 1923), p. 13.
17. Garibaldi memoirs, in Di Giura, "Meucci," pp. 13–14.
18. Di Giura, "Meucci," p. 28.
19. Ibid., p. 29.
20. Schiavo, *Four Centuries,* p. 276.
21. Ibid., p. 283.
22. Ibid., p. 282.
23. Ibid., p. 283.
24. Meucci notebooks, in ibid., p. 286.
25. Secchi de Casali, in Luciano J. Iorizzo and Salvatore Mondello, *The Italian-Americans,* The Immigrant Heritage of America (New York: Twayne Publishers, 1971), p. 27.
26. Marraro, *American Opinion,* p. 94.
27. Quoted in ibid., p. 122.
28. Quoted in ibid., p. 121.
29. Quoted in ibid., p. 120.
30. Federalist Papers, in John Higham, *Strangers in the Land: Patterns of American Nativism, 1860–1925* (New York: Atheneum, 1963), p. 3.

Chapter 6

I consulted three sources for biographical material on Luigi Palma di Cesnola. The most richly detailed one was the excellent biography by Elizabeth McFadden, *The Glitter and the Gold.* Another valuable source was Calvin Tomkins's history of the Metropolitan Museum of Art, *Merchants and Masterpieces.* Finally, Barbara Marinacci has done a fine short portrait of Cesnola in *They Came from Italy.* I also drew on Cesnola's own book, *Cyprus: Its Ancient Cities, Tombs, and Temples,* published in 1878. Two sources were used in verifying Cesnola's Congressional Medal of Honor: one an official Department of the Army publication, *The Medal of Honor,* and the other, *Above and Beyond: The Story of the Congressional Medal of Honor,* by Joseph L. Schott. Michael Musmanno's *The Story of the Italian in America* contains information on other Union soldiers of Italian descent.

Various monographs by the late Professor Marraro provided detailed information on the Italians in America at the time of the Civil War, and the Barziza book edited by P. Henderson was the source of that Confederate warrior's dramatic tale of escape.

1. New York *Herald,* 27 April 1861, in Howard R. Marraro, "Lincoln's Italian Volunteers from New York," *New York History,* January 1943.

2. New York *Herald,* 10 May 1861, in Marraro, "Lincoln's Italian Volunteers."
3. Decimus et Ultimus Barziza, *The Adventures of a Prisoner of War, 1863–64,* intro R. Henderson Schuffler (Austin: University of Texas Press, 1964), pp. 24–29.
4. Ibid., p. 45.
5. Ibid., pp. 105–107.
6. Ibid., p. 13.
7. Elizabeth McFadden, *The Glitter and the Gold: A Spirited Account of the Metropolitan Museum of Art's First Director, the Audacious and High-Handed Luigi Palma di Cesnola* (New York: Dial Press, 1971), p. 1.
8. Ibid., p. 7.
9. Ibid., p. 14.
10. Calvin Tomkins, *Merchants and Masterpieces: The Story of the Metropolitan Museum of Art* (New York: E. P. Dutton, 1970), p. 50.
11. Ibid., p. 50.
12. Anonymous letter to P. H. Watson, assistant secretary of war, 16 July 1862, in McFadden, *The Glitter and the Gold,* p. 35.
13. McFadden, *The Glitter and the Gold,* p. 41.
14. Cesnola to Stanton, in ibid., p. 43.
15. McFadden, *The Glitter and the Gold,* p. 44.
16. Cesnola to Hitchcock, in ibid., p. 45.
17. McFadden, *The Glitter and the Gold,* p. 49.
18. Ibid., p. 52.
19. Ibid., p. 65.
20. Cesnola to Hitchcock, in ibid., p. 65.
21. Ibid.
22. Ibid., p. 67.
23. Cesnola, quoted in McFadden, *The Glitter and the Gold,* pp. 70–71.
24. McFadden, *The Glitter and the Gold,* p. 76.
25. Cesnola, in ibid., p. 81.
26. Cesnola, in Tomkins, *Merchants and Masterpieces,* p. 52.
27. McFadden, *The Glitter and the Gold,* p. 149.
28. Cesnola, in Tomkins, *Merchants and Masterpieces,* p. 52.
29. McFadden, *The Glitter and the Gold,* p. 96.
30. Ibid.
31. Cesnola, in ibid., p. 97.
32. Cesnola, in Tomkins, *Merchants and Masterpieces,* p. 52.
33. McFadden, *The Glitter and the Gold,* p. 92.
34. Ibid., p. 105.
35. Cesnola to Gedeonov (Hermitage), in ibid., p. 106.
36. McFadden, *The Glitter and the Gold,* pp. 120–123.
37. Quoted in ibid., p. 120.
38. McFadden, *The Glitter and the Gold,* pp. 137–138.
39. Ibid., p. 143.
40. Cesnola to Hitchcock, in ibid., p. 135.
41. McFadden, *The Glitter and the Gold,* p. 149.
42. Ibid.
43. Ibid., p. 150.
44. Ibid., pp. 153–154.
45. Ibid., p. 156.
46. Luigi Palma di Cesnola, *Cyprus: Its Ancient Cities, Tombs, and Temples* (New York, 1878), p. 302.
47. Cesnola to Baraezi, in McFadden, *The Glitter and the Gold,* p. 170.
48. Tomkins, *Merchants and Masterpieces,* p. 57.
49. Ibid., p. 56.
50. McFadden, *The Glitter and the Gold,* p. 234.
51. Ibid., p. 187.

52. Choate address, in ibid., pp. 189–190.
53. Tomkins, *Merchants and Masterpieces*, p. 24.
54. Ibid., p. 17.
55. Quoted in ibid., p. 58.
56. Feuardent article, in McFadden, *The Glitter and the Gold*, p. 190.
57. New York *Post*, 6 August 1880, in McFadden, *The Glitter and the Gold*, p. 194.
58. McFadden, *The Glitter and the Gold*, pp. 196–197.
59. Quoted in ibid., p. 201.
60. Cesnola to New York *Times* reporter, in McFadden, *The Glitter and the Gold*, p. 204.
61. New York *Times*, in McFadden, *The Glitter and the Gold*, p. 207.
62. McFadden, *The Glitter and the Gold*, p. 215.
63. Cesnola, in ibid., p. 200.
64. McFadden, *The Glitter and the Gold*, p. 209; Tomkins, *Merchants and Masterpieces*, p. 65.
65. Quoted in McFadden, *The Glitter and the Gold*, pp. 226–227.
66. McFadden, *The Glitter and the Gold*, p. 228.
67. Ibid., p. 233.
68. Tomkins, *Merchants and Masterpieces*, p. 89.
69. Ibid., p. 84.
70. Quoted in ibid.
71. Ibid., p. 85.
72. Cesnola to Marquand, in Tomkins, *Merchants and Masterpieces*, p. 85.
73. McFadden, *The Glitter and the Gold*, p. 232.
74. Department of the Army, *The Medal of Honor* (Washington, D.C.: U.S. Government Printing Office, 1948).
75. Cesnola, in McFadden, *The Glitter and the Gold*, p. 248.
76. Quoted in Tomkins, *Merchants and Masterpieces*, p. 91.

Chapter 7

There were many valuable sources of information for this chapter. The most valuable single source, because of its early date and mass of detail, was Henry Swindburne's *Travels in the Two Sicilies*, published in London in 1790. A similar work is Patrick Brydone's *Viaggio in Sicilia e a Malta, 1770*, recently published in Italian by Longanesi.

I have quoted several times from two superb portrayals of the people of southern Italy, Carlo Levi's *Christ Stopped at Eboli* and Norman Douglas's idiosyncratic classic *Old Calabria*. Professor Procacci's history and those of Trease and Hibbert, all contained information used here, as did Denis Mack Smith's *Italy*. S. C. Burchell's *Age of Progress* in the Great Ages of Man series has a chapter dealing with Italian unification and an informative picture essay on Garibaldi describing the meeting of Garibaldi and Victor Emmanuel at Teano that marked the birth of modern Italy.

The basic work of Italian immigration is still Professor Robert E. Foerster's *The Italian Immigration of Our Times*, first published in 1919 and recently reissued. It is an invaluable work not simply for its statistical content but because it clarifies the economic basis for Italian immigration and shows how Italian male laborers fanned out towards overseas job markets.

1. Manlio A. D'Ambrosio, *Il Mezzogiorno d'Italia e l'Emigrazione negli Stati Uniti* (Rome: Athenaeum, 1924), I:32.
2. C. M. Bowra and the editors of Time-Life Books, *Classical Greece*, Great Ages of Man (New York: Time, Inc., 1965), pp. 52–53.
3. Geoffrey Trease, *The Italian Story: From the Etruscans to Modern Times* (New York: Vanguard Press, 1963), p. 6.
4. Ibid., p. 5.
5. Ibid., p. 101.
6. Norman Douglas, *Old Calabria* (Melbourne: Penguin Books, 1962), p. 149.
7. Ibid., p. 150.
8. Henry Swindburne, *Travels in the Two Sicilies* (London: J. Nichols, 1790), II:44.
9. Trease, *The Italian Story*, p. 120.
10. Ibid., p. 145.
11. Douglas, *Old Calabria*, p. 226.
12. Ibid., pp. 227–228.
13. Carlo Levi, *Christ Stopped at Eboli*, trans. Frances Frenaye (New York: Farrar, Straus, and Giroux, Noonday Press, 1969), p. 24.
14. Giuliano Procacci, *History of the Italian People* (New York: Harper & Row, 1970), p. 195.
15. Ibid., p. 194.
16. Trease, *The Italian Story*, p. 276.
17. Ibid., p. 274.
18. Ibid., p. 275.
19. Christopher Hibbert, *Garibaldi and His Enemies: The Clash of Arms and Personalities in the Making of Italy* (New York: New American Library, Plume edition, 1970), p. 197.
20. Ibid., pp. 206–207.
21. Captain H. F. Winnington-Ingram, in ibid., p. 208.
22. Garibaldi, in Hibbert, *Garibaldi and His Enemies*, p. 240.
23. Cavour, in S. C. Burchell and the editors of Time-Life Books, *Age of Progress*, Great Ages of Man (New York: Time, Inc., 1966), p. 100.
24. Ibid., p. 101.
25. Denis Mack Smith, *Italy: A Modern History* (Ann Arbor: University of Michigan Press, 1969), p. 73.
26. Ibid., p. 73.
27. Quoted in ibid., p. 74.
28. Smith, *Italy*, p. 75.
29. Douglas, *Old Calabria*, p. 298.
30. Swindburne, *Travels*, II:296–297.
31. Douglas, *Old Calabria*, p. 295.
32. Levi, *Christ Stopped at Eboli*, p. 4.

Chapter 8

Since the writings of Jacob Riis form the most detailed, comprehensive, and objective firsthand portrait of how southern Italians lived when they reached America, I have quoted extensively from him and particularly from *How the Other Half Lives*. Other valuable sources have been Oscar Handlin's many distinguished books, including *The Uprooted, Children of the Uprooted,* and *Immigration as a Factor in American History*. Eli Ginzburg and Hyman Berman's *The American Worker in the Twentieth Century* contains the long first-person narrative of the boy who was hired by the *padrone* Bartolo and set to work sifting garbage; and Antonio Mangano's *Son of Italy* contains the equally dramatic first-person narrative of the young man who found work on a railroad gang.

The details of how immigrants were processed through Ellis Island are from Willard A. Heaps's *The Story of Ellis Island*. *The Italian-Americans*, by Professors Luciano J. Iorizzo and Salvatore Mondello, in the Immigrant Heritage of America series published by Twayne, is a recent and important study of Italian-American history. Their book contains a detailed account of the New Orleans lynching and other acts of violence against Italian immigrants.

An invaluable work on nativist reaction to immigrants (and in this case, of course, Italian immigrants) is John Higham's *Strangers in the Land: Patterns of American Nativism, 1860–1925*. Other sources for this chapter include *Aliens or Americans* by Howard B. Grose, Eliot Lord's *The Italian in America,* Professor Foerster's *The Italian Emigration of Our Times,* and the celebrated Glazer-Moynihan book *Beyond the Melting Pot*.

1. Oscar Handlin, *Immigration as a Factor in American History* (Englewood Cliffs, N.J.: Prentice-Hall, 1959), pp. 29–30.
2. Robert F. Foerster, *The Italian Emigration of Our Times* (New York: Russell & Russell, 1968), p. 243.
3. Nathan Glazer and Daniel Patrick Moynihan, *Beyond the Melting Pot: The Negroes, Puerto Ricans, Jews, Italians, and Irish of New York City*, 2nd ed. (Cambridge: MIT Press, 1970), pp. 182–183.
4. Quoted in Willard A. Heaps, *The Story of Ellis Island* (New York: Seabury Press, 1967), p. 58.
5. Ibid., p. 91.
6. Jacob A. Riis, *How the Other Half Lives: Studies Among the Tenements of New York* (New York: Hill & Wang, 1957), intro.
7. Ibid., p. 1.
8. Ibid., p. 41.
9. Ibid., p. 8.
10. Ibid., pp. 50–51.
11. Ibid., p. 43.
12. Riis, "The Children of the Poor," from *Jacob Riis Revisited,* ed. Francesco Cordasco (Garden City, N.Y.: Doubleday Anchor Books, 1968), pp. 134–135.
13. Riis, *How the Other Half Lives,* p. 124.
14. Ibid., p. 47.
15. Ibid., p. 125.

16. Luciano J. Iorizzo and Salvatore Mondello, *The Italian-Americans,* The Immigrant Heritage of America (New York: Twayne Publishers, 1971), p. 49.
17. Quoted in John Higham, *Strangers in the Land: Patterns of American Nativism, 1860–1925* (New York: Atheneum, 1963).
18. New York *Times,* in Iorizzo and Mondello, *The Italian-Americans,* p. 70.
19. Higham, *Strangers in the Land,* p. 91.
20. Emerson, in ibid., p. 65.
21. Quoted in Howard B. Grose, *Aliens or Americans* (New York: Eaton & Mains, 1906), p. 3.
22. Quoted in Higham, *Strangers in the Land,* p. 66.
23. Higham, *Strangers in the Land,* p. 55.

Chapter 9

An eloquent account of the Lawrence strike is contained in Milton Meltzer's *Bread — and Roses: The Struggle of American Labor, 1865–1915.* I have quoted from an article by Ray Stannard Baker in Meltzer's chapter on Lawrence, and have relied on his text for other details of the strike. Also extremely valuable in preparing this chapter were an IWW anthology, *Rebel Voices,* edited by Joyce Kornbluh, and Patrick Renshaw's *The Wobblies: The Story of Syndicalism in the United States.*

1. This is the title of one of Danilo Dolci's books, published in English as *The Man Who Plays Alone* (by MacGibbon & Key in England and by Pantheon Books in the United States).
2. From a description by Fred E. Beal, in Joyce L. Kornbluh, ed., *Rebel Voices: An IWW Anthology* (Ann Arbor: University of Michigan Press, 1964), p. 177.
3. Milton Meltzer, *Bread — and Roses: The Struggle of American Labor, 1865–1915* (New York: Knopf, 1967), p. 170.
4. Report by the U.S. Commissioner of Labor, in Kornbluh, ed., *Rebel Voices,* p. 158.
5. Justus Ebert, "Industrial Democracy Arrives," in Kornbluh, ed., *Rebel Voices,* p. 167.
6. Ray Stannard Baker, in Meltzer, *Bread — and Roses,* pp. 172–173.
7. Patrick Renshaw, *The Wobblies: The Story of Syndicalism in the United States* (New York: Doubleday, 1967), p. 133.
8. Quoted in ibid., p. 135.
9. Baker, in Meltzer, *Bread — and Roses,* p. 174.
10. Meltzer, *Bread — and Roses,* p. 178.
11. Kornbluh, ed., *Rebel Voices,* p. 159.
12. Ibid.
13. *Outlook,* October 1912, in Renshaw, *The Wobblies,* p. 140.
14. Renshaw, *The Wobblies,* p. 135.
15. Quoted in Kornbluh, ed., *Rebel Voices,* p. 159.
16. Baker, in Kornbluh, ed., *Rebel Voices,* p. 158.
17. Meltzer, *Bread — and Roses,* p. 182.
18. Renshaw, *The Wobblies,* p. 146.
19. Ibid.
20. Haywood at Cooper Union, quoted by Ebert in Kornbluh, ed., *Rebel Voices,* p. 169.
21. Quoted in Kornbluh, ed., *Rebel Voices,* p. 162.

22. All of the quotations in this paragraph are from Renshaw, *The Wobblies,* pp. 147–148.
23. House Document No. 671, 62d Congress, 2d Session, reprinted in Kornbluh, ed., *Rebel Voices,* p. 181.
24. Renshaw, *The Wobblies,* p. 148.
25. Kornbluh, ed., *Rebel Voices,* p. 162.
26. *The Collected Poems of Arturo Giovannitti,* intro. Norman Thomas (Chicago: E. Clemente & Sons, 1962), p. 94.
27. Kornbluh, ed., *Rebel Voices,* p. 162.
28. Ibid.
29. Ibid.
30. Renshaw, *The Wobblies,* p. 140.
31. *Giovannitti,* p. 72.
32. Quoted in Kornbluh, ed., *Rebel Voices,* p. 163.
33. Kornbluh, ed., *Rebel Voices,* p. 163.
34. Ibid., p. 190.
35. *Current Opinion,* January 1913, in Kornbluh, ed., *Rebel Voices,* p. 195.
36. Kornbluh, ed., *Rebel Voices,* p. 195.
37. Renshaw, *The Wobblies,* p. 149.
38. Ibid., pp. 151, 154.
39. Ibid., p. 220.

Chapter 10

For a description of the life of Italian immigrants outside the major Eastern cities, I have relied chiefly on Andrew F. Rolle's *The Immigrant Upraised: Italian Adventures and Colonists in an Expanding America.* The information on the Italian Jesuits in the Northwest was drawn from this book, as well as other details concerning the life of Italians west of the Mississippi. The material on Siringo is from his autobiography, *A Texas Cowboy.*

Walter Lord's *The Good Years: From 1900 to the First World War* contains an engrossing description of the San Francisco earthquake, from which several details were drawn. A book by Marquis James and Bessie Rowland James, *Biography of a Bank: The Story of Bank of America,* was most useful for its abundant information on Amadeo Giannini as a banker. Also useful was a biographical sketch by Barbara Marinacci in *They Came from Italy* and the history of the San Francisco Italians in Professor Rolle's book.

1. Andrew F. Rolle, *The Immigrant Upraised: Italian Adventurers and Colonists in an Expanding America* (Norman: University of Oklahoma Press, 1968), p. 11.
2. Ibid., p. 185.
3. Ibid., pp. 195–196.
4. Ibid., p. 192.
5. Jay Monaghan, *Custer: The Life of General George Armstrong Custer* (Boston: Little, Brown, 1959), p. 386.
6. Charles A. Siringo, *A Texas Cowboy: Or Fifteen Years on the Hurricane Deck*

of a Spanish Pony, intro. J. Frank Dobie (Lincoln: University of Nebraska Press, 1966), p. 49.

7. Rolle, *The Immigrant Upraised,* p. 179.
8. Quoted in Rolle, *The Immigrant Upraised,* p. 252.
9. *Encyclopaedia Britannica,* 11th ed., s.v. "California"; Rolle, *The Immigrant Upraised,* pp. 265–266.
10. *Encyclopaedia Britannica,* "California."
11. *Encyclopaedia Britannica,* "Robert Owen."
12. Rolle, *The Immigrant Upraised,* p. 267.
13. Ibid.
14. Ibid., pp. 273–274.
15. Ibid., p. 261.
16. Ibid.
17. Walter Lord, *The Good Years: From 1900 to the First World War* (New York: Harper & Bros., 1960), pp. 121–122.
18. Ibid., p. 133.
19. Marquis James and Bessie Rowland James, *Biography of a Bank: The Story of Bank of America, N.T. & S.A.* (New York: Harper & Bros., 1959), p. 5.
20. Ibid., p. 7.
21. Ibid., pp. 7, 8.
22. Ibid., p. 10.
23. Ibid., p. 15.
24. Ibid., p. 28.
25. Quoted in ibid., p. 41.
26. James and James, *Bank of America,* p. 46.
27. Ibid., p. 48.
28. Ibid., p. 65.
29. Quoted in ibid., p. 64.
30. Ibid., p. 71.
31. Frank N. Belgrano, Jr., quoted in *Fortune,* April 1957.
32. In *Time,* 15 April 1946.
33. Ibid.
34. James and James, *Bank of America,* pp. 197–198.
35. Ibid., p. 264.
36. Ibid., p. 271.
37. Ibid., p. 274.
38. Ibid., p. 275.
39. Ibid., p. 282.
40. Ibid., p. 296.
41. Ibid., p. 297.
42. *Time,* 5 October 1931.
43. James and James, *Bank of America,* p. 327.
44. Ibid., p. 322.
45. *Time,* 5 October 1931.
46. *Time,* 15 April 1946.
47. Quoted in James and James, *Bank of America,* p. 375.
48. New York *Herald-Tribune,* 28 April 1935.
49. Time, Inc., files.
50. *Time,* 15 April 1946.
51. *Fortune,* July 1949.
52. Ibid.
53. Quoted in James and James, *Bank of America,* p. 502.

Chapter 11

The subject of Italian-American crime has received a great deal of attention recently, and there is no lack of material to read. Mario Puzo's *The Godfather* and Gay Talese's *Honor Thy Father* head the list. Another valuable source was John Kobler's *Capone: The Life and World of Al Capone.* Also useful for both its overview and its detailed information was *The Mafia Is Not an Equal Opportunity Employer* by Nicholas Gage. Giuseppe Prezzolini's *I Trapiantati* and Carlo Levi's *Christ Stopped at Eboli* also treat the subject of the Mafia. Humbert S. Nelli's *The Italians in Chicago, 1880–1930: A Study in Ethnic Mobility,* and Iorizzo and Mondello's *The Italian-Americans* both have chapters on Italian crime in America.

For detailed information on the Sacco-Vanzetti case I am indebted to two published works: Herbert B. Ehrmann's *The Case That Will Not Die: Commonwealth vs. Sacco and Vanzetti* and Francis Russell's *Tragedy in Dedham: The Story of the Sacco-Vanzetti Case.* A valuable source on the anarchist movement in Italy was George Woodcock's *Anarchism: A History of Libertarian Ideas and Movements.*

1. Quoted in Milton Lewis, New York *Herald-Tribune,* 22 May 1960.
2. Quoted in John Kobler, *Capone: The Life and World of Al Capone* (New York: G. P. Putnam's Sons, 1971), p. 48.
3. Humbert S. Nelli, *The Italians in Chicago, 1880–1930: A Study in Ethnic Mobility* (New York: Oxford University Press, 1970), p. 134.
4. Kobler, *Capone,* pp. 32–34.
5. Nicholas Gage, *The Mafia Is Not an Equal Opportunity Employer* (New York: McGraw-Hill, 1971), p. 42.
6. Ibid., p. 43.
7. Kobler, *Capone,* p. 14.
8. Ibid., p. 15.
9. Ernest R. May and the editors of *Life, War, Boom, and Bust,* LIFE History of the United States (New York: Time, Inc., 1964), p. 91.
10. Kobler, *Capone,* p. 40.
11. Quoted in Gage, *The Mafia,* p. 37.
12. Francis Russell, *Tragedy in Dedham: The Story of the Sacco-Vanzetti Case* (New York: McGraw-Hill, 1962), pp. 84–85.
13. George Woodcock, *Anarchism: A History of Libertarian Ideas and Movements* (New York: World Publishing, Meridian Books, 1962), p. 328.
14. Pisacane, in ibid., p. 329.
15. Malatesta, in S. C. Burchell and the editors of Time-Life Books, *Age of Progress,* Great Ages of Man (New York: Time, Inc., 1966), p. 120.
16. Woodcock, *Anarchism,* p. 346.
17. Vanzetti, in Russell, *Tragedy in Dedham,* p. 74.
18. Ibid., p. 75.
19. Ibid.

20. Russell, *Tragedy in Dedham,* p. 77.
21. Ibid., p. 77–78.
22. Herbert B. Ehrmann, *The Case That Will Not Die: Commonwealth vs. Sacco and Vanzetti* (Boston: Little, Brown, 1969), p. 48.
23. Palmer, in John Higham, *Strangers in the Land: Patterns of American Nativism, 1860–1925* (New York: Atheneum, 1963), p. 229.
24. In Higham, *Strangers in the Land,* p. 228.
25. Russell, *Tragedy in Dedham,* p. 87.
26. Higham, *Strangers in the Land,* p. 230.
27. Ehrmann, *The Case That Will Not Die,* p. 48.
28. Russell, *Tragedy in Dedham,* p. 59.
29. Ehrmann, *The Case That Will Not Die,* p. 73.
30. Russell, *Tragedy in Dedham,* pp. 88–89.
31. Elia affidavit, in ibid., p. 89.
32. Russell, *Tragedy in Dedham,* pp. 88–89.
33. Ibid., p. 64.
34. Vanzetti manifesto, in ibid.
35. Quoted in Ehrmann, *The Case That Will Not Die,* p. 135.
36. Ehrmann, *The Case That Will Not Die,* p. 136.
37. Ibid.
38. Vanzetti notes, in ibid., p. 459.

Chapter 12

Several first-rate writers have described life in the Little Italies. *The Fortunate Pilgrim* is a beautifully written novel that did not receive the recognition it deserved until *The Godfather* was published and made Puzo famous. Jo Pagano, Jerre Mangione, and John Fante are other writers of Italian background who have described growing up in America, and Pietro di Donato's *Christ in Concrete* is an unforgettable account of the life and suffering of immigrant laborers. Iorizzo and Mondello treat many aspects of the Italian experience, as does Joseph Lopreato, chairman of the Department of Sociology at the University of Texas in his recently published *Italian-Americans.* Other scholarly works describing and analyzing Italian-American social attitudes are Professor Irving R. Child's *Italian or American: The Second Generation in Conflict* and Herbert J. Gans's *The Urban Villagers: Group and Class in the Life of Italian-Americans.* No one writing about Italian-Americans today could fail to be unaware of Nathan Glazer's section on the Italians in *Beyond the Melting Pot* or of Nicholas Pileggi's numerous articles.

W. Warde Fowler's *Social Life at Rome in the Age of Cicero* contains much useful information on the life of the average Roman citizen, while Maurice Vaussard's *Daily Life in the Eighteenth Century Italy* was most valuable for its detailed description of festivals and religious processions.

1. William Foote Whyte, *Street Corner Society* (Chicago: University of Chicago Press, 1943), p. 11.
2. Article by Jory Graham, *Chicago Magazine*, Winter 1969.
3. Quoted in Murray Schumach, New York *Times*, 11 August 1970.
4. Ibid.
5. Mario Puzo, *The Fortunate Pilgrim* (New York: Lancer Books, 1964), p. 55.
6. Quoted in Silvano M. Tomasi, "The Ethnic Church and the Integration of Italian Immigrants in the United States," in *The Italian Experience in the United States* (Staten Island, N.Y.: Center for Migration Studies, 1970), p. 167.
7. Maurice Vaussard, *Daily Life in Eighteenth Century Italy*, trans. Michael Heron (New York: Macmillan, 1963), p. 143.
8. Ibid.
9. Quoted in Tomasi, "The Ethnic Church," p. 169.
10. Anonymous poem in Italo-American, in Carlo Sforza, *The Real Italians: A Study in European Psychology* (New York: Columbia University Press, 1942), p. 121.
11. Pagano, in Andrew F. Rolle, *The Immigrant Upraised: Italian Adventurers and Colonists in an Expanding America* (Norman: University of Oklahoma Press, 1968), p. 320.
12. Irving L. Child, *Italian or American: The Second Generation in Conflict* (New York: Russell & Russell, 1970), pp. 137, 141.

Chapter 13

The analysis of La Guardia the congressman here was based on two primary sources. One was La Guardia's own autobiography, *The Making of an Insurgent*. It ends unfortunately with the year 1919. For material on the rest of La Guardia's congressional career, I drew heavily from Arthur Mann's superlative *La Guardia: A Fighter against His Times, 1882–1933*. A shorter profile on La Guardia in Barbara Marinacci's *They Came from Italy* was also useful.

1. Arthur Mann, *La Guardia: A Fighter against His Times, 1882–1933* (Philadelphia: J. B. Lippincott, 1959), p. 135.
2. Ibid., pp. 22–23.
3. Fiorello H. La Guardia, *The Making of an Insurgent: An Autobiography, 1882–1919* (New York: Capricorn, 1961), p. 19.
4. Mann, *La Guardia*, p. 31.
5. Ibid., p. 30.
6. La Guardia, *The Making of an Insurgent*, p. 27.
7. Ibid.
8. Mann, *La Guardia*, p. 29.
9. La Guardia, *The Making of an Insurgent*, p. 31.
10. Quoted in Mann, *La Guardia*, p. 33.
11. La Guardia, *The Making of an Insurgent*, p. 33.
12. Ibid., p. 36.
13. Mann, *La Guardia*, p. 35.
14. La Guardia, *The Making of an Insurgent*, p. 37.
15. Mann, *La Guardia*, p. 36.
16. La Guardia, *The Making of an Insurgent*, p. 38.
17. Mann, *La Guardia*, p. 37.
18. La Guardia, *The Making of an Insurgent*, p. 64.
19. Ibid., pp. 54–55.

20. Ibid., p. 55.
21. Mann, *La Guardia,* p. 37.
22. La Guardia, *The Making of an Insurgent,* pp. 57–58.
23. Ibid., pp. 58–59.
24. Ibid., p. 60.
25. Ibid.
26. Mann, *La Guardia,* p. 38.
27. La Guardia, *The Making of an Insurgent,* pp. 49–50.
28. Ibid., p. 50.
29. Ibid., pp. 60–61.
30. Mann, *La Guardia,* p. 44.
31. La Guardia, *The Making of an Insurgent,* pp. 65–66.
32. Ibid., p. 69.
33. Mann, *La Guardia,* p. 46.
34. Ibid., p. 47.
35. Ibid., p. 56.
36. Ibid., pp. 47–48.
37. La Guardia, *The Making of an Insurgent,* p. 117.
38. Ibid., p. 118.
39. Ibid.
40. Ibid., p. 93.
41. Ibid.
42. Ibid., p. 95.
43. Mann, *La Guardia,* p. 58.
44. Ibid., pp. 58–59.
45. Ibid., p. 59.
46. Quoted in ibid., p. 58.
47. La Guardia, *The Making of an Insurgent,* p. 102.
48. Ibid., p. 101.
49. Mann, *La Guardia,* p. 61.
50. Ibid., p. 63.
51. La Guardia, *The Making of an Insurgent,* pp. 108–109.
52. Ibid., p. 113.
53. Harry Andrews, quoted in Mann, *La Guardia,* p. 66.
54. Mann, *La Guardia,* p. 66.
55. Ibid., p. 69.
56. La Guardia, *The Making of an Insurgent,* p. 149.
57. Ibid., p. 144.
58. Ibid., pp. 165–166.
59. Mann, *La Guardia,* p. 68.
60. La Guardia, *The Making of an Insurgent,* p. 167.
61. Mann, *La Guardia,* p. 84.
62. La Guardia, *The Making of an Insurgent,* p. 180.
63. Mann, *La Guardia,* p. 92.
64. La Guardia, *The Making of an Insurgent,* p. 198.
65. Mann, *La Guardia,* p. 96.
66. La Guardia, *The Making of an Insurgent,* p. 203.
67. Ibid., p. 200.
68. Ibid., pp. 214–215.
69. Mann, *La Guardia,* p. 116.
70. Ibid.
71. Ibid., p. 118.
72. Ibid., p. 126.
73. Quoted in Mann, *La Guardia,* p. 132.
74. Mann, *La Guardia,* p. 138.
75. Ibid., p. 142.

76. Ibid., pp. 146–147.
77. Ibid., p. 152.
78. Ibid., p. 157.
79. Ibid., p. 185.
80. Ibid., p. 189.
81. Quoted in ibid., p. 191.
82. Mann, *La Guardia*, p. 185.
83. Ibid., p. 186.
84. Andrew Mellon, in ibid., p. 208.
85. La Guardia, in Barbara Marinacci, *They Came from Italy: The Stories of Famous Italian-Americans* (New York: Dodd, Mead, 1967), p. 177.
86. Mann, *La Guardia*, p. 179.
87. Ibid., p. 234.
88. Ibid., p. 228.
89. Ibid., p. 276.
90. Ibid., p. 286.
91. La Guardia to Norris, in ibid., p. 300.
92. Mann, *La Guardia*, p. 304.
93. Ibid., pp. 281–313.
94. Ibid., p. 314.

Chapter 14

A number of published sources were useful for this chapter: Don Luigi Sturzo's *Italy and the Coming World;* Charles F. Delzell's *Mussolini's Enemies: The Italian Anti-Fascist Resistance;* Richard Collier's recent *Duce! A Biography of Benito Mussolini;* Irving R. Levine's *Main Street, Italy;* and, again, Denis Mack Smith's *Italy.*

The Tresca material was drawn chiefly from his own unpublished autobiography preserved at the New York Public Library. Other important sources were an unpublished biography by Max Nomad, which is at the Center for Ethnic Studies on Staten Island; Francis Russell's article, "The Last of the Anarchists," from *Modern Age;* Max Eastman's "Profile" of Tresca in the *New Yorker;* and, finally, clippings at the *Herald-Tribune* morgue and at the Italian Cultural Institute in New York.

1. *Fortune*, November 1940, p. 86.
2. Wilson, quoted in Humbert S. Nelli, *The Italians in Chicago, 1880–1930: A Study in Ethnic Mobility* (New York: Oxford University Press, 1970), p. 118.
3. Quoted in Richard Collier, *Duce! A Biography of Benito Mussolini* (New York: The Viking Press, 1971), p. 93.
4. Churchill, quoted in Collier, *Duce!* p. 93.
5. Johnson, quoted in Alexander DeConde's *Half-Bitter, Half-Sweet: An Excursion into Italian-American History* (New York: Scribner's, 1971), p. 185.
6. McKellar, quoted in DeConde, *An Excursion*, p. 199.
7. Irving R. Levine, *Main Street, Italy* (New York: Doubleday, 1963), p. 216.
8. Collier, *Duce!* p. 40.

9. Luciano J. Iorizzo and Salvatore Mondello, *The Italian-Americans*, The Immigrant Heritage of America (New York: Twayne Publishers, 1971), pp. 202–204.
10. *Fortune*, p. 86.
11. Ibid.
12. Emilio Segré, *Enrico Fermi, Physicist* (Chicago: University of Chicago Press, 1970), pp. 113–114.
13. Ibid., p. 116.
14. Ibid., p. 129.
15. Don Luigi Sturzo, *Italy and the Coming World* (New York: Roy Publishers, 1945), pp. 71–72.
16. Denis Mack Smith, *Italy: A Modern History* (Ann Arbor: University of Michigan Press, 1969), p. 326.
17. Sturzo, *Italy*, pp. 176–177.
18. Max Eastman, "Profile," *New Yorker*, 15 and 22 September, 1934.
19. Max Nomad, biography of Carlo Tresca, Center for Ethnic Studies, Staten Island, New York, pp. 28–29.
20. Ibid., p. 14.
21. Autobiography of Tresca, Manuscript Section, New York Public Library, p. 95.
22. Ibid., p. 103.
23. Ibid., p. 129.
24. Ibid., p. 144.
25. Francis Russell, "The Last of the Anarchists," *Modern Age*, Winter 1963–1964, p. 66.
26. Autobiography of Tresca, p. 172.
27. Ibid., p. 139.
28. Russell, "The Last of the Anarchists," p. 72.
29. American Civil Liberties Union, "Foreign Dictators of American Rights," New York, June 1925.
30. Ibid.
31. Quoted in Eastman, "Profile."
32. Ibid.
33. Pravda, quoted in Hugh Thomas, *The Spanish Civil War* (Baltimore: Penguin Books, 1965), p. 457.
34. Russell, "The Last of the Anarchists," p. 74.

Chapter 15

The material for this final chapter came mostly from newspaper files and from interviews. But I would be remiss in not mentioning Leonard Covello's *The Social Background of the Italo-American School Child*, Michael Novak's *The Rise of the Unmeltable Ethnics*, and Nicholas Pileggi's articles in *New York Magazine* for their insights into a difficult subject.

1. Judith Michaelson, New York *Post*, 28 June 1971.
2. Nicholas Pileggi, "Risorgimento: The Red, White, and Greening of New York," *New York Magazine*, 7 June 1971.
3. Michaelson, New York *Post*, 28 June 1971.
4. Ibid.
5. Norman Douglas, *Old Calabria* (Melbourne: Penguin Books, 1962), p. 268.

6. Carlo Levi, *Christ Stopped at Eboli,* trans. Frances Frenaye (New York: Farrar, Straus, & Giroux, Noonday Press, 1969), p. 143.

7. Al Silverman, *Joe DiMaggio, His Golden Year* (New York: McFadden-Bartell, 1971), p. 35.

8. DiMaggio, in Larry Claflin, *The Sporting News,* 25 March 1967.

9. Frank Capra, *The Name above the Title* (New York: Bantam Books, 1972), p. 497.

10. Bill Moyers, *Listening to America: A Traveler Rediscovers His Country* (New York: Harper's Magazine Press, 1971), pp. 50–56.

11. Nicholas Gage, *The Mafia Is Not an Equal Opportunity Employer* (New York: McGraw-Hill, 1971), p. 28.

12. Danilo Dolci, *Chi Gioca Solo* (Torino: Enaudi, 1966–1967), p. 17.

13. Giuseppe Prezzolini, *I Trapiantati* (Milano: Longanesi, 1963), pp. 45–46.

14. Stendhal, quoted in Luigi Barzini, *The Italians* (London: Hamish Hamilton, 1964), p. 56.

INDEX